How To Determine Your Stimulus Payment

If your Net Income Tax Liability is:	If your Qualifying Income is:	
* "income tax liability is tax before including the alternative um tax, less all nonrefundable other than the allowable child dit.)	(Qualifying Income is earned income, Social Security benefits, and certain veterans' payments.)	
	At least $3,000	**Under $3,000**
han zero	Your stimulus payment is your net income tax liability up to $600 (or $1,200 for joint filers).	
	However, generally your stimulus payment will not be less than $300 ($600 for joint filers).**	
))	Your stimulus payment will be $300 ($600 for joint filers).	You will not receive a stimulus payment.

** In addition, if qualifying income is under $3,000, gross income must exceed $8,750 if single or married filing a separate return, $17,500 if married filing a joint return, $11,250 if head of household, or $14,100 if qualifying widow(er).

Additional Stimulus Payment for Children. Individuals eligible for payments may also receive an additional $300 for each qualifying child for the child tax credit.

Reduction for Higher Income Taxpayers. The stimulus payments are reduced for taxpayers with adjusted gross income (AGI) of more than $75,000 (more than $150,000 if married filing jointly).

 Printed on recycled paper

* U.S. GOVERNMENT PRINTING OFFICE: 2008–341-830

Department of the Treasury
Internal Revenue Service
Andover, MA 05501-0500

Official Business
Penalty for Private Use, $300

IRS

Notice 1377 (February 2008)
Catalog Number 51255B

ENCLOSED IS AN IMPORTANT
MESSAGE FROM THE IRS ON THE
ECONOMIC STIMULUS ACT OF 2008.
DO NOT THROW AWAY!

C00584025
0000338
7
******C005***************5-DIGIT 02474
SHAUNDRA L CUNNINGHAM
389 MASSACHUSETTS AVE APT 3
ARLINGTON, MA 02474-6707

PRESORTED
FIRST-CLASS MAIL
Postage and Fees Paid
Internal Revenue Service
Permit No. G-48

Verizon Bill Issue
7 University Ave.
Medford, MA

Remaking a World

Sponsored by the Culture, Health, and Human Development Program of the Social Science Research Council

Remaking a World

Violence, Social Suffering, and Recovery

Edited by Veena Das,
Arthur Kleinman,
Margaret Lock,
Mamphela Ramphele, and
Pamela Reynolds

UNIVERSITY OF CALIFORNIA PRESS
Berkeley   Los Angeles   London

University of California Press
Berkeley and Los Angeles, California

University of California Press, Ltd.
London, England

Chapter 2 reprinted by permission from *Transcultural Psychiatry* 37, no. 1 (2000): 11–34.
Chapter 3 reprinted by permission of *Dædalus,*
Journal of the American Academy of Arts and Sciences, from the issue entitled "The Next Generation: Work in Progress," Spring 1999, vol. 128, no. 2.

Library of Congress Cataloging-in-Publication Data

Remaking a world : violence, social suffering, and
recovery / edited by Veena Das . . . [et al.].
    p. cm.
Includes bibliographical references and index.
ISBN 0-520-22329-2 (cloth : alk. paper)—
ISBN 0-520-22330-6 (pbk. : alk. paper)
1. Violence. 2. Community life. 3. Interpersonal
relations. 4. Suffering—Social aspects. I. Das,
Veena.
HM886. R45 2001
303.6—dc21

                                    00-046707

Manufactured in the United States of America
10 09 08 07 06 05 04 03 02 01

10 9 8 7 6 5 4 3 2 1

The paper used in this publication meets the minimum requirements of ANSI / NISO Z39 0.48-
1992(R 1997) (Permanence of Paper).♾

Contents

Acknowledgments

In 1993 the editors, who are members of the Committee on Culture, Health, and Human Development of the Social Science Research Council (New York), planned a series of volumes to examine anthropological questions on the relation of violence to states, local communities, and individuals. The first two volumes, *Social Suffering* and *Violence and Subjectivity*, explored the different ways in which social force inflicts harm on individuals and collectivities. In this, the third volume, we offer comparative ethnographies based upon long-term fieldwork in different regions of the world to find how communities which have been marginalized through the structured violence of historical processes or which have faced the trauma of collective violence, rebuild their lives. Rather than suggesting immediate solutions to the urgent problems posed by such violence, these accounts, embodying a cluster of conversations between the various editors and authors, are sober accounts of the manner in which communities try to regain their worlds. How, after such devastation, do communities go on? How do those who have been excluded from the political community—whose words have been drained of life through the soft knife of systematic discrimination presenting itself in the guise of "development" or "bureaucratic impersonality"—find ways of reanimating their words? How do communities respond, cope, or fail to engage with the violence and its aftermath? The knowledge may well be the grounds upon which effective policies and programs need to be fashioned at a later date.

We are grateful to the Social Science Research Council (New York) for its support for this project, and especially to Frank Kessel, who provided excellent support in the various phases of this work to all the editors and the authors. We thank Diana Colbert and Carrie Nitka for their assistance in various organizational matters and to Scott Giampetruzzi and Julie Lake for preparing the final typescript.

We thank the MacArthur Foundation for overall funding for the SSRC Committee and the Rockefeller Foundation for providing the necessary funds to support the fieldwork on which the papers are based. The opportunity to have intensive discussions among the various scholars involved in this project, and to create a network of affiliations between anthropologists working in different universities in Asia, Africa, and North America, is cherished—as are memories of the wonderful hospitality of the University of Cape Town, where the conference to discuss these papers was held in October 1995. Kenneth George gave insightful comments on several papers and especially the introduction, for which we are grateful. Discussions with Lawrence Cohen which have streched over several years now are acknowledged with pleasure by Arthur Kleinman and Veena Das. Most important have been the enthusiasm and the patience of the authors, for which we are truly grateful.

Veena Das
Arthur Kleinman
Margaret Lock
Mamphela Ramphele
Pamela Reynolds

Introduction

Veena Das and Arthur Kleinman

Social trauma and the remaking of everyday life are the subjects of the six essays in this volume. Much has been written and continues to be written on the traumatic effects of war, political violence, and systematic practices of state terror, as well as on the adverse impact of development projects on marginalized communities. Psychologists and psychiatrists are engaged in documenting, describing, and diagnosing post-traumatic stress disorder and other distressing consequences of murder, rape, torture, molestation, and other forms of brutality. The anthropological contribution to this has been of a different but no less important character. Ethnographers have described how political violence is both mobilized and targeted—and how it works on lives and interconnections to break communities. Sometimes this violence is sudden, as in the dropping of the atomic bombs on Hiroshima and Nagasaki. At other times it takes the form of a continuous reign of terror, as with the policies and practices of the brutal regime of apartheid. Even when violence is not present in such dramatic forms, there can be the slow erosion of community through the soft knife of policies that severely disrupt the life worlds of people. And yet in the midst of the worst horrors, people continue to live, to survive, and to cope. This might appear as an obvious, even banal statement, especially if we think of the everyday only as the site of the taken-for-granted, the "uneventful," from which one seeks escape in the realm of the transcendental. Yet, in relation to lives severely disrupted, to be able to secure the everyday life by individuals and communities is indeed an achievement. What is the stake, then, in the everyday after such overwhelming experiences of social suffering, and how do people learn to engage in it? Is it possible to speak of this re-engagement as a healing at the level of the community and of the individual? Are these processes similar?

In 1993, the editors, who are members of the Committee on Culture, Health, and Human Development of the Social Science Research Council (New York), planned a series of volumes to examine anthropological questions on the relation of violence to states, local communities, and individuals. The first volume, *Social Suffering* (1997), dealt with sources and major forms of social adversity with an emphasis on political violence. It gave illustrations of how transformations in cultural representations and collective experiences of suffering reshape interpersonal responses to catastrophe and terror. It also charted the effects of bureaucratic responses to human problems, and found that these institutional actions can (and often do) deepen and make more intractable the problems they seek to ameliorate.

The second volume, *Violence and Subjectivity* (2000), contained graphic accounts of how collective experience of violence can alter individual subjectivity. It questioned much of the present wisdom in subjects such as international relations and political science, which tend to conceptualize collective violence as a direct translation of social scripts through which relations between ethnic groups and identities are said to be defined, especially in parts of the world in which identity politics rather than the civilized conflict characteristic of modern polities is said to be operative. Questioning the polarity between violence and civilized politics as either a mark of social evolution or the basis of contemporary classification of societies, *Violence and Subjectivity* showed how social force transforms itself into political violence. In the process it demonstrated the entanglement of various social actors, ranging from global institutions to modern states on the one hand and small local communities inhabiting increasingly uncertain worlds on the other, in the production and authorization of collective violence. Most important, it interrogated the notion of the "ordinary" as a site for understanding the nature of sociality in local communities. A surprising finding was that actions of global institutions and agencies of the state have often inhibited the mechanisms of restraint and notions of limit that have been crafted in local moral worlds: it is not that such local worlds have some kind of natural immunity to violence, but simply that in response to the imperatives of imagining a common future such communities also have to experiment and put into place ideas of limits to violence.

The present volume, the third panel in our triptych of social danger, highlights how communities "cope" with—read, endure, work through, break apart under, transcend—both traumatic violence and other, more insidious forms of social suffering. It is the result of an effort to bring the immediacy of multifaceted, complex, and intricately woven ethnographies to describe the processes through which communities cope with various forms of social suffering. We hope the comparative ethnographies presented here are rich enough in local detail to support comparison and analysis of the societal consequences of violence, in both its spectacular and everyday forms, at the level of local worlds, interpersonal relations, and individual lives.

The process of producing this volume was itself an interesting one. While each essay describes the theoretical issues in a specific local setting, an attempt was made to stitch together the issues in a larger framing through commentaries by each editor, which have been incorporated into the essays as well as this Introduction. There were lively and intense interactions between the entire group of scholars (editors and authors), so that the chapters can be read as the result of a cumulative cluster of conversations. Though the social and cultural contexts of these studies are diverse, their resemblance lies in the crisscrossing and overlapping of certain key questions. They extend our concepts of social suffering, violence, coping, and healing, in the way one twists fiber on fiber when spinning a thread. This metaphor of spinning was explained by Wittgenstein thus: "And the strength of the fiber does not reside in the fact that some one fiber runs through its whole length, but in the overlapping of many fibers" (Wittgenstein 1953: para 67).

The fibers that overlap to make up the thread of narration in what follows may be characterized in terms of the (a) relation between collective and individual memory; (b) creation of alternate public spheres for articulating and recounting experience silenced by officially sanctioned narratives; (c) retrieval of voice in the face of recalcitrance of tragedy; and (d) meaning of healing and the return to everyday.

The social and cultural contexts of these ethnographies are varied. Yet there are important similarities in the way in which the project of re-creating "normality" seems to engage the survivors of collective tragedies in, on the one hand, creating a public space in which experience of victims and survivors can not only be represented but also be molded,

and, on the other, engaging in repair of relationships in the deep re-
cesses of family, neighborhood, and community. The recovery of the
everyday, resuming the task of living (and not only surviving), asks for
a renewed capability to address the future. How does one shape a
future in which the collective experience of violence and terror can find
recognition in the narratives of larger entities such as the nation and
the state? And at the level of interpersonal relations, how does one
contain and seal off the violence that might poison the life of future
generations? How these goals are secured is complicated, for it asks
for the simultaneous engagement of political and judicial institutions,
as well as families and local communities. While everyday life may be
seen as the site of the ordinary, this ordinariness is itself recovered in
the face of the most recalcitrant of tragedies: it is the site of many
buried memories and experiences. At the level of the public discourse
many of these communities seem to be engaged in a "politics of recognition," to use the felicitous phrase of Charles Taylor (1992), but
one has to understand also how this form of politics is itself anchored
to the material, moral, and social aspects of everyday life in marginalized communities.

It is a commonplace that underlying the contractual theories of society is a vision of the polis as a creation of its members and not simply
a reflection of either divine will or natural order. This vision of the polis
implies the capacity to speak for oneself politically—to be able to find
a voice *in community with other voices.* Emerging from the studies that
follow is the stunning fact that even in the "oneiric geography of fear"
(Pandolfo 1997), as in the postapartheid society of South Africa or during the period of terror in southern Sri Lanka in the late 1980s, the fresh
attempt to build communities or neighborhoods is never purely a local
affair. In fact, it is simultaneously an attempt to redefine and re-create
the political society. Such is the case with the Cree in Canada or the Kui
in Thailand, whose deprivation comes from the fact that they have been
consistently excluded from participation in the collective life of the polis.
Historically they have been the objects of state policies and not their
subjects; hence they cannot recognize themselves in the collective projects of the wider political community. As we shall see later, the projects
to redefine their places in the political community might be said to be a
matter of finding *voice* that appears in a complicated relation to *words.*
Sometimes, in certain spaces, words which have been frozen, removed
from circulation, are reanimated by being embodied in voice—while at
other times and in other places, stories are extracted from violent ex-

periences when fear may be given a shape in some alien voice, which comes back as the experience of dispossession.

One of the strengths of the ethnographies presented here is that these questions have been addressed by paying close attention not only to the content of narratives, but also to the processes of their formation within local communities. How are institutions implicated in allowing or disallowing voice? How does the availability of a genre mold the articulation of suffering—assign a subject position as the place from which suffering may be voiced? It may be the experience of survivors that certain categories that the culture readily assigns to them (such as the "dignified suffering mother" role often assigned to the women survivors of Hiroshima) become completely or partially disconnected from the ongoing contexts of their lives. When such subject positions are assigned they can lay to waste whole forests of significant speech—questions of representation become questions of connecting the enunciations with the lived world of the survivors. In collecting the narratives of survivors by directly participating in the contexts in which stories are made, the authors of the essays in this volume show the tremendous tensions between competing truths: they explore the shadows that fall between what is regarded as truth and what as fiction. Saying, as Pandolfo (1997) puts it, overflows the content of the utterances, for it gathers gesture, context, and signature in the process of telling.

There is clearly a tension between interpreting a violent event in the form of a text (even a text that is performed) and trying to find ways in which violence is implicated in the formation of the subject, foregrounding the category of experience. The view of culture as text has come under sustained critique, especially by those who have questioned the appropriation of ethnographic authority through different conventions of representation (e.g., Marcus and Fischer 1986). The links between aesthetic, legal, and political forms of representation are now recognized to be at the heart of the problem in the theorizing on the relation between culture and power. Yet if one were not willing to experiment with how much one's own voice finds recognition in other voices—and, conversely, with when it is that in speaking for oneself one is also legitimately speaking for another—it would be hard to conceive of any democratic processes at all. Hence the category of shared experience as a ground from which this recognition may stem has some attractive possibilities, provided we do not slip into the idea of a *pre-given* subject to whom experience happens. Thus in a salutary footnote Gupta and Ferguson (1997) state that "By decoupling the idea of experience from the vision of an ontologically prior subject who is 'having' it, it is possible to see in experience neither the adventures and expressions of a subject nor the mechanical product of discourses of power but the workshop in which subjectivity is continually challenged and refashioned" (29). Yet in the body of their own text they seem to encounter this process only in moments of resistance, as if the processes of everyday life, the efforts required to reproduce the everyday, are not equally implicated in the formation of subjectivity. The notions of sub-altern resistance, of hidden scripts, and of other such resting points where it seems possible to say no to power have obvious advantages in locating what Daniel (1997) calls agentive moments. Finding one's voice in the making of one's history, the remaking of a world, though, is also a matter of being able to recontextualize the narratives of dev-astation and generate new contexts through which everyday life may become possible. That communities formed in suffering do not always succeed in this, and that life can drain out of words that signify healing and overcoming of tragedy, and that as the scribes of such experiences we need to be able to read such experiences—that is also the burden of some of the essays. There are other positions: the Cree vigorously reject the subject position of victims; others, such as the mothers in Sri Lanka, are still too close to the deaths, torture, and disappearance of their children to even be able to own such fears as their own. They seek to hear what they fear most from the mouths of oracles. The image of culture as a workshop in which subjectivity is shaped seems to offer little scope for the understanding of this oneiric quality of fear captured especially in the chapters by Perera, Ross, and Mehta and Chatterji. In the other cases too, the relation between the formation of the subject and the experience of subjugation is shown to involve a complex pro-cess. As Butler (1997) argues in her important exploration on the psy-chic life of power, the experience of subjugation may itself, when owned and worked upon, become the source for claiming a subject position. The movement from the first person singular pronoun, the "I," to the claiming of a plural first person, the "we," calls upon ex-perience, but this does not provide some kind of unmediated bedrock on which the foundations of subjectivity can be laid. Thus while the Cree and the Kui are able to forge links of community on the basis of shared experiences of subjugation, the women *hibakusha* in Japan try to redraw the boundaries around themselves, as they do not want to lease their voices to the collective representations of themselves as the silent enduring mothers.

The rich contextualization provided in these essays, as also their vantage position in capturing not any particular spectacular moment of violence but its shadows, its reverberations years later in the lives of communities, is extremely important. Sometimes violence in one era is grafted onto memories of another, as the ethnic and communal violence that occurred in Bombay after the destruction of the Babri mosque in Ayodhya in India has become entangled with memories of the Partition of the country in 1947. As stories are layered upon other stories, the categories of history and myth collapse into each other. Thus spaces become imbued with these mythic qualities, narrations not only representing violence but also producing it. Pandolfo's evocative description of violence as inscribed in the memories of the local community in Morocco she studied ("The *fitna* of that distant past, recent past, *fitna* of the ruinous consequences of foreign invasions, *fitna* of women, of buying and selling of words" [Pandolfo 1998: 223]) provides a glimpse of how local communities might experience themselves. Her sense, though, that from such wounds springs the poetry of ruins does not seem to find any resonance in the accounts of violence presented here. If anything, there is an angry rejection of the aestheticization of their experiences by the women hibakusha, or by the slum dwellers of Dharavi in Bombay. When and how does suffering then become a source from which poetry can spring? The Cree now seem to be able to imagine how to create well-being, the Kui to be able to align with larger civic movements in Thailand to resist the appropriation of their traditions as tourist commodities. The diverse forms that the processes of coping and healing take demand the kind of thick ethnography that Geertz advocated without necessarily an allegiance to the notion of culture as text.

TRAUMA AND EVERYDAY LIFE

When I talk about language (words, sentences, etc.) I
must speak the language of everyday.
   Is this language somehow too coarse and material
for what we want to say?
   Then how is another one to be constructed?—And
how strange that we should be able to do anything at
all with the one we have!

Ludwig Wittgenstein

From the point of view of the relation between trauma and everyday life, these ethnographies can be divided into two kinds. On one side are the descriptions of the communities, the Kui in Thailand (Komatra Chuengsatiansup) and the Cree in Canada (Naomi Adelson), among whom the hurts are historical and the experience of violation is more in the nature of policies and programs of the state that have marginalized these communities and endangered their sense of identity. On the other side are the ethnographies of violence in which traumatic events seem (from the actors' point of view)[1] to have caused sudden and often inexplicable hurt on their social and individual lives. Thus there are the women hibakusha in Japan suffering from radiation diseases (Maya Todeschini); the stories of wandering ghosts that mark a geography of brutal violence in post-terror southern Sri Lanka (Sasanka Perera); the difficulties of inhabiting a common locality and of carrying life forward after a vicious communal riot in Bombay (Deepak Mehta and Roma Chatterji); and the complex interweaving of stories in the testimonies offered by women before the Truth and Reconciliation Commission in South Africa (Fiona Ross). In all these cases the societal spaces as well as individual bodies are *marked* by the signs of brutality: the violence is *visible* in radiation disease, wounds, destroyed houses, and the disheveled, dispossessed bodies of women. The process of reinhabiting these spaces of terror puts demands on the survivors for forging memory and forgetfulness in new ways. On the other hand, the call by the Kui and the Cree for recognition of their own voice in their history engages the public and private dimensions of experience by reformulating questions of history and tradition, not only within discursive formations but also in the new ways in which their identity is sought to be performed.

TRADITION, COLLECTIVE MEMORIES, AND ALTERNATE PUBLIC SPHERES

Are these harms that have too often gone unrecognized, unnamed, unaddressed? Can and should there be alternatives to traditional institutional responses? Should working through the emotions of victims and survivors figure prominently in the goals for the nation or the world, or instead find a place as by-products of fact-finding, guilt-finding, and punishment?

Martha Minow

Various writers have addressed the relation between collective memories and individual memories, highlighting the disjunction between public culture, official memories, and the "sensory" memory of individuals (Pandolfo 1997; Rèv 1997; Seremetakis 1994). Seremetakis makes the point that sensory memory does not simply repeat what is part of official memory but has the potential of challenging and transforming it. Following the trajectories laid out in the various contributions by Benjamin (1966) on this theme, she outlines a polarity between official memory and official inattention, arguing that the history produced throughout modernity, the official memory, is created as though it were a continuum from which both the mundanity of the everyday and discordant experiences are excluded through inattention. There are two themes here, that of contesting the history of inattention and that of using the sensory memory of individuals to challenge the official memory created through official record.

Chuengsatiansup's rendering of the manner in which the history of the Kui, a marginal community in Thailand, is *overwritten* by the practices of the state suggests that erasure is not achieved simply through inattention but by the production of a different kind of history by specific forms of attention. "In the case of the Kui," he says, "their memories have been taken away not only because their history has been incorporated into that of other states and written in languages not their own, but, more importantly, because official historical records take no notice of the Kui, either as a people, a race, or a nation." The colonial practices of historiography assigned a place in history to social groups such as the Kui, but in a manner which would basically support colonial claims for territorial conquest. The modern nation-state too saw them as "wild," as standing outside the definition of the nation and thus in need of being domesticated and brought within the agenda of national integration. Indeed, to contest the hegemony of the state under whose sign social history is written is the classical theme of subaltern historians. Chuengsatiansup shows, though, that more than in the texts of history, it is in the bureaucratic practices and in the particular ideology of the welfare state in Thailand that we should seek reasons for the marginalization of the Kui community. The community is now engaged in a process of social reformulation, creating networks of affiliation with the wider movement of voluntary organizations in Thailand to create new definitions of civil society and new definitions of citizenship. Thus authenticity is seen not as turning away from modernity to some distant, more authentic past, but as an engagement with the present, creating what Chuengsatiansup calls alternate "subaltern counterpublics."[2]

A similar theme appears in the efforts of the Cree, an aboriginal community in Canada, to create institutional mechanisms for transmission of tradition and hence of the creation of collective memories. Since much of the thrust of colonial educational policy was "to take the Indian out of their children," an imagination of well-being by the Cree includes the creation of pedagogic spaces in which the children can learn their traditions. Adelson is clear that in creating the subject position of a Cree nation there is a reimagination of aboriginality. Thus indigenous healing and cultural practices are reinvented, and processes are put in place through which these invented traditions can acquire authenticity. Adelson sees these as creating both transnational indigenous unity and local potential.

Neither the Cree nor the Kui present us with cases of dramatic violence or genocide of the kind that was witnessed in the case of former Yugoslavia or Rwanda, or indeed historically in many other indigenous communities. Yet the soft knife of state policies in these cases shows how experiences of violation may become embedded in the everyday lives of marginal groups. The Kui and Cree experiences bear some resemblance to descriptions of peasants in various parts of Southeast Asia whose resistance to various forms of domination has been captured by the notion of hidden scripts (Scott 1992), marked by the use of irony and other such rhetorical devices to convey passive resistance. Dumont (1992) has noted, of peasants in the Philippines, that "confronted with such violence, the Visayan peasants responded like most peasants do, that is neither with enthusiasm nor with rebellion but with increased passivity, cynicisms and witticisms included" (148). Chuengsatiansup's and Adelson's ethnographies show the capacity of marginal groups for collective action in their reimagination of well-being, which takes resentment in a different direction from either everyday passive resistance or violent confrontation. Engagement in collective action then moves resentment from the arena of private conversations towards the making of a counterpublic sphere within which notions of citizenship may be renegotiated with the state.

COUNTERING INATTENTION

Do you want me to tell you what I think, Yes, do, I
don't think we did go blind, I think, we are blind,

Blind but seeing, Blind people who can see, but do not
see.

José Saramago

Violence that is embodied in the hibakusha, the survivors of atomic
bombs in Hiroshima and Nagasaki, carries a different significance for
world history. Quite apart from the terrible suffering and death it
caused (and continues to cause) hundreds of thousands of Japanese,
the unleashing of nuclear weapons signified our entry into an era in
which the self-annihilation of humankind is now possible. Hence
the burdens of memory for the whole of mankind are of a different
order (see Lifton 1967, 1983). Yet the official Japanese response to the
bombs, on balance, was one of memory erasure. The shock of defeat
in war followed by the headlong struggle for economic recovery and
further modernization led to an official inattention, an erasure of the
pain and losses caused by the bomb. Maya Todeschini in her sensitive
ethnography of women survivors shows how this collective memoro-
politics (a term after Ian Hacking) of erasure was only partially effective: informal recording of suffering started as soon as peace was declared. But she also points out that men were seen to be so deeply
implicated in the brutality of war, especially a war of aggression and
colonization, that with the end of the war they were not considered
appropriate as cultural representatives of the nation. In defeat and
foreign occupation other images were called forth. Yet the suffering of
the women survivors was represented, even in popular novels and
cinema, only within the dominant modality of portraying them as suffering mothers. Frozen into position as mythical mothers, as women
who showed inhuman strength and endurance, the stereotypes fixed
women's experiences within certain permitted genres of expression.
Women whose children did not survive, for instance, were turned into
living memorials to these dead children. The account by Todeschini of
women as storytellers relates how women counter by various means
the social death imposed upon them: they resist both the stigma and
the cardboard heroic roles assigned to them. Listening to them as an
ethnographic stance requires that we not only assign importance to
their stories for the lessons Hiroshima or Nagasaki has to teach us in
relation to the grand projects of world history, but also tune our
ears to hear the more local pitch at which such women speak to establish a new normality for themselves. Their attempts to escape the
molds in which Japanese literature and society have fit them are as

important as any lessons against the futility of war that they have to convey.

The other essay in this volume (by Fiona Ross) that deals primarily with the testimonies of women, this time in the context of the Truth and Reconciliation Commission in South Africa, repeats the gendered nature of recounting traumatic experiences.[3] She notes that women testified primarily against the brutality committed on sons, husbands, and brothers—rarely could they speak of the harm done to themselves. The Commission had to repeatedly endorse the importance of women speaking about their own experiences of violation. The stories women tell record impossible levels of violence, but their terror lies in the manner in which the everyday punctuates these accounts. Thus one woman speaks of hearing about a police attack on supposed Russians in the genteel atmosphere of the house in which she works as a maid. Already fearful, with a premonition of disaster, she turns on the television on reaching home and recognizes one of the persons killed to be her son. The memorialization of these events is in the register of the everyday, as women speak of the dispersal of families and the extraordinary tasks of continuing to maintain relationships and provide nurturance in the context of political turmoil. The stake in heroic political struggle waged by the young in South Africa has its counterpoint in the manner in which women as mothers maintained the everyday relationships. Hence there is an interweaving in their stories of different voices—their own suffering is embodied in the suffering of their kinsmen and kinswomen. The emergence of voice in community with other voices uses the category of experience not to create neat categories of well-bounded units—it suggests rather that the bridges between everyday life and the making of a political community call upon these intertwining stories.

Can societies subjected to such continuous violence as in South Africa recover the capabilities of instituting democratic rights? The Truth and Reconciliation Commission is a dramatic effort to provide a public space in which the terror unleashed during apartheid may be articulated and publicly heard. The Commission seeks to give judicial acknowledgment to stories that may have circulated earlier in more restricted circles: the impunity with which whites killed and tortured children and adults beggars belief.[4] Though conceived on the model of a judicial commission, the mandate of the Truth and Reconciliation Commission departs considerably from the gold standard of evidence to establish guilt required under a criminal justice system. In this sense the Commission is different from, say, international tribunals to inquire into human right violations in ex-Yugoslavia or Rwanda, for the hope in South Africa is to enclose and seal a certain kind of violence as it was experienced in the past, to put a full stop to it, even as the impossibility of being able to judicially pin responsibility on individual criminals is clear.

The Commission, though, has its own genealogy. It is informed by assumptions about truth, reconciliation, and forgiveness at the level of public pronouncements. The analysis of women's testimonies in Fiona Ross's chapter points to the naïveté of the assumption that forgiveness can be easily earned. As Martha Minow has stated, "Ultimately, perhaps, responses to collective violence bear witness to it. The obligation of witnessing includes the practice of 're-memory,' which is Toni Morrison's term for practices that concretely encourage people to affirm life in the face of death, to hold onto feelings of both connection and disconnection, and to stay wide enough awake to attend to the requirements of just recollection and affirmation and the path of facing who we are, and what we become" (Minow 1998: 147).

It is perhaps also possible to argue that in testimonies offered before the Commission, one is not only reading the events through the testimonial accounts but is also being read. That is to say that while the *texts* of the testimonies might be about the experiences of violation, offering words that were earlier not permitted to be voiced, the *processes* involved in giving and receiving testimony established a new context for the interaction between the perpetrators, witnesses, and survivors. Those who had been silently complicit or actively involved in perpetrating violence had to also learn to read themselves. A recent account by Antjie Korg of her personal transformation as an Afrikaans woman while observing the processes through which the testimonies were produced provides a rare insight into this aspect of the Truth and Reconciliation Commission. She describes her own work as that of wrapping the survivors in words, so that over these past hurts they can inherit a common future. But in doing so, she also learns that she did not know how to read the body codes of black people and that she could not escape the way that genealogies of power and familiarity worked within her own body. The pedagogic task of the Commission then is not that it has offered new information, but that it has made perpetrators as well as survivors become part of the formation of knowledge through which it may become possible to create a future in which this divided and traumatic past can be inherited.

It is not only in the Commission but in small communities and families away from the eyes of the Commission that work is being done to come to terms with painful memories and to domesticate the terror of the past. Work currently under progress by several scholars suggests that communities fragmented by the violence of apartheid are also responding to fresh possibilities in different and less dramatic ways.[5] Reconciliation is not a matter of a confession offered once and for all, but rather the building of relationships by performing the work of the everyday. Such work is comparable to the reconstitution of everyday life as well as the search for the counterpublics described in the other chapters in this volume.

THE RECALCITRANCE OF TRAGEDY

Thus, the role of memory, of ancient precedents of current criminality, obviously governs our responses to
the immediate and often more savage assaults on our
humanity, and to strategies of remedial action. Faced
with such a balancing imposition—the weight of memory against the violations of the present—it is sometimes useful to invoke the voices of the griots, the ancestral shades and their latter day interpreters, the
poets. Memory obviously rejects amnesia, but it remains amenable to closure that is, apparently, the ultimate goal of social strategies such as the Truth and
Reconciliation and the Reparation Movement (for the
enslavement of a continent?). It is there that they find
common ground even though the latter does entail, by
contrast, a demand for restitution. Both seek the cathartic bliss, the healing that comes with closure.

Wole Soyinka

One of the assumptions behind the judicial reckoning of truth is of a mimetic relation between memory and event. The accounts of horrific events have made us acutely aware of the delicate work of giving testimony and of the facile assumption that our systems of representation reproduce either everything or nothing. Consider the various forms that testimony takes in Primo Lévi, who sometimes speaks of his *pathologically precise* memories and at other times of his memories as a *suspect source* that he must be protected against (Cheyette 1998). One of the most difficult tasks before survivors is to remember not only objective events but also one's own place in those events.[6]

In this context Sasanka Perera's account of ghost stories and "demon" possession provides a methodological strategy for understanding the process of coping with terror, in which the cultural, political, and experiential are deeply connected. For Perera, coping with trauma happens in both the outer space of the social memory of loss and the inner space of the intimate memories of devastation. The tactics for producing the culture of terror in Sri Lanka that he describes are all too familiar: making persons disappear and making bodies appear in strange and unexpected places (for example, severed heads lined up around an otherwise calming reflective pool near a university). Perera goes on to tell us a good deal about culturally authorized forms such as rituals, folk tales, and possession tales, through which symbolic meanings given to these horrific events and collective memory are supported in the face of official erasures.

Perera sees these culturally authorized forms as providing a coping strategy by which survivors of civil conflict continue to live in the midst of torturers and murderers, long after mass violence has ended but in settings in which there is official silence, a state compliant with offenders, and no judicial ways of seeking justice. The situation may look normal from the outside, but this is mere seeming. Memories of terror continue, as does the desire for witnessing and for a response to deep grievances responded to. Storytelling, ritual, and possession—all symbolic means embedded in folk religions—provide ways by which the traumatized continue to find meaning in their suffering, to exist and to rebuild their relationships.

One may ask, though, if communities ever heal such wounds, or are the memories simply buried for one or two generations, until such time as the perspectives and experiences of those living through the shadow of death can be articulated? The French memory of the collaborationist Vichy government and its policies of conniving in genocide and oppressing resisters is a case in point. Similarly, the examples of Stalinist terror, the discovery of pigeon graves of Serbs killed but not allowed to be officially buried during the communist regime who in turn became killers, and the inability of the Chinese to come to terms with the turmoil, terror, and loss of the Cultural Revolution point to the need for long-term studies among survivors of terror. Ethnographers perhaps need to come to terms with the Weberian logic of the tragic in history and politics (Diggins 1996). But they also need to watch against the tendency to assume that stories that are lying dormant in the time of the fathers will *inevitably* come alive in the time of the sons. We are looking not

necessarily for a grand narrative of forgiveness and redemption but for
the small local stories in which such communities are experimenting
with ways of inhabiting the world together.

COMMUNITIES AND HEALING: A COUNTERPOINT

In the penultimate chapter of this volume, Roma Chatterji and Deepak
Mehta describe how an event that is national in character, the demolition of the Babri mosque on 6 December 1992 by a crowd led by a
partisan Hindu political party, may be analyzed at a pitch that is more
local and specific. The demolition of the mosque in the city of Ayodhya
was followed by riots in several cities in India. Chatterji and Mehta
analyze the impact of this on Dharavi, a local slum in Bombay. According to the Srikrishna Commission, appointed by the government to inquire into the Mumbai riots, 900 persons died and 2,036 were injured
between 6 December and 20 January. Although the largest number of
casualties were due to the police firing, many deaths were also attributed
to attacks by local people.

This leads Mehta and Chatterji to ask, what is community? And indeed, what is the individual? They did not find evidence in Mumbai
slums of well-bounded moral communities, which could stoutly resist
corruption from outside. Instead what they found after the riots was "a
multiplicity of fragmented communities, each charting, through rehabilitation work, its strategies for survival and coexistence." Nor was it
the riots alone that were responsible for this fragmentation. Dharavi
occupies 342 acres of land and houses approximately 600,000 people,
with a population density of 187,000 per square kilometer. No wonder
the spaces that people are compelled to occupy are not even visible to
the visitor. Mehta and Chatterji thus raise important questions about
the connections between the violence of the riots and the everyday stories
of crime and violence that make up the picture of Dharavi in the popular
discourses in India.

What relation do acts of violence described in the testimonies of survivors in South Africa, or in stories related by survivors of ethnic violence in Sri Lanka and communal riots in India, bear to everyday life in
society and polity? Nancy Scheper-Hughes, who has given much
thought to this question, asks, "How shall we explain the alarming complicity of 'good people' to outbreaks of radical violence perpetrated by
the state, police, military and ethnic groups?" Her general theoretical
answer is that it is the human capacity to reduce other humans to non-

humans that allows policies of mass destruction to come into play with broad social consent (Scheper-Hughes 1997: 471).

It appears to us that the deployment of the category of "human capacity" does not offer us tools fine enough to ask how it is that this capacity is realized in some contexts and not others. It is in the extraordinary ethnographic recounting of events in Scheper-Hughes (1995, 1997) that one gets an idea of how it is that people can get *beside themselves*. That is to say, it is as if successive selves come to inhabit the same person—the disappearance or loss of context may be generative of the experience (as in possession, dispossession, or in trance) of a new kind of subjectivity. To investigate the continuity between peacetime crimes and acts of spectacular violence, for which Scheper-Hughes makes an important and convincing case, we feel that we need to examine closely what sudden removal of any access to context can do to the formation of the subject.

Especially in the case of South Africa, the various incidents of violence Scheper-Hughes discusses (1995, 1997) evoke a sense of a complete loss of context in the local worlds in which such incidents happen. For instance, a group of students coming out of a mass meeting see a car with a white driver and think she is a collaborator, a state agent, an enemy out to destroy their movement, and they attack her. This affect of panic, of being somehow endangered, is often produced through particular linguistic forms such as panic rumor—it is part of that oneiric geography of fear when trust in conventions has disappeared. Das (1997) has argued that the rumors during a riot unsettle the context to an extent that even the perpetrators can begin to feel that they are the intended victims. This removal of access to context is when language seems to take on an infectious quality and the dominant affect becomes that of panic. So in Dharavi, where even the "ordinary" act of performing the morning ablutions is fraught with tension because of fights over use of very limited spaces, some maps did exist which could tell people how they might read each other. It was during the riots that all such markers disappeared and had to be reinterpreted—the difference between interpreting a sign correctly or incorrectly became a difference between life and death. Perera similarly gives some stunning examples of the destruction of known landscapes and the production of the constant sense of fear through the circulation of stories that have an infectious quality to them.

Allow us to take the reader to one important moment that occurred in the course of our discussions in the workshop in Cape Town in 1995.

After hearing the presentation by Perera, Arthur Kleinman was moved to say that "pathos is central to historiography and it should be the ethnographer's task too." Violence surely destroys communities, and history is replete with examples of such collapse. In the earlier volume on *Social Suffering*, Lawrence Langer (1997) focused on the terror of memory for the survivors of the Holocaust: rather than using the sanitized terms like "post-traumatic stress disorder," he so resonantly calls such pain and loss the *ruins of memory*.[7] Langer's vision of the anatomy of melancholy among survivors is based on stories told by survivors on video; these tapes are part of the Furtonoff Video Archive for Holocaust Testimonies established at the Yale University in 1982 (see Langer 1991).[8] The context in which the ethnographer listens is (or could be) of a different order, for memory is articulated within local communities through several dispersed narratives in the context of everyday life—it is not seen as already part of an archive. It is this sense of presence, this idea that the events of violence are not past, that they have the potential of becoming alive any moment, which might explain how hard the survivors had to work to generate new contexts in which enough trust could be created to carry on, once again, the work of everyday life.

When Mehta and Chatterji conversed with the survivors in collecting what they call walking ethnographies (as contrasted to what they call sitting ethnographies), they participated in the everyday life of the survivors. So they were able to viscerally experience their fear and defiance. Concerned not only with "what happened?" but also how neighborhoods were now coping with that, the authors are able to document how genealogies of violence and of rehabilitation, though intersecting, have independent trajectories. In the narratives of rehabilitation the authors see the complex subjectivity of actors as they move between subject positions of victims and perpetrators, for in most local contexts these lines are not sharply divided, for precisely the reasons we mentioned earlier.

Thus efforts at rehabilitation of victims in Dharavi were themselves ambivalent and point to a precarious balance between a multiplicity of divergent forces that violent events unleash. There is the question of betrayal, both loss of trust in one's neighbors and suspicion of agencies of the state, since the police actively connived with some of the perpetrators; but there are also pragmatic concerns regarding livelihood, schooling of children, health care for the traumatized. These heterogeneous relations endure through violence. As Mehta and Chatterji state, "The altered everyday is marked by a new knowledge and memory of loss, but also a practical wisdom of negotiating this loss. It tells one that reparation cannot take the form of justice, co-existence is possible only if the past is deliberately set aside."

We return to healing and what it means. For Langer (1991, 1997) there can be no healing after an atrocity like that of the Holocaust, but he makes a distinction between the Holocaust and other kinds of atrocities. For the Hindu and Muslim communities in Dharavi, healing is described as the ability to unite sufficiently closely to allow everyday commerce between peoples to resume after violence has cut ties and broken relationships. Different sorts of healing are implicated in the definition used. Thus to cure pain or to repair loss for the individual may not be possible. Yet communities may see health as the measure of sufficient cooperation to allow for the resumption of everyday activities.

The work of anthropologists in recent years has made it sufficiently clear that locality is produced by forces that come from the outside as much as from internal developments (Appadurai 1996; Gupta and Ferguson 1997). It would thus be perilous to ignore the larger political environment which addresses the hurts that have been incurred in acts of violence that have a local signature. This entanglement of the larger political environment in both the acts of violence and in the creation of possibilities for healing seems important in all the accounts. In fact, Perera's description stands out as one in which an alternate public sphere has not yet been allowed to emerge in which the survivors can articulate their demands for justice. Clearly a double movement seems necessary for communities to be able to contain the harm that has been documented in these accounts: at the macro level of the political system it requires the creation of a public space that gives recognition to the suffering of survivors and restores some faith in democratic processes, and at the micro levels of community and family survivors it demands opportunities for everyday life to be resumed. This does not mean that success would be achieved in separating the guilty from the innocent through the working of the criminal justice system, for in most cases described here it is not easy to separate the guilty and to pinpoint legal responsibility, but it does mean that in the life of a community, justice is neither everything nor nothing—that the very setting-into-process of public acknowledgment of hurt can allow new opportunities to be created for resumption of everyday life.

RETRIEVAL OF VOICE

No foreign sky protected me,
No stranger's wing shielded my face.
I stared as witness to the common lot,
Survivor of that time, that place.
     Anna Akhmatova, "Requiem"

The survivor's tale, the sufferer's lament, even the therapeutic narrative
of pain transformed through religious or psychiatric healing, are all examples of stories called forth out of the ruins of memory. But is it this
way, or rather is it that voices speak through the wounded just as spirits
communicate through mediums, that stories call victims to say something that is not theirs to possess? These ethnographies are structured
by local narrative styles that are distinctive cultural productions. Thus
the narratives of Japanese atomic bomb survivors are a genre within the
Japanese literary tradition, as Maya Todeschini demonstrates; and the
legends of the Cree are a part of revitalization within the contours of
this indigenous North American people's tradition, as Naomi Adelson
shows. Pain is always part of a particular culture, the expression of a
local world.

Yet this is not an entirely satisfactory way of putting things. In both
traditions the choke and sting of experience only becomes real—is
heard—when it is narrativized. The expression of personal pain is also
a form of cultural representation, yet the relation is not an isomorphic
one. There is a sliding relation between social structure and the construction of personal agency in the transformations of ordering experience.
The voices of the atomic bomb survivors *resist* inauthentic distortion
into nationalist programs of denial and xenophobia; they press up
against the limits of stigma and social control to open a local space
where survivors can express their individuality as well as an alternative
collective sentiment. The therapeutic stories of the Cree establish a space
of ethnic authenticity that carries political as well as moral significance.
In each setting stories restructure moral experience, defining what matters most to local groups who have been marginalized and whose local
world has been broken apart by powerful social force. Even the Kui,
Chuengsatiansup shows, speak in order to assert an identity against the
stigmatizing alternative provided by the dominant Thai center (king)–
periphery (barbarian tributary) discourse. That speech turns against (re-

sists) dominant definitions and clichéd stories of those who appropriate and distort the local on behalf of the state or for commercial interests.

Experience moves from inchoate social and psychological processes to definable, even memorable cultural representations through its evocation or realization in stories. This does not mean that there is a pre-given subject to whom experience happens—rather, postulating the subject is a way of thinking about the possibility of experience. Thus it is that these stories provide a cultural shape that has the potential to naturalize, normalize, and thereby order experience in terms of societal processes of social control. But stories, like other social phenomena, have unanticipated consequences. This must be especially true in communities undergoing or trying to break down or break away from established conventions. The social space occupied by scarred populations may enable stories to break through routine cultural codes to express counterdiscourse that assaults and even perhaps undermines the flow of taken-for-granted meanings of things as they are. Out of such desperate and defeated experiences stories may emerge that call for, and even at times may bring about, change that alters utterly the commonplace—both at the level of collective experience and at the level of individual subjectivity. Here Todeschini's comparison of literary works and ethnographic voices suggests more than even her strong analytic line can work out.

The expression of voice is found in a dramatic form in Perera's account of possession and the stories of avenging ghosts. The psychiatric and psychological literature has replaced the term "possession" with "dispossession." Possession places emphasis on the being of the possessing agency or the person-who-is-possessed's experience of being taken over, becoming a medium for that god, ghost, demon, or ancestor. Dispossession, in contrast, refers to an experience of splitting in cognitive and affective states so that the person becomes nearly completely absorbed in that focus. During dispossession what is inner and inexpressible can be projected outward into a culturally authorized voice. We do not wish to imply that there is a completed hidden script in the inner life that is simply waiting to be projected. Rather, the states of dispossession are able to provide the external criteria by which the person traumatized by violence can overcome the suffocation of speech. Thus dispossession, possession, and even the deep call of stories may be seen as stitching together the person's inner space and the outward space. Language does not function here purely as a medium of communication but is also to be viewed as experience (see Das 1998) which allows not only a message but also the subject to be projected outwards.

We require long-term participant observation to see how such experiences may mold the subjectivity of persons traumatized by violence. We can say, though, that the yearning for recrimination and retribution can be received in the collective symbolic forms and may become a source for collective action. Alternately, voice when it comes may come too late to avert tragedy. This is the sense one has of the communities that have refused to testify before the Truth and Reconciliation Commission, or of women who did testify but found that they could speak of experience only in the third person—relating what happened to other dearly loved ones but being unable to project themselves within this genre of speech.

An altogether different meaning is given to the idea of voice in Mehta and Chatterji's chapter, because voice has here become untethered from the signature of the person. The authors describe the anonymity of the voices emanating from crowds during the killings in Dharavi. Repeatedly survivors asserted that individuals could not be recognized in these voices—the slogans became signatures of large, hostile collectivities (see also Das 1997). Although Mehta and Chatterji do not speak of possession or dispossession, their account speaks of the impossibility of giving narrative form to experience. Witness the mentally disabled child who sits by the adults overhearing their conversations and monotonically recites, "We were playing India and Pakistan." Overtly this is not a ghost story, but surely the child is *possessed* here by a jingoist nationalist discourse of boundaries that was heard in the context of a local violence that she had little means to comprehend. These fragments of floating stories now shape her memory and make her almost a victim to language. In such contexts voice appears in a lethal form, testimony to how one may be robbed of agency. Paradoxically it is not the retrieval of voice but the appearance of the face through which communities torn asunder by violence begin to accord mutual recognition to each other.[9]

CONCLUDING THOUGHTS

In a review of a volume on the Rwandan catastrophe, Wole Soyinka (1998) observes:

> The orders came from above, yes; the *interhamwe,* the Hutu militia, was
> schooled and drilled and indoctrinated into the diverse mission of liquidating

a designated other, but that so many ordinary people turned against their neighbors, blood relatives, co-workers, drinking and gossip companions— this is where the process of comprehension is stalled no matter how eloquent the argument of economics and politics, or of the deleterious role of memory—given the level of unrepentant participation, including the social ostracism of the dissenting or critical bystanders even till now, can the two main components of the Rwandan nation be expected to live together . . . that is to bring to realization the rehabilitation. . . .

This question, once their different stories are taken into account, still haunts the aftermath of ethnic cleansing in Bosnia; the crisis in Kosovo; and the South African, Sri Lankan, and Indian cases in this book. It was the defining question in our second volume, *Violence and Subjectivity,* in this series (Das, Kleinman, Ramphele, and Reynolds 2000). From the ethnographies in this book, sensitive to both the larger political context of these local stories of devastation and the dense intimate connections that have been forged in the context of everyday lives, it would appear that no glib appeal to "our common humanity" can restore the confidence to inhabit each other's lives again. Instead it is by first reformulating their notions of "normality" as a changing norm, much as the experience of a disease changes our expectations of health (cf. Canguilhem 1978), that communities can respond to the destruction of trust in their everyday lives.

The question of carrying on after political violence has a relation to the question raised by truth commissions, commissions of enquiry, or other Nuremberg-style proceedings against perpetrators. Legal procedure may well play a role, even a decisive one, in community coping, but that role cannot account for the continuity of everyday social experience, nor can it alone bring about the repair of social ties and institutions. Moral procedure in responses to mass violence—a recognizable aspect of South Africa's Truth and Reconciliation Commission—is not about judging cases to establish criminal status and determine punishment. Rather it turns on *acknowledgment* of pain of victims and the role of perpetrators in causing that pain. Acknowledgment need not be limited to individual injury: it can give recognition to the injury or deaths inflicted on a collective, and also legitimate that collective's quest for repair, revitalization, and healing. The term "healing," as it is used in truth commissions, retains its defining conflation of medical and religious action. Community healing, as we read in chapters in this volume, means repair but it also means transformation—transformation to a different moral state.

All of this sounds interesting, but can it be real? Do, in fact, broken communities that have been fractured by war and structural violence ever regenerate? Or are these simply the official words needed to authorize political processes of normalization that themselves merely prevent ultimate defeat and stanch social hemorrhage and chaos until a later time? Is "coping" then too simple and simplifying a concept to apply to communities ravaged by political terror? The chapters in this book suggest that at the level of the ordinary, the everyday social realities, states of rebuilding and accommodation are as complex as are the networks of individual lives of victims, perpetrators, victim-perpetrators, internal resisters, and critics and witnesses. There usually is no clear-cut victory, no definitive crossing over to safety and renewal. But if that sounds too bleak a conclusion, think of it the other way around: there usually is no complete defeat, no ultimate breakdown and dissolution. Even following the most horrendous ethnocides—the Holocaust, the mass murder of Tutsis—social life continues. And that is the source both of possibilities and of very deep perplexities. Recently, traveling in Poland, one of us (AK) was told by a Polish professional colleague, "Our society is so homogeneous." Stupefied by the historical amnesia of the remark, the listener could only angrily rehearse the scenario of the mass killing of Polish Jews and Gypsies, who together compromised such a large minority of pre–World War II Poland. Continuity often means collective amnesia and rewriting of the historical record. Political and social transformation that fails to engage the moral reality must be contested. Hence the value of memorialization of victims and of the political and social conditions of their victimhood, and the significance of what truth commissions need to establish as an incontrovertible record of the destruction of individuals and groups. Does there need to be an opposite form of moral engagement that limits or qualifies excessive and unending claims of victimhood that aspire to create a permanent condition of moral superiority and that prevent compromise and resettlement? And what of the commercialization of victimhood and its other abuses: political and moral? The materials in this book suggest that even this balancing act may represent too limited an engagement with on-the-ground realities. These realities cannot be adequately categorized by using coarsely definitive descriptions such as health or breakdown, healing or pathology. Local worlds are too multisided and changing to be usefully described in this way. On the other hand, large ethical formulations such as crimes against humanity, abuse of human rights, and claims of social justice seem too large-scale and clichéd to deal with the specificity of cases such as those described in the following ethnographies.

The answers to the questions we posed in the beginning of this Introduction, then, are a series of paradoxes. Ian Buruma (1994) has argued that our age is one in which victimization has become of special ontological salience. The assumption is that it helps the victims to emphasize *victimhood* as a cultural representation and collective experience. If that is true, does the appropriation of victimization as the core moral stance create a paradox in that it becomes a means to revivify the fragments of communities, one that works against reconciliation and rebuilding?

The analyses embedded within these detailed renderings of local worlds testify to the need of survivors to be able to articulate their collective hurts by the creation of alternate public spheres, but there is enough evidence of resistance to being made into icons of the status of victims. Clearly ethnography needs to document the recalcitrance of tragedy so as to avoid the sentimental view of suffering, but we also emphasize the creativity of everyday life in arriving at new norms of interrelatedness in communities. The survivors' narratives do get powerfully structured by the cultural genres that can authorize experience, but that does not preclude the appearance of voice that resists such taken-for-granted categories. We suspect that it is because the task of reformulating everyday life in the face of the radical doubts about its possibilities is fraught with unimagined dangers that we find survivors inhabiting all these contradictory positions.

There is now an increasing production of knowledge about violence by those who are the mediators and translators of collective violence to the rest of the world.[10] Images are generated by the media and reports are prepared by judicial commissions, citizens' committees, and other human rights groups in response to the question: what happened? Such images and reports are now part of national and even global patterns of consumption through which a new geography of the world has been brought into existence. The media and the human rights organizations play an important role not only in representing the violence but also in becoming actors in the anticipations of local communities on how their suffering is to be addressed. We need to realize, though, that there are strong compulsions of politics and commerce, as well as personal commitments, which inform these reports. This is true equally for anthropological reports. What may be different is that the importance of violent events lies for the media in their dramatic potential. This is why very few stories are followed over time in the media, especially when they appear to become dated. Similarly, those writing on behalf of human rights groups are constrained by the immediate needs of victims and by a mode of storytelling that is anchored in judicial ideas of what testimony can stand up in court. Typically the interaction between such fact-finding committees and the survivors of disasters is of short duration. There is rarely an opportunity to observe how everyday life is lived in such communities of survivors, no long-term relation established between those who experience the violence and those who interpret it for others. The eliciting of memory follows judicial models of witnessing: even though it is recognized that memory can only be recovered in fragments, the relation of the fragments to the event is seen as a mimetic one.[11] The commercialization and emergence of powerful global media have further complicated the situation. Not only do the media pay scant attention to long-term and "little" consequences of violence, they are also positioned to demand a sentimental view that privileges miraculous exceptions, hopeful endings, and a clarity in pronouncements. The global media, suspicious of too much local detail that may overwhelm the viewer, have created a viewing stance in which the consumers of news and documentaries are suspicious of mixed messages, paradoxes, and unfinished stories. Yet our ethnographies can only take us to resting points that are not endings but openings to new issues that require continuous working through, so characteristic of everyday life.

As against the judicial or media-oriented confessional models of truth-telling, the ethnographic method used by anthropologists in this volume is based on long-term interactions with communities of survivors. The moment of destruction is but one moment in these accounts—the narratives move to the manner in which processes of resistance, contestation, and accommodation begin to happen.[12] Sometimes it is not even a single event but a series of events spanning more than a century, embodied in the memories that are now being contested of communities such as the Cree and the Kui. Thus we may speak here not only of collective violence but also of the margins that extend the violence backwards and forwards. It is this different temporality of the ethnographic account that marks its special feature.

Since this project relied on an approach that was both ethnographic and comparative, it was able to show the diverse configurations within which the institutional and the experiential, the public and the private, the spectacular and the quotidian come together to define the realm of politics. Rather than preconceived ideas about the nature of the public sphere, the definition of citizenship, and the division between public and private, it showed how these domains are themselves constituted by the collective action of marginalized groups in some cases and those suffering from the trauma of collective violence in other cases. By simultaneously engaging the public and the private, it showed how the creativity of social action may be located in the realm of the everyday but also that the everyday itself is implicated in the creation of a new normality in areas devastated by such experiences of terror. These are not solutions to the pressing problems of violence but they point to the necessity for each one of us to engage in sober ethnographic reflection on the possibilities and the limits of the creativity of everyday life. The juxtaposition of translocal ethical perspectives on ethnographic descriptions of local moral worlds makes for a bifocality of perspective, which can illuminate the imperatives of each, as also their limits. We hope the three volumes will be read as part of the same project of addressing social suffering, violence, and the remaking of worlds—a quest which did not yield any final destinations but pointed to some resting places, some temporary closures, stories of hope and despair.

NOTES

1. This is not to say that what appears sudden and inexplicable to the actors may not be shown to be structurally embedded.

2. The idea of alternate public spheres is formulated by Nancy Fraser (1995) in opposition to Habermas's notion of the public sphere, in which the constitutional state is revealed and monitored through organs of rational and intelligent discussion. It opens up a very interesting space for discussion on the various publics that struggle for recognition in the modern democratic constitutional state.

3. The division of voices in mourning laments is the subject of much recent literature. See especially Seremetakis (1992), Das (1997), and Wilce (1998).

4. On the relation between biography and social text see Das (1995).

5. Personal communication by Pamela Reynolds.

6. In *The Periodic Table,* Lévi says: "I find it difficult to reconstruct the sort of human being that corresponded in November 1944 to my name, or better, to my number: 174517. I must then overcome the most terrible crisis, the crisis of having become part of [the] Lager system, and I must have developed a strange callousness if I then managed not only to survive but also to think, to register the world around me, and even to perform rather delicate works, in an environment infected by the daily presence of death" (139–40).

7. For a completely different way of conceptualizing memory as ruin, see Pandolfo (1997).

8. Langer warns that he is talking about the Holocaust and not every kind of violence. We do not think it is useful to enter into a debate on the uniqueness

of the Holocaust in the history of human violence, but Langer's caveat is important because the possibilities for recovery of community differ not only due to the scale of violence but also the styles of violence.

9. The concept of face is taken from Levinas (1998).

10. This theme was explored explicitly by Kleinman and Kleinman (1997).

11. For instance, Pandey (1991) speaks of the importance of fragments and the need to relinquish the idea of finding the whole truth in the context of a fact-finding mission he undertook on behalf of a human rights groups (People's Union of Democratic Rights) following Hindu-Muslim riots in Bhagalpur in the state of Bihar. He imagines these fragments to be in the nature of partial truths bearing a mimetic relation to the event in answer to the question of what happened. It is not our position that such regimes of truth-telling are not important but that fragments of traumatic memory are about the event *and the subject's place in that event,* as Lévi's various explorations with memory show.

12. We can see the temporality of long-term intimacy established by the anthropologist in the accounts of violence by Loizos (1981), Spencer (1990, 1992), and others. These anthropologists found that war and collective violence altered the very fabric of relations in the communities they had studied before the time of violence. Their accounts are therefore much more conducive to understanding the heterogeneity of everyday life—but even these accounts have not addressed issues of how new norms of sociality are established in this altered normality in the lives of communities.

REFERENCES CITED

Appadurai, Arjun. 1996. *Modernity at Large: Cultural Dimensions of Globalization.* Minneapolis: University of Minnesota Press.

Aretxaga, Begona. 1988. "What the Border Hides: Partition and Gender Politics in Irish Nationalism." *Social Analysis: Journal of Cultural and Social Practice* (Special Issue on Partition, Unification, Nation, edited by Gautam Ghosh) 42, no. 1: 16–33.

Benjamin, Walter. 1966. *Illuminations.* Ed. Hannah Arendt. New York: Schocken Books.

Buruma, Ian. 1994. *The Wages of Guilt: Memories of War in Germany and Japan.* New York: Farrar, Straus & Giroux.

Butler, Judith. 1997. *The Psychic Life of Power: Theories in Subjection.* Stanford: Stanford University Press.

Canguilhem, Goerges. 1978. *The Normal and the Pathological.* New York: Zone Press.

Cheyette, Bryan. 1998. "The Ethical Uncertainty of Primo Lévi." In *Modernity, Culture and the Jew,* ed. Bryan Cheyette and Laura Marcus. London: Polity Press.

Daniel, E. Valentine. 1997. *Charred Lullabies: Chapters in an Anthroprography of Violence.* Princeton: Princeton University Press.

Das, Veena. 1995. *Critical Events: An Anthropological Perspective on Contemporary India.* Delhi: Oxford University Press.

————. 1997a. "Language and Body: Transactions in the Construction of Pain." In *Social Suffering,* ed. Arthur Kleinman, Veena Das, and Margaret Lock: 67–93. Berkeley: University of California Press.

————. 1997b. "Official Narratives, Rumour, and the Social Production of Hate." *Social Identities* 4, no. 1: 109–30.

————. 1998. "Wittgensein and Anthropology." *Annual Review of Anthropology* 27: 171–95.

Das, Veena, Arthur Kleinman, Mamphela Ramphele, and Pamela Reynolds, eds. 2000. *Violence and Subjectivity.* Berkeley: University of California Press.

Diggins, John P. 1996. *Max Weber: Politics and the Spirit of Tragedy.* New York: Basic Books.

Dumont, Jean-Paul. 1992. "Ideas on Philippine Violence: Assertions, Negations, and Narrations." In *The Paths to Dominance, Resistance and Terror,* ed. Carolyn Nordstorm and JoAnn Martin. Berkeley: University of California Press.

Fraser, Nancy. 1995. "Politics, Culture and the Public Sphere: Toward a Postmodern Conception." In *Social Postmodernism: Beyond Identity Politics,* ed. Linda Nicholson and Steven Seidman. Cambridge: Cambridge University Press.

Gourevitch, Philip. 1998. *We Wish to Inform You that Tomorrow We Will Be Killed with Our Families: Stories from Rwanda.* New York: Farrar, Straus, and Giroux.

Gupta, Akhil, and James Ferguson. 1997. "Culture, Power, Place: Ethnography at the End of an Era." In *Culture, Power, Place: Explorations in Cultural Anthropology,* ed. Gupta and Ferguson, 1–29. London: Duke University Press.

Kleinman, Arthur, Veena Das, and Margaret Lock, eds. 1997. *Social Suffering.* Berkeley: University of California Press.

Kleinman, Arthur, and Joan Kleinman. 1997. "The Appeal of Experience; the Dismay of Images; Cultural Appropriations of Suffering in Our Times." In *Social Suffering,* ed. Arthur Kleinman, Veena Das, and Margaret Lock. Berkeley: University of California Press.

Krog, Antjie. 1998. *Country of My Skull.* Johannesburg: Random House.

Langer, Lawrence L. 1991. *Holocaust Testimonies: The Ruins of Memory.* New Haven: Yale University Press.

————. 1997. "The Alarmed Vision: Social Suffering and Holocaust Atrocity." In *Social Suffering,* ed. Arthur Kleinman, Veena Das, and Margaret Lock, 47–67. Berkeley: University of California Press.

Lévi, Primo. 1985. *The Periodic Table.* Trans. Raymond Rosenthall. London: Michael Joseph.

Levinas, Emmanuel. 1988. *The Drowned and the Saved.* Trans. Raymond Rosenthall. London: Michael Joseph.

————. 1998. *Entre nous: On Thinking-of-the-Other.* Trans. Michael B. Smith and Barbara Hershaw. London: Athlone.

Lifton, Robert J. 1967. *Death in Life: Survivors of Hiroshima.* New York: Random House.

————. 1983. *The Broken Connection: On Death and the Continuity of Life*. New York: Basic Books.

Loizos, Peter. 1981. *The Heart Grown Bitter: A Chronicle of Cyprist War Refugees*. New York: Cambridge University Press.

Marcus, George E., and Michael M. J. Fischer. 1986. *Anthropology as Cultural Critique: An Experimental Moment in the Human Sciences*. Chicago: University of Chicago Press.

Minow, Martha. 1998. *Between Vengeance and Forgiveness: Facing History after Genocide and Mass Violence*. Boston: Beacon Press.

Pandey, Gyanendra. 1991. "In Defence of the Fragment: Writing about Hindu Muslim Riots in India Today." *Economic and Political Weekly* 26, nos. 11–12: 559–72.

Pandolfo, Stephania. 1997. *Impasse of the Angels: Scenes from a Moroccan Space of Memory*. Chicago: University of Chicago Press.

Rév, Istavan. 1997. "The Necronym." Paper presented at the Getty Conference on Collective Memory and Material Artifact, Hamburg, June, 17–21.

Scheper-Hughes, Nancy. 1997. "Peace Time Crimes." *Social Identities* 3: 471–497.

Scott, James C. 1992. *Political Arts of the Powerless: Interpreting the Hidden Scripts of the Powerless*. New Haven: Yale University Press.

Seremetakis, Nadia. 1994. *The Senses Still: Perceptions and Memory as Material Culture in Modernity*. Boulder: Westview Press.

Soyinka, Wole. 1998. "Hearts of Darkness." Review of Philip Gourevitch, *We Wish to Inform You that Tomorrow We Will Be Killed with Our Families*. *The New York Times Book Review*, October 4, p. 11.

————. 1999. *The Burden of Memory: The Muse of Forgiveness*. New York: Oxford University Press.

Spencer, Jonathan. 1990. "Collective Violence and Everyday Practice in Sri Lanka." *Modern Asian Studies* 24, no. 3: 603–23.

————. 1992. "Problems in the Analysis of Communal Violence." *Contributions to Indian Sociology* 26, no. 3: 261–79.

Taylor, Charles. 1992. *Multiculturalism and "The Politics of Recognition": An Essay*. With commentary by Amy Gutman. Princeton: Princeton University Press.

Wilce, James M. 1988. "The Pragmatics of Madness: Performance Analysis of a Bangladeshi Woman's Aberrant Lament." *Culture, Medicine and Psychiatry* 22: 1–54.

Wittgenstein, Ludwig. 1953. *Philosophical Investigations*. Trans. G. E. M. Anscombe. New York: Macmillan.

Marginality, Suffering, and Community

The Politics of Collective Experience and Empowerment in Thailand

Komatra Chuengsatiansup

INTRODUCTION

The varieties of human suffering have spurred the anthropological imagination. The subject provides a critical standpoint from which anthropologists and cultural theorists can address the devastating effect of macrostructural forces on the lived experiences of the victims (Kleinman 1986, 1988; Das 1990, 1993; Good and Good 1988; Scarry 1985). Such inquiries, which aim at unveiling the social origins and structural sources of human misery, are particularly crucial for the current historical period, when the dominant voice in the discourse of power persistently and deceitfully "insists that responsibility for suffering must be acknowledged by the sufferer himself or herself" (Das 1993: 140) and thus interprets human suffering in terms of personal stake and individual accountability.

At the end of the "short twentieth century," when violence against humanity is both extreme and systematic (Hobsbawm 1994), such accounts draw critical attention to the social as a possible cause of unnecessary forms of human suffering. More recent works examine the societal and institutional responses to individual suffering, demonstrating the adverse effects of inhumane professional transformation and bureaucratic appropriation of the experience of suffering by the state, market, media, and academia (see Das 1993; Kleinman and Kleinman 1991, 1996; Lock 1996; Young 1995, for instance).

While the social origins of suffering have been critically brought to the fore by scholars, relatively few works have been written on the political significance of the lived experience of suffering in the process of collective empowerment. Transcending the individual experience of suffering is depicted in academic discourse and glorified in religious discourse as personal victory, "in the manner of the oyster whose sickness breeds pearls and of the cedar whose drooping develops its much praised knobs" (Schwarcz 1996: 141).

This personal version of healing suffering, insightful and inspirational as it is, fails to look at how the lived experience of suffering can attain a collective dimension and therefore be politically significant in forging the politics of collective empowerment. It thus inevitably runs the risk of individualizing "social" suffering and resting the burden of solving the problems of suffering on the more docile bodies of individual victims.

This chapter is about a form of social suffering that unequivocally resists such individualization. It is about the predicament of political marginality: the afflicting experience of those whose social existence has been excluded, discounted, dehumanized, and displaced by the dominant political discourse. The concept of marginalization and marginality has been employed by various writers to explore the interplay of multiple forms of asymmetrical power relations in the production of human misery.[1] John Solomos (1982), for instance, uses the concept of marginalization to examine the intertwining of class, race, and the state, which works to the detriment of black youth in Britain. Solomos shows how official discourses and practices in the implementation of public policy regarding the problems of black youth in Britain not only fail to integrate those youth at the margins into an appropriate social realm, but further marginalize them through mechanisms of discipline and control.

In a different approach, Seremetakis (1991) looks at the struggle of marginalized women of Inner Mani in patriarchal Greek society to resist domination by men, the church, the state, and medical rationality. Seremetakis shows how the margins can challenge the dominating center by creating a public space and employing "empowering poetics of the periphery" in the mourning rituals, for the aesthetic expression of a form of resistance.

Although among these writers the actual definitions and applications of the concept may vary, they share a common view that marginality as a theoretical concept offers a comprehensive understanding of the multiple dimensions of asymmetric power relations, rather than their reduction to any single dimension along lines of race, class, or gender. Anna Tsing (1993), in her ethnographic study of the Meratus Dayaks of Indonesia, suggests that the study of marginality has opened up novel ways of thinking about cultural theory. She writes:

> The "marginal" began as a point from which theoretical criticism in academe could be launched. . . . A number of critics have shown how asymmetries of race, gender and colonial status have been produced within rather than in spite of humanist standards. . . . Similarly, the marginal has been a rejoinder to Marxist class-oriented approaches that do not adequately address colonialism and racism. Unlike class, the latter power relations cannot be understood within a homogeneous, taken-for-granted cultural regime; they construct and bind systems of cultural difference. . . . From this criticism, then, marginality began to signal a discussion that moves beyond rereading dominant theories to formulate new objects of study. (Tsing 1993: 14)

In studying power relations in the "galactic polity" of Siam, where power and spatiality are interwoven by "a concept of territory as a variable sphere of influence that diminishes as royal power radiated from a center" (Tambiah 1976: 112), the notion of marginality is particularly relevant. In fact, a number of social scientists have fruitfully applied such a notion to the study of ethnic minorities, particularly hill people in Thailand.[2] My inquiry, therefore, will add to the voices of these forerunners in addressing the predicament of those whose social existence is discounted and excluded. While maintaining a focus on the dynamics of power relations in the politics of marginalization, my analysis will also link local events and the experience of marginality to the emerging political awareness at the wider level that is currently reshaping the contemporary political landscape of Thailand.

OVERVIEW

This chapter is divided into three parts. In the first part, I examine the social production of marginality among the Kui, an indigenous people residing at the borderland of the ancient kingdom of Siam. I will relate how Kui marginal identities have been constructed in historical discourse by examining the representations of the Kui in official Siamese historiography. Then, drawing on my ethnographic inquiry, I will discuss how the Kui's marginality has been re-created and perpetuated in contemporary politics, with particular emphasis on the role the state has taken in the construction of Kui vulnerability and marginality.

By examining how marginalization processes operated to exclude the voices of the Kui from the mainstream political sphere, I make an attempt to reveal the form and nature of the power exercised by the dominant sector. I will argue that at the margins of political domination, the power of the modern Thai state was constituted and maintained by the politics of exclusion. This form of power differs from the coercive power of "discipline and punish" (Foucault 1979) in that the state is not concerned with creating docile bodies or the network of disciplines and punishments. Rather, it is exclusion and indifference (Herzfeld 1992) that have provided the modern Thai state with new sources of power.

In order to place the first part in a larger context, the second part of this chapter traces an emerging political ethos—namely, skepticism about state authority—in the dynamics of the contemporary Thai political landscape. From extensive review of current academic and political discourses in Thailand, it is evident that people's organizations, NGOs (nongovernmental organizations), and concerned academicians, from grassroots initiatives to national movements, are forging a new political sphere, a sphere of deliberate citizenship in which the voices of the excluded can be heard and extreme asymmetrical power relations can be challenged. Such social movements, articulated in the notion of movements towards a stronger "civil society," are now gaining more and more political momentum in Thailand.

This review reveals an emerging collective political consciousness: a critical public awakened by shared experience of discontent with the deforming structural order of the status quo. It was within this political context that the vibrant resonance between the Kui's experience of political marginality at the local level and the emerging collective political consciousness at the macrosocial levels took place. Such resonating repercussion brought about a new awareness among local Kui leaders of being part of an "imagined community" (Anderson 1991) of dissenters seeking freedom from the prevailing cultural hegemony. This process will be described and discussed in part three, along with an account of local initiatives that linked local movements with emerging movements at the regional and national levels.

Drawing on my field experience, I argue for a more careful examination of the political significance of intersubjective experiences of suffering and their relation to collective empowerment. The intersubjectivity of social suffering, by virtue of being rooted in a shared historical and structural predicament, constitutes a sphere of shared cognizance

and shared practices which together forge a collective political consciousness of an imagined community of dissenters. Viewed from this
angle, the social ceases to be a single structure of constraint or merely
the source of unnecessary forms of human suffering. Rather, against the
official politics of exclusion and indifference, society is better conceived
as sets of multiple potential sources of collective empowerment and as
multiple spaces of resistance.

ETHNOGRAPHIC SETTING

It is among the Kui elephant people, an indigenous group living in Surin
province near the Thai-Cambodian border, that I conducted my fifteen
months of fieldwork. Surin province, although a small province, is renowned for its annual Elephant Round-Up Festival. Each year, more
than two hundred elephants gather and perform for tourists from
around the world. This annual event has contributed greatly to the local
economy. The elephant affair is so unique and significant that the province is proudly named "the Land of Elephants" and its insignia bears
an image of a sacred elephant.

A lesser-known fact is that it is the indigenous Kui people who exhibit
their elephants and perform the elephant show. Surin province is eth-
nically diverse. Besides a small number of Chinese and Thai, the bulk
of the province's population is Khmer, Lao, and Kui. These three ethnic
groups possess different social statuses within the Thai social hierarchy.
Among them, the Kui people are indisputably the most marginalized
and underprivileged. Unlike their Lao and Khmer counterparts, the Kui
have no independent nation-state with which they can identify. A high-
ranking local official remarked upon my arrival that not having a nation
of their own is unmistakably a sign of the Kui's inferiority and degradation. Stereotypes about Kui people abound: they are considered to be
deceptive, lazy, self-serving, alcoholic, and disease-laden. These social
prejudices force the Kui to veil their ethnic identity.

The Kui language is linguistically classified as part of the Mon-Khmer
language stock. Linguists identify the Kui language as the most "marginal language" in Northeast Thailand (Smalley 1989). The fact that the
Kui language has no writing system causes further difficulties for young-
sters in keeping faith with their traditional knowledge. To be socially
efficient, most Kui have to be in practice multilingual. When conversing
with outsiders, the Kui use the Khmer, Lao, or Thai languages. They

retain Kui only for intraethnic communication. This has the further effect of making the marginal Kui even more invisible—and inaudible—by the society at large.

The Kui prefer to call themselves "Kui," which means "human" or "people." But when conversing with Lao or Thai people they are often described as "Suai." Subpopulations of Kui are differentiated as Nao, Kantou, Per, Man, Bai, Yau, Lo or So, Haut, and Kandrau in the Srikhoraphum district (Prasert 1978). The Kui I study are a subgroup renowned for their ability in elephant hunting—so much so that among the Kui they are specified as Kui Ajiang, or "elephant people."

Physically, the Kui communities I studied are located at the confluence of the rivers Moon and Chee. To a certain extent, the historical settlement of the elephant people in this specific locality was ecologically determined. The banks of the rivers Moon and Chee, until the last three decades, supported large areas of forest. Dong Sai Taw in the east and Dong Poo Din in the west provided food for a herd of elephants captured by the Kui from the deep forest in Cambodia.

I. THE CONSTRUCTION OF KUI MARGINALITY

READING HISTORY AGAINST THE GRAIN

If in reading a text one looks as much for what it conceals as for what it reveals, then in reading official historical records, it is only from attending to what the texts conceal that we can reckon the historical experience of the Kui, a marginal ethnic group residing in the borderland of the ancient kingdom of Siam. In the official historical records of the Siamese kingdom, the Kui were not only "the Other Within" (Thongchai, forthcoming) but the enigmatic one whose historical existence was almost always elusive. In the course of history, their name changed as the categorization and differentiation of Siamese subjects by their rulers changed. The Kui's historicity is found in their absence; we can decipher their existence only by reading history against the grain. And this critically interpretive reading is necessary to find a place in history for the Kui.

To be sure, the Kui's existence in the Siamese historical records was tolerated, but only to a certain, very limited extent, and in a very revealing form; their historical existence was acknowledged only insofar as it served to legitimize the dominating centers. In other words, the Kui were allowed to appear in the official historiography only as a subservient, ignorant, or docile other necessarily to be protected, rescued, and conquered by the Siamese kingdom of central Thailand and the Lao rulers of Champasak. Having neither an independent nation-state nor a written language, the Kui's history has been incorporated and written by other states and in languages other than their own.

Without a system of writing, the Kui's historical knowledge has now become a subjugated knowledge struggling to survive under the hegemony of the "national print-languages" (Anderson 1991: 67). Their oral history has been increasingly overshadowed by the official national history, presently the only true and possible "autonomous history" (Smail 1993). However, the Kui are not a people without history, nor do they live outside history. To be sure, their historical consciousness and their political subjectivity have been shaped by their historical experience, the experience of fragmented identities and marginality that is embodied in their everyday life struggle here and now.

TRACING THE HISTORY OF THE KUI

Connerton, in his much-cited book on social memory (1989), relates the mutual influence between historical reconstruction and collective memory of social groups. While historical reconstruction can in important ways receive a guiding impetus from the memory of a social group, how the official historical narrative is fabricated can profoundly shape a social group's memory and identity. "A particularly extreme case of such interaction occurs when a state apparatus is used in a systematic way to deprive its citizens of their memory. All totalitarianisms behave in this way; the mental enslavement of the subjects of a totalitarian regime begins when their memories are taken away" (Connerton 1989: 14). In the case of the Kui, their memories have been taken away not only because their history has been incorporated into that of other states and written in languages not their own, but, more important, because official historical records take no notice of the Kui, either as a people, a race, or a nation. "Kui" was not even recognized as an ethnic/racial category. Other than appearing in an early Ayutthaya legal code and in one Angkor chronicle, the term "Kui" was not mentioned in the historical records of either the Siamese kingdom or the Lao rulers of Champasak.

It was not that the court of Siam at Bangkok and the rulers at Champasak were so ignorant of the ethnic/racial identity of the natives they administered that they had not considered it worthy of mentioning.

Rather, this neglect arose because the term "Kui" contains no significant meaning in the Siamese and Lao semiopolitical regime. In other words, identifying these people as the Kui had little relevance for Siamese and Lao administrative practices. In fact, the Kui were handily subsumed (and existed) under other names—names that were not self-adopted but imposed upon them by the rulers at Bangkok and Champasak in order to differentiate and categorize the subjects of their regimes. They were labeled and known as "Suai" and "Kha"—meaning tribute and slave, respectively—by the Siamese court and the rulers at Champasak. In the early Bangkok period, they were also classified and named as Khamen Padong, or "the wild Khmer," a designation indicating an exotic, un-civilized other living in an untamed space of wilderness. These officially imposed names carry an irrefutable sense of stigma, and this stigma has become part of the Kui's fragmented identities.

Although among Thai-speaking communities "Suai" has become the natural name of the Kui, such identification originated quite late. Sei-denfaden points out that its onset came as late as the middle nineteenth century. During the reign of Phra Nang Klao (Rama III, 1824–1851), an official survey of the population of the northeastern region was con-ducted by the government in order to get detailed information on the Siamese subjects for a more effective administration of tax, tribute, and corvée labor. The subjects were categorized into three main groups: Lao, Khmer, and Suai (Seidenfaden 1952: 158). The logic behind such cate-gorization is arbitrary yet understandable. For the Siamese court, Lao and Khmer had long been known as well-established racial/ethnic cat-egories, each with its distinctive language and culture. Beyond the know-able Lao and Khmer, however, there were those elusive peoples living in a terra incognita whose racial/ethnic identifications were unknown.[3] Unknown as they were, there was no need to seek out what they called themselves or what their ethnic/racial identity might have been, for there was already a serviceable category for these faraway people. Inasmuch as it was administratively sufficient for the regime to categorize them as those who were liable to pay tribute, it was enough to know and call them by their social obligation—as "Suai," or "tribute people."

THE SOCIAL ORGANIZATION OF PREMODERN SIAM

To better understand the historical experience of the Suai living at the margin of Siamese domination, one has to consider the social organi-zation of the precapitalist Siam. During Ayutthaya and the early Bangkok period, as delineated by Akin Rabibhadana's excellent account (1969), power relations were characterized by the *sakdina* system. Sakdina, literally "power/prestige over land/field," was a hierarchical system of ranking the entire population in a numerical scheme. Except for the king, to whom all land and human lives in the kingdom belonged, every adult male was designated a number as the mark of his dignity or status. Ranks ranged from 5, the lowest, to the highest sakdina, 100,000. The level of sakdina 400 was the dividing line between two major strata: "upper-class persons" and "lower-class persons." It is estimated that the small ruling stratum with sakdina 400 and higher numbered perhaps no more than two thousand people out of an estimated population of two million in the Ayutthaya period (Chai-anan, cited in Turton 1980: 253).

Every male adult from age 18 to 60 was obliged to register as a client or subject (lek or phrai) of a patron/master (*munnai*). No one was allowed to be independent without a patron/master, except for the descendants of the nobility with sakdina 400 or more. Lek or phrai were obligated to work as corvée labor three to six months out of the year until the age of sixty, without compensation or reimbursement of any kind.

SUAI: THE TRIBUTE PEOPLE

To ensure that corvée labor was effectively administered, the Siamese subjects were periodically marked by having their bodies tattooed and registered as corvée. Periodically also the government would organize expeditions to catch people who refused to register. The most extensive registration by tattooing in the northeast began in the reign of King Rama II in 2353 B.E. (A.D. 1810) and took three years to complete. All the Siamese subjects in the northeastern region from Champasak to Sisaket were ordered to be tattooed. Toem, in his voluminous work on the history of northeastern Siam, writes about this matter:

> After having all the lek in the capital tattooed, [the king] ordered officials in the tattooing unit to go tattoo lek in remote *huamuang* (domains), in the north, the northeast, and the east. [The king] ordered local lords and officials to round up and capture lek who had hidden or who couldn't name their munnai, and to tattoo them as *lek huamuang*. If any lek under any munnai was not tattooed at this time, the *chao muang* (lord) was instructed to capture and send him to Bangkok. Both the lek and the munnai who concealed such wrongdoing would be severely punished, and the lek would be sent to work cutting grass for elephants. (Toem 2530 [1987]: 139, my translation)

It is clear that commoners' resistance to registration by escaping into the forest was a common practice. Official expeditions to catch those who had fled were difficult particularly in the marginal provinces. During the reign of King Rama III, trade with China began to flourish. While the demand for indigenous products such as sandalwood, lacquer, and beeswax for export was increasing, demand for corvée decreased because Chinese laborers willing to work at a very low wage were being imported into Siam. The Siamese court turned its policy to extracting indigenous forest products instead of corvée labor.

The region from Champasak and Saravan to Attapeu which was seized during 2320 B.E. (A.D. 1677) was the site of such forest products. Local natives in this area thus were commanded to send forest products as a token of submission in place of their labor. This practice led to a new category of phrai called *phrai suai,* who were obligated to send valuable local products as tribute to the court (Jit Phumisak 2519 [1976]: 443). At first, this measure seemed to work well. Later on, however, as the tribute demanded by the court of Siam increased, phrai suai were unable to supply the tribute in kind. Subsequently, some native men were sent as tribute to the court of Siam at Bangkok. Local people in the area thus came to be known by the name of phrai suai, and eventually "Suai" (ibid.: 445). Jit Phumisak posits that "Suai is a name derived from social obligation, and not determined by race; phrai suai or Suai therefore composes many tribes and races. Given that they were obligated to pay tribute, they all were called Suai. However, in the southern region of the Moon River, the largest group of such people is those of Mon-Khmer linguistic branch. . . . The term 'suai' thus becomes their ethnic name to this day" (Jit 2519 [1976]: 445).[4] Thus the Kui were officially recognized as "Suai" or tribute people, for they were the Siamese subjects residing at the fringes of the kingdom of Siam who were liable to pay to the Siamese court. Or, more precisely, they had become human tribute.

Although, as Seidenfaden suggests, the term "suai" is of recent origin, in modern Siamese historiographies the term has been applied as the name of the Kui as if it has been their original racial/ethnic name since time immemorial. Toem Wiphakpotjanakit, for instance, describes the Kui's ancestors as "a people called 'Suai' " who migrated into Thailand from Attapeu and Saen Paang in Champasak around 2200 B.E. (Toem 2530 [1987]: 153). "Suai" thus has become the Kui's official designation and their only place in Siam historiography. Despite its recent origin, it has been naturalized and become the timeless, unbounded, infinite identity of the Kui in the Thai historical imagination.

STATE POETICS OF HEGEMONY: THE KUI IN MODERN SIAMESE HISTORY

... when there occur great changes in the contemporary scene, there must also be great changes in historiography, that the vision not merely of the present but also of the past must change.

John Smail

By the middle of the nineteenth century the traditional scene of Southeast Asia was drastically changed by the advent of Western colonialist expansion. Colonialism had transformed many traditional institutional practices of the court of Siam. Along with other modern knowledge, modern historiography was introduced into Siam. As many writers have pointed out, modern historiographic practice, as well as its counterparts in art history, anthropology, and archaeology, was part and parcel of colonial practices (see Asad 1973; Stocking 1987; and Bhabha 1985, for instance).

In the Siamese context, the French in particular had invested in extensive investigation in the Far East (Srisakara 2533 [1990]: 451–52). The reports of such investigations were utilized to support colonial claims for territorial conquest in the guise of the *mission civilisatrice*. However, notwithstanding the colonial project of constructing historical and cultural knowledge suitable for colonial claims to political conquest, the royal court of Siam had its own project of constructing historical knowledge for countering colonial claims.

The production of a new history of Siam became part of the nation-building project of securing all the marginal provinces to the national center to form a seamless political entity, the modern Siamese nation-state. The construction of a genealogy of Siamese kingdoms in central Thailand became the core of the national history, and local history was reorganized under the framework of national history with various provincial domains as its constituting units. The traditional royal chronicle of dynasties, edification of the rulers, and their successors (Wyatt 1994: 21) gave way to a new form of historiographic practice. This new form is typified by the *Chronicle of Northeastern Domain*, or *Phongsawadan*

Huamuang Monthon Isan (Amora Wongwichit 2506 [1963]), which was composed in the early twentieth century during the height of colonial conflicts. Instead of relating the edification of the kings and dynastic succession, the plot of the *Chronicle of Huamuang Monthon Isan* was about several provinces in the northeast and their historical relations to Bangkok.[5]

This modern form of history could be considered as having been constructed to unify the kingdom into a united, inseparable whole consisting of various provinces each with its deep root of historical connection to Bangkok. The task of constructing this modern history, however, did not end here. More important than a unified nation was a hierarchical one, with Bangkok at the top and the rest of the kingdom subservient. Modern Siamese national history was thus fabricated to demonstrate emphatically the submissive links by which the peripheral realms were subjugated to the center.

Toem Wiphakpotjanakit's voluminous *Prawatsat Isan* (History of Northeast Thailand), first published in 1970, provides a historical account typical of such a modern local history.[6] The book is organized into five chapters, four of which are local histories of fifteen different provinces. The accounts employ a similar plot, using the subjugation of the local chiefs as the commencement of each province. In the chapter on Surin province, the account begins with an event that brought the "Suai" into contact with the court of Siam:

> Around 2200 B.E. [A.D. 1657] a people called "Suai" migrated [into Thailand] in five different routes from Attapeu and Saen Paang (on the left bank of Mekong) . . .
>
> In the Lesser Era of 1121, year of the rabbit . . . (2302 B.E.), the reign of King Ekkatat . . . of Ayutthaya, a white elephant broke loose to the forest in the realm of Champasak. [The king] ordered that two brothers with accompanying soldiers be dispatched to capture the elephant. The brothers pursued the elephant into the realm of Phimai and entered the southern region of the Moon River. . . . Several Khmer-Suai proffered to guide the brothers and finally captured the white elephant. Some chiefs of the Suai accompanied the two brothers in escorting the elephant back to Ayutthaya. . . .
>
> With their favor [in helping to capture the white elephant], the King of Ayutthaya thus rewarded them with royal titles and honor. . . .
>
> Takaja became Luang Kaew Suwan . . . , Chiang Pum became Luang Suwan Pakdee, Chiang Si became Luang Sri Nakhon Tao. . . .
>
> With the appointment, the chiefs were granted the official authority to control the wild Khmer-Suai (Khamen-Suai Padong) within their respective locales under the supervision of Phimai domain. Because of the opinion that

the area under the control of Luang Suwan Pakdee was too diminutive, the official of Phimai domain relocated the people to Ban Ku Patai Saman, which is the site of Surin province nowadays.

Later on these local chiefs presented elephants, horses, resin, rhino horn, ivory, beeswax, etc. as tribute to the court of Ayutthaya. The King thus rewarded them with a promotion to the rank of lord (chao muang) and upgraded their hamlet from "ban" [village] to "muang" [principality]. . . . Luang Suwan Pakdee (Chiang Pum) became Phra Surin Pakdee Sri Narong, the lord in charge (chao muang chang wang) of Muang Patai Saman (later on this principality was renamed Muang Surin in accordance to the title of its lord—Surin). . . . (Toem 2530 [1987]: 153–55; my translation)

This history seems to be a straightforward depiction of the creation of several *muang* (hierarchical, semidependent principalities or states) by describing how local people were organized into principalities. But its effect is much more sophisticated. In a single trope, such a narration not only incorporates this marginal wild domain into the modern Siamese nation-state but, more important, it establishes the status of the Province of Surin, and of the Kui, in relation to Bangkok within a grid of power relations. The account fortifies the muang's subordination to Siamese rulers by illustrating its historical submission to the court of Siam. The muang's origin is the royal bestowal of title and status in return for the self-subjugation of the Kui's chiefs. In the plain language of impartial description, the account carries an unmistakable didactic value.

By framing local history within the framework of national history, the entire plot of this historical reconstruction serves mainly to herald the official commencement of Surin province under the court of Siam. The Kui were portrayed as a subservient, docile indigenous people who willingly subjugated themselves under the patronage of the Siamese rulers. Framed in this way, the history of the Kui is conflated with and becomes a subtext of the history of Surin province. The national history of a unified Siamese nation-state is created by conflating the demographic and geographic notion of historicity. Such a conflation has been pervasive and has become the normalized plot for local history;[7] it has been a way to talk around the history of local natives without talking about the historical experience of the dominated.

The Kui's appearance as a marginal, impoverished, and unacknowledged other in a kingdom where elephants are symbols of prosperity is rather repugnant. They were the elephant masters who provided the Siamese court with elephants—many of which were the sacred white elephants, the royal regalia of the king. In fact, the prosperity of an ancient Siam kingdom was expressed by one of its great kings, Ramkamhaeng, as "muang kwang—chang lai"—a vast kingdom with abundant elephants. And as Terwiel (1989: 31–33) points out, elephants had been the most pivotal animals in ancient warfare in Southeast Asia. Most of the great historical events glorified in Siamese national history involve the heroic kings whose courageous and victorious battles on the elephants have preserved the nation's independence and saved the kingdom from destruction.

The hypervisibility of elephants in the Thai historical texts as the symbol of power, together with the inaudibility of the Kui's voice, which marks their powerless state, makes any truth claim of the official historical accounts only more contestable. The Kui's voice, like most subaltern voices, must be excluded, for its existence would potentially subvert the moral and political legitimacy of the dominating centers. In a sense, the Kui's historical disappearance is but the testimony of their being deprived. History has been constructed in such a way that it has deprived the Kui even of their most intangible possession: their historical identity.

COLONIAL ENCOUNTERS AND THE EMERGENCE OF THE MODERN SIAMESE STATE

Threatened by the expansion of Western colonialism, the Siamese court under the reign of King Mongkut (Rama IV, 1851–1868) and King Chulalongkorn (Rama V, 1868–1910) rushed to consolidate centralized control over the outskirts. Several measures were declared to strengthen the state's sovereignty (Siffin 1966; Riggs 1966; Tej Bunnag 1976). The autonomy of local chiefdoms was greatly reduced in the transition to the territory-based modern nation-state from the loose organization of muang, each ruled by a lord who controlled taxation, labor, and law, linked to the Bangkok kings by means of tribute. Local lords were replaced by salaried governors dispatched from the central state government (Tej 1976). The Central Thai language was announced as the only official language to be used in schools and governmental administrative procedures; it was facilitated by print technology to become the language of power (Anderson 1991: 45).

It is not coincidental that ethnonationalist uprisings in the form of millennialist movements promptly occurred among the ethnic groups in the northeast, specifically the Khmer, the Lao, and the Kui (Keyes 1977;

Paitoon 1984). The situation was suppressed heavy-handedly, leaving a wound in the collective memory of the local indigenous people.[8] More recently, during the 1950s, a number of highly respected northeastern politicians who had come to challenge the legitimacy of the regime in Bangkok were murdered by the police. These incidents, coupled with the fact that the northeast remains the poorest part of the country, have led indigenous peoples there to see themselves as belonging to a disadvantaged regional minority (Keyes 1987). Historical discourse and the formation of the modern Thai state reveal much about the Kui's marginality as it was generated by the structural predicaments endured for centuries by the Kui. However, the change which was most threatening to the Kui Ajiang's identity took place some sixty years later.

THE END OF ELEPHANT HUNTING

During the 1950s the Kui witnessed a drastic change in their political economy. The pursuing of wild elephants into Cambodian territory became no longer possible; but moreover, in those very same years the Kui were first introduced to the modern world as entertainers who tame and train elephants for display in the elephant round-up fair. This first elephant round-up in 1958 later became the Elephant Round-Up Festival of Surin province, the festival that made the name of Surin well known to the global community as "the Land of Elephants."

Before 1957 the Kui elephant hunters used to march across the Phanom Dongrek Range into the deep forest in Cambodia to capture wild elephants. These forests extended southward into the Cambodian plain and eastward into present-day Laos. Kui elephant hunters would ride domesticated chaser elephants, and they used a sacred leather lasso mounted at the tip of a lance to loop around the rear leg of a wild elephant calf. They tamed and trained the young elephants and then sold them to the logging industry in the north or hired them out for hauling and transportation in difficult terrain, as well as for marching in the processions of traditional ceremonies in the surrounding countryside.

A regular expedition for elephant hunting involved thirty to fifty domesticated chaser elephants, which were well trained in charging wild elephants. A single chaser elephant commonly captured at least one elephant calf. For a real expert, however, the looping of two to three elephant calves in one expedition was plausible. On average, there would be more than three to four hundred elephants captured and traded by the Kui each year. Elephant hunting had been, for centuries, a pivotal economic enterprise for the Kui.

Nor was it just economically significant; Kui Ajiang's sociopolitical organizations were tightly intertwined with this elephant hunting tradition as well. Both sociopolitical structure and everyday life were organized around the salient elephant-raiding affair. Risky and pivotal as it was, it is little wonder that elephant hunting was super-ritualized. Spirit language, an exclusive sacred language known only among elephant masters, was the only communicating medium used in the hunting expedition. At the heart of the Kui Ajiang's culture is the great spirit of Phii Pakam, whose absolute power controls the lives and well-being of Kui people and elephants. Each household that possesses or used to possess a elephant would have a shrine, *san pakam,* housing Phii Pakam.

In the expedition, the great master (*kam luang pued*) took control and exerted supreme authority over all the hunting crews. *Mahouts,* or elephant keepers, who wanted to join the expedition had to get permission from the kam luang. The rituals of confession and absolution for hunting crews exemplified the authoritative status of the great kam luang. The ranking of the hunters indicated a highly hierarchical organization, with each rank entailing certain rights and duties. Mobility in this hierarchy and the sharing of captive elephants follow a certain set of elaborate rules and criteria.[9] Honor, wealth, and authority were derived from this risky elephant-hunting affair.

The elephant-hunting expeditions were disrupted due to a political dispute between Cambodia and Thailand, which eventually led to the border closing in 1957. Some later expeditions into Cambodia were fiercely attacked by the military force of the Khamen Serei, a rightist military force occupying the borderland of Thai-Cambodia that sought to destabilize the Sihanoukist regime in Phnom Penh. Coinciding with the complete halt of elephant hunting, a local elephant round-up caught the attention of the National Tourism Development Organization (NTDO). In 1961, NTDO organized a fair exhibiting Surin elephants for tourists, and provided foreign visitors a special train and motorcade package to attend the fair. This spectacular exhibition prompted the declaration of an annual Elephant Round-Up Festival beginning in 1962, and for reasons of convenience, it was moved to the provincial capital of Surin. Local informants noted that the first collaboration with the state in organizing the round-up had a hidden agenda. The Kui were hoping that such cooperation would prompt the Thai state to speak on their behalf to the Cambodian state, to allow them to hunt wild elephants in Cambodian territory. However, such efforts were of no avail. Elephant hunting is now a thing of the past, only worth recounting to foreign visitors—and researchers.

Within a few years the pivotal elephant-hunting enterprise, which long served as a referential political center bestowing charismatic power, political authority, and economic wealth over those masters and mahouts, evaporated. Clifford Geertz's elaboration on the notion of "center" is illuminating in this instance. In "Centers, Kings, and Charisma: Symbolics of Power," Geertz puts forward some aspects of Max Weber's notion of "charismatic power." Taking Edward Shils' refinement of the idea of charisma as the repercussion of social location stressing the connection between the symbolic value individuals possess and their relation to the active centers of the social order, Geertz writes:

> Such centers, which have "nothing to do with geometry and little with geography," are essentially concentrated loci of serious acts; they consist in the point or points in a society where its leading ideas come together with its leading institutions to create an arena in which the events that most vitally affect its members' lives take place. It is involvement, even oppositional involvement, with such arenas and with the momentous events that occur in them that confers charisma. It is a sign, not of popular appeal or inventive craziness, but of being near the heart of things. (Geertz 1983: 122–23)

The center of the Kui's sociopolitical order was thus decomposed by the reorganization of modern geopolitics. Once the centrality of the elephant-hunting convention disappeared, the charisma, authority, and wealth conferred by that pivotal center deteriorated. A great master of elephant hunting, well respected by the people of his generation, turned into an amateur actor performing empty rituals for a few nostalgic documentary moviemakers and journalists and the odd tourist who travels off the well-beaten path.

THE EMERGENCE OF A NEW POLITICAL CENTER

This traditional center of political order was replaced by the emergence of a new center that exerted a modernized form of authority through an officially sanctioned agency. The new agency achieved its effect of command and control over its subjects by registering itself in the officialdom of the centralized bureaucratic polity. In this new social field of the modern bureaucratic state, how things worked was astonishingly different. Here it was Central Thai, and not the spirit language, that was the sacred lingua franca in communicating with the poltergeist of modern politics. Lacking necessary cultural capital, the Kui were simply rendered irrelevant and thus excluded from this new political field.

During the 1960s, under the influence of the World Bank and the United States, Sarit's military regime turned state policy towards privatization, facilitating gradual control over the Thai economy by locally influential Chinese traders. Chinese influence over the economy coincided with the expansion of the state's authority into villages in remote areas. A great number of local Chinese entrepreneurs became affluent and cautiously took over public office, particularly at subdistrict levels. Although subdistrict headmen were mostly elected, the electoral process in general was, and still is, corrupt. Vote buying has been common practice and became a means for clientelistic incorporation of the poor.[10] Local law enforcers turned a blind eye to vote buying; they enjoyed a relationship of reciprocity with these influential and affluent "elected" headmen. Within the span of three decades, some influential subdistrict headmen (*kamnan ittiphon*) expanded their influence into regional and national politics (Pasuk and Sangsidh 1994: 11–12). Quite a number of them came to be known as local "godfathers" (*jao pho*)[11] and were allegedly involved in unlawful activities such as illegal logging, cross-border smuggling, trafficking in women, seizing public land, using connections with civil servants to issue land titles, and deforesting reserve forest for cultivating cash crops.

The new social field was thus characterized by bureaucratic clientelism controlled by ethnic Chinese political entrepreneurs and their allied bureaucrats. Local bureaucrats were prompted to provide the ethnic Chinese kamnan, most of whom were also construction contractors of some sort, with governmental construction contracts or other concessions and in turn received a kickback of 15 percent of the whole grant. Once this process of corrupt reciprocity started, it fed on itself. The backhoes, bulldozers, tractors, and dump trucks operating in most of the public construction projects belonged to the private firms of influential local politicians. The trucks had the name of their owners with their official political titles, either Kamnan, Provincial Council Member, Municipal Council Member, or Member of National Parliament, displayed immodestly on their windshields or the sides of the trucks. Fed by the state, local headmen turned into handmaidens of the state and thus defended and protected the bureaucracy. Such structural order precluded any meaningful participation of local natives in the mainstream political sphere that would disturb the status quo. Among the Kui communities the situation was no exception.

The negative stereotypes of the Kui lent further legitimacy to their exclusion. The images of the Kui as extra-rebellious, untrustworthy, self-serving, and thus difficult to deal with were magnified in the official discourse. The fact that Surin province has the annual Elephant Round-Up Festival as its emblem made controlling the Kui even more critical. The jao pho capitalized on these stereotypical images and represented themselves as an indispensable tool for taming the natives, for they possessed "cultural knowledge" and the clientelistic control essential in domesticating the stubborn and rebellious Kui. The provincial administration had to rely on these local headmen as arbiters or the rebellious natives would not cooperate and perform in the festival. Such a political positioning had a twofold strategic edge: on the one hand, by portraying themselves as the indispensable apparatus to control the Kui, local headmen established official connections and thus gained access to the inner circle of power. On the other hand, by registering in the state's official-dom, the local elite became the embodiment of state authority to whom local natives were subjugated. It was within this context that a new form of domination was imposed upon this marginal people.

STRUGGLING TO REPRESENT ONESELF: THE CONSTRUCTION OF THE TRADITIONAL KUI HOUSE, BAN BORAN

Informed that the local situation was politically charged, I began my fieldwork by staying at a Buddhist temple in the village and confined myself primarily to observing communal religious life. The realm of the religious, seemingly the least politicized aspect of the community, turned out to be precisely what was at stake in local politics.

The twenty-second of July, 1994, was not just another full moon night at this local village temple. It marked the inauguration of Buddhist Lent at the beginning of rainy season, one of the most virtuous moments for merit-making and offering. In fact, most of the villagers did gather at the temple to attend this meritorious ceremony. It was on this special occasion that Kru Ba Panya, acting abbot of the temple, announced the project of constructing a traditional-styled Kui house, or Ban Boran. The aim, according to his announcement, was to preserve the vanishing tradition of the Kui's indigenous ways of house construction.

The Ban Boran would be built according to Kui Ajiang's traditional convention. There was to be a high-roofed shelter under which elephants were kept during the night. A spirit shrine would also be constructed to house the sacred lasso, one of the most important objects in Kui Ajiang's cultural practice. To demonstrate everyday Kui life, a pigsty, a cow pen, a foot mortar, and an area for raising silkworms and for silk weaving would all be assembled on the ground floor of the house. A baby cradle and swing were also to be featured, to reflect the traditional child-rearing practices of the Kui. The project seemed to me a novel local initiative in a time when concrete block buildings were aggressively replacing local-styled housing. However, this seemingly simple plot turned out to be one of the most disputed issues in local politics for years to come.

Kru Ba Panya is an indigenous Kui monk who has long been active in working for the community. In 1991, one of his family's elephants gave birth to a new calf. The mother elephant didn't have enough milk to feed her baby. He soon found the calf starving. Struggling to save his elephant calf, Kru Ba Panya went to the provincial administrative office for help. Since elephant affairs are so salient to the province, he reasoned, support during a crisis would be not only permissible but obligatory. However, his quest for help was to no avail. Muddling through the bureaucratic structure of a province named the Land of Elephants, he couldn't find any agency responsible for elephant welfare.

Determined to battle this predicament, Kru Ba Panya later established a local mahout association, Chomrom Phoo Liang Chang, to voice the needs of the elephant people. With support provided by the Asian Elephant Foundation, a high-profile NGO working to preserve elephants in Thailand, the association launched a welfare program for local elephants without recourse to official authority and support.

Within the authoritarian clientelism of the Thai bureaucratic polity, getting people organized without capitulating to the paternalism of official authority was a form of crime, precisely because it made local people politically more conscious and independent. Kru Ba Panya was promptly accused of being a Communist, a label familiar to most social activists in rural areas even to this day. Although there has been no official charge or prosecution, such a political accusation asserted an irrefutable form of domination.

Five months after the announcement of the Ban Boran project, as the construction of the Kui traditional house was on its way, local officials started opposing the construction. They accused Kru Ba Panya of challenging the official authority and competing with the government in launching such an important project in the name of the Kui people. There was, in fact, an official project for a "Museum of Elephant Village." The National Tourism Development Organization funded a four-year construction budget to build a local museum starting in 1992. However, since the construction of the first phase was completed in 1992, the project had come to a complete halt. The first two buildings looked remarkably awkward. Instead of using the local architectural form, the buildings were designed by a civil engineer in the provincial administrative office with neither knowledge of Kui culture nor experience in museum design. The official museum's pseudo-Japanese pagoda look, as described by an anthropologist from the University of Washington, Peter Quasay, was totally alien to the local landscape. Besides this physical estrangement, there was no representative from the village on the administrative committee. Local people did not have any idea what was going on. Local officials seemed harsh and agitated when local people raised questions about the project's plan and the museum's administration.

Nevertheless, when the official museum was in its early gestation, villagers were eager to be involved in the project. Many villagers donated cultural objects from their family's heritage, many of which were not only of sentimental significance but also financially valuable, to the organizing committee. Kru Ba Panya's collection of artifacts was among them. Although most of the contributors were promised certain compensation and acknowledgment in exchange for their donations, the promise has been hanging in the air. At this writing, nobody knew the whereabouts of the cultural artifacts, and the buildings have been left unattended. The lawn has become grassland for feeding the appetite of villagers' buffaloes and cows.

Building a Kui traditional house in the face of a stalled official museum placed official dominance in an awkward situation. The Ban Boran project not only asserted the right to represent oneself but, more important, opened up a parallel discursive space within which official accountability was called into question and its legitimacy contested. The extreme contrast in the physical appearance of the two buildings made such contestation exceedingly visible. Soon after, official discourse against the Ban Boran project abounded. Among several recurrent arguments against the project, the most prominent one circulating in the community portrayed Kru Ba Panya's effort as indecent, an offending act aimed at rivaling and sabotaging the official project.

Despite the failure of the official project, official discourse asserted that only the state and its officially appointed agent had the legitimacy to represent and to act on behalf of the Kui community. In other words, Kui culture and identity have been taken over by and now belong exclusively to the state. Other representative claims were not only considered illegitimate but were depicted as threats, sabotage, and bad faith. The Kui were deprived of the legitimacy to represent themselves; their agency was denied and their identity did not belong to them. They were called upon to display their identity in the annual Elephant Round-Up Festival only under the signature of the state agencies. The Kui's marginality was fabricated in the language of official claims that rendered voices other than the official one irrelevant, illegitimate, and discounted.

The Kui certainly were internally differentiated and their relationships to this form of domination varied—ranging from total incorporation to forthright challenge. But once the issue was cast by the official discourse in terms of a threat to state authority that could jeopardize "public order," it forced the Kui into an either/or choice between being subjugated or revolting. To be sure, official discourse did not allow an ambiguous political identity to exist within its realm of authority. The Kui were compelled to bring together their fractured subjectivities to create collective agency in the political sphere. What can we learn from this, as people who have suffered political marginality tried to gain control over their own communal affairs while the state refused them the legitimacy to do so? What were the structural causes of the marginalization process that has been imposed upon local Kui by the Thai state? What is the form and nature of power as it was exercised by the state agencies and how does this form of power achieve domination?

PROBLEMATIZING THE POWER OF THE STATE

It is worth noting that in community studies the role of the state, its forms and functions, and its relations to citizens have come under critical scrutiny (see, for instance, Robertson 1984; Norgaard 1994). The myth of the state as a neutral, impartial structure—neither an instrument serving to protect the interests of the dominant class, nor a structure with a logic and interest of its own—is being demystified (Evans, Rueschemeyer, and Skocpol 1985). In what follows, I explore the root of the persistent problematic encounter between the modern Thai state and its people. I will argue that the role the state took in constructing the Kui's marginality was generated by the state's self-perpetuating structural flaws.

Alan Wolfe, in his analysis of the capitalist state (Wolfe 1993), describes the statization process by which virtually every sphere of societal
life is subject to state's authority. He writes:

> A central political development of late capitalist society has been an increase
> in the tendency to view the state as capable of solving problems that lie
> outside its competence. As the ascription of ability and magical powers to
> the state fails to solve these problems, advocates of statization press their
> claim for even stronger potions, producing a cycle in which impotence results
> in calls for greater potency, which bring about higher levels of impotence.
> The more the state fails, the more it is worshipped, and the more it is wor-
> shipped, the greater will be its failure. (Wolfe 1993: 192)

Alan Wolfe calls the process by which the state is assigned a wide
variety of mythic powers "the reification of the state." The more reified
the state, the more people are deprived of their ability to represent themselves and to solve their own problems. The more the people lose their
self-assuredness, the more the state expands its authority. It is this self-
repeating, spiraling procedure of power reproduction that creates an
illusion of the all-powerful state. But, in the case of the Kui, what is the
specific mechanism of power reproduction that enables the state to reify
itself? What are the structural sources that, while lending legitimacy to
the official claims of being the sole collective voice, systematically marginalize and exclude the Kui from the mainstream political sphere? How
does the official discourse work to render other voices irrelevant, illegitimate, and discountable?

It is not that the state lacks recognition of local desires for participation. Rather, people's voices and local initiatives are excluded from
participating in the state's affairs for both historical and structural reasons. The historical development of the Thai bureaucratic polity has
occurred in such a way that the state and its bureaucracies have always
been the only legitimate representation of Thai society. Such political
representations are built into the Thai semiology. As Thanes (1992)
points out, "the Thai word 'kong luang' or 'kong rachakarn' (state's
property or bureaucratic property) can be generally used as substitution
for 'kong suan ruam' (public property)." But bureaucratic property or
state property is not regarded as property for the general public, and
more often than not people's accessibility to such property is restricted
or prohibited (Thanes 1992: 208). Such a semiopolitical regime insists
that there must be only one "public sphere,"[12] which has been made
sacred and which only the officially appointed can enter. Officially ap-

pointed headmen become the embodiment of state power, and thereby
contribute towards the maintenance of the structural order from which
they draw their authority, thus eliminating any possibility of meaningful
local "participation" which does not fully conform to the state's authority and official command.

The politics of exclusion works not only by invoking the negative
stereotypes to maintain the Kui as rebellious "Other within" (Thongchai, forthcoming), but also by systematically imposing the state's structural order as the only legitimate, officially sanctioned political order
upon the local community's organization. The "public" realm has been
conflated with the official, formal, and bureaucratic realm. It is by this
process, the statization of the public sphere, that vertical forms of state
power are reproduced at the community level and other forms of local
political claims in the community are precluded.

COUNTERHEGEMONIC PRACTICE

It is within this context that the Kui have been excluded from the mainstream political sphere. They lived, experienced, and suffered the marginality imposed on them by the particular formation of the Thai bureaucratic polity. Not only were the state's bureaucracies incapable of
handling the problems, but the state administrative practices themselves
were dehumanizing and further rendered those already at the margin
even more vulnerable. However, the state was far from a monolithic
hegemonic institution of social control, and the villagers were not passive clients. Villagers selectively appropriated certain elements of the
bureaucratic practices to construct their own counterhegemonic practices. The construction of a secondary school in the Kui community is
a case in point.

Despite the 1990 expansion of compulsory education up to the ninth
grade, in 1992 there was no high school within the subdistrict of Supho.
Established in 1921, Supho has a population of 14,328 in nineteen villages. According to a former village headman, once the old kamnan's
right-hand man, during the last two decades the Department of Education proposed on several occasions to construct a high school in the
subdistrict. However, the late kamnan, citing unavailability of land, allegedly discarded the proposal. "That was not the real reason why the
proposal was discarded," proclaimed the ex-headman. "It was that education will make the villagers difficult to keep under control."

However, this time the demand was from below. In early 1992, Kru Ba Panya and Ajarn Korn, acting principal of a high school in a nearby subdistrict who was in charge of a high school extension program, drafted a proposal requesting the construction of a high school campus in the village. For governmental budgetary support, official administrative practice required the proposal to be submitted through a bureaucratic channel, stepwise: from village to local subdistrict council, to district office, to provincial office, and then to the Ministry of Education in Bangkok. Initial endorsement by the subdistrict council (or *sapha tambon*) according to the standard procedure was therefore a must. However, such a procedure would only detain the project, since the subdistrict council was nothing but the handmaid of the kamnan. Also, each and every step in the standard procedure was beyond the control of local community leaders. Instead, local elites with official titles and connections were the ones who could move effectively within the bureaucratic structure and could obstruct the project at any point. To bypass the endorsement—or, rather, the disapproval—of the sapha tambon, community leaders managed to contact select sectors of the local bureaucratic structure for support.

They first contacted the Treasury Department and proposed donating their land to the state specifically for the construction of a high school campus. The land was contributed by Luang Pu Lee, the abbot of the village temple, and six other villagers. In the meantime, initial support from the then-popular holy monk, Phawana Buddho, who had been passionate about elephants, contributed to the construction of temporary school buildings and the purchase of other office equipment. Upon the issuing of a document stating that the land was legally available for a public school, community leaders discovered that the District Administrative Office, afraid of being involved in conflict with the influential kamnan, refused to process their proposal. Struggling to overcome the impasse, they submitted their project through a personal connection directly to the Provincial Educational Office.

Provincial educational officers had a shared interest in building the school in the area. They would gain credit not only for being able to construct a high school campus in a subdistrict where the rate of attaining compulsory education has been the lowest in the region, but also for being able to mobilize local resources, particularly precious land and temporary buildings. The proposal was approved and sent to Bangkok. Although it took some time for Kru Ba Panya and Ajarn Korn to travel back and forth to Bangkok to lobby for the case, the project was eventually approved and the school has now been constructed.

The construction of a high school certainly created a sense of discomfort among some political factions in the area, and the power play within the educational bureaucracy was far from over. However, children were now, for the first time, able to attend high school without traveling to other subdistricts. The existence of a high school campus at Suklang village instead of at Supho, an official center of the subdistrict, is a testimony of the possibility of the excluded to appropriate certain cultural knowledge of bureaucratic practices and radicalize it for their own advantage.

Now that I have delineated local phenomena in some detail, I will examine recent social movements at the macro level, which have been acquiring momentum in Thai politics.

II. AN EMERGING POLITICAL ETHOS

In contemporary Thai politics, discontent toward state authority has not been sporadic. A study of political conflicts and public demonstrations reveals that 739 events of political protest were organized between October 1993 and September 1994 (Institute for Policy Study 1994), the majority of which (510 events, or 68.9%) were conflicts between the state and the local communities. Compared to the year of high political tension after the 14 October 1975 popular uprising, the incidence of political demonstrations and contests during the study period was twice as high (two events per day to one). It is also noteworthy that the majority of political organizers were local community leaders. Only a few events involved leaders who were NGO workers or student activists. One can hardly deny that in the present political climate officially authorized forms of power are being questioned. Indeed, as we have seen, though the state was still the central authority, its power was no longer monolithic.

The aim of this second part is to examine an emerging political consciousness, namely civic consciousness, in contemporary Thai politics. I will attempt to demonstrate that this emerging consciousness has triggered a new political orientation and generated much skepticism at the societal level regarding the previously unquestioned authority and legitimacy of the state. I will examine recent academic and political discourses to reveal this political ethos of discontent and its articulation in the idea of "civil society." The review will provide a background for further discussion of how the experience of political marginality among the Kui attained a collective dimension and became politically salient in forging the politics of empowerment among a marginal people.

CIVIL SOCIETY AND THE STATE

In theorizing on revolution in Europe, Antonio Gramsci juxtaposes two models of sociopolitical orientation: a primarily agrarian society like prerevolutionary Russia and a more advanced capitalist society. Gramsci points out that in advanced capitalism, political control is achieved as much through popular consent as through force. Based on this insight, Gramsci distinguishes two fundamental forms of political power: "domination" (direct physical coercion) in the realm of state and "hegemony" (consent, ideological control) in the realm of civil society (Boggs 1976: 39).

According to Gramsci, in advanced capitalist societies, the development of a skilled labor force with specialized technical knowledge, the role of the mass media, the availability of more sophisticated techniques of ideological control, the importance of knowledge and education, all require the state to increasingly build its authority upon hegemony rather than force. Thus, the growing complexity of advanced capitalist societies, accompanied by the strengthening of "civil society," inevitably raises ideological-cultural struggles to a new level.

In so theorizing, Gramsci proposes a "war of position" as a main strategy for social change in advanced capitalist societies, in contrast with Lenin's notion of "war of movement." By "war of position" Gramsci means the long-range contestation of cultural-ideological hegemony for the gradual shifting in the equilibrium of social forces. Politics in Gramsci's sense is thus more moral-intellectual and cultural-ideological, rather than political in the narrow sense of struggle for seizing state power, as connoted by Lenin's "war of movement."

In the case of a middle-income country like Thailand, a country typified by its rapid economic transition and industrialization, what is the accurate reconnaissance of the existence of civil society, its strength, and its relation to the state? Akom Chanangkura has conducted an early investigation of this issue. Akom's article "Thai Bureaucratic Capitalist State: An Essay on State and Civil Society in Thai Capitalism" is cited in Thanes Arpornsuwan's analysis of state and politics in Thailand: "Blurred demarcation between civil society and political society is expressed in the forms of relationship deeply embedded in the Thai

bureaucratic system, namely, paternalism, nepotism, and a highly hierarchical, ranked system of relation. Even on the level of basic understanding, Thai people are not aware of the distinction between the state
and society. They seem to wrongly assume that society is the state and
vice versa" (Akom, cited in Thanes 1992: 208).[13]

Chai-anan (1992) offers an explanation of this phenomenon by
pointing out the historical evolution of the Thai state. Chai-anan contends that the formation of the modern Thai state was basically a response to the external challenge from colonialism. The expansion of
colonial power threatened the sovereignty of the Siam court. The modernization process has been a response to this threat and thus was mainly
a process of strengthening the state machinery so as to maintain a
stronger grip on political power and sovereignty. The focus of modernization was on creating a more effective centralized bureaucratic body,
which would secure the state's authority over its territory. It has been a
state-building process and not a nation-building one.

According to Chai-anan, the consolidation of the Thai state machinery and the centralization of governmental organization have created a
monopolistic bureaucratic polity. Civic organizations outside the realm
of the state have been disdained. Chai-anan notes that in Europe and
Britain the process of state formation was accompanied by a coevolution
of an economic sector, to the extent that a civic sector developed and
was able to take a decisive role in political evolution, eventually over-
turning the absolutist regimes. The Thai state developed without this
concomitant growth in the civic sector.

However, the last decade has witnessed drastic changes in the Thai
political and economic scene. Rapid economic growth has accelerated
and increased the role of the middle class in Thailand. In the May 1992
upheaval, it was the middle class who gathered and protested against
the military junta, and eventually cast the coup leader out of the pre-
miership. The mob was called the "mobile-phone mob" by news reporters, for participants in this political demonstration carried pocket
mobile phones which they used to describe the situation to their friends
and families. Previous descriptions of Thai society as a "bureaucratic
polity" have been challenged by Anek Laothamatas, who posits that the
Thai state has been transformed from a bureaucratic polity into a state
of "liberal corporatism" or "social corporatism." Such a transformation
is marked by the emergence of a powerful middle class in Thai politics
and the consolidation of economic sectors (Anek Laothamatas 1992).

Therayut Boonmee, a prominent social activist, proposes a ground-breaking analysis of Thai politics and suggests a strategy for social change which takes into account the crucial role of "civil society" (Therayut 1993). He points to an emerging civic consciousness, expressed in popular and professional movements in the last few decades. This movement, according to Therayut, is more diffuse in its character, emphasizing popular involvement rather than the highly centralized, hierarchically organized movements that were popular among socialist-minded activists during the 1960s and 1970s. This civic movement is also characterized by an emphasis on local initiatives and the empowerment of organizations outside the realm of the state, such as NGOs, businesses, and professional organizations.

According to Therayut, the existing national ideological construction, namely "nation" (*chat*), which has been employed by the state to promote nationalist loyalty and social cohesion, has lost its compelling power and become irrelevant. Therayut contends that civil society as an ideological construct has been emerging and replacing the old nationalist construct. The ongoing process of institutionalization of civil society will eventually cultivate "sustainable political development." Therayut spells out four steps towards the strengthening of civil society: the emergence of collective consciousness at the societal level, the formation of various civic organizations, the crystallization of civil society as an ideology, and the institutionalization of civil society. Therayut suggests that in the last three decades, Thai society has been in the third step, with "civil society" emerging as a new political ideology.

Prawase Wasi, a senior citizen who has been contributing to a careful examination of social and political development for more than three decades, wrote an article in 1993 entitled "Societal Powers in Balance," or "Sangkomsamanubhap." In the article, he advocates the role of "collective/societal power" in balancing centralized state/bureaucratic power and capitalist dominance. Prawase points out that the state and capital are megapowers which together act as a "social black hole," sucking up all social institutions and societal resources without accounting for collective well-being and morality. To counterbalance these megapowers, collective/societal power in the form of various civic organizations must be created and empowered (Prawase 1993a: 15–18, and 1993b: 31–34).

In the prestigious Komol Keemthong Lecture, Phra Paisal Wisalo, a social activist and leading Buddhist monk, scrutinizes the implacability of an all-powerful state and market. Phra Paisal posits that "vertical forms of social relation" such as those between individual person and state and individual person and market have to be counterbalanced by "horizontal forms of social relation": personal relations, friendship, neighborhood organizations, informal and nongovernmental organizations, professional organizations, and relationships within small communities. Phra Paisal calls for the strengthening of this horizontal, nonhierarchical social organization as an important long-range strategy for creating and empowering "civil society" as a means to achieve a peaceful society (Paisal Wisalo 1994).

Coinciding with the critical awareness in academia, social movements have also been gathering strength in Thailand, in the last ten years especially. Nidhi Aeusriwongse, a major figure engaged in social critique, reveals the power dynamics in contemporary Thai society using a case of communal resistance to local government disposing of garbage in their community. Nidhi, in his article entitled "Garbage Flooding the State in Chiengmai" in *Matichon* newspaper, 29 August 1994, gives an account of the event: villagers from Tambon Mae-hiah who had long endured the dumping of garbage from the city of Chiengmai near their communities refused to allow it any longer.

The city administration tried to dump the massive garbage in Sansai district instead. An agreement with local communities was reached that certain measures would be used to prevent environmental contamination (such as placing plastic sheets in the burrow before dumping garbage, covering garbage with soil of a certain thickness to prevent flies and odor, being careful when transporting garbage not to drop it on the road, and so on). Except for the plastic sheets, none of these promised measures ever materialized. The villagers, finding themselves betrayed, started protesting against the city administration. The administration, however, viewed the conflict as a conspiracy led by opposition politicians and nongovernmental organizations, and with assistance from military forces, proceeded to dump garbage in a "secret place," possibly in the military-controlled area. Soon villagers around the Mae Aalai area in Mae Taeng district started complaining about the dumping of urban garbage in their district. The city administration was unable to handle the problem and hopelessly left mountains of odious garbage on the sides of streets in Chiengmai City. Nidhi observes:

> The outpouring of garbage in the city of Chiengmai at the moment substantively reflects the weakness of the state and its governmental machinery. In whatever kind of activity, any level of government will be unable to achieve

its objective or to accomplish its mission effectively without agreement and cooperation from the people concerned. . . . Thailand is moving to an era in which the state cannot simply hang over people's heads. Instead, the state has to work with and to negotiate with people on an equal basis. The state can no longer rest its power solely on legal legitimacy. . . . Unless it turns to work side-by-side with the people, the state will not be able to accomplish its duty and will become paralyzed in the near future. (Nidhi Aeusriwongse 1994: 20, my translation)

Of utmost importance in these civic movements was the community struggle to control local natural resources. The conference on Community Rights and Decentralization of Natural Resource Management, held on 11–12 February 1993 at the National Assembly, called into question the state's monopolistic authority over natural resources. The forum, a collaborative effort between the House Standing Committee on Environment, the House Standing Committee on Justice and Human Rights, and twenty-two nongovernmental organizations and institutes of higher learning, was attended by more than three hundred participants, including members of parliament, NGO workers, public servants, academics, mass media personnel, and the general public.

Prawase Wasi, in his keynote address, contended that the Thai state's claim to ownership over all the nation's natural resources might not be problematic since, in popular understanding, the state is the unquestionable legitimate representative of the whole nation. However, the state's centralization of authority over management of natural resources has caused severe devastation of these resources and profound degradation of the environment. This environmental deterioration has been so detrimental that the state's claim has to be re-examined. Prawase asserted that the mission of environmental preservation cannot be achieved by relying solely on the state (Wiwat 1993: 45–50).

The conference pointed to the root of the problem: "Local people's organizations are not accepted by the state as being legal entities and hence cannot be entrusted with the authority to manage and control their own resources" (Wiwat 1993: 16). The conference appealed for "community rights and community-based natural resource management." The conference summary suggested that civic organizations at the grassroots level must be strengthened, accredited, and provided with the authority to control their local natural resources. At the core of the conference was skepticism about the legitimacy of the absolute authority of the state (see also Saneh and Yos's trilogy on community forestry, 1993).

As with the expansion of the power of the middle class, the business sector is now more than ever interested in the public sphere and has been active in initiating programs for public service. Examples of such programs are Krongkarn Ta Wises, a campaign project for better environment; the Think Earth Project; antismoking campaigns sponsored by the Central Department Store; the Creative Media Foundation (supported by Bang Chak Petrochemicals); and the Population and Community Development Association's Thailand Business Initiative for Rural Development (TBIRD). Professional organizations are also beginning to be aware of their roles as civic organizations: for example, the Rural Doctors' Foundation, Thailand's Medical Council, the Lawyers' Council of Thailand, the Social Workers' Association. Several NGOs are now networking with civic organizations and local initiatives at the grassroots level. Of particular importance are LDI (the Local Development Institute), RDI (the Research and Development Institute, at Khon Kaen University), THIRD (Thailand Institute for Rural Development), and the Social Research Institute of Chieng Mai University.[14]

With these political developments in mind, the third part of this chapter will describe the resonance between local experience of political marginality and the emerging political awareness among Thai people in a wider context. Such a resonance has opened up the possibility for a politics of collective empowerment through the linking of local initiatives to a larger network of civic movements.

III. POLITICAL SUBJECTIVITY AND ALTERNATIVE DISCURSIVE SPACES

The emergence of a critical public in the current Thai political scene has challenged the notion that the reified state has the unbridled power to govern in the name of and at the behest of "the people." The discrepancy between what the state claims to be and what the marginalized really experience has undermined the hegemonic control of the modern bureaucratic Thai state.

The arbitrariness of a reified state becomes most visible when it is challenged in a crisis. However, crisis is not the most significant moment for change. Quite to the contrary: if the main objective of social change is to create a long-lasting equilibrium of power, we have to look for a more gradual, democratic, and sustainable transformation in everyday forms of struggle, roughly comparable to what Gramsci called the "organic dimension of change." Gramsci argued that Lenin's model of revolution that stresses the "conjunctural dimension" of change is not workable in most advanced capitalist societies. The conjunctural dimension of change stresses the passing and momentary period of crisis in which the contesting political forces struggle for seizure of state's power. The "organic" aspect of political struggle, on the other hand, refers to the long-range contestation of ideological hegemony, to the gradual shifting in the equilibrium of social forces that must precede any "conjunctural" moment (Boggs 1976: 114–15). Therefore, the "moral-intellectual" phase of ideological contestation, rather than a catastrophic phase of revolution, is of strategic importance.

The most important question, then, is from what point can the marginalized launch their contest in order to challenge the established cultural hegemony, since those who are marginalized have already been excluded from the mainstream political sphere? Susan Herbst (1994) looks at the relation of marginal groups, the public sphere, and social movements. Herbst agrees with scholars who study social movements that the establishment of alternative discursive public space is a prerequisite for the development of any social movement initiated by the marginal. "When people who hold similar ideas, or share particular social characteristics, form communities, they sometimes develop what Aldon Morris has called "oppositional consciousness"—an understanding of the flaws in mainstream social life, and a shared approach to challenging conventional politics" (Herbst 1994: 15). The primary task of this moral-intellectual struggle, therefore, is to create an alternative discursive space, what Fraser calls "subaltern counterpublics," a parallel public arena "where oppressed or minority groups invent and circulate counterdiscourses to formulate oppositional interpretations of their identities, interests, and needs" (Fraser, cited in Herbst 1994: 14).

The Kui's struggle to represent themselves can be seen as just such an effort to create an alternative discursive arena, or a resistance space in which "an agentive moment" (Daniel 1996: 189–92), a shift in the sense of oneself from an object being acted upon by the world to a subject acting upon the world, can take place. In my fieldwork experience, the ethnographic encounter itself can also create a space in which such alternative political discourse can occur. Constantly asking questions about local politics, social exclusion, suffering, and the predicament of political marginality not only creates a discursive space for the expression of political discontent but, to a certain extent, obliges people to contemplate their history and to reflect critically on their experiences. The process of anthropological inquiry itself is a conscientization

process through critical reflection. Critical reflection, as McLaren puts
it, "is a form of social empowerment . . . and is part of a long political
process, a battle waged on behalf of the peripheralized subordinate class
who seek freedom from the totalizing constraints of the prevailing cultural and moral hegemony" (McLaren 1992–93: 12).

SOCIALLY ENGAGED ANTHROPOLOGY

As a domestic anthropologist exploring the misery of a marginalized
people in my home province, I found that it was not detachment but
involvement that instructed my inquiry. Involvement, however, is not
for the sake of gaining access to deeper sources of anthropological
knowledge, but is a situated act driven as much by situational exigency
as by humanistic impulse. As my fieldwork progressed, I became more
and more involved in exchanging ideas and working with indigenous
leaders on their community problems. My fieldwork was tied closely to
the contingencies and immediate needs of practical political involvement. By the end of my fifteen months of fieldwork, I found myself much
involved in supporting local community leaders to create and link local
movements to social movements in larger networks of community organizations, NGOs, and local academic institutions.

As my review below of the contemporary Thai political context attests, such networking is strategically important, for it connects local
movements that face isolation and limits of scale with other social movements that have been gaining broader power. Networking independent
movements and collectives is a process of gradually constructing an alternative sphere within which the marginal can enact their own political
agenda. Networking cultivates a new collective identity and fosters a
sense of community working together for a noble cause, an imagined
community without which those who are marginalized can have very
little sense of their own political efficacy.

Working with community leaders in a politically charged environment also provided me with an acute understanding of the role objectivity and neutrality in anthropological practices can unwittingly and
inevitably play in legitimating a repressive structural order (Das 1994).
Under the banner of "objectivity" anthropologists can easily become "a
part of the tribe that creates discourses of power on the pretext of understanding suffering, or that uses the suffering of the people only as
occasion for professional intervention and transformations" (Das 1993:
164).

In discussing community problems with indigenous leaders, I found the exchange of stories with Kru Ba Panya particularly constructive. I recounted the life stories of some of the activist monks I knew who were involved in, for instance, forest preservation, community organization, or herbal medicine, by applying Buddhist teaching to community work. I shared with Kru Ba Panya my copy of Mahatma Gandhi's book on civil disobedience, books on local initiatives in rural development, traditional medicine, alternative agriculture, and the life stories and experiences of local community leaders.

In addition, I accompanied Kru Ba Panya and local villagers on some field trips to visit several nearby rural development projects—organic farming, silk weaving, production of earthen bricks (for house construction, to reduce the number of trees cut down)—as well as visiting some local NGOs, academic institutions, and social activists. During these trips, experiences of suffering and struggle were exchanged. There was a certain disparity and distinctiveness in each of these local experiences. Nonetheless, the stories bore some crucial similarities and resonated greatly with one another.

The most prominent and recurring issues in these stories surrounded the problem of state intervention. An organic farmer in Sanom district, for instance, ridiculed the state's agricultural officers as being shamelessly instrumental. Local agricultural officers claimed in their official reports and on television that the success of his integrated organic farming was the result of their supervision, despite the fact that the farmer worked for fifteen years without a single visit from local agricultural officers.

One of the most important movements was the networking with a coalition of Buddhist monks engaged in community and spiritual development, the Sekiyadharm. The coalition was headed by Abbot Nan Sutasilo of Samakkhii Temple in Surin province. The abbot himself persevered in working with his community. At first, thinking of development as modernization, with electricity and new roads, he tried hard to convince reluctant villagers to give up their land to build a road to link their homes with the city. The result was a "modernization without development." Motorcycles started roaring into the village. TV antennas quickly followed electric poles, consumer goods advertised on television flooded villagers' lives, and gambling and drinking became more widespread. And the villagers plunged deeper into debt. Convincing himself that without "spiritual immunity" it was difficult for villagers to fight the influx of consumerism, the abbot started applying Buddhist meditation to the development process. Meditation has enabled the villagers to realize that self-betterment is possible through one's own effort. Soon after, the abbot set up a fertilizer bank so that villagers would not have to borrow money from loan sharks. A village rice bank followed to ensure that no one in the village would starve and to ease the hunger caused by drought.

The most difficult project, which also placed Abbot Nan in a troublesome relationship with the state, was the "friendship farming," or *na krachab mit*. In the project, villagers donated their labor to plant rice on a communal piece of land, also donated. The rice that was harvested went to the village rice bank to help the needy. More important than the rice harvest, the abbot contended, was the return of the fraternal spirit of the community (for a concise description of Abbot Nan's initiatives see Sanitsuda 1994). However, his communal approach to solving a village's problem made him a target of suspicion. He was accused of being a Communist by the right-wing regime in the mid-1970s, a familiar experience for community activists.

When the state turned its policy from military security toward community development in the 1980s, the predicament persisted. Abbot Nan's relationship with the state community development officials continued to be troublesome. The state development agency often appropriated the projects the abbot initiated. It erected signs claiming that the projects were under its support and administration and tried to impose the standardized official model of development upon local styles. "Most of my projects, soon after they were intervened in by the state's officer, became defunct. I am now busy following up and restoring these collapsed projects," said the abbot on a visit to Suklang village, invited by Kru Ba Panya. In his visit, the abbot gave a talk to the local mahout association at the Ban Boran, encouraging local people to get organized and be self-reliant.

Within the coalition, there are other energetic monks. Phra Ajarn Somneuk Natho of Plak Mai Lai monastery in Nakhon Pathom province is active in forest preservation and herbal medicine. After Kru Ba Panya met Phra Ajarn Somneuk at a meeting of the coalition, he started working on his own project of preserving and growing herbal plants for treatment of elephant ailments, while encouraging a nearby forest hermitage to collect herbal plants for human ailments. A project of producing earthen bricks using local material was also begun after a three-month exchange of ideas and assessment of possibilities with villagers and a technical expert from a local NGO. Locally made bricks from locally available resources will substitute for trees in building houses. The aim is to stop deforestation, which has threatened elephants with severe loss of habitat.

However, what is more important than these activities, which may wax and wane depending on multiple exogenous factors, is the connection that links local, indigenous Kui leaders and their initiatives to the greater collective of fellow activists. It is the process of forming a community, which is both experiential and structural at the same time (Calhoun 1980). Such a community within a broader civic culture is made possible not by interpersonal relationships alone; rather, it is constituted within the intersubjective realm of contemporary experiences of dissent among people outside the mainstream. The shared cognizance which forms the infrastructure of this "imagined community" has two roots: one penetrates into the deforming structural order of the modern Thai state, the other goes deep into the intersubjectivity of the lived experience of subordination and marginality.

The networking of local initiatives and the construction of "imagined community" within this intersubjective space have certain empowering characteristics. Learning processes are shared among local activists through constructive exchange of perspective. Material support, in addition to creative ideas, can also be mobilized. As Paul Starr puts it, "without groups built on mutual trust, people can have little sense of their own political efficacy" (Starr 1994: 7). Most important, this imagined community of fellow activists induces the spirit of companionship. As Seremetakis succinctly describes the communities of marginalized women in Inner Mani: "Composed of entire categories of persons in conflict with the social structure, such communities of shared emotional inference and reference correspond to Bauman's (1977) notion of performance spaces as disruptive and disjunctive and as alternative social structure within or at the margins of a social structure" (Seremetakis 1991: 5).

Networking also promotes dialogue and creates a parallel public space within which critical opinions, which are otherwise excluded and marginalized by the dominant discourse, can be expressed and publicized. Within this civic network, those who are marginalized are invited to tell their stories. It is not that the marginalized don't know what is at odds with them. Rather, the question is how individuals can narrativize their suffering, name their own histories, and claim the necessary personal and collective force to resist the deforming effects of social power (McLaren 1992–93: 9).

CONCLUSION

On 11 November 1994, as the annual Elephant Round-Up Festival was approaching, the provincial governor visited Suklang village to oversee a rehearsal of the elephant show. The official museum buildings were reopened and restored to accommodate district officers' presentation of the long overdue Elephant Village Development Project to the governor. Except for a few official headmen, local villagers were not invited to the event. The participants in this exclusive event were local politicians, provincial and district officers, local headmen, and a troop of media people.

A few hundred meters away, a housepost-planting ceremony was being held to inaugurate the construction of Ban Boran. Beautifully dressed in their traditional costumes, hundreds of local villagers cheerfully participated in this event, preparing and serving food and drinks for guests, arranging ritual items, and holding and helping to upright the housepost. The juxtaposition of the two events was coincidental but revealing. While the event at the official museum excluded local participation, the Ban Boran's event mobilized a multitude of local people; it belonged to local people. It is in this realm of the informal and unofficial that the local Kui realize their shared goals and a profound sense of what is right for their community.

The construction of Ban Boran was but one among a number of such activities that drew together members of a community and helped them to elaborate their common purpose, to negotiate their identity, to assert their autonomy, as well as to realize their political potentiality. It was through their discursive participation within this alternative political sphere nurtured by local initiatives that individual members were transformed into citizens, conscious citizens with a shared sense of purpose. Against the politics of exclusion, the Kui constructed their alternative sphere of autonomy, which expanded to include themselves as legitimate new actors. This sphere of autonomy in the local Kui community, as well as its counterparts in the contemporary Thai political landscape, was the site in which aspirations for a stronger civil society were materialized. And this is how the predicament of political marginality and its intersubjectiveness valorized political consciousness and political action in a marginal Kui community; how the lived experience of marginality attained its collective dimension; and how the intersubjective experience became politically significant in forging a politics of collective empowerment in Thailand.

NOTES

This research was supported in part by a grant from the Social Science Research Council, WHO, and Redd Barna (Thailand). I also wish to acknowledge colleagues at the Local Development Information Center, particularly the director, Preecha Uitrakul, for help with my field research, which was conducted during June 1994–August 1995. Names of people and places have been changed to prevent unexpected adverse consequences and to protect their confidentiality.

1. As Spivak (1993) tells us, there has been "an explosion of marginality studies" in the United States, particularly in postcolonial studies. For interesting ethnographic works on marginality and the marginalization process, see Tsing (1993), Seremetakis (1991), Bourgois (1995: 114–73), and Solomos (1982). See also Ferguson et al., (1990), Herbst (1994), and Spitzer (1989).

2. See for instance Alting von Geusau (1983), Radley (1986), and Hutheesing (1990).

3. In 1891, a commission was formed to reform the administrative structure of the northeastern provinces. Two translators were included in the commission to help facilitate communication with the local natives. The official titles of the translators are revealing: Khun Kambhuchbhaja and Muen Bhasamilukhu. *Khun* and *Muen* are ranks of nobility. *Kambhuchbhaja* suggests the recognition of the court of Siam of the ethnic Khmer in the northeast (*Kambhuch* = Cambodia or Khmer, *Bhaja* = language, conversation), while *Bhasamilukhu* means literally "savage/barbaric language" (*Bhasa* = language, *Milukhu* = savage or barbaric).

4. Jit suggests that such a term has been naturalized to the extent that the Kui themselves have taken its meaning for granted and don't dislike the name. Villagers I encountered during my fieldwork in Kui communities, however, seemed to have diverse opinions on this matter, ranging from indifference to strong distaste.

5. Such an effort of constructing local history within the framework of a nation-state by emphasizing the constituting units and their relations to Bangkok continued well into the middle of the twentieth century. In 1957, the year of Twenty-fifth Century of the Buddhist Era celebration (marking the midpoint of the five thousand years of the Buddhist era), the government launched a project of publishing provincial histories of each of the seventy-one provinces in a uniform national historical framework.

6. The content of Toem's book (2530 [1987]) is very similar to the *Phongsawadan Huamuang Monthon Isan,* or the official *Chronicle of the Northeastern Domain.* Toem's materials are from the same sources as that of the official chronicle. In fact, Toem's father was a high-ranking officer in the northeastern domain and played an important role in writing the official chronicle. Toem's book was based on historical materials from his father's notebook that he found in 1947. I choose to discuss Toem's text here because of its accessibility and availability. The book was published by Thammasat University and is widely used as a standard reference for the history of the northeast provinces.

7. This conflation of demographic and geographic notions of history is by no mean a novel invention of the Siamese rulers. It can even be considered a relic of colonial practices of territorial conquest and political domination. Colonial practices involved a discernible pattern of wavering between demographic and geographic notions of political jurisdiction to create a pretext for colonial intervention (see Streckfuss 1993 and Thongchai 1994).

8. For accounts of millennialist movements in Thailand, see Keyes (1977); Murdoch (1974); Tej Bunnag (1967); and Tambiah (1984: 293–320).

9. For detailed accounts of ritual practices in elephant hunting see Giles (1929); Rote (1972); and Chuen 2533 (1990). See also my analysis of the contestation within the Pakam's structural order (Komatra 1998: 121–99).

10. During my fieldwork, I witnessed three elections—two for village headman and one for member of national parliament—in all of which widespread buying of votes, in cash and in kind, was commonplace. "Bullets," a term coined for loose cash for buying votes, were systematically distributed particularly among the poor on "the nights of dog howling" (*kuen ma hon*), one to three days prior to the election. Villagers express their feeling against vote-buying through iconoclastic idioms like "Phuyaiban ngern muen, kamnan ngern saen, phootan ngern lan" (Village headman worth ten thousand, subdistrict headman worth a hundred thousand, member of parliament worth millions). For a detailed account of corrupt electoral practices in contemporary Thai politics see Sombat Chantornvong (2536 [1993]).

11. For extensive analysis of *jao pho*, see Pasuk and Sangsidh (1994: 50–97).

12. For the notion of multiple "public spheres" as opposed to Habermas's (1989), see Fraser (1995).

13. Such an analysis is not at all peculiar. The distinction between civil society and the state is historically as well as discursively constructed, and negotiated, through competing political discourses. In Europe the historical development that led to the distinction took place in the middle of the seventeenth century (see Keane 1988: 35–71).

14. For a review of Thai NGOs at a grassroots level, see Vitoon Panyakul (1992); Preecha Uitrakul et al. (1990); and Office of National Culture Commission (1990 and 1991). For an excellent account of local initiatives see Sanitsuda Ekachai (1994).

REFERENCES CITED

Akin Rabibhadana. 1969. *The Organization of Thai Society in the Early Bangkok Period, 1782–1873.* Ithaca, N.Y.: Cornell University Southeast Asia Program, data paper no. 74.

Alting von Geusau, L. 1983. "The Dialectics of Akha Zang." In *Highlanders of Thailand,* ed. John McKinnon and Wanat Bhruksasri. Kuala Lumpur: Oxford University Press.

Amora Wongwichit. 2506 (1963). *Phongsawadan Huamuang Monthon Isan* (Chronicle of the Northeastern Domain). In *Collection of Chronicles* 3: 184–395.

Anderson, Benedict. 1991. *Imagined Communities: Reflections on the Origin and Spread of Nationalism*. Rev. ed. London: Verso.

Anek Laothamatas. 1992. *Business Associations and the New Political Economy of Thailand*. Boulder: Westview Press.

Asad, Talal, ed. 1973. *Anthropology and the Colonial Encounter*. Atlantic Highlands, N.J.: Humanities Press.

Bhabha, Homi. 1985. "Signs Taken for Wonders: Questions of Ambivalence and Authority under a Tree Outside Delhi, May 1817." In *"Race," Writing, and Difference,* ed. Henry Louis Gates, Jr. Chicago: University of Chicago Press.

Boggs, Carl. 1976. *Gramsci's Marxism*. London: Pluto Press.

Bourgois, Philippe. 1995. *In Search of Respect: Selling Crack in El Barrio*. Cambridge: Cambridge University Press.

Calhoun, C. J. 1980. "Community: Toward a Variable Conceptualization for Comparative Research." *Social History* 5: 105–29.

Chai-anan Samutwanich. 2535 (1992). *Nueng roy pee haeng karnpatiroop karnmuang Thai* (A Century of Thai Political Reform). Bangkok: Chulalongkorn University.

Chuen Srisawat. 2533 (1990). *Prawatsat lae wattanatham karn liang chaang khong chaw Kui (Suai) nai Changwat Surin* (History and Culture of Elephant Raising among Kui [Suai] People in Surin Province). Surin: Dept. of Organizational Management, College of South Isan.

Connerton, Paul. 1989. *How Societies Remember*. Cambridge: Cambridge University Press.

Daniel, Valentine. 1996. *Charred Lullabies: Chapters in an Anthropology of Violence*. Princeton, N.J.: Princeton University Press.

Das, Veena. 1990. "Our Work to Cry, Your Work to Listen." In *Mirror of Violence: Communities, Riots and Survivors in South Asia,* ed. Veena Das. Delhi: Oxford University Press.

———. 1993. "Moral Orientations to Suffering: Legitimation, Power, and Healing." In *Health and Social Change in International Perspective*, ed. L. C. Chen et al. Cambridge: Harvard University Press.

———. 1994. "The Anthropological Discourse on India." *In Assessing Cultural Anthropology,* ed. Robert Borofsky, 133–43. New York: McGraw-Hill.

Evans, Peter B., Dietrich Rueschemeyer, and Theda Skocpol, eds. 1985. *Bringing the State Back In*. Cambridge: Cambridge University Press.

Ferguson, Russel, et al., eds. 1990. *Out There: Marginalization and Contemporary Cultures*. Cambridge, Mass.: MIT Press.

Foucault, Michel. 1979. *Discipline and Punish: The Birth of the Prison*. New York: Vintage Books.

Fraser, Nancy. 1995. "Politics, Culture, and the Public Sphere: Toward a Postmodern Conception." In *Social Postmodernism: Beyond Identity Politics,* ed. Linda Nicholson and Steven Seidman. Cambridge: Cambridge University Press.

Geertz, Clifford. 1983. "Centers, Kings, and Charisma: Symbolics of Power." In *Local Knowledge,* 121–46. New York: Basic Books.

Giles, Francis H. (Phya Indra Montri Srichandrakumara). 1929. "Adversaria of Elephant Hunting." *Journal of the Siam Society* 23, no. 2: 1–36.

Good, Mary-Jo, and Byron Good. 1988. "Ritual, the State, and the Transformation of Emotional Discourse in Iranian Society." *Culture, Medicine, and Psychiatry* 12: 43–63.

Gramsci, Antonio. 1971. *Selections from the Prison Notebooks.* Ed. Quintin Hoare and Geoggrey Nowell Smith. London: Lawrence & Wishart; New York: International Publishers.

Habermas, Jurgen. 1989. *The Structural Transformation of the Public Sphere: An Inquiry into a Category of Bourgeois Society.* Trans. Thomas Burger with Frederic Lawrence. Cambridge, Mass.: MIT Press.

Herbst, Susan. 1994. *Politics at the Margin: Historical Studies of Public Expression Outside the Mainstream.* Cambridge: Cambridge University Press.

Herzfeld, Michael. 1992. *The Social Production of Indifference: Exploring the Symbolic Roots of Western Bureaucracy.* New York: Berg.

Hobsbawm, Eric. 1994. *The Age of Extremes: A History of the World, 1914–1991.* New York: Pantheon.

Hutheesing, Otome Klein. 1990. *Emerging Sexual Inequity among the Lisu of Northern Thailand: The Waning of Dog and Elephant Dispute.* Leiden: E. J. Brill.

Institute for Policy Study. 2537 (1994). "The Study of Conflicts between State, Business Sector, and Popular Sector during One Year of Chuan's Administration (October 1993 to September 1994)." In Thai. Bangkok: Institute for Policy Study.

Jit Phumisak. 2519 (1976). *Kwampenma kong kam Siam, Lao, Thai lae laksana tang sangkom kong chue chon chat* (The Origins of the Terms *Siam, Lao, Thai,* and the Social Characteristics of Ethnic Names). Bangkok: Krong karn Tamra, Thammasat University.

Keane, John. 1988. "Despotism and Democracy: The Origin and Development of the Distinction between Civil Society and the State, 1750–1850." In *Civil Society and the State: New European Perspectives,* ed. John Keane. London: Verso.

Keyes, Charles. 1977. "Millennialism, Theravada Buddhism, and Thai Society." *Journal of Asian Studies* 36, no. 2: 283–302.

———. 1987. *Thailand: Buddhist Kingdom as Modern Nation-State.* Boulder, Colo.: Westview Press.

Kleinman, Arthur. 1986. *Social Origins of Distress and Disease: Depression, Neurasthenia, and Pain in Modern China.* New Haven: Yale University Press.

———. 1988. *The Illness Narratives: Suffering, Healing, and the Human Condition.* New York: Basic Books.

Kleinman, Arthur, and Joan Kleinman. 1991. "Suffering and Its Professional Transformation: Toward an Ethnography of Interpersonal Experience." *Culture, Medicine, and Psychiatry* 15: 275–301.

———. 1996. "The Appeal of Experience, the Dismay of Images: Cultural Appropriations of Suffering in Our Times." *Daedalus,* winter: 1–23.

Komatra Chuengsatiansup. 1998. "Living on the Edge: Marginality and Contestation in the Kui Communities of Northeast Thailand." Ph.D. diss., Department of Anthropology, Harvard University.

Lock, Margaret. 1996. "Displacing Suffering: The Reconstruction of Death in North America and Japan." *Daedalus,* winter: 207–44.

McLaren, P. L. 1992–93. "Critical Literacy and Postcolonial Praxis: A Freirian Perspective." *College Literature, Teaching Postcolonial and Commonwealth Literatures,* double issue 19, no. 3 (Oct. 1992) and 20, no. 1 (Feb. 1993): 7–27.

Murdoch, John B. 1974. "The 1901–1902 'Holy Man's' Rebellion." *Journal of the Siam Society* 62, part 1 (January): 47–66.

Nidhi Aeusriwongse. 1994. "Garbage Flooding the State in Chiengmai." *Matichon Newspaper,* 29 August, p. 20.

Norgaard, Richard. 1994. *Development Betrayed: The End of Progress and a Coevolutionary Revisioning of the Future.* London and New York: Routledge.

Office of National Cultural Commission. 1990. *Local Wisdom: Proceedings of a Seminar.* Bangkok: Office of National Cultural Commission.

———. 1991. *Local Wisdom, Cultural Attainment, and Rural Development.* Bangkok: Office of National Cultural Commission and Thailand Institute for Rural Development (THIRD), Village Foundation.

Paisal Wisalo, Phra. 1994. *Duay palang haen panya le kuamrag Sangsan tanglueg pue sangkom tai nai satawat na* (With the Power of Wisdom and Love: Creative Alternative for Thai Society for the Next Century). Bangkok: Song Siam.

Paitoon Mikusol. 1984. "Social and Cultural History of Northeastern Thailand from 1868–1910: A Case Study of the Huamuang Khamen Padong (Surin, Sangkha, and Kukhan)." Ph.D. diss., University of Washington.

Pasuk Phongpaichit and Sangsidh Piriyarangsan. 1994. *Corruption and Democracy in Thailand.* Bangkok: The Political Economy Centre, Chulalongkorn University.

Prasert Sriwises. 1978. *Kui (Suai)–Thai–English Dictionary.* Bangkok: Chulalongkorn University Language Institute.

Prawase Wasi. 1993a, 1993b. "Naewkid lae yuttasat sangkom samanubhab lae Wicha" (Concept and Strategies for Wisdom and Intercursive Power Society). *Matichon Weekly,* 23 July (1993a): 15–18; and 30 July (1993b): 31–34.

Preecha Uitrakul et al. 1990. "Sakkayaphab lae kreu kai punum chowban" (Community Leaders' Potentiality and Network). Bangkok: Local Development Institute.

Radley, H. 1986. "Economic Marginalization and the Ethnic Consciousness of the Green Mong (Moob Tsuab) of North Western Thailand." Ph.D. thesis, Oxford University.

Riggs, Fred W. 1966. *Thailand: The Modernization of a Bureaucratic Polity.* Honolulu: East-West Center Press.

Robertson, A. F. 1984. *People and the State: An Anthropology of Planned Development.* Cambridge: Cambridge University Press.

Rote Sodesiri. 1972. "Changing System of Belief of the Elephant Hunters of Surin, Thailand." M.A. thesis, Dept. of Anthropology, University of Western Australia.

Saneh Jammarik and Yos Santasombat, eds. 1993. *Pachumchon: Naew tang karn pattana* (Community Forestry: An Approach for Development), 2d ed. Bangkok: Local Development Institute.

Sanitsuda Ekachai. 1994. *Seeds of Hope: Local Initiatives in Thailand*. Bangkok: Thai Development Support Committee (TDSC).

Scarry, Elaine. 1985. *The Body in Pain: The Making and Unmaking of the World*. New York: Oxford University Press.

Schwarcz, Vera. 1996. "Pane of Sorrow: Public Use of Personal Grief in Modern China." *Daedalus*, winter: 119–79.

Seidenfaden, Erik. 1952. "The Kui People of Cambodia and Siam." *Journal of the Siam Society* 39, no. 2: 144–80.

Seremetakis, Nadia. 1991. *The Last Word: Women, Death, and Divination in Inner Mani*. Chicago: University of Chicago Press.

Siffin, William J. 1966. *The Thai Bureaucracy: Institutional Change and Development*. Honolulu: East-West Center Press.

Smail, John. 1993. "On the Possibility of an Autonomous History of Modern Southeast Asia." In *Autonomous Histories, Particular Truths: Essays in Honor of John R. W. Smail*, ed. Laurie J. Sears. Madison: University of Wisconsin, Center for Southeast Asian Studies, Monograph Number 11.

Smalley, William. 1989. "Thailand's Hierarchy of Multilingualism." *Language Sciences* 10, no. 2: 245–61.

Solomos, John. 1982. "Black Youth, Economic Marginalization and the State in Britain." In *Cultural Identity and Structural Marginalization of Migrant Workers*. Strasboug Cedex, France: The Europe Science Foundation.

Sombat Chantornvong. 1993. *Leuktang wikrit: Phanha lae tang ok* (Election in Crisis: Problems and Solutions). Bangkok: Kobfai, Social Science Association, Thammasat University.

Spitzer, Leo. 1989. *Lives in Between: Assimilation and Marginality in Austria, Brazil, and West Africa, 1780–1945*. Cambridge: Cambridge University Press.

Spivak, G. C. 1993. *Outside in the Teaching Machine*. New York: Routledge.

Srisakara Vallibhotama. 2533 (1990). "Si Sa Ket: Srisaket Khet Khamen Padong" (Si Sa Ket: The Area of the Backward Cambodians). In Srisakara Vallibhotama, *Aeng Arayadharm Isan* (A Northeastern Site of Civilization), 448–87. Bangkok: Silpawattanadharm.

Starr, Paul. 1994. "The Disengaged." *The American Prospect*, fall: 7–8.

Stocking, George W., Jr. 1987. *Victorian Anthropology*. New York: Free Press.

Streckfuss, David. 1993. "The Mixed Colonial Legacy in Siam: Origins of Thai Racialist Thought, 1890–1910." In *Autonomous Histories, Particular Truths: Essays in Honor of John R. W. Smail*, ed. L. Sears, 123–53. Madison: University of Wisconsin, Center for Southeast Asian Studies, Monograph Number 11.

Tambiah, Stanley. 1976. *World Conqueror and World Renouncer: A Study of Buddhism and Polity in Thailand against a Historical Background*. Cambridge: Cambridge University Press.

———. 1984. *The Buddhist Saints of the Forest and the Cult of Amulets*. Cambridge: Cambridge University Press.

Tej Bunnag. 1976. *The Provincial Administration of Siam, 1892–1915*. London: Oxford University Press.

Terwiel, B. J. 1989. *A Window on Thai History*. Bangkok: Duang Kamol.

Thanes Arpornsuwan. 1992. "State and Thai Politics in 1990s." In Thai. In *State, Capital, Local Godfathers and Thai Society*, ed. Pasuk Phongpaichit and Sungsidh Piriyarangsan, 197–233. Bangkok: Center for Political Economy Study, Faculty of Economics, Chulalongkorn University.

Therayut Boonmee. 2536 (1993). *Sangkom Kemkaeng* (Strong Society). Bangkok: Ming Mitr.

Thongchai Winichakul. 1994. *Siam Mapped: A History of the Geo-Body of a Nation*. Honolulu: University of Hawaii Press.

———. Forthcoming. "The Others Within: Travel and Ethno-spatial Differentiation of the Siamese Subjects 1885–1910." In *Civility and Savagery: The Differentiation of Peoples within Tai Speaking Polities of South East Asia*, ed. Andrew Turton.

Toem Wiphakpotjanakit. 2530 (1987). *Prawatsat Isan* (History of the Northeast). Bangkok: Social Science Association.

Tsing, Anna. 1993. *In the Realm of the Diamond Queen: Marginality in an Out-of-the-Way Place*. Princeton, N.J.: Princeton University Press.

Turton, Andrew. 1980. "Thai Insitutions of Slavery." In *Asian and African Systems of Slavery*, ed. J. L. Watson, 251–92. Oxford: Basil Blackwell.

Vitoon Panyakool. 1992. *The Experience of Hope*. Bangkok: Local Development Institute.

Wiwat Katidhamanit, ed. 1993. *Sitthi choomchon: Karn krajai umnaj jadkarn sappayakorn* (Community Rights: Decentralization of Natural Resource Management). Bangkok: Local Development Institute.

Wolfe, Alan. 1993. "The Reification of the State." In *Power in Modern Societies*, ed. Marvin E. Olsen and Martin N. Marger, 286–94. Boulder, Colo.: Westview Press.

Wyatt, David. 1994. *Studies in Thai History*. Bangkok: Silkworm Books.

Young, Allan. 1995. *The Harmony of Illusions: Inventing Post-Traumatic Stress Disorder*. Princeton, N.J.: Princeton University Press.

Reimagining Aboriginality

An Indigenous People's Response to Social Suffering

Naomi Adelson

The pain is about being Aboriginal.
> *Stephanie Gilbert*

The issue of (Native) identity continues to be contentious. It has its own very interesting and troubling history(ies), changing by the decade to match the times.
> *Gerald R. McMaster*

INTRODUCTION

SOCIAL SUFFERING IN INDIGENOUS CANADA

Social suffering, and responses to it, are social and political phenomena. Given that among Indigenous Canadians[1] social suffering and responses to it are linked to the history and politics of Canada, philosophical reflection on suffering must ultimately give way to concrete, viable solutions and change. Specifically, real social or health improvements will only take place in conjunction with the attainment of economic and political autonomy on an Indigenously controlled land base (O'Neil 1993; Salée 1995). Until any of those processes of autonomy are fully realized, the "yoke of colonialism"—manifested in political alienation, poverty, despair, substance abuse, violence, and suicide—will continue to plague far too many Indigenous Canadian communities (O'Neil 1993).

"Aboriginal children are still dying, Aboriginal youth are still committing suicide and the aged are still either in pain from personal oppression or numbed by the anaesthetic of oppression which attempted
to force the discarding of their self-respect and confidence in their culture. All of this is the cumulative effect of two hundred years of racism,
hatred and white arrogance" (West 1990, quoted in Gilbert 1995: 147).
This quote summarizes the situation that far too many Indigenous Canadians face today. That it was written about Australian Aboriginal
peoples reminds us that the internally colonized nations of Australia and
Canada share far too many traumatic histories of marginalization, exclusion, and institutionalized racism (RCAP 1995). This is a time, in
other words, of competing and difficult histories, histories that reflect
the dampening pall of sustained, neglectful, and discriminatory practices. This is the kind of long-term, institutionalized, and ultimately invisible suffering that has been referred to as the "soft knife" of long-
term oppression (Kleinman et al. 1996). Indeed, so invisible is the
suffering of the so-called fourth world of the internally colonized that it
is often overlooked in the global context.

Despite this relative invisibility both nationally and globally, in Canada its continued effect is manifest in the excessively high rates of interpersonal violence, alcohol abuse, and related accidental deaths and
suicides reported in so many Aboriginal communities today (Waldram
et al. 1995). Native populations in Canada are diverse and live in urban, rural, and remote areas of the country. Despite linguistic, cultural,
and imposed classificatory variations amongst the groups,[2] and despite
differences between generations or genders, Indigenous Canadians
unite under the thumb of a history of oppressive Canadian governmental policies and insidious racist practices. Whether overrepresented
in the prisons and in disease and suicide statistics or underrepresented
in "mainstream" Canadian society, and despite clear and exciting exceptions to this norm, Indigenous Canadians as a group are living out
the effects of a chronology of neglect, indifference, and systematic oppression. High rates of poverty, unemployment, dropping out of
school, infant mortality, and death by nonnatural causes are far too
common in Aboriginal communities across Canada (AFHJSC 1993).
Thus we can speak of social suffering amongst Aboriginal Canadians
as an example of the process which "ruins the collective and the intersubjective connections of experience and gravely damages subjectivity.
. . . [I]t results from what political, economic, and institutional power

does to people, and, reciprocally, from how these forms of power themselves influence responses to social problems" (Kleinman et al. 1996: xi).

Shared cultural and community traumatization are the product of two centuries of internal colonization, neglectful government practices, suppression or banning of Indigenous cultural practices, dislocation (in some cases) of entire communities, and separation of children from families by means of virtual incarceration in residential schools or long-term hospital facilities (Kirmayer et al. 1993). Cultural decomposition was also part of the missionization process, which began over two hundred years ago, and later (more explicitly) with the often brutally enforced educational programs of residential schooling. Church-run residential schools for boys and girls closed permanently only in the latter half of the twentieth century but have had a profound and lasting effect, having been written about both in scholarly and literary terms as places of resignation and submission, systems established to "take the Indian" out of these children (Johnston 1988; Lomawaima 1993). While such schools did provide educational skills, they took a profound toll on the individuals who had "the Indian" trounced out of them. Residential schools alone, of course, do not account for the high rates of violence, abuse, poverty, disease, suicide, or incarceration among Aboriginal Canadians today. The residential experience, however, remains a key factor singled out by Indigenous peoples as contributing to their current status as among the most disenfranchised in Canada (O'Neil 1993).

Irrespective of its roots or effects, social suffering must not be viewed simply as a destructive or, for that matter, a creative force. The effects and processes of inequality can be dangerously romanticized simply by naming them. To be identified as either "sufferer" or "victim" shackles individuals and groups to a particular history and burdens them with the responsibility for a history that was never theirs to decide. I cannot imagine that Indigenous Canadians want to be defined exclusively from within the narrow confines of "sufferer" or "victim." Nevertheless, it is evident that far too many of the prevailing and often awful circumstances in their lives are inextricably linked to past and present native/nonnative relations in this country (Waldram et al. 1995).

It is not surprising then that so many Indigenous leaders across Canada are calling for a time of community healing. How that healing is to take place, however, is not readily defined. As stated at the outset, community healing in its broadest sense can only occur with real economic and political autonomy. Autonomy, however described or enacted, will not be realized until the issue of native self-government is resolved at the federal and provincial levels of Canadian politics and until all Indigenous Canadian nations have been fairly dealt with in terms of land rights and treaty negotiations (where none yet exist). The increase in public protests, blockades, and demonstrations held by Indigenous groups across Canada in the last few years points to the growing frustration with the slow pace of and injustices in this process.

An extensive review of the national situation for Aboriginal Canadians was undertaken through the first half of this decade by a federally instituted Royal Commission on Aboriginal Peoples (RCAP). Despite the inherent problems of such a massive undertaking, Indigenous and non-Indigenous experts alike confirmed that greater attention must be paid to community initiatives and local-level efforts that directly and indirectly improve social and economic conditions and, ultimately, social health (Kirmayer et al. 1993). In a summary of their findings, the authors note in particular that "government responses to social pathologies of simply providing more health care avoid the more fundamental causes. Serious effort must be applied to developing full employment and to actively preserving and enhancing community and cultural esteem. The most obvious and direct way of doing this is by political and social empowerment. [Further,] it is crucial . . . to find and promote images and activities representative of the vitality, renewal and rebirth of Aboriginal communities and traditions" (Kirmayer et al. 1993: 56). Responses to social suffering in the context of Aboriginal Canada, in other words, must be processes that originate within and evolve from local efforts of social (re)construction. From the Northwest Territories to central and coastal towns and villages, there are examples of community-based programs of "healing" that incorporate approaches that are both appropriate and culturally sensitive (RCAP 1995; AFHJSC 1993). Increasingly, but by no means invariably, those efforts incorporate "traditional" Indigenous values and practices that are being reinvigorated in North America (O'Neil 1993). Both in reaction to the social ills and as efforts to encourage self-esteem, Indigenous healing and cultural practices, including the use of medicine wheel teachings, sweat lodges, and pow-wows, have flourished across eastern Canada in the last decade in particular.[3] These practices, rooted in various Indigenous histories across the Americas, are increasingly coming to symbolize transnational Indigenous unity as well as local potential.

Health and well-being, in other words and in the broadest meaning of the terms, are a reflection of social and economic circumstances

(Adelson 1998). By putting into the foreground the social and political bases of health, I argue that social pathologies—that is, the expressed forms of social suffering—cannot only be relegated to the level of the individual. To always view these problems simply as individuated "health" issues constrains the analysis to the far-too-narrow domain of the medicalization of social distress. By contrast, in this paper I explore a *social response* to social suffering and, in particular, describe the concept of aboriginality as part of the fundamental matrix of this response.

ABORIGINALITY AS RESPONSE

Aboriginality, for Indigenous populations everywhere, is a claim to distinctiveness based on the assertion of original occupancy, of land rights and the concomitant spurning of colonial influences. Aboriginality, by definition, occurs within the constraints of current political and social relations linking representations of the past with identity constructions in the present. However it is locally defined, aboriginality is the negotiation of the political, cultural, and social space of Aboriginal peoples within the nation-state (Archer 1991). Interpretations of historical relations and present-day circumstances thus influence the ways in which aboriginality is constructed. Indigenous culture and identity in Canada, for example, is always linked to issues of self-determination and land rights (Bennett and Blundell 1995). In particular, the metaphors and images used today by Indigenous Canadians to describe and justify their cultural and political autonomy are made necessary by the continual need to validate claims of legitimacy. Aboriginality is thus a critical political tool: an essential "space of otherness that is shifting, complex, and dynamic [yet] in which Aboriginal imagination can produce an identity" (Beckett 1992: 167; Bennett and Blundell 1995; see also Santiago-Irizarry 1996; Légaré 1995). In this analysis I examine the contingency, fluidity, and vitality of aboriginality as it is shaped and expressed by the Cree people of northern Québec, Canada.

Conflicts around land rights and political autonomy form the (seemingly) permanent backdrop to this analysis. Specifically, for the Whapmagoostui Cree of Great Whale, Québec, discussions of aboriginality must be contextualized not only within a long history of institutionalized neglect but, more recently, with an attempt to further erode their social and economic base. In 1989 a massive hydroelectric project was slated for development on the Great Whale River. That project had a profound effect on the people of Whapmagoostui and has ultimately led to a rethinking of what it means to "be Cree." Articulations of aboriginality certainly did not begin with the battle against the hydroelectric project, nor have they ended with its ultimate cancellation in 1994. Yet, as I describe later, the very real threat of the tremendous changes to their lives if the project had been completed and the seemingly interminable fight with its concomitant media attention were instrumental to that process. This, in combination with ordeals faced by other Indigenous nations in Canada, the nationalist agenda in Québec, and the growing affirmation of Aboriginal identity in the rest of North America, set in motion a conscious shift in the way the Whapmagoostui people think about and act upon a particular sense of themselves—what it means, in other words, to be Cree.

But what of the idea of "aboriginality as response"? What sort of cultural "renewal" is taking place? In asking these questions I do not in any way challenge the tremendous healing efforts, programs, and initiatives that are having real effects throughout Indigenous Canada. I am, though, interested in the links between social suffering and concepts of cultural renewal as social response. And as I suggest below, aboriginality is part and parcel of that response.

It is that inventive and vitally political process which I address in this discussion of a relatively new annual event that has been taking place in Whapmagoostui: the summer Gathering. The Gathering can be described as an interlude, a time and a place where people can come together as a group. The Gathering, of course, represents but one modality of social response and does not seek to address directly the individual problems such as unemployment, poverty, or related social ills to which some people must return home once the event is over. The Gathering is not a panacea. It is nonetheless an important local initiative: a deliberate attempt to improve, in the long term, the social welfare of this small community. Elsewhere I have written about the Gathering specifically in relation to meanings and interpretations of aboriginality (Adelson 1997). In this essay I shift the analysis to how these ideas of aboriginality are part of the larger project of response to social suffering. This study draws from ethnographic fieldwork conducted at the three Gatherings that have been held to date, along with discussions with members of the community at other times of the year. That work is informed by close to a decade of working and living with members of the Whapmagoostui community.

In the next section, I introduce the specific case study central to my analysis. I begin with a contextualization and brief historical review of

the Eastern James Bay Cree, the Whapmagoostui people and their annual Gatherings. I end the essay with a discussion of the relationship
between social suffering, aboriginality, and social response.

THE JAMES BAY CREE NATION

The Whapmagoostui Iiyiyuu'ch[4] are members of the James Bay Cree
Nation, a political alignment of the eight Eastern James Bay Cree communities of northern Québec, Canada. This alignment was formalized
in the early 1970s, when the James Bay Cree suddenly found themselves
having to fight for their ancestral lands against a formidable opponent.
Political, legal, and media battles were waged in 1971 against the province of Québec, which had unilaterally announced plans to create a
massive hydroelectric project in the James Bay (La Grande Rivière) region of northern Québec.

Because they had not initially been consulted or apprised of the project plans, the Eastern James Bay Cree were at first unprepared to contest
the planned massive hydroelectric project. Initial encounters with the
government of Québec were hindered by the limited experience and resources available to the Cree in dealing with an issue of this magnitude
(Richardson 1977; Salisbury 1986). That soon changed, however, as a
new young leadership began to hire lawyers and consultants to assist it
in launching challenges to the proposed plan. The long and arduous
legal battles that ensued resulted in the James Bay and Northern Québec
Agreement (JBNQA) between Québec's Cree and Inuit populations and
the provincial and federal governments (Feit 1985; Richardson 1977;
Salisbury 1986).[5] Ultimately, the James Bay Cree (and Inuit) of Québec
relinquished Native title to approximately 647,000 square kilometers of
land in exchange for benefits, payments, and specific land rights. The
JBNQA and the Northeastern Québec Agreement that followed were
hailed at the time as dynamic treaties which, importantly, overrode the
mandate of the Indian Act of Canada[6] for the Cree of Québec. Further,
the Cree-Naskapi (of Québec) Act, resulting from the agreements, established the legal basis for a form of Indigenous self-government. Sur-
rendering the land in exchange for financial compensation and a (limited) self-government was not simple or easy. That decision can be
viewed as more than a modest victory for the Cree, however, since without the legal battle the land would have been appropriated with no
compensation whatsoever. Indeed, this response to the Québec government's hydrodevelopment project in the early 1970s remains a compel-

ling—if ultimately flawed—example of modern-day relations between Indigenous populations and the nation-state.

The individuals who spearheaded that fight against the government's plans emerged as the first organized leaders of the Eastern James Bay Cree people as a group distinct from other Indigenous groups in Canada. The "Cree Nation" is thus a recent political phenomenon that arose out of necessity to represent the Cree position in the transactions and negotiations with government bodies over the James Bay hydroelectric projects. The Grand Council of the Cree of Québec (GCCQ), the unified political voice of the Eastern James Bay Cree Nation, ultimately became their first regional government.

Despite involvement in negotiating the JBNQA, the people of Whapmagoostui were relatively isolated from the political disputes surrounding the construction of the La Grande Rivière hydroelectric dams. In fact, prior to the 1970s, the Whapmagoostui Iiyiyuu'ch had remained relatively isolated from the politics and economics of the rest of the province. This all changed by the late 1980s. In 1989 the Québec provincial government renewed its interest in northern hydroelectric development, and specifically in the development of the Great Whale River waterway. This project would have an enormous, direct impact on the Whapmagoostui people, who rely on this waterway and its tributaries for food and travel. The blueprints planned the diversion of three rivers north of the Great Whale River into it, connecting them all to an immense system of dams, dikes, reservoirs, and power stations built to generate a maximum of 2,890 megawatts of power.[7] A new airport, the first road into the region, and development previously unseen in this remote coastal region were all being discussed by Hydro-Québec.

The Cree were not persuaded by these plans, and opposition to the Great Whale hydroelectric project was swift and focused. The Grand Council of the Cree of Québec, now with an established team of legal and environmental experts, began to prepare legal, environmental, and media challenges to the Great Whale River project. Compared to the legal battles with the government of Québec over the James Bay I project, this second campaign by the Cree leadership was much more successful in terms of the speed at which it was able to react to the provincial government. It should be noted that the environmental experts, legal advisors, and provincial Cree leadership did not take on this battle without the directive of the community of Whapmagoostui. The primary consideration for the Whapmagoostui Cree, as for their leaders and experts, was the welfare of the land and the effect that this project

would have had on the wildlife and the vegetation upon which the animals depend. Implicit in this consideration of the land and the animals
was of course a fundamental concern for the people themselves.

Compounding the basic concerns about the project was a skepticism
shared by the Cree leadership and people about the motives of the provincial government. It was clear to the Cree that the province of Québec
had never lived up to the promises written into the original JBNQA,
and therefore it would be increasingly difficult to enter into any new
form of negotiations with either the provincial government or Hydro-
Québec (GCCQ 1990; Salée 1995). For these reasons, in 1989 the Cree
opted to halt further talks or negotiations with representatives of Hydro-
Québec and initiated political and legal steps to cancel the project. One
of the more successful aspects of these efforts was to tie the project
nationally and internationally into global concerns about pollution and
the protection of natural environments.

Lobbying by the Cree and their supporters led to the cancellation of
important energy contracts in several northeastern U.S. states. Those
cancellations, compounded by the impediments of a very expensive yet
flawed environmental review process and a change in the Québec provincial government in 1994—from Liberal to Parti-Québecois—and the
concomitant change in governmental priorities led to the (quite sudden)
shelving of the Great Whale hydroelectric project on November 18,
1994.

From 1989 until 1994 the people of Whapmagoostui found that they,
their lifestyles, and their small, remote community were the focus of
national and international media attention. Reporters from Europe, the
United States, and Canada regularly came north to record the images
and words of the Cree—images more often than not of people working
on the land which they were fighting to protect. The fight as well as the
media attention took a tremendous toll on the people of Whapmagoostui, so that, despite the successful outcome, the years of struggle culminated in what can only be described as communal exhaustion. People
were worn thin by having to contemplate the immense changes that
would have come with the hydroelectric dams while continually justi-
fying their very existence and worth at the provincial, national, and
international levels.

Just as the Great Whale River battle abated, another issue began to
escalate. The same government that had halted the hydroelectric project
began to step up its sovereigntist agenda. Included in that agenda is the
claim of sovereign title to all of Québec, irrespective of signed treaties

or agreements. Land and ethnocultural distinctiveness are, not surprisingly, the two most important issues at stake for the sovereigntists and the Cree nation alike. The small village of Whapmagoostui, despite its relative isolation, thus remains immersed within the (post)colonial enterprise.

THE WHAPMAGOOSTUI IIYIYUU'CH

Whapmagoostui is located approximately 1,400 kilometers north of Montreal, on the northern edge of the mouth of the Great Whale River. Like many remote Indigenous communities in Canada, Whapmagoostui is the by-product of a history of contact. Travel by nonnatives into the Great Whale River region began in the mid-1600s, when prospectors and traders arrived in the region, but it was not until the mid-1700s, when the highly aggressive whaling industry was in full operation, that there was any sort of regular trading post activity at Great Whale River.[8] With Little Whale River and Richmond Gulf to the north, the area at the mouth of the Great Whale River was one of a number of known summer meeting places for the northern, caribou-hunting Cree. The Cree traveled along set hunting and trapping routes, arriving at the (now established) posts to trade in furs or perhaps work in the whaling industry, visit with families who would also congregate at these sites, and then move on before the fall freeze-up of the waterways.

Now numbering over six hundred, the people of Whapmagoostui did not consider this site a permanent "home" until relatively recently. Less than fifty years ago most people were born on the land and lived by hunting, fishing and trapping. People would travel to the post site as part of a regular hunting route in order to trade for, and later purchase, dry goods such as flour, tea, tobacco and ammunition.

Beginning at the end of the nineteenth century, some individuals always remained at the post site, sometimes because of cyclical declines in the animal populations, sometimes because of work opportunities or incapacitating illness. With a depressed fur market in the early part of the twentieth century, the number of permanent post residents grew, as fewer families could sustain themselves with full-time trapping. Facilities and services arrived much later, coming sometimes from an unexpected resource. In the 1950s, for example, Great Whale became a site for the Distant Early Warning radar station. Even today the Cree speak of how the Canadian Armed Forces seemed to just appear one summer, barricading the station and its personnel behind high wire fences. As the need for the Distant Early Warning lines waned in the late 1950s, the armed forces corps left. Not too long after, some of their barracks were turned into a school for the children of Great Whale.

That first school was rudimentary at best, with classes held only in the summer months. Great Whale got its first full day school in the 1960s as more families came to live at the village site. Living in the village took a devastating toll on this new population of village dwellers, however. Infectious diseases such as tuberculosis and influenza were rampant at that time, attesting to the extreme poverty and squalid conditions in which the Cree were living.

With the changes brought about since the early 1980s as a result of the JBNQA, the village now resembles a far more permanent site, with modern houses, a new band (local government) office, a community hall, a school, and an indoor hockey arena. Three stores, a post office, a church, a small hotel and restaurant, sports fields, a machine shop, a construction warehouse, and other services and facilities also dot the rather barren landscape that comprises the immediate Whapmagoostui area. There is, however, a growing shortage of housing. With the exorbitant cost of housing materials in the north, diminishing funds available through the transfer payments to each of the Cree communities, and a young and thriving population, an increasing number of multiple-generation families are living in less and less space.

Today fewer than twenty percent of the Whapmagoostui adults remain full-time hunting and trapping families, living the majority of the year on the land.[9] Trade in furs is no longer lucrative and hence forms a much smaller part of the local economy. Hunting for food remains an important resource, though, and thus, while most Whapmagoostui people now either live in or are employed in the village, many spend a portion of their time out on the land. Groups of men or entire families regularly go out for the day or weekend throughout the year to hunt caribou, shoot birds such as ptarmigan, or to fish. Twice a year, during the annual spring and fall migrations of the Canada goose, the village resembles nothing short of a ghost town, as entire families move to their respective camps for these key hunting periods.

Great Whale consists of two official municipalities, Whapmagoostui (Cree) and Kuujjuarapik (Inuit), and three unofficial communities: Cree, Inuit, and nonnative.[10] The nonnative teachers, government employees, Hydro workers, police, employment officer, postal employees, aviation workers, and engineers all live near their respective offices. This entire section of town is considered "up the hill" from the two Native communities. For the most part there is very little social interaction between those up the hill and the Indigenous communities. There are of course other layers of political import here, as those who live up the hill are primarily well-employed French Québecois.[11] Communication between the three (unofficial) communities occurs most often in a fourth language, English. Since Cree and Inuit speak different mother tongues, hunt in different areas, and tend to socialize largely within their own extended kin groups, there is only limited socializing between the two communities. The children, for example, have for a long time attended different schools and the Cree and Inuit take part in separate church services. The JBNQA only increased the separation, with the implementation of separate governments, municipal services, and medical clinics, and the creation of invisible jural lines to divide the two communities.[12]

With no roads into this northerly region of Québec, Whapmagoostui can only be accessed by either plane or watercraft. This physical isolation is increasingly diminished, however, not just by air transport but by the telephones, fax machines, satellite dishes, and computers that are an indispensable part of life in the Canadian north.

As much as television, radio, and the Internet bring a heightened awareness of Aboriginal issues across North America into the community, these media are held partially responsible for the continued insinuation of a nonnative ideology into the lives of the people of the north. As I have noted elsewhere, while a range of goods and services have been accommodated and incorporated into Indigenous lifestyles, there remains a sense that nonnative/"white man"[13] beliefs writ large represent a greater threat than any material item per se (Adelson 1997, 1998).

Whapmagoostui is, by comparison to many other Indigenous communities in Canada, doing well. Services, schooling, and warm homes are all available, and a local municipal government is in control of community services. Many, but by no means all, of the adults have given up alcohol. There has not been a completed suicide in Whapmagoostui. Yet still there are women and men who are physically and emotionally traumatized or abused, who drink to excess, who hurt their children or who were themselves hurt as children. The homes and services provided are more than adequate but, in a sense, camouflage the continuing hardships and traumas that define life for too many of the people of Whapmagoostui. This kind of despair, insidious as it is in the lives of the people, was only exacerbated by the struggle that took place over the last few years as the members of the community fought to save their river and themselves from the massive hydroelectric project.

In the next section I describe Whapmagoostui's Gatherings, the first of which coincided with the final year of the battle against the hydro-electric project slated for the region. The Gathering has since changed its primary focus somewhat, yet it remains a compelling example of a collective process of cultural assertion and response.

THE WHAPMAGOOSTUI GATHERINGS, 1993–1995

This Gathering is a result of a resolution of the Whapmagoostui First Nation who called for a gathering of
this kind to be able to assess the influence of modern
impacts on our culture. . . . There are many reasons for
this Gathering but the most important is to revisit our
culture.

> Matthew Mukash, Whapmagoostui Chief,
> Opening Ceremony speech excerpt,
> Gathering 1993

The annual summer Gathering began, in part, as a local response to the hydroelectric project and as a venue to promote Cree cultural knowledge and values. As members of the community recall:

> The first summer, 1993, was a very exciting time because it was something new to do and was for a special and specific reason which was to show the outside world that we are still alive and well and practicing our way of life.

> [The first Gathering] was quite the learning experience, everybody was there. Because you understood how confused you were and that it was the political fight for the river, but in turn you were going across on the river. . . . It made it more real; that if this river is gone you won't be able to go across it.[14]

The first Gathering was a relatively large event, held across the river from the community. People came from up and down the Hudson Bay coast to participate at this Gathering, including a caravan of canoes from Chisasibi, a Cree village to the south of Whapmagoostui, and a group of Povugnituk Inuit, who arrived by trawler from their northern coastal village.[15] Spiritual leaders, or elders, from the provinces of Manitoba, Ontario, and New Brunswick were brought in to perform various cer-emonies.[16] As well, there were professional photographers, film, televi-sion, and radio crews, and anthropologists recording the entire event. Canvas tents were set up in family groupings and tipis in order to ac-commodate the more than three hundred participants. While families were responsible for cooking their own meals, small canteens were also set up at various sites, at which women cooked and sold everything from soft drinks and hot dogs to fish roe bannock and a full range of official Gathering memorabilia.

The first week-long Gathering officially opened on the afternoon of 26 July 1993 with an honor song sung by local drummers, a prayer by a highly respected local catechist, and speeches by the event coordinator, the Whapmagoostui chief, and the mayor of Kuujjuarapik. The speeches revolved around the general themes of the event: teaching and learning about the ways of the Cree people, rekindling the practices and knowledge that have been suppressed. The controversy surrounding the Hydro-Québec issue was explicitly raised by some of the speakers, although politics were not the central focus of this first Gathering. The Gatherings, from the outset, constituted a place for young people to learn from their elders and a time for people to relax and enjoy themselves away from the village, to "revisit their culture." This is, as one woman described, "rejuvenating to the spirit and to the history of the Whapmagoostui [people] and other Indigenous peoples who join our Gatherings. It is a peaceful and exciting time."

The Gathering site—across the river from the village of Whapmagoostui—is viewed as particularly important. The village is recognized as a useful but ultimately imposed structure and a reminder of a colonial history. Home after all has far less to do with village houses than it does with family and the expanse of land to the north, south, and east of the village. Home is defined quite simply as the land—the mountains, wooded regions, open expanses, and rivers upon which the Cree and their ancestors have lived and traveled. One might even argue that the week-long Gathering instills more of a sense of permanence than the concrete-based houses back in the village.

The temporal and social space of the Gathering are thus significant and evocative. The planning, preparation, and readying of the site itself with stage, tents, firewood, fir boughs, and even adequate waste facilities all signify the importance of the place. Having the Gathering in the summer and at this site establishes a link to the congregations of family ancestors who traveled to this very spot for their summer respite from the harsh winter of work and travel. As one of the coordinators of the Gathering put it: "The Gathering has to continue because it supports the revival of the culture here. Like . . . the site is appropriate, it is where our people used to gather. And even just by gathering there we preserve that site."[17]

Scheduled events of the 1993 Gathering began early for those few
who attended the sunrise ceremonies. A few hours later, the rest of the
day's events got underway with an opening drumming honor song, a
Christian prayer recited by a church elder, and then a full morning of
speeches. The afternoons were filled with scheduled workshops. Workshops were designed to highlight both men's and women's activities and
were conducted by both local and visiting elders. These teaching sessions
included such topics as traditional trap building, lodge building, tool-
making, and wood carving (all men's work), or knotting fishnets and
the proper handling of caribou hides (women's work). Other workshops
included sessions on the proper use of the Cree language, legends from
the past, medicines made from plants or animals, and the importance of
respectful behavior and practices. A number of sessions were geared
specifically toward the youth, touching on subjects such as married life,
"traditional" versus "modern" ways, alcohol and drugs, spiritual and
physical healing, and the problems of peer pressure. Workshops were
held either out in the open or in one of the several *iyiyuukimikw* (Cree
dwelling, tipi) built for that purpose. A typical craft workshop consisted
of an elder member of the community talking about and demonstrating
how to go about making a particular item, be it a wooden snow shovel,
a diaper of absorbent moss, or spruce gum glue. These workshops were
for the most part well attended in the first year of the Gatherings.

Evening and night activities were crowd-pleasers and included some
pow-wow dancing, a concert by the popular Innu duo Kashtin,[18] Cree
versions of softball or soccer, and square dancing. An elders' feast was
held for all present at the Gathering on the last evening of the 1993
event. And finally, there were the closing speeches, an integral—if at
times lengthy—part of the event. Thus the first Gathering ended successfully, serving its dual purpose of bringing the community together
and reflecting a unity to the outside world via the various media recordings of the event.

The 1994 and 1995 Gatherings differed somewhat from that original
event. Even before the shelving of the hydroelectric project (which took
place between the 1994 and 1995 Gatherings), and especially after, the
consensus was that the Gathering no longer had to be a production for
anyone but the Whapmagoostui people themselves. The band council
and community at large felt that the Gatherings should, however, continue, since as one organizer succinctly said, they had become integral
to "the revival of culture here." This attention to things Cree is viewed
as beneficial to the long-term social well-being of the community. The

annual Gathering has thus quickly evolved into a forum for the conscious affirmation of particular notions of local Indigenous identity; a specific time and a place, in other words, for rethinking and renegotiating specific cultural practices.

The second and third Gatherings were quieter than the first in that there was virtually no outside media (and only this one anthropologist) present. Within Whapmagoostui, however, the Gatherings have become anything but quiet, and indeed begin months prior to the actual event. Preparations for the Gatherings, along with discussions by elders about what should and should not take place, occur all year round. As one woman noted:

> I have noticed when I am at the [local] store, I hear people talking of buying something that they will need for the Gathering, things like pots, foam mattresses, sleeping bags, new canvas for a tipi or a new tent. The people seem to prepare for the Gathering all year round. . . . The people start getting firewood and poles for the tents and tipis when the weather starts to warm up, in March. As soon as the river is navigable, in early June, some people will already be putting up their tents and tipis and spend weekends there. People will start packing their stuff as soon as they can to be ready to go at a moment's notice for the actual Gathering, which takes place sometime in the middle or near the end of July. . . . The families will urge the young people to participate in the preparation of the camps. The youth are employed to make ready the guest tents and tipis. They help to erect the dwelling, gather firewood and the [fir] boughs [for the floors]. They get and chop firewood for the elders long before the Gathering. When the time comes, everything is ready. All the tents and tipis have already been made.

Both the 1994 and 1995 Gatherings were well attended by the Whapmagoostui Cree and Chisasibi Caravan visitors. More than sixty tents and tipis were set up in and around the new location, with about three hundred people once again living at the Gathering site. In accord with the request of the Whapmagoostui elders' council, scheduled events were planned somewhat differently from the first year. Specifically, there were fewer speeches and no honor drumming in the mornings. Workshops were scheduled throughout the latter half of the day, and speeches relegated to the evenings. This format accommodated those who felt that the first Gathering had far too many scheduled activities, speeches, and "traditional drumming" sessions. The evenings were filled with social activities, square dancing, and games. Church services, held at the Gathering site, were incorporated into the 1994 and 1995 schedules. Included as well in the second and third Gatherings as "other daily activities" were morning and evening sweat lodges which were conducted by the

visiting elders and attended in particular by those who share a growing
interest in Native spirituality.

People regularly commented to me on the enjoyment they derived
from being together and socializing in this communal camp setting. They
focus on the past, on what will be lost with the passing of the elder
members of the community. Reflecting on the meaning of the Gatherings, one woman who is particularly concerned about what is at stake
with the loss of the older generation noted that:

> When people are at these Gatherings they visit each other more often and
> they see each other at the outdoor events. They help each other out. Some
> will get water and chop firewood and cook food to share with all the family
> members. It is a time of getting closer to your own family members because
> you are living in the same tent with them. Some family groups will even join
> their tents together. In this way, there are more open discussions about things
> in general and personal family member things. . . . When I was there with
> my mother, she would start telling us a story that she had heard her mother
> tell her about her parents—an event that happened right there on those
> [Gathering] grounds. It made my ancestors more real and I felt closer to them
> and wanted to know about them when they were alive.

Another remarked,

> It is at these events where our language comes out strong. Living here in [the
> village] without associating with the nature part of our language means that
> [so much] is not used. Whereas if we live in the bush or at camp, words and
> expressions in Cree come out, which we don't normally use here in the com-
> munity. Best of all, the teachings from our elders come out so strong, they
> have so much to teach us and we have so much that we need to learn.

A notion of what it means "to be Cree" draws extensively from the
oral historical record and interpretations of the past as it is constituted
through the retelling of stories of hunting and survival in the bush. The
most profound images are those of past hunting days when families
traveled and hunted on the land on a full-time basis (Adelson 1998;
Masty 1995). These stories connect present-day "traditional" activities
such as hunting and a myriad of other bush-related activities to a social
past and hence become more than "what the Iiyiyuu'ch do." These acts
assert a particular contemporary identity and focus.

The physical space of the Gathering is equally important to that sense
of identity. Not only is the Gathering site of historical relevance, the
layout of the tents is significant in the contemporary context. The proximity of one family dwelling to the next and the soft, permeable walls

of a canvas tent are, as people note, far more conducive to communication than the permanent houses back in town.

> Then there is the community togetherness that is not here [in the village].
> Because it's very hard. Even with my next door neighbor—we have walls . . .
> [on] both sides, we would live this close if we were in a tent side by side. All
> those barriers that were put around us, barriers that isolate us from one
> another, are taken away when we live in our traditional way, on the tradi-
> tional site. . . . just the setting is different because if you are in a school or in
> a—even a community home, you're being taught—there is a constant re-
> minder of what was taken away.

The permeable walls mean something else as well for members of the
community: "You look around and people are happy . . . you don't
hear—one of the things that I am very glad about because there are no
physical outbursts of family violence in the tents," said one young
woman. Linked to this is the fact that the Gathering is a "dry" event:
alcohol is not allowed at the site.

Let me now comment briefly on the theme and events of the 1995
Gathering. I do this to highlight the dynamic nature of aboriginality;
that essential "space of otherness" that is defined as much by context
as by content. What I point to here specifically is the heterogeneity of
Aboriginal identities as they are created in the (post)modern context.

The theme of the 1995 Gathering was "Protecting our Lands and
Traditional Way of Life." "Tradition," however, was renegotiated at
this Gathering, since it was here that the community organized its first
formal "traditional pow-wow." Traditional pow-wows are large dancing and drumming events with particular universal features such as the
dancers' regalia, honor songs, healing dances, and a tributary gifting
practice known as a giveaway. In Whapmagoostui, as is practiced elsewhere, drumming groups, dancers, an elder, and an emcee were invited
in from various other Canadian Indigenous communities in order to
enhance the local event. Pow-wow dancing activities have, in the last
decade in particular, become part of the surge of trans-Indigenous (spiritual) identity in North America. Elder Whapmagoostui men whom I
have recently interviewed have commented that the dancing and drumming is reminiscent of drum dances of their past, but that this formalized
version is quite new to the region. This first "traditional pow-wow" thus
hailed the incorporation of transnational "traditional culture" into
Whapmagoostui. It also marked a time of contradiction and some degree
of turmoil. The pow-wow, postponed until Sunday evening because of

inclement weather, conflicted with regularly scheduled church services. Some of those who attended the pow-wow commented to me that there might have been a better turnout without this scheduling conflict. Sunday remains a Sabbath day whether one attends church or not,[19] and the weak attendance at the pow-wow attests to the mixed reactions within the community about this particular event. In fact workshops were not that well attended either, but for another reason entirely: people were content to spend a great deal of time at the Gathering site just visiting with one another. Indeed, a general comment that I often heard was that the best thing about the 1995 Gathering in particular was the time it afforded people to enjoy each other's company in familiar camp surroundings in a way that is structurally impossible in the village. People passed their time at the Gathering cooking or eating bush foods, talking, playing checkers, drinking tea, and listening to or telling a story. They also spent part of their days as they might typically at any hunting camp—cutting and splitting wood for the fire, hauling water, or collecting fir boughs.

Men and women may have been conscious of doing "things Cree" at scheduled events, but those planned "cultural" activities, such as the wooden fishhook-making workshop or the canoe-building workshop, were ultimately not central to the success of the Gathering. The opportunity to be at a camp site and amongst family for an extended period of time, whether learning from them or simply just relaxing with them, was viewed as more significant than any of the planned activities. Whether eating goose, caribou, bannock, hot-dogs, or layer cake; purchasing commemorative mugs or sweatshirts; or participating in practices such as sweat lodges or pow-wows, the people of Whapmagoostui were creating a new composite of what it means to be Cree.

For the Whapmagoostui Iiyiyuu'ch, the issue of hydroelectric development was the impetus for the first Gathering. It was, to a large degree, the constant eye of the camera on the community during the lengthy opposition to the hydroelectric project that instigated this search for Cree identity. The first Gathering was planned as a media event but also as an opportunity for people to "revisit their culture." The second and third Gatherings were no longer public displays for the outside world but rather time set aside for the people of Whapmagoostui to reflect upon their contemporary situations while living in a communal setting away from the village. As such the Gatherings continue to provide a time and a place for the people of Whapmagoostui to reflect and act upon their sense of "being Cree," however that was defined.

REIMAGINING ABORIGINALITY,
RETHINKING RESPONSE

Aboriginality, as I stated at the outset, encompasses contemporary political and social relations as Indigenous peoples negotiate their identities
within the nation-state, and is manifested in part through the telling and
acting upon a particular historical identity, however that history is negotiated in the present (Friedman 1992). Yet aboriginality is not simply
a rejection of all things nonnative. It is a melding of concepts and practices, so that pow-wows, square dancing, playing checkers, living in
tents, hearing stories from the past, videotaping the present, scraping
hides, drinking sodas while eating bush foods, and purchasing Gathering
memorabilia all authenticate identity. There is a conscious fusion of old
and new, as people are not so much revisiting the past as negotiating
and constructing a contemporary sense of themselves as Indigenous peoples. It is for this reason that we must not, in the analysis, "strip away
the invented portions of culture as inauthentic, but . . . understand the
process by which they acquire authenticity" (Hanson 1989: 198; cf.
Scott 1993). All traditions are invented—and the Gathering exemplifies
that process by which traditions "present and reflect contemporary concerns and purposes rather than a passively inherited legacy" (Linnekin
1991: 446). Aboriginality is constructed as an exchange, layering, and
intermingling of old, new, adopted, and created Cree practices. People
are making their own history, hybrid as it may be, melding influences,
commodities, practices, and products (Clifford 1995). Further, it is in
this assertion of a particular and particularly political stance that we
find the basis of local strength and empowerment. Culture is used to
authenticate (or contest) identity in ways that are creative and transfor-
mative. People use various resources, manipulate their realities, formulate their projects to "both become and transform who they are, [to]
sustain or transform their social and cultural universe" (Ortner 1995:
187). Power thus, perhaps paradoxically, lies in contingency and in ambiguity. As Salée notes,

> The ancestral customs and practices, however thin they may wear in some
> cases, serve as ideological mooring where the collective imagination can an-
> chor and elaborate a concrete identity. This identity, even if invented, even
> if tainted by borrowings from the very culture it claims to oppose politically,
> constitutes the impregnable rock on which Aboriginal [peoples] lay their ter-
> ritorial claims, mobilize themselves, and express their desire to gain auton-
> omous control of their collective destiny. (1995: 293)

And, I would emphatically add, even if borrowed from nonnative or distant Indigenous neighbors, the question of authenticity is moot. There is no one particular configuration of what being Cree, or Indigenous, "means." It is the "historical reality and agency of human diversity" (Clifford 1995: 100) that ultimately defines aboriginality. Questions should not revolve around whether pow-wow dancing is authentically Cree or how much people choose to integrate Indigenous and non-Indigenous materials or practices. Rather, one must ask what purpose aboriginality serves, and to what ends?

It is, I think, sadly ironic that the Iiyiyuu'ch must strive to build, let alone assert, cultural identity. Yet it is that sense of aboriginality—what was not that long ago either forbidden or trounced right out of people—that now serves as one of the incremental steps toward social and political awareness, strength, and, thus, social healing. Culture does not "cure" (cf. Santiago-Irizarry 1996) but in the negotiation of what it means to be Cree there is an attempt to control the creation of identity and its significance and implications which, in turn, is fundamentally—and increasingly—part of the larger recuperative process. People in Whapmagoostui are renegotiating the terms and conditions of identity in the face of direct and indirect threats to their land, lives, and livelihoods. The annual summer Gatherings thus link this community not just to a precolonial past but to a present and future that include a growing range of what will constitute Indigenous beliefs and practices. We see through the example of the Gatherings that aboriginality is constructive in two senses of that word: both produced and beneficial.

In their discussion of the invisibility of everyday social suffering, Kleinman, Das, and Lock (1996) speak about the fragmenting effect of the bureaucracy of aid.

> Because of the manner in which knowledge and institutions are organized in the contemporary world as pragmatically-oriented programs of welfare, health, social development, social justice, security and so on, the phenomenon of suffering as an experiential domain of everyday social life has been splintered into measurable attributes. These attributes are then managed by bureaucratic institutions and expert cultures that reify the fragmentation while casting a veil of misrecognition over the domain as a whole. (Kleinman, Das, and Lock 1996: xix)

This is, to be sure, a bleak view. Its futility lies, in particular, in the presumed limits of human agency. As O'Neil (1993) reminds us, though, the recourse can never be limited to shaking a collective fist at a colonial oppressor. Rather, we see in examples such as the one that I have de-

scribed an attempt to solder together the fragmented—and fragmenting—effects of social suffering. If social suffering derives from a colonial
and postcolonial history of disenfranchisement and attempts to eradi-
cate a cultural history, then the proper response to that suffering must
include the reconstitution and reaffirmation of social identity. In Whapmagoostui this ongoing, conscious, and imaginative process begins with
the summer Gatherings but resonates within the community the rest of
the year, as people continue to reimagine and renegotiate their cultural
and political worlds.

NOTES

I thank the people of Whapmagoostui for their continued support of my
research. As well, I would like in particular to thank Margaret Lock, Mamphela
Ramphele, Arthur Kleinman, Laurence Kirmayer, J. Teresa Holmes, Daphne
Winland, Lisa M. Mitchell, and Arthur Cheechoo for their insight as well as
their thoughtful and stimulating commentary on previous drafts of this work. I
gratefully acknowledge research funding provided by the Social Science Research Council, York University Faculty of Arts, and the Social Science and
Humanities Research Council of Canada.

1. Terms that are used synonymously today to indicate autochthonous status
include Aboriginal Peoples, Indigenous Canadians, Native Canadians, and First
Nations People. "Indian" is deemed incorrect in any public usage but remains
a neutral colloquial term in many Indigenous communities.

2. The approximately one million people of Indigenous ancestry living in
Canada are divided by government legislation into treaty, status, nonstatus, on-
reserve, off-reserve, Métis, and Inuit. Reserves are parcels of Crown land designated for Native use.

3. The people of Whapmagoostui have only in the last few years begun to
regularly invite elders/healers into the community. Their work specifically includes performing ceremonies (blessing homes, feasts for the departed), running
sweat lodges, and conducting individualized healing sessions as well as group
medicine wheel (Indigenous spiritual) teachings. My current research in this
community includes assessing the responses—be they acceptance, rejection, or
indifference—to these practices, and in particular the negotiation between Indigenous "traditional" ways and the teachings of the Anglican mission present
in this community for the last 150 years.

4. "Iiyiyuu'ch" translates into English as *person,* and more specifically Indigenous person. It is used in this paper interchangeably with the more familiar
English term, Cree (Eastern Sub-Arctic [Algonkian] Indigenous peoples).

5. Incorporated into the Agreement is control of wildlife resource management, as well as input into environmental impact assessments, a program of
guaranteed income for hunting families, and guaranteed native economic and
social development. Other fundamental benefits include administrative control

over local and regional governments, education, health, housing, and the administration of justice (Cree-Naskapi Commission 1986).

6. The Indian Act, recognized now as an extremely paternalistic document, remains the principal federal statute dealing with Native status, local government, management of reserve land and monies.

7. The original intention of the government of Québec had been to build these dams and power stations over a decade ago. Those plans were halted in the early 1980s because of a temporary surplus of hydroelectric power and a shift of government priorities. In 1989, with rising energy concerns, lowered water levels in the James Bay I reservoirs, greater public opposition to nuclear and coal energy, and the increasing cost of fossil fuel power, the dormant Great Whale project plans were revived by the provincial Liberal government and Hydro-Québec.

8. A full-time post and Anglican mission station were established at Great Whale in 1857. Prior to that traders and missionaries passed through the region en route to points north or south of this site (Francis and Morantz 1983).

9. An Income Security Program set up through the JBNQA financially assists those families who opt to spend the majority of the year hunting and trapping as their primarily livelihood (see Salisbury 1986; Scott 1979).

10. In contrast to most Native communities across Canada, where English has become the sole language, Cree is widely spoken by all generations in Whapmagoostui.

There are approximately 300 Inuit living in Kuujjuarapik and 150 nonnative Francophones living primarily on Inuit 1A lands. It is only in the last few years, since many Inuit moved to the newly created village of Umiujaq, that the Cree outnumber the Inuit. Umiujaq, located about one hundred kilometers north of Great Whale, is a village that was petitioned for by Kuujjuarapik Inuit as part of the compensation package in the JBNQA. The construction and eventual move to this new coastal village took place in the early 1980s.

11. Given the current nationalist debate in Québec there are issues related to the relationship between these disparate groups that are interesting but tangential to those raised in this essay (see, e.g., Salée 1995).

12. The village of Kuujjuarapik is run by the mayor and his council, while Whapmagoostui elects a chief and council to these municipal government seats. One new recent change is worth noting, given that it was the focus of a great deal of attention and concern over the last few years. As of December 1995, there is a newly built nursing clinic located halfway between the two villages which services Cree and Inuit patients.

13. "White man" is the common translation of the term *waamistikushiiu*. More specifically, it refers to people from far away or to English-speaking people. While there are other terms for Francophones and people of other nationalities, the word that is used most often and which generally connotes *any* outsider is *waamistikushiiu*. While not necessarily derogatory, neither is it a term of endearment. Subsumed within the meaning of *waamistikushiiu* is the sense of a prevailing uneven balance of power, favoring the nonnative.

14. Ongoing research in Whapmagoostui includes interviews with community members about the Gatherings. While that research involves a substantially

larger cohort of participants, I have selected comments from three adult women, each of whom spoke to me specifically about that first Gathering.

15. Approximately fifty members of the Cree village of Chisasibi, about one hundred kilometers to the south, paddled up to Great Whale River in seven canoes in order to participate in the Gathering. The caravan trip and their stay at the Gathering were recorded on video by a Chisasibi production crew. In addition, Inuit guests had come by trawler from Povungnituk, a community further up the Hudson Bay coast, in order to actively show their alliance with the Cree and Inuit of Great Whale in their struggle against Hydro-Québec.

16. Native spirituality was certainly a part of the 1993 Gathering and an even greater part of the 1994 and 1995 events. The elders were active participants in the Gatherings, leading various teaching sessions as well as performing the sunrise ceremonies, conducting sweat lodges, and delivering healing services as requested. As noted earlier, this shift to—and friction around—increasing Native spirituality in Whapmagoostui is a separate but related issue.

17. The particular site was selected because it was the summer meeting site of the ancestors of Cree and Inuit of the northeastern region of Quebec. A recent archaeological survey as well as old debris found around the campsites attest to the numerous dwellings in and around this area. In the process of preparing the ground for their tents, people at the Gathering came across items such as an old pipe, a copper nail, and desiccated whale bone. Family camps were dispersed about the entire Gathering site, with tents accommodating in excess of three hundred people. Many people spent the entire week at the Gathering, returning by canoe to the village briefly to shop or shower.

18. The Kashtin concert was held at the large gym in the village and was attended by hundreds of Cree and Inuit. There was a complaint by the Cree elders, however, that the people should not have left the Gathering site en masse as they did. All activities in 1994 were kept at the site. In 1995, the pow-wow was postponed so often due to inclement weather that the decision was finally taken to move it to the village band hall.

19. The literal translation of the Cree word for Sunday is "prayer day."

REFERENCES CITED

Aboriginal Family Healing Joint Steering Committee. 1993. "For Generations to Come: The Time Is Now—A Strategy for Aboriginal Family Healing. Final Report." Unpublished report prepared for the government of Ontario (submitted to the ministers of Women's Issues, Native Affairs, and Social Services).

Adelson, Naomi. 1997. *Gathering Knowledge: Reflections on the Anthropology of Identity, Aboriginality, and the Annual Gatherings in Whapmagoostui, Québec.* Aboriginal Government, Resources, Economy, and Environment Discussion Paper Series, no. 1. Montreal: McGill University.

———. 1998. "Health Beliefs and the Politics of Cree Well-Being." *Health* 2, no. 1: 5–22.

Archer, Jeff. 1991. "Ambiguity in Political Ideology: Aboriginality as Nationalism." *TAJA* 2, no. 2: 161–69.

Beckett, Jeremy. 1992. "Comment on Hollinsworth." *Oceania* 63: 165–67.
Bennett, Tony, and Valda Blundell. 1995. "First Peoples." *Cultural Studies* 9, no. 1: 1–10.
Clifford, James. 1995. "Paradise." *Visual Anthropology Review,* 11 no. 1: 93–117.
Cree-Naskapi Commission. 1986. *1986 Report of the Cree-Naskapi Commission (Commissioner's 1st Biennial Report).* Ottawa: Cree-Naskapi Commission.
Feit, Harvey. 1985. "Legitimation and Autonomy in James Bay Cree Responses to Hydro-Electric Development." In *Indigenous Peoples and the Nation State: Fourth World Politics in Canada, Australia and Norway,* ed. Noel Dyck, 27–66. St. John's, Nfld.: Institute of Social and Economic Research of Memorial University.
Francis, Daniel, and Toby Morantz. 1983. *Partners in Fur: A History of the Fur Trade in Eastern James Bay, 1600–1870.* Montreal: McGill-Queen's University Press.
Friedman, Jonathan. 1992. "Myth, History, and Political Identity." *Cultural Anthropology* 7 no. 2: 194–210.
Gilbert, Stephanie. 1995. "Postcolonial Aboriginal Identity." *Cultural Studies* 9, no. 1: 145–49.
Grand Council of the Cree of Québec (GCCQ). 1990. *1989/1990 Annual Report of the Grand Council of the Cree of Québec and the Cree Regional Authority.* Nemaska, Québec: GCCQ.
Hanson, Allan. 1989. "The Making of the Maori: Culture Invention and Its Logic." *American Anthropologist* 91, no. 4: 890–902.
Johnston, Basil. 1988. *Indian School Days.* Norman: University of Oklahoma Press.
Kirmayer, Laurence J., Barbara C. Hayton, Michael Malus, Vania Jimenez, Rose Dufour, Consuelo Quesney, Yeshim Ternar, Terri Yu, and Nadia Ferrara. 1993. *Emerging Trends in Research on Mental Health Among Canadian Aboriginal Peoples: A Report Prepared for the Royal Commission on Aboriginal Peoples.* Report 2. Montreal: Culture and Mental Health Unit (Sir Mortimer B. Davis–Jewish General Hospital).
Kleinman, Arthur, Veena Das, and Margaret Lock. 1996. "Introduction to 'Social Suffering.'" *Daedalus* 125, no. 1: xi–xx.
Légaré, Evelyn I. 1995. "Canadian Multiculturalism and Aboriginal People: Negotiating a Place in the Nation." *Identities* 1, no. 4: 347–66.
Linnekin, Jocelyn. 1991. "Cultural Invention and the Dilemma of Authenticity." *American Anthropologist* 93, no. 2: 446–49.
Lomawaima, K. Tsianina. 1993. "Domesticity in the Federal Indian Schools: The Power of Authority over Mind and Body." *American Ethnologist* 20, no. 2: 227–40.
Masty, Emily. 1995. *Women's Three Generation Life History Project in Whapmagoostui, Québec (A Report to the Royal Commission on Aboriginal Peoples).* Ottawa: Royal Commission on Aboriginal Peoples.
McMaster, Gerald R. 1995. "Border Zones: The 'Injunuity' of Aesthetic Tricks." *Cultural Studies,* 9 no. 1: 74–90.

O'Neil, John. 1993. "Report from the Round Table Rapporteur." In *The Path to Healing: Report of the National Round Table on Aboriginal Health and Social Issues* (Royal Commission on Aboriginal Peoples), 13–24. Ottawa: Ministry of Supplies and Services Canada.

Ortner, Sherry B. 1995. "Resistance and the Problem of Ethnographic Refusal." *Comparative Studies in Society and History* 37, no. 1: 173–93.

Richardson, Boyce. 1977. *Strangers Devour the Land: The Cree Hunters of the James Bay Area versus Premier Bourassa and the James Bay Development Corporation.* Toronto: Macmillan.

Royal Commission on Aboriginal Peoples (RCAP). 1995. *Choosing Life: Special Report on Suicide among Aboriginal People.* Ottawa: Canada Communication Group.

Salée, Daniel. 1995. "Identities in Conflict: The Aboriginal Question and the Politics of Recognition in Québec." *Ethnic and Racial Studies* 18, no. 2: 277–314.

Salisbury, Richard. 1986. *A Homeland for the Cree: Regional Development in James Bay, 1971–1981.* Montreal: McGill-Queen's University Press.

Santiago-Irizarry, Vilma. 1996. "Culture as Cure." *Cultural Anthropology* 11, no. 1: 3–24.

Scott, Colin. 1979. *Modes of Production and Guaranteed Annual Income in James Bay Society.* PAD Monograph no. 13. Montreal: McGill-Queen's University Press.

———. 1993. "Custom, Tradition and the Politics of Culture: Aboriginal Self-Government in Canada." In *Anthropology, Public Policy and Native Peoples in Canada,* ed. N. Dyck and J. B. Waldram. Montreal: McGill-Queen's University Press.

Waldram, James B., D. Ann Herring, and T. Kue Young. 1995. *Aboriginal Health in Canada: Historical, Cultural, and Epidemiological Perspectives.* Toronto: University of Toronto Press.

West, Errol. 1990. "Towards a bran nue [sic] day: a discussion about the present and the past for the future." Unpublished thesis.

The Bomb's Womb?

Women and the Atom Bomb

Maya Todeschini

> If the radiance of a thousand suns would burst forth at once in
> the sky, that would be like the splendor of the Mighty One. I
> am become death, the destroyer of worlds.
>
> > From the Bhagavad-Gita, *the Song of God.*
> > *Reportedly cited by Robert Oppenheimer after*
> > *the first atomic explosion in Alamogordo,*
> > *16 July 1945*

> My heart is moved by all I cannot save:
> > so much has been destroyed
>
> I have to cast my lot with those
> > who age after age, perversely,
>
> with no extraordinary power,
> > reconstitute the world.
> > > *Adrienne Rich*

INTRODUCTION

The two atom bombs that were dropped on Hiroshima and Nagasaki
on 6 and 9 August 1945 massacred and injured human beings—men,
women, old people, children—indiscriminately, regardless of background or nationality. They also erased gender, dehumanizing both men
and women and stripping them of their health, families, and communities. And the bombs' most insidious feature, the delayed effects of radiation,[1] of course affected all *hibakusha* (literally, "atom-bombed persons")[2] alike. Yet gender played an important role in shaping the manner
in which individuals and the larger community interpreted these traumatic events, as well as the responses they elaborated to deal with them.

This essay explores the relationships between women and the bomb. How did the bomb, and particularly the threat of delayed radiation effects, shape women's sense of subjectivity and sexuality? How did officially sanctioned discourses on hibakusha (both the medical/legal discourses and popular, nonformalized representations) provide appropriate ways of interpreting hibakusha experiences, as well as of embodying suffering for women? And how did women themselves negotiate their identities as "hibakusha women" and create a sense of political agency?

I focus on women who were adolescents or children when the bombings occurred; most of the women in the study were born in the early 1930s. They have experienced the most crucial years of their lives, from late adolescence into adulthood, as hibakusha women. This distinguishes them from older women, who were already settled in their family or professional lives when the bombs fell. I argue that for women of the generation I studied, problems of feminine self-worth, identity, and sexuality were particularly profound: seen as tainted by radiation, and thus counter to the dominant gender ideal of the childbearing, nurturing woman, they were cast into the role of "undesirable others" in Japanese society. At the same time, as I discovered when doing fieldwork in Hiroshima and other cities between 1991 and 1993, women of this generation have been particularly successful in carving out an important role in the hibakusha literary and grassroots movements, as peace activists, writers, founders of self-help groups, and oral storytellers (kataribe).[3]

For this essay, the writings by and interviews with Hayashi Kyōko, a prominent author and Nagasaki survivor who lives in Tokyo, were my most important resource. Hayashi has been acutely concerned with questions of gender and sexuality in her writings, and has produced several autobiographical collections centering on the experiences of hibakusha women.[4] I also draw on the narratives of two hibakusha women's groups: the Osaka Association of Female Atom Bomb Victims (henceforth, the Osaka Group) and the Yamashita Group, based in Hiroshima, both of which formed in the late 1960s as forums for female self-expression and activism. The Osaka Group is currently one of the most active self-help groups in Japan; it not only publishes members' life histories but also is involved in advocacy and counseling on behalf of hibakusha (cf. Bruin and Salaff 1982). It has most consciously deployed a motherly identity to legitimize its activities. The Yamashita Group, named after its founder, Yamashita Asayo, began as a "hibakusha mother study group," where members discussed their bomb experiences in the context of larger social and educational issues. Members have written detailed accounts of their experiences, published in a series of pamphlets. During the 1970s and 1980s, the group had considerable influence in Hiroshima as a model for a grassroots hibakusha movement. Officially the group is no longer in existence, but former members still meet regularly and organize public events focused on hibakusha women's experiences. To complement this primary focus on mothers and housewives, I also draw on the narratives of single women like Yamaoka Michiko, a former "Hiroshima Maiden"[5] who lives in Hiroshima and is active as a kataribe today.

Fieldwork was crucial to this project, because it provided access to women's informal accounts, such as grassroots publications, pamphlets, and brochures as well as oral testimonies and interviews. There are also important tensions between publicly sanctioned "scripts" that tend to reproduce dominant assumptions of how a good hibakusha woman should behave, and women's personal narratives, including gossip. Though often intended for internal consumption by peers and friends, they are also meant to create alternative subject positions and publics, and to contest dominant discourses on the atom bomb and hibakusha.

Theoretically, this essay draws on gender studies and feminist criticism in anthropology, history, and literature, and particularly on research on Japanese women and gender (Lock 1993; Lebra 1984). I follow Joan Scott's definition of gender as social and cultural construction used to "articulate the rules of social relationships, and to construct the meaning of experience," and also as a "primary way of signifying relationships of power," thus serving important strategic and political functions (1988: 38, 42). As recent studies on the construction of suffering in various societies have shown, the public acknowledgment and appropriation of illness, loss, pain, and grief, and the establishment of gender categories in connection with suffering, are profoundly political acts, which draw boundaries and determine "appropriate" expressions of suffering. (Compare Kleinman 1991; Kleinman and Kleinman 1996; Das 1992, 1996; Ramphele 1996; Pandolfi 1991.) In this respect, my paper is meant as a contribution to the work of other researchers who emphasize the interrelations between gender and suffering, particularly in societies where gender bifurcation remains a central principle of social and symbolic organization.

The essay is divided into three major parts. In the first, I focus on the ongoing suffering created by the bomb and radiation illnesses, as they affected my informants at various stages in their life cycles, leading them to consider their fertility as a liability and preventing them from fulfilling their expected roles as "wise mothers and good wives." In the second, I examine dominant discourses on the bomb and hibakusha women, in both official, scientific/legal constructions and in informal, popular representations. In the third section, I analyze women's relationships to such discourses, and their attempts to elaborate alternative positions as hibakusha women.

As I attempt to show, "hibakusha women," and hibakusha women's "experience," were contested and dynamic categories, with officially sanctioned discourses often at odds with the women's own interpretations. Yet I argue that individual and collective narratives on hibakusha women have one important point in common: an acute concern with the bomb's perceived threat to biological (and thus social) reproduction, a concern that became focused on women's "tainted" bodies.

I. DANGEROUS BODIES

My informants' life histories are unified by one overarching theme: the bomb's pervasive influence throughout their lives, from adolescence to middle age, through marriage and work, childbirth, child-rearing, and aging. Thus, in contrast to the more conventional testimonial accounts, the main thrust of their narratives is not so much a preoccupation with the atomic explosion itself and its immediate aftermath but with what came later, the years and decades after the bomb. In Yamaoka Michiko's words, "the real war started after the war ended." This war focused primarily on one battleground: bomb-related illnesses, and the various meanings they took on for women and the larger community.

One major theme in women's narratives, and in collective responses to women, is anxiety surrounding women's bodies, and women's life-giving or nurturing capacities as childbearers and mothers. Women's bodies acquired a special resonance in connection with radiation pollution: female bodies (particularly young bodies) were felt—by the larger community and often by the women themselves—to be particularly vulnerable to radiation-induced illnesses, including sterility, and were thus seen as primarily responsible for the potential transmission of genetic effects. (Scientists have found no evidence for singling out women's bodies as somehow more sensitive to radiation.) Moreover, radiation-induced illnesses were also viewed as a threat to women's maternal capacities, and their ability to take care of others. Thus, the female body became a danger and liability, a disrupter of family and community life.

THE INJURING

A man can marry someone completely unrelated to the
bomb, but we women, we're stuck with it. It's a problem of the womb [*botai*].

> *Teramae Taeko, fourteen at the time*
> *of the bombing*

For my informants, two atomic bombs heralded their entry into the world of adults. But aside from the psychological trauma wrought by the explosion itself, the young women were forced to grapple with the delayed effects of radiation and their protracted threat to their bodies. Aside from external injuries, and even in the absence of external wounds, most of my informants received extensive doses of radiation, and suffered from acute radiation symptoms, such as hemorrhaging, hair loss and a low blood cell count. Hayashi Kyōko, fourteen at the time of the bombing, sustained no obvious injuries but suffered hair loss, diarrhea, and purplish spots on her limbs. Seventeen-year-old Takagi Shizuko, cofounder of the Osaka Group, was injured by flying glass splinters and suffered from severe anemia as well as disfiguring reddish facial scars. Such symptoms, and the fact that countless other survivors, who seemed apparently healthy, died from radiation illnesses in the weeks and months following the bombing, quickly led them to internalize a sense that their bodies had become irremediably "other," aggressors that could turn against them at any time.

Such feelings greatly intensified when it became apparent that plants and vegetation had been affected by radiation, sometimes exhibiting mysterious deformations, and rumors arose in the two cities that "no grass and no trees would grow in Hiroshima and Nagasaki for seventy-five years" (cf. Lifton 1961: 68, 131). As one informant put it: "When grass stops growing, everything is finished." Needless to say, to adolescents, at the threshold of adult life, the assumption that natural cycles had been profoundly disturbed was horrifying beyond belief.

Among the radiation effects that caused the greatest agony in the community were those related to human reproduction. Young and proliferating cells and tissues are very sensitive to radiation, and radiation damage to babies born to pregnant women was particularly severe. Many were stillborn, born with major congenital abnormalities (especially microcephaly), or suffered from growth disorders. There were also frequent cases of miscarriage and premature birth among exposed pregnant women (Committee 1981: 218–19, 156). It was no wonder that hibakusha feared that their reproductive functions had become perverted or even destroyed by radiation.

Such fears had an especially devastating effect on young women's emerging sexuality and self-image: Hayashi wrote that she came to see her pubescent body as a "shrunken, worm-eaten apple," devoured from the inside by radiation and hopelessly unattractive in comparison to the "fat, healthy" bodies of her non-hibakusha sisters (*Shōwa nijūnen no natsu*, 258–76). She added that "Nagasaki's [barren] landscape reflected my own self" (*Naki ga gotoki*, 292). Takagi confesses that she wondered who would marry such an "ugly, deficient woman" as herself.

Menstruation disorders, including amenorrhea, irregular and excessive bleeding, which were frequent among hibakusha women (Committee 1981: 153), also intensified anxieties that women's bodies had been somehow devitalized by the bomb. Takagi, who had menstruated normally up until the bombing, stopped menstruating for an entire year: "I didn't bleed for such a long time, and was wondering if I could ever have children." The younger Hayashi and her friends dreaded the onset of menarche—which they associated with massive hemorrhaging, one of the symptoms of radiation illness—and confessed their fears about childbearing in the face of rumors of monstrous babies quietly disposed of by their mothers, too ashamed to show them: "We were afraid we'd give birth to abnormal children. It was such a contradiction: More than most people, we were aware of the value and weight of human life, its preciousness, yet we were terrified that we should nip unborn life in the bud" (*Naki ga gotoki*, 339). Thus from the very beginning, women's bodily anxieties extended beyond the self, encompassing the child to come.

Although scientists concluded that fertility, whether male or female, was not lastingly affected by radiation (except among those who were exposed to extremely high doses, many of whom died in the weeks or months after the bombing) and that the high incidence of abnormal births was limited to fetuses exposed in utero (Committee 1981: 151–56, 212–14), it makes little sense to contrast a "scientific truth" with victims' fears. Aside from the fact that such scientific studies were unavailable to hibakusha at the time—partly due to the censorship code

that had been instituted by the Occupation authorities in October 1945
on all information on the atom bombings, especially radiation effects
(Braw 1990)—the very fact that hibakusha's reproductive functions at-
tracted the interest of researchers sent the implicit message that there
was a problem. More important, it is likely that the linking of the bomb
to (female) bodily corruption was one way of giving meaning to an
abnormal, unprecedented event, and a new and mysterious form of contamination. Since younger people were generally more vulnerable to radiation, it was inevitable that young women who had not yet given birth
were feared to have been especially affected.

"ATOMIC MAIDENS"[6]

Such feelings must also be placed against the cultural and symbolic context of traditional pollution beliefs, and the perception of radiation as
the "pollution of death." Japanese society is characterized by a complex
system of beliefs and practices about purity and pollution (Namihira
1978; Lock 1980; Miyata 1996). Generally, transitional and marginal
states (such as death, illness, crime, or other abnormal events) are considered to be "polluted" because they suggest displacement from permitted categories, and transgression of boundaries and accepted rules
(cf. Douglas 1966). In a wider sense, then, everybody who was in Hiroshima and Nagasaki on the day of the explosion, in contact with
corpses afterward, or associated with "atom bomb disease" in any form
was polluted.

Such beliefs have special relevance for women. Women's bodies, and
especially their reproductive capacities and blood, are considered to be
ritually polluted in Japan (as in many other societies), and female hibakusha, who combined the impurities of death (radiation) and of blood
(reproduction), were perceived as doubly dangerous, thus evoking contamination anxieties that were particularly intense. Moreover, in another pattern that applies cross-culturally, it is women, rather than men,
who are blamed for sterility or abnormality in offspring (Héritier 1984:
129–33). Clearly, then, such women represented a great danger to the
community—they could pass on pollution not only through bodily contact, but also through their children. In fact, their mere existence as
"liminal beings" (Victor Turner) was an implicit threat to the community. To use Judith Butler's terms, these women's bodies were literally
"abject," "unlivable," and "uninhabitable" (1993: 3).

Even if such notions did not always operate on a conscious level, there is evidence of intense fear of contamination surrounding hibakusha women, especially in rural areas (Kamisaka 1987). These fears were magnified when women bore keloids (burn scars), taken as "evidence" of bodily contamination. Informants like sixteen-year-old Yamaoka Michiko, who sustained extensive and extremely disfiguring burn scars on her face, arms, and breasts, were in a particularly tragic situation, having suffered a quite literal "loss of face" in addition to having been irradiated. Yamaoka spent several years in near-seclusion, leaving her home only when strictly necessary. She recalls that she was treated like "a leper" by others.

The "Hiroshima Maidens" project, initiated by an American, Norman Cousins, which brought a group of keloid-scarred young women to the U.S. for plastic surgery in 1954, yielded undeniable medical benefits for such women, but also had the undesirable effect of focusing media interest on disfigured female hibakusha (Barker 1985; Chūjō 1984).[7] Yamaoka is grateful for the surgery she received in the U.S., but she has bitter memories of the Japanese media, which feasted on lengthy descriptions of the women's scars ("their rosy and glowing adolescent flesh had been turned into masses of horrifying keloids"). TV stations featured lengthy programs that rhetorically wondered all the while how they could broadcast images of a "face that was unbearable to look at." As Ōta Yōko, one of Japan's premier women hibakusha writers, remarked in her typical scathing style, "these female freaks [bakemono] made big money in Japan" (Hiroshima kara kita musume-tachi, 282). Cast into the role of the eternal maiden, the women had to contend with the image of themselves as love-starved virgins whom no man would have as his wife (after all, the very term "maiden" [otome] seemed to prescribe virginity in such women). When such women married, against all expectation, these marriages became sources of endless fascination with "love born by the bomb" and "exceptionally courageous" husbands (cf. Barker 1984 for media reports on the "maidens"). Needless to say, such depictions contained a great deal of hostility toward women. Most important, no matter how much plastic surgery was applied or how skillful the surgeons' knife, external intervention could not efface the stigma of "radiation-taint," deeply seated inside the body. In the eyes of their community, the "atomic maidens" remained eternally conjoined to the agent of their suffering, as though locked in a mutual and deadly embrace.

BAD WIVES AND UNWISE MOTHERS

We women can give life; but if we transmit something
impure to the children, we become carriers of death.
This is an unforgivable crime.

Takagi Shizuko

The perception that their bodies were dangerous proved often devastating for young women about to enter marriageable age and eager to
become full members of society. In traditional patriarchal family structures—which were in many ways still operative in the early postwar
years—a young bride (*yome*) is recruited into the husband's home, often
by means of an arranged marriage, for the purpose of reproducing an
heir for the family line, and so for continuing the house-line (*ie*). A
woman's first duty is to bear children. Sterility is considered to be the
woman's fault, and when the children are handicapped in any way, it is
often women who are blamed. In the words of Takagi, "Japan is still a
feudal society, and the first thing people are interested in, except for
personal fortune, is the standing of a family [*iegara*]. By marrying a
hibakusha woman, a man destroyed his iegara."

It is important to note here that marriage is not only an obligatory
social ritual. It is also considered to be an important step toward adulthood and psychological maturity—an unmarried person, especially a
woman, is considered to be both socially and psychologically "incom-
plete" and even deprived of meaning in her life (Lebra 1984). Women
must also marry at the right time, during the period called *tekireiki,* or
marriageable age, between the ages of twenty-two and twenty-five. For
the hibakusha women of the generation I studied, tekireiki was in the
early 1950s, when anxieties surrounding radiation-induced leukemia
and aftereffects on children were at their height.

Women who married non-hibakusha men, such as Takagi or Hayashi, generally married in "love marriages," against the opposition of
their husbands' families. Takagi's husband's family refused to come to
the marriage. "They were sure that I would give birth to a cripple," she
recalls. Many others, such as Hashimoto from the Yamashita Group,
married fellow hibakusha: "For lack of a better choice," she laughed,
yet adding that being married to a hibakusha doubled her anxiety about
possible genetic effects on their children. Still other women, certainly a
very large number, married without telling their husbands about their
hibakusha status.

I met several women who had desperately wished to marry but had given up because of repeated rejections. One member from the Osaka Group, a striking woman who had worked as a bar hostess after the war, said that "many men were interested in me but when they found out I was a hibakusha, they disappeared." Another woman from the same group, orphaned by the bombing, added that she had given up hopes for marriage, since "being an orphan and a hibakusha woman was a double handicap."

Many single women (and also those who were divorced or widowed) ended up in low-paying or demeaning positions. "Hiroshima Maiden" Yamaoka Michiko survived by doing sewing work at home, transforming old kimonos and military uniforms into Western-style clothes. Members of the Osaka Group worked as waitresses and in pachinko parlors; one woman worked as a menial laborer and garbage collector in the cities of Hiroshima and Osaka. In fact, a considerable number of hibakusha women worked as day laborers in the 1950s and 1960s, when the country was rebuilding, with many ironically involved in the construction of Hiroshima's "Peace Park," destined to become the official expression of the city's atom bomb memory (Genbaku-hibakusha-sōdan-in no kai 1989: 42). Aside from economic problems, single women also had to contend with an image of themselves as psychologically warped or even sexually insatiable, an image that was heightened by the perception that their bodies were somehow abject or abnormal (cf. Natsubori 1983).

A considerable number of women decided to remain single for health or other reasons. Some felt physically unable to take care of a family, and the continued uncertainty about delayed radiation effects, including potential genetic effects, could act as powerful deterrent to marriage and childbearing among the women themselves. In the words of one informant, "how could I presume bearing children with this body?" (*kono karada de umu wake de wa nakatta*). Still others renounced marriage for ideological reasons, an extremely rare occurrence among women of this generation. But no matter what particular path a young hibakusha woman chose, the decision to marry and bear children or not was often an agonizing one. Though these problems were shared by many hibakusha males as well, men to a certain extent were able to efface the stigma of the radiation taint through an active work life. In addition, childless males are not considered as socially anomalous as childless females. In my interviews with male hibakusha, I have generally found less emphasis on the fear of transmitting radiation damage to children and a greater emphasis on professional difficulties and achievement than in female narratives.

Yet women's anxieties did not end with marriage, or with childbirth. It is in the nitty-gritty of daily life, of dealing with husbands, parents, and in-laws, and raising children, that many women most strongly felt the bomb's lasting impact. As a consequence of a gender ideology that evolved from the "good wife and wise mother" (*ryōsai kenbo*) of the Meiji period, a woman is considered to be largely responsible for the health and well-being of her children, husband, in-laws, and often her own aging parents as well (Uno 1995; Lock 1993). It is the mother who is blamed when the child falls sick, or when the family looks ill-kept or neglected. A good wife and mother is also expected to manage all aspects of the household, including the budget, children's education, the family's social life, and ritual aspects such as gift-giving and ancestor-worship (Vogel 1978; Fujita 1989). In short, a family's psychological, physical, and social health rests entirely on the woman's shoulders. As we can see, such a notion of mother- and wifehood has little place for women who are ill or incapacitated, or who are unable or unwilling to nurture others.

Such views were internalized by most of my informants. They have agonizing stories to tell about conflicts in their families, and their own guilty feelings at their incapacity to provide "proper" care. Given the general ignorance about delayed radiation symptoms, families and in-laws had little understanding for mothers who were perpetually sick, or who lived with a paralyzing fear of future illness. As Hayashi said in the interview, "It's the women who must do all the homework. Until I was thirty, I couldn't even get to Tokyo, I was so weak. But I had a family, a mother-in-law, a household to take care of, and was afraid of being accused of being 'neglectful' when I took a rest." Another woman tells of difficult relations with her husband and in-laws: "Whenever I would go to the hospital for a medical exam, they would frown and say 'again' [*mada ka*]? They knew that I was a bomb victim and tried to sympathize with me, but they just couldn't accept the thought that I might get sick." Such problems were exacerbated in lower-class families, where women had to work for income as well, thus doubling the burden on the mother's shoulders. A few working mothers of the Osaka group refused to be hospitalized for treatment even when they were quite ill, because this would have meant not only an unacceptable loss of income but also "abandoning" their children, who had no one else to take care of them.

Among hibakusha intrafamilial problems, none were equal in intensity to anxieties over children's health. Childbirth was fraught with fear for many; as Hayashi put it, "the child belonged as much to August 6 as it belonged to me." Imposing additional stresses on an already weakened body, childbirth often involved medical problems. Even if the children were apparently healthy, the slightest fever or nosebleed could precipitate fears that they were falling seriously ill. Women's fears of transmitting illness to their children must partly be related to the strong cultural emphasis on the "unbreakable" mother-child tie (Takie Lebra calls it "mammalian symbiosis," 1984: 175–78). Children are often seen literally as a "split part" (*bunshin*) of the mother's body. This makes it difficult for mothers to conceive that their own children might be in perfect health if they themselves are not (and vice versa).

But such anxieties about radiation damage were also intensified by historical factors: about a decade after the explosion, the incidence of leukemia among atom bomb victims reached an unprecedented peak (Committee 1981: 255–61) and in 1954, the "*Lucky Dragon* incident," in which a Japanese fishing boat was contaminated by radioactive fall-out from U.S. nuclear testing and a member of the crew died from acute radiation illness, further highlighted the dangers of radiation. Scientists denied that second-generation victims were at a greater risk for leukemia, but there were some tragic, well-publicized cases of children of hibakusha who died of leukemia in the late 1950s and 1960s (cf. Nagoya 1985). One of the members of the Osaka group lost both of her adolescent children (a son born in 1958 and a daughter born in 1959) to leukemia. The group has published an extensive account of her son Ken'ichi's illness. Even if such cases were statistically rare, it was only natural that even one such tragedy should prove devastating to parents who already felt guilty about having given birth at all. As Takagi wrote forcefully:

> It is true that the great majority of hibakusha children are as healthy as ordinary boys and girls. But it is also a real fact that Ken died. Suppose a child born and bred as a treasure of a family should be killed in time of peace by weapons used in a war before the child's birth! Who could have imagined such cruelty? The number of second-generation victims who suffer from fatal diseases is not important. Even one case of hereditary effects of radioactive matter constitutes an unforgivable sin against justice and humanity.

Women's fears that the bomb might catch up with them or their children put uncommon pressures on their family relationships. In Hayashi's case, conflicts with her non-hibakusha husband contributed to the failure of her marriage. She recounts the tense mood in her family in the following passage:

When our son was born, all my fears of bomb-related illnesses were transferred to him—even though he seemed to be quite healthy. For example, it's
not unusual for growing boys to have occasional nosebleeds. My son was
no exception. But I made a big fuss about it, even if it was little more than
a few drops. "Has it stopped? Has it really stopped?" I asked him over and
over. I stuffed his little nostril with a tight, sterile cotton ball the size of a fat
bean. I couldn't stop thinking about it, blood dripping away like a leaky
faucet. My husband lost patience with me. "Are you enjoying yourself?" he
asked. This really got to me. "How would you know? You weren't bombed,"
I said to him angrily. . . . My husband got very angry with me. "Why do you
ask me to do the impossible?" he shouted. . . . But even though he gets im-
patient with my morbid fears, my husband pays close attention to the health
of our son. . . . I wonder if when my son finds out about my past, my husband
might take him and leave. . . . It's like taking a child away from a parent
who's contracted leprosy. As a parent, he naturally wants a healthy environment for his child, both physically and emotionally. And even if your son is
physically healthy, despite my genes, there is always the possibility of psychological damage if he lives with me. For a father who is not himself a bomb
victim, this may be too much to bear. (*Kumoribi ho kōshin*, 21–22)

Hayashi's case may be extreme, and one can fathom the difficulties
faced by non-hibakusha husbands, no matter how sympathetic. Yet
Hayashi's fear that her "impairment" might damage her son, as well as
her sense of psychological isolation, was shared by many women I interviewed, even if they had closer family relationships. Many told me
that they were completely unable to communicate with their husbands
and children about such feelings.

Also, long after they married and bore children, many women continued to experience their bodies, including their fertility, as a liability
and a source of danger. Hayashi never overcame fears of massive bleeding: "I couldn't help thinking about the time when . . . my menstrual
blood won't stop flowing. . . . Many of my friends died because their
bleeding never stopped" (*Kumoribi no kōshin*, 16). Her painful ambivalence about her reproductive capacities ironically led her to look forward to an event which many women dread: "A definite end to all this
will come with menopause. This day will be a day of celebration" (*Kompirasan*, 143–44). Several of my informants suffered from menstrual
disorders and excessive bleeding, in some cases requiring surgical intervention.

In addition to menstrual disorders, the theme of "perverted blood"
provides a constant undercurrent in hibakusha women's health histories.
According to recent unpublished statistics by medical social workers in
Hiroshima, "blood disorders" are the most frequently cited "subjective

symptom" by women who apply for medical aid, and a comparatively higher number of female victims complain of such ailments than their male counterparts (one-third as opposed to ten percent). This would further suggest women's internalization of culturally constructed beliefs about their contaminated bodies and ambivalence about their fertility.

Yet female vulnerability to radiation was not "merely" imagined or subjectively experienced: women's reproductive organs were highly sensitive to radiation damage, resulting in abnormally high levels of ovarian, uterine, and breast cancers among exposed women, especially those who were bombed at a young age. Such data, the significance of which fully appeared only two decades after the bombing or even later (due to the long incubation period of these cancers), led Hayashi—who saw many of her friends die of such cancers—to conclude that "radiation was particularly bent on destroying women's reproductive organs" (*Naki ga gotoki,* 145). Thus, to some extent, female sensitivity to radiation was borne out by scientific data.

To conclude this section, we can see that cultural discourses on "women's pollution" intensified anxieties (both the women's and society's) concerning reproductive abnormalities. They became further magnified by a gender ideology that makes women primarily responsible for maintaining the family (and thus the community at large), and which thus has no place for "deficient" maternal bodies, incapable of providing the nurturance required. Yet as we shall see in the next section, in the official discourses on hibakusha and hibakusha women, such anxieties become suppressed—they are replaced by "medical facts" that erase the possible existence of genetic effects, and a mythifying discourse on motherhood that obliterates women's dangerous bodies.

II. SILENT BODIES

Hibakusha have been seen by their society primarily, if not exclusively, as a medical problem, and we must begin by examining the effects of scientific and biomedical discourses on hibakusha, particularly as they relate to anxieties about delayed and potential genetic effects. The biomedical approach lent radiation illnesses the aura of scientific fact but also led to a delegitimization of hibakusha's concerns about potential hereditary consequences—a process that was magnified by the bureaucratization of hibakusha status, which transformed the victims into a deficient group, in need of government assistance. These processes constitute what I call the politics of care, the medico-legal and institutional framework elaborated to deal with hibakusha existence.

I also consider the politics of representation, which assigns socially and culturally sanctioned meanings to hibakusha women's experiences. Popular and fictional representations of hibakusha women are dominated by the idealized figure of the self-sacrificial, heroic mother. While this figure confers an aura of moral dignity and historical innocence to hibakusha women (and to atom bomb memory as such) and thus partly subverts the depersonalization processes inherent in the medicalization and bureaucratization of hibakushahood, its effects are remarkably similar: anxieties about women's bodies, which symbolize overall anxieties about biological and social reproduction, are sublimated.

EXPELLING SUFFERING: HIBAKUSHA AND SCIENCE

Making the suffering at Hiroshima and Nagasaki disappear . . . was . . . a long-term act of scientific work.
            M. Susan Lindee, Suffering Made Real

I distinguish two interrelated themes in my informants' narratives of their encounters with "science": the perceived misappropriation of their bodies for the sake of scientific research divorced from all other concerns, and the delegitimization of their fears concerning genetic effects. Though such themes are also found in male narratives, they are particularly resonant in the women's accounts, partly as a consequence of the association between masculinity and science (and thus also masculinity and the bomb), which encouraged a perception of women as victims par excellence, whose bodies were objectified for the sake of a military and medical experiment carried out largely by males.

My informants recall that their bodies, and especially their reproductive functions, came under intense scrutiny by medical researchers. Hayashi, for example, remembers that she and her classmates were interrogated by Japanese scientists in embarrassing detail about their periods:

> Just after the war, in October, as classes were about to begin, teams of researchers from the Nagasaki Medical School and the Faculty of Medicine at Kyūshū University came to my school to examine us. Doctors asked fifteen- and sixteen-year-old girls personal questions such as, "How about your periods? Do you bleed more than before? Have you stopped bleeding altogether? Did you get your first period after being exposed?" At the time, girls like us never even pronounced the term "menstruation," and we couldn't

stop blushing. As we stood there, flustered, Teiko [one of Hayashi's class-mates] . . . walked in and said quietly but firmly: "Those who don't want to answer, don't have to. We don't need to be part of any more radiation ex-periments. (*Kumoribi no kōshin,* 13)

Moreover, as this reference to "radiation experiments" suggests, scien-tific studies on fertility quickly came to be seen as politically and morally suspect.

The Atomic Bomb Casualty Commission (ABCC), dispatched by the U.S. government in 1947 for a long-range study into the bomb's physical effects, including genetic effects, contributed in a large measure to a highly negative image of "science" among my informants. The ABCC's notorious "no treatment" policy (it limited itself to investigating the medical effects but provided—at least in principle—no medical care to victims) was the primary reason for its disastrous reputation among the local population, leading to charges that it abused victims as guinea pigs for scientific research. The ABCC's aggressive diagnostic policies—carrying out detailed physical examinations, including taking blood and urine samples and X-rays, as well as postmortem examinations—exac-erbated such claims and contributed to the sense among hibakusha that their bodies were misappropriated and objectified. Emotional accusa-tions of the ABCC as a sinister, even diabolical institution must be placed within this context. In fact, the ABCC would never have been able to conduct its activities without the consent and active cooperation of Jap-anese government officials, researchers, municipal authorities, and med-ical practitioners such as local physicians and midwives (cf. Lindee 1994), but a negative image of the ABCC as typically American insti-tution persisted, even after it became a joint Japanese-American insti-tution in 1975 (rebaptized the RERF, Radiation Effects Research Foun-dation).[8]

The ABCC remains a vivid memory for many of my informants. As Harada Fumiko from the Yamashita group recalled:

They were always polite and friendly, asking me about how I was feeling and so on and giving me coffee and sandwiches. But they never told me about the results. Young and married as I was, I had to undress and put on a white cloth, and they'd examine me thoroughly. I had problems with my uterus and they wanted to keep examining it. And they took countless X-rays, de-spite the fact that I'd received so much radiation anyway! I wasn't allowed to wear socks, and my feet would get cold. They just told me that I was extremely anemic and gave me some sort of medicine, but it made me terribly sick and I stopped taking it. Perhaps they were testing the medicine, too? It gradually dawned on me, why as a victim do I help the aggressor? Why do

I have to get examined, give my urine and blood? You feel uncomfort-
able and cold. You don't know what's going on. Indeed, I was stupid
[*baka*].

Being subjected to humiliating examinations is a recurrent theme in hibakusha narratives on the ABCC, and particularly in the women's accounts. One can readily imagine that such exams could be traumatizing
to women raised in the prewar education system, who had been taught
to be chaste and to fear Americans as "devils." The theme of the violation of women's bodies at the hands of foreign scientists reverberates
to this day and is one example of the manner in which the scientific
response to hibakusha became gendered, as well as conflated with race,
in individual and collective memory—women's violation can also be
read as penetration of Japanese culture by the foreign other.

Such sentiments were reinforced by the closed character of the ABCC;
as an Occupation-era agency, most of the studies were carried out in
secret. Thus the dispossession of women's bodies by science and the quite
literally physical intrusion of an external authority upon the body took
place in a highly charged political context.

The ABCC has often been accused of minimizing the effects of radiation for covertly political aims. The ABCC's genetics studies occupy a
special place in such debates, having followed a consistent policy of
publicly denying the existence of genetic mutations and contributed to
an extremely optimistic image of delayed radiation effects, an image that
is perpetuated by the RERF and often used to advertise the bomb's supposed harmlessness in affecting victims over time, including succeeding
generations. In fact, as Susan Lindee's analysis shows persuasively, the
ABCC's famous genetics study—which was initiated in the late 1940s
and involved extensive research on pregnant women, mothers, and babies—was shaped as much by Cold War politics and public concerns
about radiation as it was by pure science. The very manner in which
"genetic mutations" were defined and studied was highly selective to
begin with (for example, researchers chose to focus only on mutations
believed to be "threatening for the future survival of the species"), and
thus investigated certain indicators (such as sex ratio, lower birth weight
or retarded growth, and higher rates of malformation, stillbirth, and
neonatal death) while rejecting others (such as reduced fertility or sterility, early spontaneous abortion, and minor malformations) (cf. Lindee
1994: 178–79, 223, 228). Moreover, the study's planners were pres-
sured to downplay genetic alterations in their official publications due
to rising public concern about radiation risks. For example, the authors

of a 1953 report chose to discount stillbirth effects and minimize "sex ratio effects" to "avoid misinterpretation by the popular press." The American press readily reported (and often exaggerated) such statements: for example, after an interview with then-ABCC director Robert Holmes, *U.S. News and World Report* in 1955 ran the exuberant headline "Thousands of Babies, No A-Bomb Effects."

Other observers point out a whole series of methodological problems with the genetic study, including insufficiently sensitive research methods and the possibility of recessive mutations that could show up in later generations (Barnaby 1977). These debates only serve to highlight the considerable uncertainty that still persists in the area of radiation effects, including on "permissible doses" of radiation. To be sure, ABCC-RERF officials are well aware of such problems, even if they choose not to emphasize them in official publications. For example, the RERF's American chief of research, whom I interviewed in 1992, admitted that an "overly crude test methodology" might have played a role in the fact that his team had found "absolutely nothing" on genetic effects on the second generation. He stated matter-of-factly: "It all depends on your research methodology, and on the manner in which you interpret the facts; science is nothing else but a public consensus." This surprisingly candid remark should give us pause, considering that the ABCC had a virtual monopoly on studies of delayed radiation effects for nearly a decade. All the more, what counts as "science," and what is left out, should be submitted to critical scrutiny.

It is not my purpose here to cast wholesale doubts on the scientific accuracy of the ABCC-RERF's studies; all facts, including scientific facts, are also social and ideological fabrications, and should be interpreted as such. My point here is the manner in which scientific facts, presented as unassailable truth, can be used to delegitimize victims' fears of delayed effects, including potential genetic effects. In fact, science had deeply ambiguous effects for hibakusha: on the one hand, to paraphrase the title of Susan Lindee's study on the ABCC (1994), it "made their suffering real," stamping hibakusha's complaints with scientific approval, but it also erased their suffering when biological "facts" could not be documented.

The delegitimization of hibakusha experiences through scientific discourses has reached a new peak in recent years. As Hayashi predicted in the interview, "The fact that we've lived so long, and that our children are healthy, will no doubt be used against us." Researchers have issued soothing statements about the "unexpected longevity of hibakusha" and the lack of genetic effects on hibakusha offspring; studies that give higher risk rates are belittled as "advocacy documents." The RERF reported in 1991 that the overall risk of death from cancer among bomb survivors "has proved *only* 2.5% higher than normal" (emphasis added). In 1995—not coincidentally, the bomb's fiftieth anniversary— a former director of the department of statistics and epidemiology at the National Academy of Sciences concluded that "only about 1,500 people have died from radiation-caused cancers in fifty years," and "that the original fears of other long-term effects like accelerated aging and ge- netic damage among the survivors and their children have proven almost entirely unfounded."[9] Perhaps the most glaring example, which also il- lustrates the peculiar effects of scientific jargon, is a 1992 article that appeared in the influential journal *Science* (Marshall 1992): it claimed that "radiation emitted by the bomb was less effective in producing cancer than has been assumed."

It is ironic and cruel that hibakusha, after having offered their bodies for radiation research for fifty years, are being told today that their fears or anxieties about their own health or that of their children are, and have been, unfounded and irrational. The rhetorical question Hayashi asks in one of her novels remains an open one: "Are we women living witnesses to the inhumanity of the bomb, or living proofs to its harm- lessness? Will we be used as 'medicine' against the nuclear allergy?" (*Naki ga gotoki*, 316.)

PROBLEM PATIENTS

I wonder whether there is not a way to wipe out hibakusha [*zetsumetsu ho hōhō*]. In view of the
hereditary risks of "atom bomb disease," we should
think about applying the eugenics law, and the city
should initiate policies to prevent hibakusha from
bearing children. This would also be better from the
point of view of government finances.

> A municipal assemblyman, at the occasion
> of a Diet session held in Tokyo on the
> "problem of medical relief for second-
> generation hibakusha," quoted in Mainichi
> shinbun, 2 July 1978

The ABCC was extreme in its disregard of hibakusha, but it was ex- pressive of a larger tendency: the overwhelmingly medical orientation in both treatment of and research on hibakusha, which have tended to focus only on "disease" (a core of bodily symptoms believed to be related to the bomb), and neglected "illness," the various psychological and sociocultural factors that influence victims' illness experiences (cf. Kleinman 1980: 72–73). To the hibakusha, the very uncertainty about his or her future, including that of offspring, is a source of enormous suffering, and thus devastatingly real; but such suffering has no place in the biomedical model.

To some extent, the medicalization of bomb-related illnesses must be seen in the context of a larger pattern in Japan (and East Asia) to emphasize physical symptoms and to consider psychological suffering as somehow less real. But when applied to bomb-induced illnesses, the disease model was all the more problematic, since there is no specific clinical pathology of long-term radiation illness—radiation-induced cancer, for example, is no different in form from any other cancer, and in most cases there is no way for the patient or doctor to establish a definite proof that an illness is indeed due to radiation exposure. The hunt for objective symptoms put a lot of unnecessary pressure on hibakusha (and well-meaning doctors), and also probably led many victims to over-emphasize their bodily complaints in order to receive treatment at all. Bodily complaints thus can also be interpreted as a form of resistance against normative biomedical definitions of illness, which tend to exclude many subjective symptoms (Lock 1980, 1987).

These problems were greatly exacerbated with the institution by the state of the hibakusha relief laws in 1957 (a full twelve years after the bombings), which provided free health check-ups and medical treatment as well as financial allowances for certain designated illnesses. Today, hibakusha are eligible for all kinds of benefits (including a health management allowance, a nursing allowance, a "special certification" for especially disabling diseases, and even funeral expenses).[10] Hibakusha's stake in having their complaints legitimized and authorized by medical diagnosis thus acquired a starkly material dimension in addition to the moral and psychological ones, also creating a lopsided dependency upon doctors.

It might be worth noting here that according to medical social workers, more than two-thirds of the recipients of the health management allowance, allocated for a wide range of disorders believed to be due to radiation, are women (65.9 percent of female hibakusha, as opposed to 31.4 percent of males, received it in 1993). This could mean two things: a generally lower socioeconomic status among female victims (this benefit is subjected to an income limit, and poorer victims might have felt more motivated to apply for the allowance), and/or a comparatively higher number of women who complain of various bodily (and especially blood-related) ailments.

Hibakusha have sometimes been accused by exasperated doctors of being neurotically preoccupied by their illnesses and fears. Specialists have even coined a term for hibakusha's perpetual anxiety about their bodies: "atom bomb neurosis" (*genbaku-noirooze*).[11] Incidentally, similarly "pathological behaviors" have been observed among other radiation victims, including U.S. atomic veterans (the so-called "Radiation-Response-Syndrome" [RRS]; Vyner 1983). Even if such categorizations were understandable responses by the medical community, they also increased pressure on hibakusha to provide their sufferings with a "biological" basis. As a result of this vicious circle, many hibakusha have grown increasingly frustrated and defensive with doctors. As Ōta wrote: "I know something is wrong with my body. I know my body better than any medical equipment. . . . The term 'atom bomb neurosis' is just a sly label for something doctors can't figure out" (*Watashi no genbaku-shō*, 304–6). Indeed, many of my informants feel that their anxieties are transformed into pathological "syndromes" to be overcome. Psychiatric categories perpetually risk psychologizing victims' suffering, deflecting attention away from larger political, historical, and moral issues, and pressing hibakusha responses into stereotypes that deny the complexity of memory—these are the charges made by one of the most vocal detractors of the psychiatric approach, noted woman hibakusha poet and essayist Kurihara Sadako (1975).

If doctors were ready to point out neurotic tendencies among their patients, medical care did not provide the therapeutic framework that would have allowed the patients to discuss their problems; consultations were limited to "purely medical" issues. The stigma associated with mental illness in Japan probably further discouraged many victims from seeking out professional aid; mental problems, often regarded as signs of moral weakness, were supposed to be resolved by the individual alone or within the family, which in most cases meant that they remained unspoken. Recent reports draw attention to the serious problems in Japan's mental-health-care system, including overcrowded wards, involuntary and extremely long hospitalizations, the lack of rehabilitation facilities, and rampant patient abuse (Salzberg 1994). It is evidently not in the hibakusha's interest to be classified and treated as mental patients.

The basic problems in hibakusha health care—an exclusively medical orientation, and the lack of appropriate counseling facilities—are reflected in the institutions that have been set up in the two bombed cities specifically to deal with hibakusha's medical needs. Until recently, the Hiroshima Atom Bomb Hospital and other hibakusha health centers solely provided medical treatment and free medical exams; hibakusha without a "real illness" had no one with whom to discuss their problems, or to cope with the trauma that could be caused by negative examination results. It was only in the 1980s that a group of medical social workers in Hiroshima began counseling hibakusha in Hiroshima hospitals, but because of an endemic lack of personnel and facilities, few hibakusha can take advantage of such counseling. An interview with the atom bomb hospital's sole social worker, who treats non-hibakusha as well, revealed that she is clearly overwhelmed by her caseload and feels frustrated with the fact that there are no psychiatrists at her hospital who specialize in hibakusha issues.

Today, it is undeniable that a great deal of money is being spent on health care facilities for hibakusha, even if they are still considered inadequate by many hibakusha and their advocates.[12] Yet a biomedical approach, no matter how well funded, is simply insufficient for dealing with hibakusha's problems and the moral questions they raise by their very existence. We should note in this connection that despite an ongoing struggle by hibakusha and antinuclear groups, the government has consistently refused to pay compensation to atom bomb victims. There is a fundamental moral difference between state compensation, which acknowledges a collective responsibility, and medical relief, dispensed to the weaker members of society, who must qualify to receive such aid. Several of my informants refuse to apply for the benefits, though they are eligible; they don't want "charity" (omegumi) from their government.

To conclude this section, we should note that the institutionalization of hibakusha status, while it brought much-needed medical and financial benefits to many hibakusha, came at a high price for the victims: Anything that could not be contained within the biomedical and bureaucratic categories provided by medical and legal experts was not taken into consideration, and thus became nonexistent or even illegitimate. The burden of proof was shifted to the victims, who had to be both "sick" and "deficient" to fit into the medico-judicial categories of hibakushahood as defined by the state.[13]

Yet the transformation of hibakusha's bodies into a series of medical and legal data, neatly circumscribed by experts, can also be seen as a subliminal collective attempt to control bodies that in fact were far more threatening than was publicly acknowledged. The proliferation of disease categories in connection with hibakusha was also meant to contain the disturbing characteristics of such bodies as repositories of a mnemonic substance (both the memory of suffering and of "radiation contamination") that could not be expelled. Women, more closely associated with corporeality and procreation than men, elicited a particularly intense response; it is no accident in my view that the Hiroshima Maidens project focused on young women, and that the genetics study involved large numbers of mothers. Women's bodies acquired a special resonance, and one which subsists subterraneously no matter how powerful the medico-legal apparatus. This becomes especially clear when we look at popular representations of hibakusha women.

HIBAKUSHA WOMEN AS CULTURAL HEROINES: MAKING THE OTHER INTO THE CENTER

In looking at images of hibakusha women in the mass media and in popular fictional constructions (filmic, literary, or iconic), it is apparent that the notion of the pathetic female victim is almost overdetermined and overcoded: media images are replete with representations of female suicide, unhappy spinsters, impoverished widows, and grieving mothers. This would suggest that it is women, far more than men, who have been associated in the collective memory with the "human cost" of the bombs; we can even argue, as Lisa Yoneyama asserts in her anthropological study of Hiroshima memories, that atom bomb memory as such as been "feminized" (1999: 187–210).[14] Yet popular narratives of female hibakusha all too often end up essentializing women's suffering and submerging it into idealized notions of maternal self-sacrifice.

Among images of hibakusha women, I distinguish two recurrent symbolic figures: the first, applied to young, unmarried women, is the dying maiden, condemned to die of radiation effects before she reaches the bloom of full womanhood; the second, used for older, "mature" women, is the eternal mother,[15] who sacrifices her life to save and nurture her children. Both figures appear frequently in filmic and literary narratives, whether fictional or journalistic. The eternal mother in particular is also deployed as an integral part of Hiroshima's public memorialization as "the atom bombed city," and used in iconic representations, such as

commemorative statues. In both cases, hibakusha women are transformed into cultural heroines and their dangerous bodies domesticated.

DYING MAIDENS, OR THE LURE OF UNTIMELY DEATH

The image of a woman suffering uncomplainingly can
imbue us with admiration for a virtuous existence almost beyond our reach, rich in endurance and courage.
One can idealize her rather than merely pity her, and
this can lead to what I call the worship of womanhood, a special brand of Japanese feminism.

Satō Tadao

In looking at images of young hibakusha women, it is striking that they
have been linked almost systematically to fatal illness. Leukemia, especially, became a kind of paradigmatic "female disease," just as hysteria
was considered a "female illness" in nineteenth-century Europe. As a
local journalist has written sarcastically, "While Godzhilla is one ficti-
tious result of radiation, women suffering from 'atom bomb disease' or
leukemia make popular tragic heroines. . . . Men don't seem to go along
very well with leukemia, and are therefore hardly depicted as victims of
the disease."[16] It is clear that the leukemic maiden, who reveals social
anxieties about hibakusha women's "contaminated blood," represents
the romanticized counterimage to the keloid-struck atomic maiden, who
for obvious reasons could not very well be transformed into a beautiful
heroine.

Two Japanese films, *The Diary of Yumechiyo* (*Yumechiyo nikki*,
1986), a popular TV melodrama that was made into a motion picture,
and *Black Rain* (*Kuroi Ame,* 1982) a well-regarded feature film made
by renowned director Imamura Shōhei and based on the famous novel
by Ibuse Masuji, provide revealing insights into the iconic figure of the
"leukemic maiden."[17] They portray the final months in the lives of two
beautiful young hibakusha, Yumechiyo (whose name means "a thousand dreams") and Yasuko, whose hopes for love and marriage are
dashed when they develop leukemia, years after having been exposed to
radiation.

Yumechiyo, which might most appropriately be called an atom bomb
soap opera, opens with Yumechiyo's visit to the hospital, where the
doctor announces that she has "six more months left—maybe less," and
recommends immediate hospitalization. But Yumechiyo, who takes the

news stoically, resolves to return to her village to take up her usual profession as a geisha. Halfway through the film, Yumechiyo falls in love with an actor, who comes to the village to perform with his troupe. When she finds out he is a murder suspect (suspected wrongly of patricide), she refuses to disclose his whereabouts to the police. Her lover takes refuge on a secluded island, and Yumechiyo makes the exhausting trip to the island to join him. During their climactic reunion and lovemaking, Yumechiyo gasps, "I love you so, but I am not worthy of loving anyone, in my condition." "Please give me your child," she implores him, only to add sadly, "it's no use—it's too late for me anyway. . . ." After having made her confession, she lapses into a comatose state and dies shortly thereafter, surrounded by her wailing geisha friends. Her lover is arrested by the police. The film closes with a long shot on the crestfallen, handcuffed lover, on whose portrait is superimposed the phantasmagoric vision of Yumechiyo in all her splendor, in a beautiful kimono and dancing to a traditional tune.

At first sight, Imamura's film has little in common with this contrite melodrama. Avoiding all sentimentality, Imamura offers a deeply felt portrait of hibakusha who struggle with the bomb's effects long after the war has ended. Set in a small village in the 1950s, the film focuses on three Hiroshima survivors: an elderly couple, Shigematsu and Shigeko, and their young niece, Yasuko, who is of marriageable age. All are plagued by radiation effects, but the most tragic victim is Yasuko, whose prospects for marriage come to naught due to the social stigma attached to radiation exposure. The plot revolves primarily around Shigematsu's vain efforts to find a bridegroom for his niece. Yasuko has a brief romance with a young man, but marriage talks are broken off when his parents oppose their marriage. Yasuko gives up hope for marriage altogether, aware that she is developing serious radiation symptoms. She begins a friendship with the village outcast, a man traumatized by his wartime experiences; he falls in love with her, but she is no longer willing to get married. In the end she is hospitalized, and though the film ends on an open note—her uncle hopes for a "miracle"—we know that Yasuko will never return home but die of leukemia.

Despite the important differences in treatment and plot, the films make use of similar strategies: they provide an aestheticizing view of atom bomb disease by drawing on the pathos of young beautiful women falling before their prime, and thus on culturally potent notions of the ephemerality of life and the "suchness" of our brief existence (Lebra 1976: 166–67). This partly explains their considerable success with moviegoers and television viewers, but in the process, hibakusha women are pressed into a romanticizing framework, and their suffering and deaths naturalized, just as flowers are condemned to fade one day. In *Yume-chiyo,* illness and decay are not presented as demeaning experiences but as an adjunct to female beauty and value; fatal illness seems to lend Yumechiyo, who grows fashionably thinner and paler as the film goes on, a dignified and noble aura lacking in the other women, who are unfashionably healthy and plump. The final image of the film, when we see her weeping lover with a vision of Yumechiyo floating up before his eyes, is particularly suggestive—living on in his memory, she is more beautiful and splendid than ever. True to the cultural ideal, she died "like a flower," before old age and decay could affect her. Imamura's depiction is far more subtle, but even he cannot resist an aestheticizing tendency in some of the scenes focusing on Yasuko alone in her room or bathroom. When we see her bathing, brushing her hair, powdering her nose, or otherwise tending to her body, there is a persistent ambiguity: while for any other girl these scenes might signify a natural, girlish curiosity about her own body, the viewer knows that Yasuko is falling ill with radiation effects, and so the scenes (further aestheticized by the use of soft light and fluid camera movements) create a sense of apprehension, even suspense, founded on the juxtaposition between her virginal beauty and impending illness.

The two women are also depicted as paragons of the ideal, selfless woman who confronts her suffering with forbearance, dignity, and stoic endurance. Though in constant agony because of their illness, Yumechiyo and Yasuko continue to serve the family and community as good daughters and substitute mothers; it is they who nurture and take care of others, asking little in return. In fact, their spiritual qualities seem to grow in inverse proportion to their deteriorating physical condition. Yumechiyo devotes her entire remaining six months to nurse, comfort, and provide for her geisha friends, giving them sentimental advice and material support, and in one instance keeping one from committing suicide. Similarly, Yasuko stoically accepts the breakup of her engagement with her prospective bridegroom and replaces her romantic interest in men with a sisterly (or maternal) one, taking care of the village outcast. In both cases, the bomb provokes a shift from a feminine-sexual identity (a woman in search of love) to a maternal-nurturing one (protecting an even weaker male partner).

The emphasis on stoic endurance also subverts any meaningful voice by the woman herself; the films give little weight to the heroines' subjective experiences of suffering and provide no narrative space for the victims. Though *Yumechiyo* is ostensibly based on the heroine's diary, there are only three short scenes in the three-hour film in which she confesses her own feelings, and these descriptions are too stereotypical to add any depth to her portrayal. Similarly, we learn little of Yasuko's own views. Though the film starts out promisingly, with an excerpt from her diary narrated by the heroine, her voice becomes more and more muted throughout the film: it is usually Shigematsu, through his diary or in his discussions with his wife, who provides information with regard to Yasuko's state. As a consequence, in both films the women's experiences are seen from the outside, from an essentially voyeuristic point of view, and submerged in a patina of stolid emotional sameness.

To be sure, images of long-suffering hibakusha are part of a pervasive pattern in collective representations that emphasizes stoic endurance and self-sacrifice, among both men and women. In a representative example, the writer Ōe Kenzaburō expressed admiration for hibakusha who "live bravely" and "who do not pity themselves in spite of everything" (Ōe 1969: 85). Conversely, hibakusha who appear angry, hostile, or rebellious, and especially hibakusha women who do not fit the category of the wholesome "maidens" depicted here, have been chastised for being "bad" survivors. As film critic Satō Tadao put it, the Japanese want to see hibakusha whom "viewers can safely feel sorry for: we can shed warm tears, believing that even if the bomb can destroy a person's destiny, it cannot even scratch at the victim's humanity. This is the world of drama" (1960: 835). Satō's comment is astute, but contrary to what he says, such depictions are not limited to the world of drama: they have found their most extreme expression in a documentary film that presses hibakusha women into essentializing notions of motherhood.

THE ETERNAL MOTHER: FANTASY OF SALVATION

In precisely the moment in which the world becomes
apocalyptic, through our own making, it presents us
with the aspect of a fata morgana, a paradise inhabited
by innocent murderers and hateless victims. There is
no trace of malevolence, only ruins.

Günther Anders

A documentary produced by the city of Hiroshima called *A Mother's Prayer* (*Hahatachi no inori,* 1990) provides revealing insights into images of hibakusha mothers. Produced by an official organ of Hiroshima's "peace administration" and routinely shown to city visitors and especially schoolchildren, the film purports to tell the entire "story" of Hiroshima, from the atom bombs to the present day, "through the eyes of mothers." Narrated entirely by a motherly woman's voice, it juxtaposes scenes of atomic devastation and bodily injuries (including delayed radiation effects) with a counternarrative of Hiroshima's "rebirth" as a "mecca of peace."

In fact, the film is not so much about Hiroshima or its history as about the collective suffering and sacrifice of hibakusha mothers. It is quite relentless in pursuing an image of the heroic mother who protects and nurtures her own, even at the cost of her own life. Throughout its most harrowing sections, the documentary carefully alternates scenes of destruction and death with the supposedly self-sacrificial behavior of mothers. For example, when faced with disturbing images of burnt, disfigured, and crying children, we are told that many mothers desperately searched the city and first-aid stations for their offspring, heedless of their own injuries, and that some died while taking care of them. The mother's altruistic actions extend well beyond the bombing; despite their own fragile health, they courageously nurture and tend to their sick children. Throughout, the film establishes a uniform picture of maternal love and devotion that remains unwavering no matter how catastrophic the situation. Those mothers guilty of surviving their children are portrayed as darkly clad figures whose only purpose in life is to serve as a living memorial to their loved ones, and to pray tearfully for the "sake of world peace." Such saccharine depictions place the documentary squarely into the most popular genre of all, the "mother story" (*hahamono*), dedicated to maternal suffering and self-sacrifice (cf. Buruma 1984: 24–29).

The most compelling iconic representation of the eternal mother—and the film's final image—is undoubtedly a monument that figures prominently in Hiroshima's Peace Park: a bronze statue titled "Mother and Child in the Storm," which shows a mother grasping an infant tightly in her right arm and holding another child with her left, leaning forward in a protective gesture.[18] The statue is popular with many visitors; they say that it expresses a mother's love that can withstand any storm, and which survives even a nuclear blast. Moreover, the statue is

in a prime strategic location, in front of the museum; it seems to guard
the museum entrance, and emerges as a symbolic counterpoint to the
"cold memory" of the atom bomb museum, which limits itself to dis-
playing the anonymous artifacts of atomic destruction. The fact that the
mother's gesture is laughably inadequate to the effects of the blast, which
the museum documents in scientific detail, makes her only more pathetic
and touching. On the other hand, the mother represented here is clearly
meant as a timeless figure who could exist in any epoch and could confront any "storm," whether nuclear or other. It makes little difference
what external obstacle she is fighting; what counts is the indestructible
bond that links her to her children. The Mother exists outside of, or
despite, history, politics, and ideology.

In fact, this ostensible celebration of motherhood in connection with
the bomb has been instrumental in the creation of the ahistorical and
apolitical orientation in Hiroshima's public memory—what German
philosopher Günther Anders refers to as "fata morgana." It also allowed
the city to inscribe the atom bomb experience into a redemptive narrative of destruction and rebirth, from catastrophe to its self-proclaimed
identity as "motherland of peace" (which includes a partial suppression
of the city's wartime past). This narrative is rendered unassailable by the
mother figure, into which individual victims are co-opted and recuper-
ated.

But let us return to women. The Eternal Mother only serves to ob-
fuscate the concrete difficulties hibakusha mothers have experienced
in dealing with their children, families, and communities, and diverts
attention away from the fact that the bomb prevented many women
from becoming mothers at all. And although some mothers (and certainly fathers too!) surely accomplished particularly courageous and
heroic feats to save or help their children, it is also a fact that others
abandoned their children after the blast, too frightened or simply
too preoccupied with their own survival to take care of them. Surely
it is cruel to chastise such women as unmotherly. Again, the figure of
the Eternal Mother entails, and is constructed upon, the suppression
of women's own voices and subjectivity. It also denies the devastating reality of nuclear weapons, which no amount of maternal heroism
and self-sacrifice can counter. The mother myth also overpowers the
experiences of fathers; they are completely absent from this documentary. Apparently, selflessness and nurturance are uniquely motherly
qualities. Moreover, no single adult male is depicted as a victim; the
oldest male to receive some attention is a five-year-old boy, and the

only male featured on the brochure introducing the film is Pope John Paul II.

Despite their openly sympathetic guises, Maiden and Mother send the same message to hibakusha women: a woman's lot is to suffer, and to do so uncomplainingly. Women thus become associated with what I would call a "larmoyant memory"—a memory in which tragedy and suffering occupy a central place, but which has been purged of any contestatory element. While young women are told in no uncertain terms that they have no place in society (or even in life), older women are supposed take their struggles uncomplainingly upon themselves, up to the point of sacrificing their lives for their children. Women's own need for nurturance and care is denied.

Yet both Maiden and Mother clearly reflect anxieties surrounding women's sexuality and reproductive powers. It is no accident that the Maiden, who is still dangerous because potentially sexually active and capable of giving birth, is afflicted by fatal illness (and dies off conveniently in the end), whereas the Mother, who has already given birth, can be pressed into the nonthreatening, maternal image of the nonsexual woman. In both cases, women's "dangerous body" is transformed into the quintessential maternal body. The glorified mother sublimates troubling knowledge about radiation damage and the possibility of hereditary effects, symbolized by the monstrous babies of Hiroshima women. Can we even read a fantasy of salvation into the collective fascination with the Eternal Mother in a country traumatized by the memory of the apocalyptic destruction of two cities?

III. KNOWING BODIES

Several colleagues and I were working on modeling counterforce attacks, trying to get realistic estimates of the number of immediate fatalities that would result from different deployments. At one point, we remodeled a particular attack, using slightly different assumptions, and found that instead of there being thirty-six million immediate fatalities, there would only be thirty million. And everybody was sitting around nodding, saying, "Oh yeah, that's great, only thirty million," when all of a sudden, I *heard* what we were saying. And I blurted out, "Wait, I've just *heard* how

we're talking—*only* thirty million! *Only* thirty million
human beings killed instantly?" Silence fell upon the
room. Nobody said a word. They didn't even look at
me. It was awful. I felt like a woman.

> *A nuclear weapons physicist, quoted in*
> *Cohn 1993: 227. He added that hence-*
> *forth he was careful never to blurt out any-*
> *thing like that again.*

Let us turn to the final theme: How do women themselves negotiate
their identities as "hibakusha women"? In their activities as writers,
storytellers, and members of self-help groups, my informants have
drawn on two dominant, gendered themes that have emerged in connection with collective responses to women: embodiment (woman's
body as privileged repository of radiation damage) and maternity (hibakusha women as mothers par excellence). Yet they have deployed
these images to reclaim their bodies and voices in the public landscape,
and to contest official discourses that transform them into disembodied
and mute actors, fixed in frozen positions.

Many of my informants' interpretations might seem essentializing,
and women's interpretations are often more complex than this short
paper can convey. Nevertheless, I should add that insistence on motherhood and experiences in family and household, and a tendency to
emphasize gender differences (including biological differences), are common features of most Japanese women's movements; motherhood in
particular occupies a central place in both prewar and postwar feminist
movements, including the more radical ones (Mae 1997). This in itself
would attest to the high cultural evaluation of motherhood in Japanese
society, though centralizing notions of "maternal instinct" have come
increasingly under attack.

In a different context, Fiona Ross (in this volume) argues that the
testimonies of South African women to the Truth and Reconciliation
Commission often focus on apartheid's disruption of domestic and family life, and on the suffering experienced by others rather than the self.
Women, Ross asserts, use images of domesticity to "map the interpo-
lation of violence in their lives." Her analysis brings out intriguing similarities between the narrative strategies of women in different cultural
and historical locales.

BREAKING THE SILENCE, CREATING SELVES

In examining the informants' life histories, a similar pattern emerges: the women were relatively silent for the first twenty to twenty-five years after the bomb (from 1945 to 1965–70); they began writing or speaking about their experiences only when they were in their late thirties or forties. There is a striking correspondence in dates: the Osaka and Yamashita Groups were founded, independently, in 1967; Hayashi wrote her first autobiographical essay in the same year.

Though this lapse in time was due partly to the trauma of the experience, which women took time to digest, it is more closely related to changes in women's life cycle. In their twenties or early thirties, the informants were too preoccupied with finding marriage partners, raising children, working, and material survival to have time to reflect upon their experiences. It was only when children were grown and women achieved a certain amount of stability, as well as a measure of confidence about their own health, that they became more interested in exploring the meaning of their experiences and in interacting with their peers.

Women's activism in the latter part of their lives is also suggestive with respect to the sociocultural meanings of female life-cycle changes: younger women and mothers with little children, in the structurally weak position of the bride (*yome*), tend to be isolated and enjoy little social recognition. It is only when women reach the more respected position of middle-aged woman or "lady" (*fujin*) and thus gain access to the culturally respected status of mature motherhood that their power in the family and in the larger community increases (cf. Lebra 1984). To some extent, this bias is expressed in a popular Japanese saying: *Onna wa yowashi, haha wa tsuyoshi* (woman is weak, mother is strong). This is borne out by the fact that my informants became more and more active as time went on: it was in the 1980s, thus when they were in their fifties or older, that their activities in women's groups and as individual writers/storytellers reached a peak.[19]

Once women began writing or speaking about their experiences, they took an important step toward the remaking of their selves and life-worlds, fragmented by the bomb's violence and disempowering official discourses. My informants describe the narrativization of their experiences as a transformatory and eye-opening process. As Yamamoto from the Yamashita Group put it, "Writing allowed me to release all the pent-up feelings I'd kept locked inside myself for so many years. I could finally admit that I was a hibakusha." However, the production of narrative—

often referred to by hibakusha as *kataru* (narrating or telling)—was not simply therapeutic, but also a creative reworking of the meanings of their experiences, often in interaction with peers and audiences. In so doing, my informants insist both on the idiosyncrasies of their life histories as well as on the perceived commonalties between their own experiences and those of other women. A recent collection of writings by hibakusha women is significantly titled *Women Tell of Hiroshima* (*Onna ga Hiroshima o kataru*, 1996), emphasizing women's subjectivity and active role as agents of interpretation, but also indicating the search for the contours of an (albeit emergent and contested) collective identity of "women hibakusha" (Esashi et al. 1996).

DEPLOYING MOTHERHOOD

How do my informants use the maternal trope when speaking about their activities and legitimizing their passage to the public realm?

We have seen that gendered ideologies which confined women to the domestic sphere and put the burden of child care and household management squarely on women's shoulders added uncommon stresses to hibakusha women's lives. Yet women like Hayashi, Takagi, and the members of the women's groups consciously deploy traditional notions of the "good wife and wise mother" to denounce the bomb. They assert that the source of their suffering does not lie in these gender roles themselves, felt to be natural or desirable, but rather in their inability to fulfill them properly due to the bomb. In this, hibakusha women are no different from most Japanese women, who generally endorse the role of mother and housewife, and "do not experience an ideology of service to others as oppressive" (Lock 1993: 202). Hayashi's remarks, conveyed in the interview, are emblematic: "Maybe it's bad to speak of gender differences in connection with the bomb, but a woman takes care of the small but essential things in life: giving birth, rearing children, bathing and clothing them, preparing food, and so on. This is the basis of human life, different from men's lives, and that's where the bomb's influence was greatest. . . . I know it's different for younger women, but this is the way things were for my generation."

In addition, my informants (though this applies especially to the older members in the women's groups) tend to stress that it is precisely the mothers' separateness from official power structures which endows them with a pure, uncorrupted mentality, closer to the realities of daily existence, and thus the moral authority to speak for the suffering of the community. They tend to endorse the separation between women's domestic and men's public sphere, which, they feel, corresponds to the opposition between a softer, humane form of knowledge based on human bonds and emotions, and a colder, inhuman form of knowledge epitomized by scientists, military men, and politicians.

In the maternal discourse, women appropriate images of endurance and self-sacrifice, and in some cases draw on culturally potent notions of the "mother instinct," but they use these notions in creative ways. As Hayashi put it:

> I, as a mother, have lived with the weight of August 9, and the woman who will marry my son will in a sense carry on my problems, also giving birth to a hibakusha child. So I thought, simply brushing away the problem, acting as if it didn't exist, this I couldn't allow myself, as a woman [*josei toshite yurusenai*]. . . . Being a hibakusha doesn't limit itself to the past. If it was the problem only of me, of one generation, I wouldn't write about it. But it continues to the present.

Hayashi's remark "it continues to the present" is crucial for a better understanding of the maternal idiom—the latter allows women to speak of the bomb in the present tense, of the manner in which it continues to overshadow their lives and those of loved ones in the seeming normalcy of postwar Japanese society. By drawing on "motherhood," women create a position from which they speak authoritatively about the suffering of others—a strategy that is all the more potent in a society that privileges allocentric idioms of suffering (that is, suffering experienced by others, rather than the self), and that encourages reflection on "suffering inflicted" rather than suffering received (cf. Reynolds 1980). Though males can also make use of the maternal idiom when talking about their experiences—and some have done so quite successfully—it is more easily accessible to female hibakusha because of the cultural obsession with motherhood. Significantly, I found that the most active male hibakusha tend to be teachers or doctors, professions that allow them to reproduce a "nurturing" framework, and thus to eliminate the burden of being associated with soldierhood, science, and warfare.

Mothers' groups such as the Osaka and Yamashita Groups have made the most explicit use of maternal authority: their testimonial accounts and narratives have often been framed and presented as "gifts to the children." Yet the Osaka Group's series of life histories, which carries the title *Mother's Heritage* (*Haha no Isan*), contains upon closer inspection many narratives by women who never had children, and addresses a wide range of concerns faced by women and hibakusha in general.

Similarly, when Yamamoto of the Yamashita mothers' group claims that
"in writing for our children, we could show that our accounts were not
just self-indulgent 'remembrances' [*omoide-banashi*] by ignorant housewives, but true testaments to the next generation," we can see that this
is also a rhetorical strategy, allowing women not only to counteract
charges of selfishness but to speak of the suffering of the community.

In many ways, the idiom of maternity can thus serve as a cover for
creating a forum for female expression, one which includes the experiences of a great many different women—whether married, divorced,
single, or widowed. The lives of her single women friends occupy a large
place in Hayashi's work, and both the Osaka and Yamashita Groups
include quite a few single or childless women. Women themselves are
well aware that their lives do not begin or end with childrearing, but
children, and the domestic realm, have been their most effective weapons
to bring hibakusha experiences into conceptions of social reality.

BODY AS WEAPON

Secondly, the most active women tend to emphasize that they incarnate
the bomb with their very bodies. In so doing, they often invoke a gender-
based "bodily vulnerability" to radiation. Hayashi's words are emblematic: "We women carry human life in our bodies, and we transmit it directly. This is something basic. When the sperm of some male hibakusha
from Nagasaki was examined, it turned out that all the sperm were
killed, too; so men were also influenced. But still, I believe that the most
vulnerable thing, that which received the most influence, was women's
uteri [*shikyū*]." Another woman put it this way: "A man can marry a
woman completely unrelated to the bomb. But as a woman, you're stuck
with it. It's a problem of the womb [*botai*]." Some informants claim that
they feel that the bomb is literally inside their cells [*saibō*] or their blood.
In another example, in a recent book on women hibakusha, the editor
roundly asserts that "radiation, whether it be released through atom
bombings or in nuclear power plant accidents, affected women's bodies
differently from men's bodies" (Esashi 1996: 5). With respect to this literal inscription of the bomb in women's bodies, blood is particularly
suggestive;[20] women's blood is a symbolically loaded substance that
crosses the margins of the individual body and circulates in the social
body. Women's suffering is also the corporeal suffering of the other.

It is precisely because they literally embody the bomb, my informants claim, that they know the devastating reality of nuclear weapons and their threat to human beings much better than the "experts" who have the power to legitimize (or pathologize) hibakusha existence. Hayashi, for example, gives a quite literal meaning to the term *taiken* ("body-experience") when talking about the bomb; the body is the repository of a memory that can be unbeknownst even to the hibakusha herself. As she wrote in one of her novels: "The woman has the authority of one who experienced [*taiken shita*] the terror of radiation. She is not necessarily conscious of it, but it is the truth to her. . . . She is aware of her existence as a fact of August 9" (*Naki ga gotoki,* 349–50). Members of the Yamashita Group make a similar claim, adding that their incorporation of the bomb propelled them to action: "We members felt intuitively, in our own bodies, that the bomb was a problem of the human race. This gave us a sense of mission, and the strength to confront our experiences."

Women's embodiment of radiation also makes their bodies recalcitrant to any external intervention aimed at "eliminating" radiation pollution. As Yamaoka Michiko argued: "Once you have this bomb inside, modern medicine can't do anything about it. Surgery doesn't work for our bodies." Anxieties about future generations cannot be argued away by scientific assertions of the absence of genetic effects; nor can they be domesticated by bureaucratic measures. By invoking a gendered vulnerability, my informants attempt to transform their tainted bodies, the fear of producing abnormal offspring, into a weapon to reclaim the bomb as a moral and ethical issue that concerns the community as a whole.

To be sure, there are important differences in the ways in which my informants use the tropes of maternity and embodiment to bring their experiences to public attention. Below, I provide detailed analyses of three individual examples that illustrate important differences in strategies and rhetoric: the Osaka Group, oral storyteller Yamaoka Michiko, and writer Hayashi Kyōko.

"UNVANQUISHED WE MARCH":[21] THE OSAKA WOMEN'S GROUP

I was unfortunate to be a victim, but still I feel I'm
lucky. Through my experiences, I understood the value
of human life, of human suffering. I say to my husband:

I suffered, but I received such important lessons
through it. I woke up as a woman, and became actively involved in trying to change society.
                    Itō Sakae, hibakusha activist

The Osaka Group provides revealing insights into the manner in which
hibakusha women use essentialist gender definitions to create a sense of
community among women, and to legitimize their struggles on behalf
of other hibakusha. Interestingly, the group began its career as a
woman's section *(fujinbu)* attached to the official, male-dominated Municipal Association of Osaka Hibakusha, and its formal name is still
Women's Section of the Osaka Association of Hibakusha. In reality,
however, the "women's section" has overtaken its parent-group in both
resources and community impact. Takagi laughs, "These men are just
figure-heads. It's we women who are doing the real work."

   In recounting the history of her group, Takagi asserts honestly that
the use of a woman-centered language, one which emphasizes mothers
and children, was the only way to attract a wider membership: "We
quickly realized that women tended to be intimidated by complicated
legal or medical issues, so we had to use easy [*yasashii*] and womanly
[*josei-rashii*] language. That was the true beginning of our group—the
search for a positive identity as hibakusha women." In private conversations, Takagi stated that "what's most important is women's courage
or pluckiness [*takumashisa*], women's active attitude toward life. We're
different from other people, and we must affirm this difference if we
want to achieve something." She ties hibakusha womanhood to "human
being–ness" (*ningen-rashisa*), as well as to "human rights" (*jinken-
rashisa*), repeatedly taking issue with the fact that in Hiroshima motherhood (*hahaoya-rashisa*) is "prayers only": "Mothers do not just grieve
and pray for the dead; they want to take their destiny in their own
hands."

   While such notions reflect the group's interest in Western feminism
and Western notions of human rights, they also draw explicitly on indigenous notions of female power, or powerful female figures in Japanese history and mythology, such as goddesses, empresses, peasant reb-
els, women anarchists, and the feminists of the Meiji and Taishō periods.
They claim that "Japan used to be a matriarchal society," and are fond
of quoting the title of Hiratsuka Raicho's 1911 classic: "In ancient times,
woman was the sun" (*Genshi, josei wa taiyō de atta*).

That the group has been able to translate contestatory views of motherhood into concrete action is reflected in their counseling activity and their advocacy on behalf of hibakusha. The members are extremely well-informed on the complex web of medical, social and financial benefits available to hibakusha, and they have often waged lengthy battles on behalf of their clients. The group also keeps extensive medical files on the regular and more loosely affiliated members, allowing them to contest medical and judicial diagnoses. As Takagi said, "We're like the ABCC, keeping files on everybody; only we use it for a better purpose." These women have effectively reappropriated knowledge about their bodies that was taken from them.

During the three afternoons I spent at the group's office in downtown Osaka, more than a dozen hibakusha (both men and women), sometimes from outlying prefectures, came to the office to receive counseling. Takagi insists that women are much better counselors than men because they are "naturally kinder," and because their knowledge is more "humane" than technical. Women also "know how to create a warm environment for people," she says. Indeed, much thought has gone into the design and arrangement of the counseling room, which is distinctly traditional, with tatamis, folding screens, and flower bouquets. In such an atmosphere, many hibakusha feel at ease talking about their problems. The room is quite a contrast to the counseling facilities in the Hiroshima hospitals, often cold, stark hospital rooms, decorated by a simple curtain to protect victims' privacy.

In recent years, the group has shifted its activities from advocacy to the publication of members' life histories (*jibunshi*). These life histories are distributed to the public when the group campaigns for government compensation and the outlawing of nuclear weapons. It is significant in this context that Takagi, when talking about the members' accounts, deliberately contrasts *kataru* (narrating) with *shōgen suru* (witnessing), a term commonly used in legal settings, in which hibakusha must bring some kind of factual or verifiable proof to substantiate their claims for benefits; kataru is thus quite consciously tied to the creation of a sense of critical agency and resistance vis-à-vis the imposition of external authority upon hibakusha experiences.

Despite such weighty issues, the mood in the office is extremely cheerful. When women interact with their peers, there is always much gossiping and laughter. The Osaka Group struck me as especially irreverent, which might have something to do with the Osaka local culture, which is known as somewhat rebellious: group members merrily criticized husbands, town officials, prime ministers, and other authority figures. Widows who depict themselves as forlorn figures in their life histories confessed that they are quite happy living alone, not having to take care of troublesome husbands, and laughed at men's notorious inability to survive without women and wives. Mothers spoke about feelings of hostility and frustration toward their children, and quite a few women openly admitted that they didn't care for children at all, confessions which were greeted by expressions of feigned shock by the mothers in the group. Clearly, such talk was directed not just against men but also toward a sense of unity and community among women. Paradoxically, this was done by consciously undermining supposedly natural female characteristics.

STORYTELLING: PERFORMING HIBAKUSHA WOMANHOOD

A single bomb turned my life around, but once I
started telling about my experiences, I felt that I was
able to rise up [*agaru*] in the world. My words are my
only fortune.

                                        Yamaoka Michiko

Gender ought not to be constructed as a stable identity
or locus of agency from which various acts follow;
rather, gender is an identity tenuously constituted in
time, instituted in an exterior space through a stylized
repetition of acts. . . .

                                        Judith Butler

Women have been quite successful in carving out a prominent role in the *kataribe* (oral storyteller) movement. It began in the late 1970s, when hibakusha began talking to schoolchildren about their experiences, and over time such sporadic encounters grew into a full-fledged movement, peaking in the 1980s. Oral transmission has become by far the most popular method for transmitting memories of the atom bomb, and the term *kataribe* is widely used today. There are both male and female kataribe, but women have come to occupy a prominent place in the grassroots kataribe movement, in contrast to the more official hibakusha groups, where they tend to exercise at best a backstage form of leadership. Hibakusha organizations such as the Osaka Group also employ their own kataribe, who give their testimonies in local schools. Kataribe employ a wide range of practices and strategies that cannot be summarized here, but what I am principally concerned with is the manner in which oral storytelling can be used by women as a quite literal "politics of the body" and a performative enactment of the gendered tropes of embodiment and maternity.

Former Hiroshima Maiden Yamaoka Michiko provides a striking example. I attended several of Yamaoka's performances and was struck by the skill with which she enacted a public persona as a maternal hibakusha woman while still communicating her own, deeply disturbing messages about suffering from the bomb. As a single, childless hibakusha woman, she is excluded from the dominant model of the reassuring mother, but she successfully posited herself as a substitute mother when interacting with the children, thus re-creating the culturally accepted paradigm of the transmission of knowledge from mother to child.

In addition to assuming a vicarious parent role, Yamaoka resorted to several related strategies to accrue moral face in the eyes of the audience: she emphasized several times that she was "saved thanks to [her] mother," explaining at length how her mother "pulled [her] out of the flames" and "took care of [her] day and night," presenting herself as a daughter saved by her mother and thus reintegrating her persona into the mother-child link. She also insisted on how selfish she was in her youth, having found out only after her mother's death "how much my mother had suffered." She further emphasized that she was grateful for all the people who helped her survive, and used the expression *ikasareta* ("I was caused to live," or "I was given the favor to live") several times.

In private conversations, her mother emerged as a far less idealized figure, resentful of her daughter's handicap and dependency upon her. Yamaoka also emphasized quite forcefully that she survived only thanks to her own efforts ("Nobody helped me after my mother died"). To be sure, at an experiential level, these apparently contradictory interpretations are not necessarily distinct; people's relationships with socially sanctioned idioms are always dynamic and fluid. To Yamaoka, I am certain, this flexibility does not create any internal conflicts, but rather extends her field of action.

As further evidence of this, in her kataribe performances she could quite easily switch from the reassuring maternal idiom to profoundly disturbing descriptions of the devastation wrought by the bomb. After a breathtaking immersion in harrowing scenes of the bombing and its immediate aftermath—which left the audience quite shaken up—

Yamaoka ended with the rather incongruous remark, "You know, a mother's love is so important. Parents must love their children. My mother really took care of me. Now they talk about abolishing school lunches, and it's important that mothers take care of their kids." Or another time, she said: "Many adults say today the bomb couldn't be helped, but I don't want you to think like this. The bomb shouldn't be a tale of the past [*mukashi-banashi*]. You must think about all the things in the world, and have the strength to make your own judgments. We were brainwashed and ignorant. You have the chance to think clearly for yourselves. You know, Hiroshima was to kill people [*Hiroshima wa hito o korosunda*]." This powerful statement was followed by the rhetorical coda: "You must become good children, obey your parents; then there will be peace, love, and life."

Yamaoka also illustrates how hibakusha can use their maimed bodies quite literally as weapons to bring home the corporeal reality of suffering. Pointing to her scars, keloids on her face and chest that are still visible despite extensive surgery, she described the manner in which she and her friends were injured and burned, and questioned the manner in which the atom bomb museum represents such bodily destruction: "We didn't look as beautiful as the wax dolls in the atom bomb museum."

Another form of body language, which reflects kataribe's historical roots in the oral and performative traditions, appears in Yamaoka's skillful use of gestures, noises, and tears to underline particularly dramatic episodes in her account. Yamaoka asserts that she cultivates a deliberately awkward narration, felt to reflect the authenticity of her experience: "If people become too skillful speakers [*jōzu ni naruto*], their testimony becomes artificial," she asserts. Other kataribe, including members of the Osaka group, make similar claims; as Takagi holds, "Women are much better storytellers than males; they always stick to their experiences and feelings."

The fact that Yamaoka has succeeded in becoming one of the more popular kataribe in Hiroshima today, despite her frankness (which has earned her many enemies among city officials and other hibakusha), is a testimony to the success of her strategy. To her own amusement, the media have recently baptized her the "born-again atomic maiden" (*saisei shita genbaku-otome*). For further evidence that she has succeeded in rehabilitating her image, recent articles commented on the "new, feminine glow" in her eyes—a "transformation" that is attributed to her discovery of her own maternal instincts (Hiroshima josei-shi kenkyūkai 1987: 140ff). As one journalist put it, "Her face is bright, like that of a mother thinking of her child." Though Yamaoka seems happy with her new-found popularity and enjoys her interactions with the children, she does get annoyed at the eagerness of the media to attribute a new brightness to her persona. In one instance, when told by a journalist, "You seem so bright and cheerful today," she said, "I feel smoldering discontent" (*mon-mon shite imasu*). To me, Yamaoka's persona, and indeed her very physical presence, epitomizes the paradox of the figure of the woman kataribe: as dangerous body, a disturber of peace, wrapped in the reassuring clothing of the maternal woman.

IMPOSSIBLE LIVES, POSSIBLE BODIES: THE BODY POLITICS OF HAYASHI KYŌKO

Isn't the final goal of writing to articulate the body?
. . . Words have the power to deny destruction and our
writing must prove this. We need languages that regenerate us, warm us, give birth to us, that lead us to act
and not to flee. . . . If a music of feminity is arising out
of its own oppression, it materializes through the redis-
covered body. . . . Feminine language must, by its very
nature, work on life passionately, scientifically, poeti-
cally, politically in order to make it invulnerable.
                         Chantal Chawaf, "Linguistic Flesh"

Hayashi Kyōko exemplifies the painful if productive dilemmas inherent in a politics of embodiment, and of a self-conscious engagement with the bomb's threat to biological reproduction. As John Whittier Treat remarks, Hayashi Kyōko symbolizes a kind of female writing that deals with "the very issue of biology and culture, and thus our literal and symbolic survival" (1995: 347). To Hayashi, the question "What was the bomb for us hibakusha women? What are we exactly, compared to other human beings?" (*Naki ga gotoki,* 302) remains an open one, and she considers her self-chosen role as woman kataribe to be a lifelong task.

Her most successful narratives are short vignettes focusing on her experiences with family members or friends, such as a walk on the beach, a train ride with her son, a visit to her friend's house. It is in these fragmentary, slice-of-life depictions, and via small, seemingly insignificant details—a child's fallen sock, a doll covered with dust, a broken teacup—that the narrator perceives the lived truth of atom bomb suffering, in her own life and the lives of her peers. It is these small events, rather than the big occurrences like fatal illnesses or deaths, which occupy the greater space in her narratives.

However, these chronicles of "hibakusha women's everyday lives" have a deeply disturbing, cumulative effect: they actually illustrate the very impossibility of an ordinary life for such women. No matter how normal their lives might seem on the surface and to others, Hayashi and her friends can never escape the bomb; their lives are impregnated by the ubiquitous, embodied presence of death.

In the interview, however, she was quite explicit about the fact that her own life had in many ways been "quite normal," and that she had been able to raise her son well despite the failure of her marriage. This, she added, "was not the case for many of my peers who died, or were unable to have children." Obviously, Hayashi has also rewritten her life into an impossible life for strategic purposes, motivated by a sense of mission and responsibility. The following passage put it most explicitly:

> The woman [Hayashi's alter ego] wanted to live, and she'd gone on living after August 9. It was the very everydayness of women's lives which would give testimony to the meaning of the elimination of nuclear weapons. We never once doubted the weight [*omosa*] of every single day in our lives. . . . The fact that we've survived so long, that the country had prospered, would no doubt be used against us. . . . But we women are the only truth [*tsuiitsu no jijitsu*] of that moment. (*Naki ga gotoki,* 349–50)

Hayashi has been most explicit in her intent to construct a "communal experience" of hibakusha women. As is suggested in the passage, the narrator variously posits herself as "I" (*watakushi*), "the woman" (*onna*), or "the women" (*onna-tachi*), indicating that the three terms can be used to some extent interchangeably: this "I/woman/women" carries the "weight" of a community of sufferers, and is also meant as a counterpoint to official discourses that relegate atom bomb suffering to the past or convert it into a medical or bureaucratic issue. As Hayashi stated in the interview: "Human bodies, human lives, cannot be exchanged against anything else or compensated for by anything else."

The author also deploys a potent body politics in her writings. She consistently brings the bomb back to the most basic bodily realities of women's existence, shying away from more theoretical or abstract formulations—the body occupies a central place in all her narratives. Her accounts are replete with references to women's bodily processes and experiences: women menstruating, and giving birth; women getting blood tests, and getting examined in the gynecologist's chair; women

dying from massive hemorrhaging in the hospital, or having their can-
cerous insides taken out by surgery. Hayashi's attachment to the body
has led some critics to accuse her of "body-absolutism" (*karada zettai-
sei*) (Kinoshita et al. 1978), yet this is precisely where Hayashi seeks to
locate, or relocate, the memory of the atom bomb experience: into the
raw physicality, even animality, of women's bodies. By refusing to abandon the body and women's sexuality to theoretical exegesis, by reso-
lutely sticking to the most basic processes of life and death, she feels that
she can provide a much more realistic, and authentic, picture of the
reality of nuclear destruction.

Equally suggestively, however, against the background of massive
bodily destruction wrought by the blast itself and the more insidious,
extended process of injury by radiation, women's bodies take on an
added, symbolic quality: they embody the memory of destruction but
also the possibility of transcending it, through the creation of new life,
new memories—no matter how compromised, how fragile, this life
might seem to those who bear it. As Simone de Beauvoir put it, "The
female, to a greater extent than the male, is the prey of the species." In
Hayashi's vision, women's bodies expose them to greater risks in connection with radiation, but they also persist, stubbornly, irresistibly, stu-
pidly, in "preparing for fertilization every month" even if they have been
damaged by radiation. Woman's biological functions keep compelling
her toward life no matter how saturated with death her own body and
memories. It is significant in this regard that Hayashi ends her full-length
novel, which looks back on thirty years of existence as a hibakusha
woman, with a poetic depiction of the birth of her child; as she wrote,
"In all of the woman's life, it was in this moment, and on August 9, that
she had most keenly felt the meaning of what it meant to be alive" (*Naki
ga gotoki,* 399). The birth epitomizes a painful but ultimately hopeful
paradox: the coexistence of life and death, in hibakusha women's very
bodies.

Recent writings by other hibakusha women would seem to elaborate on
Hayashi's vision; they reject a disembodied notion of the mother myth,
but insist on women's procreative capacity as an opportunity for appre-
hending the atom bomb experience. As feminist activist Kanō Mikiyo
asserts:

> Women, more than men, have a direct relationship with life, and the manner
> in which human lives are linked. This is not due to a supposed mother

instinct, but simply due to the fact that women are the "sex that bears life."
. . . The mother instinct has been invented by men suffering from mother's
complex. . . .

Women, more than men, are able to endure suffering, and be stoical. This
is partly due to gender [*jiendā*], which was forced upon them by history and
society, but this is not all: it is also due to women's biological functions, of
bleeding every month, of giving birth. . . . In today's situation, in which ir-
responsible, selfish men are destroying the earth, women must actively teach
men about the value of self-control and stoicism.

Our bodies synthesize the egg and the sperm, and they can give life. This
simply happens to be women's function. I believe that each life . . . is a small
universe, self-sufficient in itself. Our bodies harbor little universes, and they
insure the continuity of life. . . . Women must awaken men to do the same.
Men, it is certain, will never become aware of it otherwise.

Now, fifty years after the war, when women tell about Hiroshima [*onna
ga Hiroshima o kataru to*], they are not merely telling about the damage they
received; in showing what was brought about by human arrogance and scientific triumphalism, they reclaim the meaning of Hiroshima in the history
of human life and the earth. Thanks to this, Hiroshima can be truly given a
place as a revelation [*keiji*] for the future. (Kanō 1996: 240, 243)

With Kanō's remarks, we have come full circle in this exploration of
women and the bomb: while female gender roles and biological functions are felt to make women more receptive (corporeally, morally, socially) to atom bomb suffering, they are also seen as endowed with the
potential to disrupt the destructive momentum initiated by the bomb.
The maternal body becomes the bearer of a biological teleology which
is felt uniquely (solely?) capable of confronting the apocalyptic impulse.
For all its essentialism, the maternal trope emerges as a powerful language to articulate atom bomb suffering, for hibakusha women and the
community at large.

CONCLUSIONS

The war of genders is wonderful for re-winning lost
wars because of its very certain results: men never lose,
women have to.
          Klaus Theweleit, "The Bomb's Womb"

In the register of the imaginary, the pain of the other
not only seeks for a home in language but also seeks a
home in the body.
          Veena Das

The example of hibakusha women would suggest that the links between women and the bomb have been deeply paradoxical, both for individual actors and the larger community. In fact, intriguing connections can be made between women and the bomb, not only at the level of individual experience and symbolic representation, but also with respect to historical changes in the perception of women hibakusha. This would bear out my contention and that of other scholars that women, and women's bodies, often become a kind of terrain where sociocultural and symbolic contradictions are played out (cf. Das 1996; Pandolfi 1991; Ramphele 1996).

First, at the level of women's individual experiences, we have seen that the cultural conflation between women and motherhood, and women and the body, transformed hibakusha women into undesirable others but also provided them with effective idioms to legitimize their passage to the public arena and contest the bomb. I have stressed that these effects were often played out at different stages in women's life cycles, and that most women were able to take advantage of the empowering effects of these gendered discourses only when they became mothers or reached middle age.

At the level of symbolic representation and collective images of hibakusha women, women seem to occupy an ambiguous status as dangerous others and redeemers of society. We have seen such contradictory images in the "atomic maiden," aligned with fatal bodily pollution and danger, and the "eternal mother," aligned with moral purity and self-sacrifice in the service of the community. These ambivalent images, which cast women simultaneously as destroyers and protectors of life, expressed in the interrelated processes of women's exclusion and idealization, reveal considerable social anxiety about the female body. They must also be placed in the larger context of the social and symbolic ambiguity surrounding women's roles in Japan, and particularly attitudes toward mothers, who seem to be endowed with quasi-mythical powers, capable of alternately destroying or healing the social fabric. Such beliefs seem to characterize many societies marked by a strong gender division (cf. Martin 1990). They appear most strikingly in times of social crisis or change, which brings me to the next point.

For Japanese society, the atom bomb was a deeply traumatic event, the epitome of a more general breakdown, and it heralded enormous changes in Japan's social and moral landscape, beginning with nearly ten years of Occupation (by the very power which had used the bombs). In this context, it is possible that larger social anxieties caused by these traumatic changes were projected onto women (particularly those who bore the visible marks of the bomb), who were seen as the most pathetic, if historically innocent, symbols of defeat and national inferiority. The intense contagion fears expressed vis-à-vis such women can be interpreted as a self-protective social mechanism in the face of the sociopolitical and cultural changes engendered by defeat and foreign occupation. This might partly explain why pollution fears were so strong in the late 1940s and early 1950s (when Japan was occupied), reflecting a more general preoccupation with the preservation of boundaries, both of individual bodies and of the national body politic (*kokutai*, "nation-body").

The dynamic relationship between images of women and historical change is also central to understanding why the generation of hibakusha women I am focusing on became active at the time it did. We have seen that these women's activities reached a peak in the late 1970s and 1980s. Though this timing partly reflected the coming of age of a generation of women bombed as teenagers, the period also coincided with a crisis of community, one which paradoxically facilitated women's passage to the public realm: Japanese society became increasingly disenchanted with the darker sides of economic success, including materialism, Westernization, and social alienation. Such disenchantment often focused on the breakdown of the family, for which mothers, supposed to be the traditional pillar of family stability, were held to be primarily responsible. Thus, images of the bad mother as the root of all evils, including new forms of adolescent pathologies and even illnesses "caused by mother" (*bogenbyō*), came to haunt the popular imagination, with an attendant nostalgia for more traditional women who knew the value of motherhood and femininity (Lock 1993; Jolivet 1997).

In this context, hibakusha women were able to cast themselves as repositories of an authentic morality, intensely concerned with the well-being and future of their children and families. Women's considerable success in local hibakusha politics, both as activists and storytellers, was also due to the social perception that hibakusha women had something to tell not only about the bomb but about the bonds of love, friendship, and solidarity that bind families and communities together. At a time when many Japanese were concerned about selfish mothers who were unable to properly educate and care for their children, or even unwilling to give birth at all, images of wise hibakusha mothers devoted to the well-being of their families acquired an uncommon appeal. It is thus

somehow ironic that women who were previously excluded as dangerous others were held up as truly good mothers two decades later.

This brings me to what I see to be the greatest limitation in the hibakusha women's movements: women still tend to endorse a basic
framework which places them in home and family, away from the outside world of politics and history. Though such notions must also be
seen in the context of a woman's culture of politics that is highly developed in Japanese society and almost invariably based on motherhood
and experiences in family and household (Vogel 1997), insistence on
domesticity, biological differences, and the separation between male and
female realms prevented many women from attempting to play a larger
role in the more official political movements.

To my knowledge, no hibakusha woman occupies a key position at
the levels where the actual decisions are made, either in the politics of
care or the politics of representation with respect to hibakusha. For
example, there are no hibakusha women in important positions in Hiroshima's municipal organ charged with the management of atom bomb
commemoration (the museum, the Peace Park, the annual ceremonies),
no women who are doctors or psychiatrists in the atom bomb hospitals,
and no women in the Welfare Ministry commission which makes the
ultimate decision on allocating benefits. The more official antinuclear
and hibakusha movements are invariably headed by men. To be sure,
this partly relates to a larger problem in Japanese politics, which bars
women from holding powerful positions: in 1992, Japan ranked 110th
out of 130 countries in the percentage of women in the legislature.

Yet to measure the potency of images of femininity and maternity in
connection with the bomb by means of statistical representation of
women hibakusha in official survivor organizations or the more formal
political landscape is surely misleading. It remains that women's dangerous bodies emerged as potent signifiers for atomic suffering and the
bomb's threat to this and future generations, no matter how much effort
was applied to silence these bodies, by medico-legal discourses or glorified representations of mothers. We should not limit this symbolism to
Japan. Now that more than half a century has passed since the bombings, and in an international context in which the bomb enjoys continued legitimization by the world's major powers, hibakusha women's
bodies take on an added symbolic significance, as repositories of a suffering that recedes increasingly into oblivion. Women's sense that they
and their children are stuck with the bomb stands more generally for

humanity's postnuclear condition. By casting themselves as the "bomb's womb," the resolute women in the study seek to embody, and re-member, bodies that have been, or are threatening to become, dis-membered, in the past, present and the future.

NOTES

I wish to thank the editors of this volume as well as the anonymous readers for advice on earlier drafts of this essay. I also thank members of the SSRC (especially Frank Kessel, Diana Colbert, and Julie Lake) for their support and assistance. My special thanks go to the hibakusha who shared their experiences with me, and my family and friends for providing nourishment and help.

1. Among the most serious aftereffects are cancers, blood disorders (includ-ing leukemia), and eye cataracts. A large group of "divergent conditions" are attributed to ionizing radiation—including keloids (hypertrophic burn scars), anemia, liver diseases, endocrine and skin disorders, impairment of central ner-vous system function, and general weakness. For a detailed summary of the bomb's physical effects, see Committee for the Compilation of Materials on Damage Caused by the Atomic Bombs in Hiroshima and Nagasaki, henceforth Committee 1981: 105–334.

2. The term *hibakusha* includes people who were in the cities at the time of the bombings, those who were contaminated by radioactive fallout in the days following the explosion, and people affected in utero. There are about 350,000 officially registered hibakusha in Japan today, but the actual number is probably much higher because many survivors never declared their victim status for fear of discrimination. Moreover, the statistics don't include the thousands of foreign victims (especially Koreans) who moved back to their home countries after the war. The same term (though written differently in Japanese characters) is applied increasingly to other radiation victims and survivors of nuclear fallout or power-plant accidents all over the world. It is in the same spirit that I use the term as it is, without italics.

3. The term *kataribe* dates back to preliterary Japan, when oral storytellers were employed by the imperial court for reciting genealogies and cosmologies. When literacy was introduced, *kataribe* became linked with the oral and per-formative transmission of lore and folklore, including counts and legends (cf. Treat 1995: 318). The term fell into disuse until the late 1970s, when it was resurrected in connection with hibakusha, to indicate oral testimonies as op-posed to written ones. I will elaborate on this issue in a later section.

4. Hayashi won critical acclaim with her now-famous account of the Na-gasaki bombing (*Matsuri no ba,* 1975; translated as "Ritual of Death" by Kyoko Selden), which earned the prestigious Akutagawa prize, but she has written many other narratives that have not been translated into Western languages. Her works have been the object of extensive literary analyses (Treat 1995; Ku-roko 1983).

5. The "Hiroshima Maidens" were a group of twenty-five young hibakusha women disfigured by keloids who were taken to the U.S. in 1954 for plastic

surgery, in an effort organized by Norman Cousins and Japanese church leaders (cf. Barker 1985; Chūjō 1984).

6. Though the term "atomic maiden" (*genbaku-otome*) was first applied to the famous "Hiroshima Maidens" (see note 5), it has become a set expression to designate young female hibakusha suffering from bomb-related keloid scars.

7. It is striking, in this regard, that the Japanese media and public never adopted the more neutral term employed by U.S. journalists, "Hiroshima maidens," but opted for the more dramatic "atomic maidens" to designate not only the members of the Hiroshima Maidens project but young female victims suffering from bomb-related keloid scars or illnesses more generally (cf. Kamisaka 1987).

8. I provide a more detailed discussion of the ABCC, and medical discourses on hibakusha, in Todeschini 1999b.

9. Quoted in "50 Years Later, Scope of A-bombs' Horror Is Unclear," *International Herald Tribune,* Monday, August 7, 1995.

10. The average benefit is about $300 a month, though the "special certification," which goes to less than one percent of the hibakusha population, is more than $1000 a month. For detailed summaries and recent amounts of these allowances, cf. Nihon-gensuibaku-higaisha-dantai-kyōgikai 1992 and Todeschini 1999a.

11. Robert Lifton describes it as a "lifelong preoccupation with [leukemia]—with blood counts and bodily complaints, particularly that of weakness, to the extent of greatly restricting their lives or even becoming bedridden" (1967: 119).

12. The Welfare Ministry's budget for these expenses totaled over 126 billion yen in 1990; for 1995, it has risen above 145.15 billion yen. The municipal government spent the equivalent of $229 million in 1990. These amounts include the costs for medical check-ups and facilities as well as financial provisions.

13. For similar processes in a different cultural context, see Veena Das's analysis of Bhopal victims: patients who couldn't provide documentary evidence in the form of hospital records were declared "uninjured" regardless of the state of their health, and transformed into "malingerers" (Das 1992: 163).

14. Yoneyama places this feminization in a larger historical and sociopolitical context, but she is more closely concerned with the way in which dominant representations come to be marked and distinguished exclusively as those of Japanese women. I focus here on the impact of this feminization on images of hibakusha women, to bring out the contrasts between these images and women's own narratives.

15. The expression is inspired from Ian Buruma, who devotes a chapter to "The Eternal Mother" in his book on Japanese popular culture (1984: 18–37).

16. Kazuo Chujo, "The World of Fiction," *Asahi Evening News* (English edition), August 22, 1985. There is no scientific evidence for greater incidence of leukemia among women; in fact, statistics reveal that the rate of leukemia in women is consistently lower than in men, for any age group (Committee 1981: 256).

17. For a more extensive analysis of these two films, see Todeschini 1996 and Todeschini 1999a.

18. A photograph of this striking monument is reproduced in Treat 1995: 228–29. The monument and its symbolism are also discussed in Yoneyama 1999: 194–96.

19. The 1980s also coincided with a turning point in the hibakusha movement; a growing number of hibakusha formed grassroots groups and became engaged in the transmission and memorialization of their experiences.

20. With respect to women's embodied memory of suffering in another cultural context, cf. Mariella Pandolfi's suggestive study on women's "language of the body" in southern Italy. She argues that women's suffering becomes inscribed in the body, and particularly blood (*sangue*) (1991).

21. This is the slogan that the group has adopted for its English-language publications.

REFERENCES CITED

ABBREVIATION

NGB: Kaku-sensō no kiken o uttaeru bungakusha no seimei no shōmeisha, eds. *Nihon no genbaku bungaku* (Japanese A-bomb literature). Tokyo: Horupu Shuppan, 1983.

Anders, Günther. 1952. *Der Mann auf der Brücke: Tagebuch aus Hiroshima und Nagasaki.* Reprinted in *Hiroshima ist Ueberall.* Munich: Beck Verlag, 1982, 1–189.
Barker, Rodney. 1985. *The Hiroshima Maidens: A Story of Courage, Compassion, and Survival.* New York: Viking.
Barnaby, Frank. 1977. "The Continuing Body Count at Hiroshima and Nagasaki." *Bulletin of Atomic Scientists,* December.
Braw, Monica. 1990. *The Atomic Bomb Suppressed.* New York: Sharpe.
Bruin, Janet, and Stephen Salaff. 1982. "'Never Again': The Organization of Women Atomic Bomb Victims in Osaka." *Feminist Studies* 7, no. 1: 5–18.
Buruma, Ian. 1984. *Behind the Mask: On Sexual Demons, Sacred Mothers, Transvestites, Gangsters, and Other Japanese Cultural Heroes.* New York: Pantheon Books.
Butler, Judith. 1990. *Gender Trouble: Feminism and the Subversion of Identity.* New York: Routledge.
———. 1993. *Bodies That Matter: On the Discursive Limits of "Sex."* New York: Routledge.
Chūjō, Kazuo. 1984. *Genbaku-otome* (Atomic Maidens). Bilingual edition: *Hiroshima Maidens: The Nuclear Holocaust Retold.* Tokyo: Asahi Shimbun.
Cohn, Carol. 1993. "War, Wimps and Women: Talking Gender and Thinking War." In *Gendering War Talk,* ed. Miriam Cooke and Angela Woollacott. Princeton: Princeton University Press.
Committee for the Compilation of Materials on Damage Caused by the Atomic Bombs in Hiroshima and Nagasaki, comp. and ed. 1981. *Hiroshima and Nagasaki—The Physical, Medical, and Social Effects of the Atomic Bombings.* New York: Basic Books.

Das, Veena. 1992. "Moral Orientations to Suffering: Legitimation, Power, and Healing." In *Health and Social Change in International Perspective,* ed. Lincoln C. Chen, Arthur Kleinman, Norma C. Ware. Cambridge, Mass.: Harvard Series on Population and International Health.

———. 1996. "Language and Body: Transactions in the Construction of Pain." *Daedalus* 125, no. 1: 67–91.

Desser, David. 1988. *Eros Plus Massacre: An Introduction to the Japanese New Wave Cinema.* Bloomington: Indiana University Press.

Douglas, Mary. 1966. *Purity and Danger: An Analysis of the Concepts of Pollution and Taboo.* Reprint, London: Routledge and Kegan Paul, 1984.

Esashi, Akiko. 1996. "Hajime ni" (Introduction). In *Onna ga Hiroshima o kataru* (Women Tell of Hiroshima), ed. Esashi Akiko, et al. Tokyo: Impakuto shuppan.

Fujita, Mariko. 1989. "'It's All Mother's Fault': Childcare and Socialization of Working Mothers in Japan." *Journal of Japanese Studies* 15, no. 1: 67–91.

Genbaku-hibakusha-sōdan-in no kai (Association of Counselors for Hibakusha), ed. 1983–1989. *Hibakusha to tomo ni ikiru* (Living with Hibakusha), nos. 2–10. Hiroshima: Genbaku-higaisha-sōdan-in no kai and YMCA.

Hayashi, Kyōko. 1967. "Kumoribi no kōshin" (Procession on a Cloudy Day). Reprint, NGB vol. 3: 9–28. Trans. as "Procession on a Cloudy Day" by Kashiwagi Hirosuke, *Bulletin of Concerned Asian Scholars* 25, no. 1 (1993): 58–69.

———. 1975. *Matsuri no ba* (The Place of Ceremony). Reprint, NGB vol. 3: 26–68. Trans. as "Ritual of Death" by Kyoko Selden, *The Japan Interpreter* 12 (1978): 54–93.

———. 1978a. "Kompirasan" (Mount Kompira). In *Gyaman Biidoro* (Cut Glass). Reprint, NGB vol. 3: 138–48.

———. 1978b. *Shōwa nijūnen no natsu* (Summer 1945). Reprint, NGB vol. 3: 258–76.

———. 1980. *Naki ga gotoki* (As Though Nothing). Reprint, NGB vol. 3: 277–403.

Héritier, Françoise. 1984. "Stérilité, Aridité, Sécheresse." In *Le Sens du mal: Anthropologie, histoire, sociologie de la maladie,* eds. Marc Augé and Claudine Herzlich. Paris: Editions des Archives Contemporaines.

Hiroshima josei-shi kenkyūkai, ed. 1987. *Hiroshima no onnatachi* (The Women of Hiroshima). Tokyo: Domesu Shuppan.

Jolivet, Muriel. 1997. *Japan: The Childless Society? The Crisis of Motherhood.* Trans. Anne-Marie Glasheen. London and New York: Routledge.

Kamisaka, Fuyuko. 1987. *Amami no genbaku otome* (The Atomic Maidens of Amami). Tokyo: Chūōkōron.

Kanō, Mikiyo. 1996. "Onna ga Hiroshima o kataru to iū koto" (What It Means When Women Tell of Hiroshima). In *Onna ga Hiroshima o kataru,* ed. Esashi Akiko, et al. Tokyo: Impakuto Shuppan.

Kinoshita, Junji, Takhashi Hideo, et al. 1978. "Miseisan no kako ni tsuite" (On the Unmastered Past). *Gunzō* 33, no. 3: 272–92.

Kleinman, Arthur. 1980. *Patients and Healers in the Context of Culture: An Exploration of the Borderland between Anthropology, Medicine and Psychiatry.* Berkeley: University of California Press.

———. 1991. "Suffering and Its Professional Transformation: Toward an Ethnography of Interpersonal Experience." *Culture, Medicine and Psychiatry* 15, no. 3: 275–301.

Kleinman, Arthur, and Joan Kleinman. 1996. "The Appeal of Experience; the Dismay of Images: Cultural Appropriations of Suffering in Our Times." *Daedalus* 125, no. 1: 1–23.

Kurihara, Sadako. 1975. *Hiroshima no gen-fūkei o idaite* (Embracing Hiroshima's Nuclear Landscape). Tokyo: Miraisha.

Kuroko, Kazuo. 1983. *Genbaku to kotoba* (The Atom Bomb and Language). Tokyo: San-ichi shobō.

Lebra, Takie Sugiyama. 1976. *Japanese Patterns of Behavior.* Honolulu: University of Hawaii Press.

———. 1984. *Japanese Women: Constraint and Fulfillment.* Honolulu: University of Hawaii Press.

Lifton, Robert Jay. 1967. *Death in Life: Survivors of Hiroshima.* New York: Random House.

Lindee, M. Susan. 1994. *Suffering Made Real: American Science and the Survivors of Hiroshima.* Chicago: University of Chicago Press.

Lock, Margaret. 1980. *East Asian Medicine in Urban Japan.* Berkeley: University of California Press.

———. 1987. "Protests of a Good Wife and Wise Mother: The Medicalization of Distress in Japan." In *Health, Illness, and Medical Care in Japan: Cultural and Social Dimensions,* ed. Edward Norbeck and Margaret Lock. Honolulu: University of Hawaii Press.

———. 1993. *Encounters with Aging: Mythologies of Menopause in Japan and North America.* Berkeley: University of California Press.

Mae, Michiko. 1997. "Die Frauenbewegungen im japanischen Modernisierungsprozess." In *Getrennte Welten, gemeinsame Moderne? Geschlechterverhältnisse in Japan,* ed. Ilse Lenz and Michiko Mae. Opladen: Verlag Beske und Buderich.

Marks, Elaine, and Isabelle de Courtivron, eds. 1980. *New French Feminisms: An Anthology.* New York: Schocken Books.

Marshall, Elliot. 1992. "Study Casts Doubts on Hiroshima Data." *Science* 258 (October): 349.

Martin, Joann. 1990. "Motherhood and Power: The Reproduction of a Women's Culture of Politics in a Mexican Community." *American Ethnologist* 17, no. 3: 470–90.

Miyata, Noboru. 1996. *Kegare no minzoku-shi—sabetsu no bunkateki yōin* (An Ethnological History of Pollution Beliefs: The Cultural Roots of Discrimination). Tokyo: Jinbu-shoin.

Nagoya, Misao. 1985. *Hiroshima haha no ki—Naoki no "shi" o ikite* (A Hiroshima Mother's Record: Experiencing Naoki's Death). Tokyo: Heiwa bunka.

Namihira, Emiko. 1978. "Pollution in the Folk Belief System." *Current Anthropology* 28, no. 4, Supplement: 65–74.

Natsubori, Masamoto. 1983. "Seichi no onna" (Woman of the Holy Ground). Reprint, NGB vol. 11: 311–26.

Nihon gensuibaku-higaisha-dantai-kyōgikai (Hidankyō: Japan Confederation of Atom and Hydrogen Bomb Sufferers). 1992. *Hibakusha-engohō: 20-mon, 20-tō* (The Hibakusha Relief Law: 20 Questions and Answers). Tokyo: Hidankyō.

Ōe, Kenzaburō. 1969. *Hiroshima Notes.* Trans. Toshi Yonezawa and David L. Swain. Tokyo: YMCA Press.

Ōnuki-Tierney, Emiko. 1984. *Illness and Culture in Contemporary Japan.* Cambridge: Cambridge University Press.

Ōta Yōko. 1952. "Hiroshima kara kita musume-tachi" (The Girls from Hiroshima). Reprint, NGB vol. 2: 281–86.

——. 1955. "Watashi no genbaku-shō" (My Atom Bomb Disease). Reprint, NGB vol. 2: 294–300.

Pandolfi, Mariella. 1991. *Itirenari delle emozioni: Corpo et identità femminile nel Sannio Campano.* Milan: Franco Angeli.

Ramphele, Mamphela. 1996. "Political Widowhood in South Africa: The Embodiment of Ambiguity." *Daedalus* 125, no. 1: 99–117.

Reynolds, David K. 1980. *The Quiet Therapies.* Honolulu: University of Hawaii Press.

Salzberg, Stephan. 1994. "In a Dark Corner: Care for the Mentally Ill in Japan." *Social Science Japan,* no. 2: 1–4.

Satō, Tadao. 1960. "Gensuibaku to Eiga" (Atom and Hydrogen Bombs and Film). *Bungaku* 28, no. 8: 823–30.

Scott, Joan W. 1988. *Gender: A Useful Category of Historical Analysis.* New York: Columbia University Press.

Theweleit, Klaus. 1993. "The Bomb's Womb and the Genders of War (War Goes On Preventing Women from Becoming the Mothers of Invention)." In *Gendering War Talk,* eds. Miriam Cooke and Angela Woollacott. Princeton: Princeton University Press.

Todeschini, Maya. 1996. "Death and the Maiden: Female Hibakusha as Cultural Heroines, and the Politics of A-bomb Memory." In *Hibakusha Cinema: Hiroshima, Nagasaki, and the Nuclear Image in Japanese Film,* ed. Mick Broderick. London and New York: Kegan Paul International.

——. 1999a. "Bittersweet Crossroads: Women of Hiroshima and Nagasaki." Ph.D. dissertation, Harvard University.

——. 1999b. "Illegitimate Sufferers: A-Bomb Victims, Medical Science, and the Government." *Daedalus* 128, no. 2: 67–95.

Treat, John Whittier. 1995. *Writing Ground Zero: Japanese Literature and the Atomic Bomb.* Chicago: University of Chicago Press.

Uno, Kathleen S. 1995. "The Origins of 'Good Wife, Wise Mother' in Modern Japan." In *Japanische Frauengeschichte(n),* eds. Erich Pauer and Regine Mathias. Marburg: Förderverein Marburger Japan-Reihe.

Vogel, Kerstin Katharina. 1997. "Von der Unmöglichkeit, Politikerin werden zu wollen und von der Möglichkeit, es zu sein." In *Getrennte Welten, Gemein-same Moderne? Geschlechterverhältnisse in Japan,* eds. Ilse Lenz and Michiko Mae. Opladen: Verlag Beske und Buderich.

Vogel, Suzanne H. 1978. "Professional Housewife: The Career of Urban Middle Class Japanese Women." *The Japan Interpreter,* 12, no. 1: 16–43.

Vyner, Henry M. 1983. "The Psychological Effects of Ionizing Radiation." *Culture, Medicine and Psychiatry* 7, no. 3: 241–61.

Yoneyama, Lisa. 1999. *Hiroshima Traces: Time, Space, and the Dialectics of Memory.* Berkeley: University of California Press.

Spirit Possessions and Avenging Ghosts

Stories of Supernatural Activity
as Narratives of Terror and Mechanisms
of Coping and Remembering

Sasanka Perera

INTRODUCTION

Between 1988 and 1991 southern Sri Lanka experienced the most intense period of political violence and terror in modern memory, with a violent insurrection led by Janata Vimukti Peramuna (JVP) and an equally violent counterinsurgency campaign by the state.[1] The violence was unprecedented not simply because of its scale but because of its incredible brutality and its relatively sudden appearance in the sociopolitical landscape. In addition to the hundreds of bodies that littered the countryside, this period also introduced altered meanings of words, such as *beeshanaya* (terror), *wadhakagaraya* (torture chamber), *issuwa* (kidnapped), and *athurudahanwoowo* (the disappeared), into the journalistic as well as popular discourse. Such words were not new to the Sinhala language, but they were now used with substantially altered meanings, specifically marked by the experiences of terror. This is what Taussig (1987), referring to a different site of violence, describes as a "culture of terror," which has its own vocabulary as well as its own overall structure. The primary aim of the insurgency as well as the counterinsurgency campaign was to physically and psychologically terrorize the population in order to exert total control over that population. As a methodology of governance, the process of terror in Sri Lanka was similar to those that emerged in Guatemala and other parts of South and Central America (Davis 1983, Brown 1985).

By mid-1991 the physical wave of violence had stopped as suddenly as it had started, even though most of the terror-generating apparatus—especially of the state—was still intact. This does not mean, however, that the actual experience of terror had ceased. For survivors of direct violence and the kith and kin of the disappeared and the dismembered, an undying sense of terror would continue, perhaps for generations. Memories of the murdered and the disappeared cannot be easily erased from the individual and collective conscience of the people.

In this chapter I attempt to deal with two interrelated issues. First, I would describe and place in perspective the appearance of certain narratives that describe two different categories of supernatural experiences: ghost stories and narratives of spirit possession. In a number of southern Sri Lankan villages where political violence was most acutely experienced, many people claim to have encountered ghosts. According to these narratives, the ghosts or spirits involved are those of people who perished during the terror (beeshanaya). Some of the narratives I am concerned with in this chapter were published in the Sinhala weekly Irida Lankadipa in the latter part of 1992. Others have been collected from the field. The narratives of spirit possession come from people who have directly or indirectly experienced terror. According to these narratives, certain people who have experienced terror are possessed by gods (deva, deviyo) and beings called yakku[2] capable of malevolent activities.

Second, I will attempt to understand the role these and other aspects of traditional spirit religion and ritual play in the context of postterror Sri Lanka, particularly as mechanisms for remembering the past as well as coping with the trauma resulting from extensive political violence—particularly in a context where secular systems of justice, coping, and healing are not available or where trust in these systems has considerably deteriorated. I will also place in context how certain aspects in the construction of the self vary between "normal" and altered states of consciousness (under spirit possession, for example), and how such variations are directly correlated to victims' perceptions of justice and revenge.

In examining the narratives I am concerned with, it is necessary to situate them within the sociopolitical and historical context in which they initially emerged, and to comprehend the manner in which the narrators and their audiences understand the narratives within that particular context. If the narratives are removed from the context in which they were constructed, their meanings and the manner of understanding tend to get altered.

In general, many of the narratives I am concerned with were constructed immediately after the wave of violence ebbed somewhat, and it is clear that the intense experience of violence structured the construction of these narratives. Some people, however, used specific linguistic forms and terms of reference that relocated the experience of acute violence from the recent to the remote past—a desperate attempt, perhaps, to distance from the present an intolerable experience in the immediate past. But the experience of terror was always present. While many did not want to discuss the experiences of that period in any great or specific detail in initial interviews, references to the period came up in all routine conversations. As Warren has documented for Guatemala, the period of terror was used as a temporal marker (Warren 1993). A similar situation existed in Sri Lanka, where references to the period of terror were formulated within a temporal idiom: before beeshanaya, during beeshanaya, beeshanaya may happen again.

The relative silence of the people who have suffered the most needs to be taken into account in all situations involving the study of human suffering. One reason for such silence is perhaps the victims' or survivors' fear that the immediate past may repeat itself. That is one reason why many are wary of strangers asking questions. It is difficult to trust strangers after living through a situation in which people could not even trust members of their own community: security forces compelled people to supply lists of others who were deemed to be antigovernment, while on its own side, the JVP insurgency also maintained death lists compiled with the help of local people. The collapse of trust may be graphically illustrated through the *goni billo,* masked men who assisted the army in identifying people who were arrested (later to be interrogated, tortured, and murdered). For the local community, the identity of the goni billo— were they friends, relatives, neighbors?—made everyday relations fraught with apprehension and distrust.

Another reason for this silence is victims' perception that those who have not experienced what they have simply would not understand or care. As Last observes, "there is a strangeness to others' experience, especially of violence, that has made many victims feel that their listeners simply cannot understand, and hence keep their silence and suffering to themselves" (Last 1999). In this particular context, "listeners" must be defined clearly. Not all listeners are confronted with such silence. As the

Sri Lankan experience amply demonstrates, in most situations victims
and survivors perceive themselves as an aggrieved community. Within
that community there is no silence: all are victims, survivors, and listeners. It is mostly outsiders—researchers, journalists, and the like—who
are confronted with silence.

Thus, while this phenomenon of relative silence is itself a legacy of
terror, there are indications that the change of government in August
1994 has changed the situation somewhat. More people seem willing to
talk. This enthusiasm, as well as expectations of justice, is clearly exemplified in the high rate of response and provision of information to
the government-appointed commissions investigating disappearances
and other cases of political violence. On the other hand, some were
always willing to talk, and others did so when they got to know outsiders
better. But it is unlikely that the overall experience of terror can ever be
documented in any real sense. This is a significant methodological problem that will always confront researchers. The narratives of anthropologists and sociologists describing the human experience of suffering will
always have gaps, in terms of experience, perception, and the nature of
pain itself.

However, the emergence of the types of narratives I have already
identified also seem to suggest that people wanted to remember that
period, or could not forget. This was particularly significant in a situation where justice in the secular and legal sense had not yet been
achieved, and the legal process ideally entrusted with delivering such
justice had itself been severely subverted.

RELIGIOUS BELIEFS AND TERROR: A COMPARATIVE PERSPECTIVE

Anthropologists working in societies of terror, particularly in Africa
and South America, have produced a substantial body of literature
demonstrating the different and significant roles certain aspects of religions (particularly those aspects dealing with spirits) in each society
have played in the implementation of terror, as well as in helping people cope with the experience of terror in the postviolence period. While
the manifestations of the processes of terror and the way religions operate in different societies will have obvious sociocultural variations,
the overall structure of these combined experiences would have certain
recognizable patterns. I would suggest that this is particularly true in

the context of popular religion as a mechanism of coping in most societies of terror.

Ranger (1985) and Lan (1985) suggest that spirit mediums played an important role during Zimbabwe's war of liberation. Ranger argues that these spirit mediums offered guerrillas a certain historical legitimacy in their struggle while offering the peasants some sense of control over these armed youth (Ranger 1985: 208). In his view, the spirit mediums in the Zimbabwean war of liberation effectively established the "moral economy of the war" (Ranger 1985: 212). Among other things, they offered protection to the "comrades" but advised that they should refrain from killing the innocent. One of Ranger's primary arguments is that the Zimbabwean war was essentially a peasant struggle undertaken to recover lost land (Ranger 1985: 182).

If we compare Ranger's and Lan's ethnographic details with those of the Sri Lankan situation, one of the fundamental differences is in the realm of influence. Sri Lankan spirit mediums and other aspects of popular religion do not appear to have played as influential a role as Lan and Ranger have argued for Zimbabwe. (Kriege and Bourdillon, however, have both argued that spirit mediums did not have as much influence in Zimbabwe as Lan and Ranger claim [Bourdillon 1987, Kriege 1988].)

At the moment, there is not much information from Sri Lanka suggesting that popular religion played a significant role in the violence itself, on the side of either the state or the insurgents. The only exceptions to this would be the *bodhi pooja* rituals conducted by Buddhist monks as well as some laity to bless soldiers engaged in counterinsurgent activities, and the charms that some individuals engaged in violence reportedly wore to ward off gunshots. Sri Lankan spirit mediums, however, played and continue to play a significant role in addressing questions as to what happened to the disappeared and suggesting ritual measures for assuring their safe return, or for making their afterlife more comfortable. Their influence, I would argue, is more pronounced in the overall structure of coping and possible healing.

Comparative ethnography from the Musami area of Zimbabwe suggests a similar role for traditional healers in the postwar context. Pamela Reynolds documents how people who had been involved in the violence of war, including killers, came to seek the help of healers. She points out that many spirit mediums and healers seem to have believed that their role was to protect and help, not to destroy (Reynolds 1990). Such a frame of mind would be particularly useful in offering help coping with trauma as well as guilt.

As Reynolds observes, "On returning from the war, men and women who had fought on either side visited healers to be cleansed," which she suggests was an important catharsis for both individuals and communities (Reynolds 1990: 12). The notion of cleansing has significant sociopsychological connotations in postviolence situations. But cleansing refers not merely to the process of helping a person cope with his or her feelings of guilt—particularly the guilt of having committed violence. It also refers to the cleansing of spaces marked by violent death in order to make them suitable for human habitation again. As Last points out, such polluted spaces have been spatially identified in parts of Nigeria: "There are no monuments, no cemeteries; no lists of the fallen dead. Indeed, there is in some areas a strong feeling that the soil remains polluted by the blood spilt and is still uncleansed; that the community is not yet put to rights" (Last 1999). As in Nigeria, Zimbabwe and elsewhere, such marked spaces of violence are located in many parts of Sri Lanka. In such places both spirit religion and mainstream Buddhism as well have provided ritual expertise of cleansing. Moreover, in many societies of terror there is a lingering belief that the spirits of the innocents who died remain disturbed because of the unnatural nature of their deaths.

The Sri Lankan material—both spirit possessions and ghost stories—constantly makes symbolic reference to the problem of conscience and guilt among both the survivors of terror and the perpetrators. There are particular kinds of ghosts that have been experienced only by soldiers. In other cases, the community's guilt over having been unable to save loved ones manifests itself in possessions as well as in encounters with ghosts. However, such manifestations of guilt are not peculiar to the Sri Lankan situation. Suarez-Orozco points out that many Central American refugees who escaped to the United States expressed a sense of "terror and guilt over selective survival in the face of often inexplicable death and suffering in their Central American homelands" (Suarez-Orozco 1990: 355, 357). Similarly, researchers into post-traumatic stress disorder have documented that many veterans of combat "experience guilt over surviving the war, and the loss of buddies who died" (Johnson, Feldman, Lubin, and Southwick 1995: 293). As this discussion progresses, I would like to raise the issue of whether it is in fact possible to consider perpetrators of violence (at least some of them) also as victims of the very violence and terror they helped to create. Such a question has to be raised, both in the context of available comparative ethnography from different parts of the world and of the Sri Lankan material.

Warren's work in Guatemala also demonstrates the importance of specific aspects of traditional religion as a mechanism of coping in societies of terror. She refers to a category of conventional interactive narratives that are usually narrated by individuals for extended families or larger groups. According to Warren, these narratives constitute Mayan histories, presenting things that were believed to have happened in specific localities. These stories are also "systematic expressions of Mayan cosmology and social ideology as practiced by past generations" (Warren 1993: 39–40). The narratives deal with a category of people who have the power to transform themselves into animal and human forms under certain conditions. These people are known as *rajav a'a'* (masters of the night), and their identities are usually unknown to the people, including close kin. In daytime they behave as normal people, and at night they transform themselves into animal forms with supernatural powers. They roam around at night causing various kinds of mischief (Warren 1993: 39–43).

On one level, these are narratives of secret lives. On another level, they are stories about doubt—particularly the doubts the community has about its own members. It is within these parameters that the popularity of the narratives makes sense, and can be located in the context of the period of *la violencia* in the 1970s and 1980s in Guatemala. What is also important is that the people in the region (San Andres) perceived that the narratives and the experiences of terror during *la violencia* were closely linked (Warren 1993: 45–46). According to Warren, the narratives describe a spirit world parallel to the existential dilemmas of the people (Warren 1993). These narratives as a mechanism of coping make more sense when one considers another significant legacy of *la violencia*. As is the case in many societies of terror, the Guatemalan situation imposed a period of relative silence on the victims and survivors, both during the terror and immediately thereafter. In such a context of silence, traditional narratives would have served as a mechanism to talk about these existential dilemmas, and in that sense cope with the problem itself.

THE NATURE OF TERROR AND THE REALITY OF POSTTERROR EXISTENCE

It would seem that terror has some basic similarities irrespective of where it happens, what specific forms it takes, or who experiences it.

One cannot lump together the collective human experience of suffering demarcated by political violence; but a cross-cultural comparison of terror would seem to indicate a basic similarity of experience. I would call this experience the "shadow of death."

Many of those who lived through the terror have had similar experiences, though they may have formulated them in different ways. The shadow of death must ideally be understood as a particular stage in a journey or path that any individual may have to go through at some point in time in a society of terror. The shadow of death is akin to a dark space in that journey or path, a space that, once one has entered, one may or may not exit. Thus the shadow of death has an element of uncertainty. Clearly, its outcome or persistence is the source of that uncertainty, an uncertainty that realizes the existential predicament of masses in societies under terror. Until one enters it and experiences it, one cannot be sure if the shadow of death will be a terminal stage for him, a stage in which he will cease to exist; even when he has experienced it, until the very last moment he cannot be sure of the continuity of life beyond the shadow of death. It is this uncertainty in the shadow of death which mystifies and terrifies. Even when death appears certain, the form it will take—through slow torture or bodily mutilation—remains ever uncertain.

Even if life continues beyond the shadow of death, many of the experiences of those who could not transcend the shadow will have been experienced by those who did. The only difference is that those who are lucky (or unlucky, depending on how one defines the situation) enough to escape will live to talk about their experiences, or be perpetually tormented by memories of those experiences. In any event, if terror is supposed to play a coercive function in a society, which is usually the case, the perpetrators of terror must ensure that some of their victims actually transcend the confines of the shadow of death. If not, some of the necessary foundations of a society in torment cannot be properly established. Experiences of terror, therefore, necessarily have to be transmitted to others, who as a result can be coerced into submission, making the task of torturers and political leaders easier.

In this regard, I would also like to draw attention to a comment Taussig makes in his book *Shamanism, Colonialism, and the Wild Man.* Describing a phenomenon he calls the "space of death" (which is essentially similar to what I have referred to as the shadow of death), Taussig makes the following observation:

> Yet this space of death is preeminently a space of transformation: through the experience of coming close to death there well may be a more vivid sense of life; through fear there can come not only a growth in self-consciousness but also fragmentation, then loss of self conforming to authority; or, as in the great journey of the Divine Comedy with its smoothly cadenced harmonies and catharsis, through evil, good. Lost in the dark woods, then journeying through the underworld with his pagan guide, Dante achieves paradise, but only after he has reached the lowermost point of evil . . . (Taussig 1987: 7)

This idea of transformation consequent to experiencing the space of death or shadow of death is of paramount importance. Such a transformation can only occur through terror itself. Unless a population is exposed to terror on unprecedented levels for unbearable periods of time, there is no compulsion to fight it. But once individuals are exposed to the shadow of death or terror in general, the next natural step may be resolution to fight the forces of terror. Once this stage is reached, the reign of terror has turned a full cycle: finally it has reached the stage where the population is determined to challenge the original perpetrators of terror, the individuals who first controlled the shadow of death. The tormented can now use against their tormentors tactics similar to those earlier used against them. In the context of Sri Lanka, however, the tormentors themselves suspended their activities at a certain point in time, thereby not allowing the cyclical process identified above to be completed. But Sri Lankans did experience the shadow of death, and they continue to experience its social and psychological repercussions.

In the context of the beeshanaya, norms and cultural paradigms governing ideas of "good" or "natural" death among the Sinhalas were completely shattered. Death and terror were abnormal to the point of being surreal. For example, consider the eighteen bloodstained heads found gazing at the water from the banks of a circular pond near the University of Peradeniya in central Sri Lanka. Scenes like this seriously undermined the realm of mundane social symbolism. Water is seen as a source of life in many sociocultural systems. The university is a source of knowledge, especially in the context of the modern world. The university and the pond in question are located near the city of Kandy, which is the location of the Temple of the Tooth, the most hallowed shrine of the island's Buddhist majority, and thus has special religious and spiritual significance to Sinhala Buddhists. But the severed heads completely contradicted the usual symbolism of the water, the university, and Buddhism. Does it make sense to the average Sinhala to see mass human destruction (heads separated from bodies) near a source of life (the pond) in the shadow of modern knowledge (the university) and a traditionally nonviolent religion (Buddhism, especially in the vicinity of the Temple of the Tooth)? Such a scene by its very brutal and surreal nature imposes an extra element of terror on those who witness it. It questions the moral values of the society, religious ethics, and the nature of reality itself.

This sense of surrealism is not restricted to the nature of terror or the ultimate product of terror. Surrealism can be a part of the manner in which individuals deal with terror. In this case victims, or the masses in a society, may attempt to construct an alternate reality and cling to it despite the illusory and fragile nature of that reality. When corpses were discovered in most parts of Sri Lanka between 1989 and 1991, many middle-class and upper-class Sri Lankans who were unable to leave the country constructed an alternate reality within the air-conditioned and refrigerated existence of suburbia. "Nothing's happening in Colombo," and "Kandy is quiet," many of them stated. Within the relatively secure environs of the cities there was some room to construct this alternate reality or to maneuver the truth to a more tolerable degree. Such alterations of reality continued until some of these individuals saw bodies floating in the scenic Kandy Lake, or half-burned corpses in Colombo streets. Such denial, while understandable, has nevertheless an element of surrealism to it, a detached strangeness. It is a mechanism that helps people cope with an intolerable situation.

Moreover, experiences of unnatural and violent death, and the narratives of experiences such as ghost stories, have to be understood in the context of a language of incompleteness, suddenness, darkness, and endless unfulfilled continuity (Perera 1995). Das observes that death is marked by its nonnarratability and its rupture of language: ordinary language becomes transformed in the process of making death narratable, especially when death has occurred in violation of cultural norms governing good death (Das 1990b: 345–46). In such cases survivors cannot easily resort to conventional means of mourning and expression of grief. When the body is lost, the normal expression of grief is further subverted in many cultures of terror. Ariel Dorfman's powerful novel *The Widows* also deals with this theme: a group of peasant women all claim a body that comes floating down the river as that of their disappeared husbands, sons, or brothers (Dorfman 1988).

In Sri Lanka, the initial manifestation of the disappearances was the unnatural nature of mutilated or burned bodies that were scattered around. People soon realized that every time they discovered bodies in places where they were not supposed to be, real people had disappeared from places where they should have been. Such bodies usually disappeared into mass graves or went up in smoke in mass pyres of tires. As in all societies of terror, in Sri Lanka the lack of a body created serious social problems other than that of grieving. Deep wounds are never really allowed to heal. No compensation can be paid to the kin of those who had disappeared until they can be legally defined as dead. Young wives of disappeared men are not legally recognized as widows, making it difficult for them to remarry and reconstruct their lives and frame their futures (Perera 1995).

Therefore it was no surprise that many people turned up to witness the rather amateurish excavation of mass graves in Suriyakande in southern Sri Lanka in January 1994, initiated by some members of the present government (though in the opposition at the time). The skeletal remains were dug up by people who were not competent in either forensic anthropology or forensic medicine. Neither were the diggers amateur archaeologists. The discoveries (skeletal remains and clothes) were simply collected into used fertilizer bags and taken to the local Magistrate Courts complex. Soon afterwards, an identification parade was organized in an attempt to identify the skeletons. Identification parades are usually held to identify persons, and perhaps corpses, but not skeletons or skulls. Those who allegedly identified the remains also had no training in what they were doing (Perera 1995).

In one case a woman "recognized" the sarong that belonged to her husband while two other women "recognized" the batik and Duro sarongs of their sons, all of whom had disappeared.[3] Two persons recognized skulls as those of their disappeared loved ones, one on the basis of a false tooth and the other on the basis of a protruding tooth (*Irida Lankadipa,* 11 January 1994). In the light of scientific inquiry or cold logic, of course, none of these identifications would have been possible. Sarongs are things people buy in stores, and very few of them have truly individual features. Similarly, without expert knowledge, specific training, or dental records to corroborate, firm identification of skulls is not possible (Perera 1995).

However, these are extraordinary circumstances where ordinary or scientific rationality is suspended. As far as survivors are concerned, what governs events such as these are emotional and social compulsions. Thus the usual "reality" is replaced by a powerful belief and the necessity to believe in *something* that constructs an alternate reality. In this

case that something is a symbol that people can identify with their disappeared loved ones—sarongs, protruding teeth, and so on.

Such symbolic indicators help to put an end to that terrible and traumatic uncertainty that only the kin of disappeared persons truly experience. Such symbols indicate that their loved ones are actually dead,
and thus the necessary rituals and funeral rites can commence. Merit
can be transferred in the hope that the disappeared—now "confirmed"
dead—will be less unfortunate in the other world. Even tombstones may
be erected. Because now they have come into possession of a body or
something that can symbolize a body (the skulls or sarongs), the process
of usual mourning denied to these people would finally be available to
them. In the long run, this is precisely what is necessary for all survivors
of political violence and the kin of the disappeared—a viable means of
coping. Thus, irrespective of criticisms by UNP (United National Party)
supporters and some sections of the print media, such excavations may
have to continue until such places are no longer found or until the survivors deem otherwise (Perera 1995). None of the kin of the victims
have criticized the excavation process. They are still awaiting a body.

What happened in Suriyakande, I suggest, has provided a few people
the long-overdue first stage in coping with endless grief and framing their
futures. Others still await their chance, though many may never get it.
In general, then, the construction of ghost stories and the experience of
possession as a narrative of terror and unnatural and violent death have
to be placed in a context where the normal processes of mourning as
well as law and order have completely failed.

GHOST STORIES AS VOICES OF THE DEAD

Narratives of experiences with spirits are hardly new phenomena among
the Sinhalas. They are components of the popular lore of the Sinhalas
as well as an integral part of spirit religion. For generations, women
have been warned of Kalu Kumaraya (the black prince), a malevolent
yaka who preys on solitary women loitering in lonely places after dark.
Similarly, men have been warned against the evil designs of Mohini, a
female yaka or *yakinni*. Such experiences, associated narratives, and the
proposed action to be taken in case of possession are part of the Sinhala
ritual discourse. As a result of negative karma, deceased relatives can be
reborn as *prethayo* and *kumbandayo*, defined as lowly spirit life forms
in the Sinhala Buddhist scheme of karma, demerit, and rebirth. As op-

posed to these traditional categories of spirits, the words *holman* and *avatara,* meaning ghosts, seem to be comparatively recent constructs.

If *yakku, pretha,* and *kumbanda* have specific technical connotations in ritual and religious discourse, *holman* and *avatara* do not. On one level they appear to be nonspecific references to apparitions of deceased individuals commonly and popularly used by those who are not ritual or religious experts. On another level, the two words refer to the idea of ghosts as borrowed from popular Christianity, which recognizes no categorization of the community of spirits as do Sinhala Buddhists. Irrespective of the terms' ultimate genesis in popular culture, as far as the contemporary usage is concerned, ghosts (holman and avatara will hereafter be referred to as ghosts) are mostly perceived as the wandering and *unhappy* spirits of dead relatives or neighbors, who more likely than not have died unnatural deaths. Ghosts also tend to be considered in popular belief as apparitions of particularly unpleasant people. In this sense, it is understandable that the spirits associated with terror and violent death are ghosts. If death was unreal, surreal, or scary, then the use of similar means to narrate such experiences makes sense.

The ghost stories I am concerned with have clearly identifiable structural features insofar as their narrative format is concerned:

(1) Some narratives are incident-specific, which means that ghosts are specifically associated with a certain incident that the community is acutely aware of (like the beheading of a particular youth).

(2) Some are area-specific, which means that the purported supernatural activities are associated with areas where violent deaths are known to have occurred, such as an area where bodies were burned on a pyre of tires.

(3) Some are both incident- and area-specific.

(4) Some are general narratives which reflect the general turmoil of the period.

(5) Most narratives combine two interrelated narrative components. The primary narrative directly describes the reported supernatural activity. The secondary narrative is a brief commentary explaining the sociopolitical and personal context within which the supernatural incident is located. Secondary narratives usually precede primary narratives and are generally used if the intended audience contains outsiders.

According to the first narrative in my collection, many people have reportedly seen the figure of a white-clad weeping woman walking along
the street at night. If a solitary individual happens to run into her, she
utters the following words before disappearing: "I am going to see my
two sons." On certain days at midnight the voice of a woman lamenting
for her sons (*ane mage puthune*) can be heard along the street (*Irida
Lankadipa,* 1 Nov. 1992).

The secondary narrative associated with the above attempts to place
it in the context of an actual incident. Two sons from a single family
living nearby were arrested one day. Their mother went to the place
where they were detained and pleaded with the officers to let her see
them; but by then both of them had been killed. During the whole day
the mother cried bitterly, rolling on the ground and cursing the military
officers who killed them. Her lamentations and cursing could not be
stopped. She used to do this every day from dawn to dusk. Unable to
put a stop to this, the military personnel eventually killed her (*Irida
Lankadipa,* 1 Nov. 1992).

According to the second narrative, some people saw the headless
body of a young man walking along the street crying "Mother, Mother"
at midnight. He was followed by a well-built monkey (*Irida Lankadipa,*
1 Nov. 1992). I suggest that the function of these narratives and many
of those to follow is to construct a continual set of experiences parallel
to the traumatic experiences of the immediate past. Tormented individuals searching for their loved ones were and are a common experience
in the south. These narratives are also reflections of the distraught conscience of the community. Until the community is able to come to grips
with the experiences of the past, its collective conscience would remain
tormented and unhealed. It must be borne in mind that in the secondary
narratives of most ghost stories, people stress that the reason for the
existence of these apparitions is the violent nature of the deaths in their
community: "The ghost of a young woman who was killed [after a
group of unidentified persons slashed her throat] haunts her former
home, banging on the doors and windows. Her voice can be heard when
her mother worships the Buddha. When she observes *sil* in the temple,
the voice of the dead woman calls out 'Mother'" (*Irida Lankadipa,* 1
Nov. 1992). The mother of the dead woman is convinced that her
daughter is haunting her home because she died a terrible death, and is
reborn as a low/bad life form (*naraka athmaya*). The mother laments
that she cannot transfer to her daughter the merit she so urgently requires because she (the mother) cannot afford an alms-giving. This sec-

ondary narrative is an example of the role certain aspects of Buddhist ritual can play as an intermediate phase in the process of healing. Many people have traditionally believed that merit transferrals can alleviate the suffering of the dead in the afterworld. Such mechanisms are commonly utilized in the case of confirmed violent and sudden deaths, and to a lesser extent in disappearances, which in the long run would seem to tend to lessen the burden in the conscience of most bereaved families.

The next narrative in my collection describes a community of ghosts at sea. I would hasten to note here that most Sri Lankan ghosts I have heard of are very much based on land, and in that sense this narrative as a ghost story is unusual:

> A little bit offshore there is wonderful rock formation. Four or five people can hide on the side of it. One day when a group of fishermen were fishing in this vicinity they heard some terrible sounds from atop the rock. Then suddenly a well-built man wearing a black jacket and a hat appeared. Making a loud noise, he jumped into the sea. After a while the fishermen saw the man climb onto the rock again. Then another man appeared and both of them jumped into the sea. The fishermen returned home and consumed a fish curry made out of the fish they had caught. That night all three started purging. Their excrement was black. Other fishermen have seen groups of strangers sailing towards them in the darkness who disappear before contact can be made. (*Irida Lankadipa,* 8 Nov. 1992)

The secondary narrative associated with the above notes that four people who took refuge on this particular rock to avoid the military had been shot, and jumped or fell into the sea. They were all killed. Others are reported to have hidden in the sea masquerading as fishermen. Moreover, it notes that during the terror many corpses washed ashore along the coast. The color black, so prominent in the narrative, is associated with death and mourning in contemporary Sinhala society, and the imagery of the tale is relevant to the experiences of the immediate past: the ghosts were sighted at night; they wore dark clothes; the witnesses got sick the following night; the excrement of the sick was black; and most violent deaths and disappearances of the immediate past occurred under cover of the night. In a sense this is a re-creation of recent experiences; but it is also more.

It should be noted that the ghosts are supposed to be those of people who hid in the ocean. People do not usually hide in the ocean. A source of danger, death, and mystery as well as sustenance, it is a space over which humans have little control. The sea is situated beyond the immediate space of human habitat and civilization. Thus the mere suggestion that humans had to seek refuge in a space they had little control over, and beyond the safety of their own social environment, is a strong statement of the threatening nature of that social space and civilization itself.

Moreover, all three fishermen became violently sick after consuming the fish they had caught. Traditionally, Sinhalas who see a ghost, a yaka, or any other potentially malevolent being are more likely than not to fall sick. Many witnesses of ghosts in this southern Sri Lankan village seem to get sick. As far as conventions are concerned this is only to be expected. But these are not conventional ghosts. In this sense I believe that such sicknesses, which are never long-lasting, are symptomatic of the inability of individuals to come to grips with a tormented past where justice failed to prevail. More important, I believe these sicknesses to be expressions of personal guilt. Despite being alive, these individuals could not prevent the deaths of many in their community.

Moreover, they have not been able to seek justice or spiritual salvation on behalf of those of their community who were violently killed. But the sickness in the case of this narrative goes further than this general explanation. The fishermen fell sick specifically as a result of eating the fish, not simply of seeing ghosts. Note that the secondary narrative refers to corpses being washed ashore. The fishermen clearly ate tainted fish, fish that had fed upon humans, possibly members of their own community. I believe that the revulsion at possible indirect cannibalism would have been in the collective consciences of communities such as these. After all, during the terror the fish market was known to have collapsed precisely for this reason, until collective efforts, the necessities of nutrition, and Sinhala ingenuity managed to come to grips with the situation.

Other narratives also clearly indicate the potential for violent but brief sicknesses consequent to seeing ghosts. In one case a young man suffered from severe shock after he saw a huge black dog standing on its hind legs as if to pounce on him. It had vicious teeth, and its eyes shone like balls of fire (*Irida Lankadipa*, 15 Nov. 1992). Significantly, this fearsome ghost or apparition bore no human resemblance, but it was seen at the precise spot where the corpses of four young men had been set on fire in a pyre of burning tires. We see again that spaces which had been specifically demarcated by violent death are among the most favored haunts of ghosts. This formulation is significant in that such narratives assure that spaces of violent death remain in the conscience of the community.

Similarly, a public library and a government-owned rest-house in Uva Province, as well as a building owned by the Electricity Board in a village off Colombo, have been identified in the local popular discourse as spaces where supernatural activity took place. As the physical wave of violence decreased and many of these places became functional again, people began to complain of ghosts and supernatural interventions within the buildings. Students who visited the public library complained that their books were grabbed from their hands and thrown away by unseen hands, and that they heard screams in the evenings. Those who worked at the rest-house also complained of screams at night. The night watchman at the Electricity Board building refused to work at this particular location because he heard screams emanating from within the building.

In local narratives of violence and terror, all these places had been marked as spaces where torture and violent death took place. According to these narratives, the library was used as a torture chamber while the rest-house was used as both a hostel for death squad members and a torture chamber. The Electricity Board building is specifically identified as the area's most notorious torture chamber. Many people from the communities concerned probably experienced torture and died in these places. It would not have been easy to start work in such places as if nothing had happened. Work in these three places resumed on a regular basis only after *pirit* ceremonies were organized, utilizing state funds but with public participation. Etymologically speaking, *pirit* means "protection." What usually happens in a pirit ceremony is the consecration of water and thread for protective purposes. The thread can then be worn around people's wrists and the water sprinkled on the body or around houses, offering protection.

As Gombrich and Obeyesekere have pointed out, pirit has traditionally been a public ceremony, normally recited by a group of monks (Gombrich and Obeyesekere 1988: 394). What is more important, perhaps, is the public perception of how pirit ceremonies are supposed to work. One perception (in the view of Gombrich and Obeyesekere the most sophisticated and orthodox) is that the pirit "texts are in fact sermons being preached to convert malign spirits to Buddhist ethics so that they will give up doing harm" (1988: 394). Yet another perception is that the merit gained by participants in the pirit ceremony is offered to the gods, who in turn offer their protection (1988: 394). In this context, the selection of pirit as the means to "purify" these public spaces "polluted" by unnatural and violent death as well as by torture makes a lot of sense to Sinhala Buddhists. The pirit ceremonies, along with other, associated rituals that were organized, were supposed to bless these places, ward off evil spirits, protect those who had to work in these places, and transfer merit to people who had been tortured and killed in these places. When ghost stories marked these places as spaces where violent death and torture took place, essential services that had to be carried out from such places could commence only after a minimum of ritual requirements were met. The rituals also allowed some element of collective coping and healing for the communities concerned, particularly for those who could not afford individual rituals. I would also suggest that the state sponsorship of these rituals was indicative of the state's responsibility for some of these deaths. In fact, some individuals made this connection in interviews.

In the narratives I have considered so far, all the major players have been the ghosts of people who were killed during the terror, and ordinary villagers who were sometimes confronted by these ghosts. However, there is a special category of narrative in which those who experience ghosts or apparitions happen to be members of the security forces. Let us consider two examples I have in my collection. (I hasten to note that security personnel in most cases were not members of the community, and that on many occasions they were the primary source of terror and violent death.) The first narrative in this category deals with a group of soldiers who were patrolling the streets one night. On seven occasions that night they were showered with stones that never actually hit them. The first stone-throwing occurred at a place where the head of a disappeared youth had been found. The last occurred in the vicinity of the house where the beheaded youth once lived. Despite having weapons the soldiers were terrified, and they could not find any human culprits around. The next morning three of the five soldiers were down with fever (*Irida Lankadipa*, 1 Nov. 1992).

Note that the stones were thrown at patrolling troops and never at ordinary villagers. This I believe is indicative of the community's ability to identify the primary culprits of their problems and their associated desire to punish them. But the stones themselves did not actually hit the soldiers, and their weapons obviously were of no use. This I suggest reflects the community's wish for "proper" justice, as opposed to the wild justice meted out to them by soldiers and death squads. The act of stone-throwing was a mere reflection of the need for justice, not justice itself. The nonutility of weapons is indicative of the fact that when the

time comes guns cannot help the culprits, a notion closely associated
with Buddhist karmic principles. Getting frightened and falling sick is
clearly indicative of what the community construed as the guilt of soldiers, and by extension of the state.

According to the second narrative, an army officer arrested a youth
wanted for subversive activities and placed him under detention in the
nearest army camp. That night when he was returning to camp from
the nearby city of Matara he saw the same youth standing by the road
covering his head with his hands. No one else in the officer's jeep saw
him. On his return to camp he found out that the youth had been shot
dead attempting to escape a while earlier. The narrative supposedly emanated from the officer himself, which I believe is a reflection of the
officer's state of mind, his guilt. Many youths who were arrested never
returned home, joining thousands of others who had simply disappeared—forever. As in the Zimbabwean material presented earlier, guilt
over the fates of the disappeared surely would have affected some officers and soldiers.

EXPERIENCES OF POSSESSION
IN SRI LANKA AFTER THE TERROR

THE STRUCTURE AND NATURE
OF POSSESSIONS IN SINHALA SPIRIT RELIGION

As mentioned earlier, the idea and experience of possession is an integral
part of Sinhala spirit religion and the general experience of altered states
of consciousness. As a prelude to the discussion that is to follow, I would
like to make certain fundamental clarifications with regard to the hierarchy of spirit forms[4] in Sinhala spirit religion as well as the entire notion
of possession as perceived by the Sinhalas. Scott suggests—quite correctly—that the metaphor of possession has to be specifically qualified
in order to make it relevant to the Sinhala body:

> This body offers a conception of spatial organism that cannot be assimilated
> to the possessed body of Christian and psychoanalytic discourse. The Sinhala
> body is an organism constituted by energies and normalized by an ethic of
> composure; it is differentiated not by a luminous inner essence radically
> marked off from an exterior materiality, but systematically by the regulation
> of levels and flows. It is a body vulnerable not to invasion as though it were
> a "house" or a "temple" whose owner could be usurped, but to reconstitu-
> tion of its elements precipitated by contact with other energies. Malevolence
> and benevolence are two such energies. (Scott 1994: 58)

It must be noted, then, that throughout this discussion, the concept of possession is used and understood in the manner outlined above. On the other hand, in terms of power, authority, knowledge, and virtue, all beings are considered to be subordinate to the Buddha. As such, he is at the apex of this hierarchy. Below the Buddha are the gods or deities (*deviyo, devivaru*). The Sinhala Buddhist pantheon of gods is quite extensive, and I do not intend to go into details of this pantheon here. Below the pantheon of gods are humans. It is below the level of humanity that one may find malevolent beings. At the top of this pantheon of malevolent beings are the yakku. As Scott has observed, "*Yakku* are *yakku* not because of some inherent 'evil,' but because of their bad *karma*. It is in their nature as *yakku* to harm without cause, and at their malevolent whim, they continue to accumulate bad *karma*" (Scott 1994: 21). Below the yakku are the prethayo. They are the dissatisfied spirits of dead relatives whose vocation is to harass the living and cause misfortune (*dosa*). As with deviyo and yakku, there are numerous kinds of prethayo.

According to Sinhala perception, possession as such is not considered a problem that needs to be dealt with. This differs from certain other cases of possession recorded in the anthropological literature. For instance, according to Boddy's description of the Zar cult in northern Sudan, "Zar influence, being possessed of and by a spirit, is considered an affliction and expressed as illness" (Boddy 1989: 133). In the Sinhala case, whether the possession is considered an illness or not depends on the nature of the spirit form involved. Sinhalas believe that yakku as well as spirits of dead relatives can possess humans. In addition, they believe that gods or deviyo can also possess humans.

Sinhalas refer to possession by yakku as *yaka vehila,* which literally means "covered by a yaka." They may also refer to the same condition as *distiya vehila* ("covered by the distiya") or *distiya lebila* ("has received the distiya"). If the possession involves a deva, the phrase used to describe the situation is usually *deviyo arudha wela* ("the god has possessed [the person]"), but they may use the concept of *distiya* to refer to this situation as well.

It is primarily through distiya that yakku operate in the Sinhala universe. Yakku as well as deviyo influence humans through their glances (*belma*). The Sinhalas refer to this as *belma helanawa,* the focusing of the eyesight. Scott suggests that the best way to understand the distiya of yakku (*yaksa distiya*) is to perceive it as the "malign *energy* or essence of the eyesight of *yakku*" (Scott 1994: 48). If a yaka has cast his look and his distiya has entered the body of a person, that person is considered to be possessed. Such possession involving clearly malevolent beings such as yakku is perceived as an affliction and is dealt with accordingly. Such malign glances have to be neutralized or expelled from a person's body by performing a form of ritual known as *yakthovil*. Offerings given and the details of the yakthovil vary in keeping with the nature of the specific yakku concerned.

It is important to remember that a distiya is not always a malign force; deviyo also operate through distiya. This is known as *deva distiya* and essentially refers to the beneficial essence or energy of the eyesight of a god. In cases of possession involving deva distiya, there are no overtones of ailment or affliction; rather, the distiya is considered a source of power and healing. Such possessions can occur at particular points in time or at regular intervals. Under these circumstances, as agents of deviyo, the possessed individuals are in a position to offer certain favors and services to the community. Such favors will be considered the favors granted by the particular deva or deviyo concerned.

On the other hand, possession by a certain category of ambiguous being is not perceived as an ailment. Their disti is not seen as merely malevolent but as powerful. That power, however, is capable of both malevolent and beneficial activities. For instance, Suniyam has features of both a yaka and deva. He is referred to using both words, and people seek his intervention for both malevolent and nonmalevolent purposes. Possession by his disti is not perceived as an ailment. Similarly, Kali is identified clearly as a *yakinni*, a female yaka, but according to Sinhala Buddhist tradition she is one of the few yakku saved from their malevolent and destructive practices as a result of Buddha's personal intervention (Obeyesekere 1991: 98–106). As such, her disti is not perceived as in need of neutralization.

What I propose to do in this discussion is to place conventional experiences such as possession, and the narratives associated with such experiences, in the context of terror, or more specifically in the context of coping with the realities of postterror society. I offer two examples: the first a brief report from a newspaper, the second an extensive case study from the Northwestern Province that I compiled in September 1993. Many similar cases have been recorded from around Sri Lanka and have become part of the popular discourse on terror.

The first example I would like to discuss belongs to the first type of possession. In this narrative, the sister of a disappeared person is said to have been possessed by her brother. Technically, for such a possession to take place the individual whose disti possesses the sister has to be dead. According to the narrative, when the ritual expert exorcised the woman she spoke in the voice of her brother and stated that he had been murdered after torture. This narrative format is an important construct in that it devises a mechanism that could, to a certain extent, help survivors of terror come to terms with the disappeared.

Through this narrative, the fate of the disappeared brother becomes known. Such a state of mind is a precondition for the process of reconstructing the lives and futures of survivors. In a sense, such narratives are structurally similar to seeking advice from spirit mediums regarding the fates of the disappeared. Such advice usually tends to suggest that the disappeared have died and that certain rituals need to be undertaken to alleviate their suffering in the other world. Once their fate is known and the necessary ritual obligations are fulfilled, an important requirement of the individual healing process would be established.

DENIED JUSTICE AND POSSESSION:
THE CASE OF SUMANAPALA AND HIS DAUGHTER

Sumanapala[5] lives in an interior village in the Northwestern Province. His wife and three of his four children (two sons and one daughter) were killed by a government death squad in September 1989. As the physical wave of violence subsided, Sumanapala began to experience possessions. He claims that he is alternatively possessed by six deities: Suniyam, Ratna Kalukambili, Waduru Kali, Sohon Kali, Riri Kali, and Badra Kali. Except the first two, all are different manifestations of Kali. His eldest daughter, the one who survived, also gets possessed (by Pattini). The manner of the killings as well as the structure of the possessions and the various strands of narratives of explanation have to be considered as a cluster of collective ideas if we are to understand the function of these possessions.

According to Sumanapala and other villagers, the reason for the massacre was his suspected involvement in JVP activities. Sumanapala claims that he was not involved in JVP activity even though the movement had forced him to put up posters near the small kiosk he owned in the village. Every morning these posters were removed by the police, and each night the JVP provided him with new posters and gave him strict orders to put them up. Like many people at the time, Sumanapala was in an unenviable situation. He could not disobey JVP orders or get caught by the police. In either eventuality, since this was the height of both the insurgency and the state's counterinsurgency campaign, he would have had to face dire consequences, if not death. Sumanapala contacted a village elder who had access to politicians from the local UNP (the ruling party at the time) as well as the military and explained his plight. The elder contacted a relative who was a junior military officer attached to a military detachment nearby and asked him for advice. According to Sumanapala's narrative, the officer consulted his commanding officer and offered him the following advice: "We understand your problem. We have no information or orders to take you in. But do not go to the police station now. The ASP's [Assistant Superintendent of Police] law is too harsh at the moment. Even if you go and tell him the truth you will be killed and burned. It would not matter whether you are innocent or not. So do your best to stay alive until the terror subsides."

It was this advice that saved Sumanapala's life. He began to sleep atop a large rock outside the village surrounded by scrub jungle. The night his family was murdered he was asleep at this location, having left his elder daughter at another house since it was too dark (and thus unsafe) to take her home. Immediately after the massacre Sumanapala surrendered to the military, and was released from detention after three months consequent to investigations which revealed that he was not associated with the JVP. During the terror, six people from Sumanapala's village were killed by the military, police, or "unidentified gunmen," while eleven have disappeared.

Even though Sumanapala does not claim that the killers were agents of the state, he observes that the JVP would not have harmed him or his family, since "I did everything they asked me to do." In general conversation both he and his daughter seem to have come to terms with their loss. But such a frame of mind is not the ideal outcome given the gravity of the crime committed by agents of the state and the relatively few positive interventions of the secular legal and social welfare apparatus. The state has estimated that it would cost Sumanapala twenty-one thousand rupees to rebuild his destroyed house. Out of this, fourteen thousand rupees has already been paid in installments of two to four thousand. But like the rebuilding of their lives, the rebuilding of their house has been difficult. The monetary compensation paid has been grossly inadequate. The remainder of the money is scheduled to be paid only to build the roof, which (like many aspects of their life) is nowhere near completion.

However, no compensation has been paid for the loss of the four lives. For such compensation to be paid certain preconditions have to be met, including a coroner's report, magistrate's report, and a police report describing the manner of death. All those who have received compensation have had documentation from the police with statements such as "shot and killed and the bodies set on fire by unknown persons." Initial indications are that very few people have received such compensation. Many who did had suffered at the hands of the JVP, not the state or UNP agents.[6]

According to Sumanapala's daughter he was not compensated for the loss of his family because of a technical problem in the initial police report:

> When the police asked my father what happened, he got scared and told them that he did not know what had happened. He told them that when he went to the house in the morning the whole place had been burned down. So the police provided a certificate stating that the death was caused by burning. When I submitted that to the office [Social Services and Rehabilitation Dept.] the person there suggested that they [his family] probably set fire to the house themselves and committed suicide. After that I did not pursue the matter. Besides, we can never enjoy ourselves with the money paid on behalf of murdered people. But if we receive this money we can offer some alms to the monks and transfer merit to them so that they will not face this kind of fate in their next life.

Because of this state of affairs Sumanapala has been unable to do the very least an average Buddhist can do to alleviate the negative karma of deceased kin: offer some alms to the monks in the village temple. Such a ritual process is an important aspect of the overall process of healing and coping. Despite the almost total failure of the state in helping Sumanapala and his daughter cope with the trauma of their past and frame and reorganize their future, ideas of revenge and expectations of justice do not emerge in their narratives. Instead they have framed their loss within a karmic paradigm and have blamed the victims themselves for their plight.

I would suggest that blaming the victims is also a mechanism of coping. In this context what is important initially is the nature of the killing. The four victims were shot inside their home, and the house was set on fire. Sumanapala claims that the reason for their fate was a crime the four victims had committed in their previous lives. His narrative of explanation is as follows:

> They were born as members of the same family in the previous life as well. One morning [in that life] while the four of them were attempting to cross a

stream they saw a nest with three little birds. They started throwing stones at the nest and started to torture them. The mother bird also stayed in the nest attempting to protect the little ones. Later, the entire nest with the four birds inside was set on fire. In this life they paid for their earlier sin. When you commit that kind of crime sometime in *samsara* you will encounter enemies, and they will have to pay for their crimes in one life or another.

According to Sumanapala the information regarding the victims' karmic past has been provided by Pattini through the medium of the daughter. In this case, as well as in some others that I have recorded, there is a clear structural similarity between the specific incidents of terror and sudden death and the narratives of the karmic past. The father and daughter also claim that Pattini has provided other information relevant to the killings. Later in his narrative, Sumanapala says, "Pattini *meniyo* has told us that three people in the village were responsible for this crime. They are the people who have sent petitions to the police falsely implicating me. Meniyo [mother, a reference to Pattini] has identified them by name. But she has advised us not to get angry or quarrel with these people. One of them has already died in an accident." Pattini's final advice is significant when we place this narrative in the context of a society where the apparatus of law and order in the secular world has been completely subverted. In fact, the police and the military, which are integral components of that law and order system, have been directly responsible for many of the violent deaths, disappearances, and experiences of torture. In such a context many people have lost faith in the secular legal system and do not expect justice to be served in the legal sense. Many also do not have the physical, mental, or financial means to seek such justice through the secular legal system. A lone fight, as some have attempted, could lead to their own elimination. Thus many people in such situations seem to believe in divine or demonic intervention as the only hope for justice or revenge available to them. As far as Sumanapala is concerned, one of the culprits is already dead and the others will be taken care of by Pattini or any of the other deities who possess him.

The above component of the narrative indicates another significant aspect of the overall experience of terror. That is, the terror was not merely an external force or intervention imposed on the local people by strangers who were agents of the state or the JVP. According to Sumanapala, Pattini has informed him that people within the village had falsely implicated him. Sumanapala, who owned a kiosk and some cattle, was relatively prosperous by the standards of this particular village; such a

situation could easily lead to jealousy, and an unsigned letter to the
military or police. Such incidents occurred in the context of the 1971
JVP insurrection as well.[7] Thus on many occasions the terror was locally
constructed or instigated and secondarily carried out by external forces.

Although an expectation of justice and revenge is absent from the
explanations of Sumanapala and his daughter and they seem to have
accepted their fate, all the deities that possess Sumanapala are malevolent deities closely associated with revenge and destruction. The manifestations and functions of Kali are well known. Suniyam is a former
yakka whose position has been upgraded to that of a deity over the last
few decades, particularly in urban areas. This and similar changes in the
pantheon have come about in the context of rapid socioeconomic and
political upheavals and transformations experienced by those in the cities, particularly those of low-income groups (Kapferer 1988, Gombrich
and Obeyesekere 1988). Ratna Kalukambili, who is usually known as
Kalukambili, is sometimes associated with Suniyam as part of his en-
tourage. He is one of a group of seven yakku whose intervention many
people seek when they want to punish enemies or to seek revenge or are
denied justice. However, it must be noted that people seek their intervention for other, more routine purposes as well.

Pattini, who possesses the daughter, is also closely associated with
justice and revenge. According to one myth associated with Pattini, the
original fire and drought in the human world were caused by her anger.
Moreover, in mythic times Pattini is believed to have set fire to the city
of Madurai, in which the evil were destroyed and the good were spared
(Obeyesekere 1984: 43). One of the consistent themes that emerged under possession was revenge. For instance, Pattini (through the voice of
the young woman) repeated the following words consistently during the
half-hour she was possessed: "This little girl has suffered much. I know
who the culprits are. They will all be punished once this girl is mature
enough to wield all the powers of Pattini." Thus, I would suggest that
the whole phenomenon of possession in this case manifested itself within
the context of lack of justice and the desire of the survivors to seek justice
and revenge through means other than those available in the secular
world, which were for practical purposes not functioning. The range of
experiences involving the possessions has provided these individuals
some mechanisms of coping.

The possessions and the narratives are also mechanisms of remembering. For instance, according to Sumanapala's narrative Pattini is supposed to have disclosed that the child born to his new wife, whom he

married in early 1992, is the reincarnation of his eldest son. Moreover, his second son has been reincarnated as the newborn son of his late wife's sister. Sumanapala is hopeful that the murdered daughter would also be reborn and that Pattini would inform him of this event. Sumanapala also says that Pattini has revealed that once his newborn son begins to talk he will explain the circumstances of his death in the previous life. Says Sumanapala: "The day before he was killed the two of us took the cattle to graze. He plucked some mangos for me. When I remind the little one of this, his entire face wrinkles up and gets dark. He remembers." In the perception of Sumanapala and others in the village, at least some of the victims continue to be with the family, which I believe also plays a constructive role in the ultimate long-term process of rebuilding the shattered lives of this particular family. This and similar cases do not merely constitute individual efforts of coping with the consequences of political violence. Such individual efforts succeed only because there is wider community recognition, acceptance and legitimization of such efforts. In that sense, they are community efforts of healing and coping.

OTHER MECHANISMS OF COPING AND INTERVENTION: THE STORY OF TILAKA

Ghost stories and spirit possessions are not the only aspects of popular religion that play a significant role in postterror coping in Sri Lanka. In many small shrines around the country, spirit mediums have been consulted in attempts to locate disappeared relatives and loved ones; *bodhi poojas* and other meritorious acts have been undertaken to bless disappeared relatives or to transfer merit to and alleviate the suffering of loved ones in the other world, if they have been deemed dead; conventional mechanisms of bringing misfortune such as *was kavi, kodi vina,* and divine and demonic intervention have been utilized to punish culprits who are beyond the grasp of the law; and ritual experts have been consulted to obtain charms to ward off gunshots. Almost everyone who came before the government-appointed commissions inquiring into the disappearances, forcible removals, and extrajudicial executions in southern Sri Lanka during the 1980s stated that they had resorted to one or more of the ritual processes referred to above in a bid to locate their loved ones or to seek justice and revenge on their behalf. What is clear, then, is that an entire spectrum of activities from popular religion and ritual play a significant part in the healing and coping process in postterror Sri Lanka.

Here, I would like to present a brief summary of the story of Tilaka.[8] She is a young mother who was thirty-two years of age when her husband did not come home from work one day in September 1989. She lives in a small village quite close to the southern market town of Matara. Her daughter, who was less than one year old when her father disappeared, has no recollection of him, except for the framed black-and-white photograph hanging in their living room next to the images of the Buddha and the god Kataragama. Tilaka's immediate activities consequent to her husband's disappearance are typical of the activities undertaken by numerous others under similar circumstances. Accompanied by a number of elderly relatives, she went to all the police stations and military detachments in the vicinity in search of the disappeared man. According to Tilaka, officers in the military detachments simply told her that they never detained her husband. In the police stations her complaints were not recorded, and the officers there also told her that they had not arrested him. Moreover, they discouraged her from coming to their stations in search of him. According to Tilaka, "They said that if there was any news, they would let me know."

According to neighbors as well as Tilaka and her relatives, her husband was not involved in JVP politics, or in the politics of any mainstream political party. The family had a number of friends in the nearby police station, and while this connection has made some people suspect the JVP in the disappearance, members of the family were never known to be supporters of the ruling party. The refusal to record her complaints came irrespective of these connections. For their part, the police were not keen to record the incident in case those responsible for the disappearance happened to be a government unit. Even now there is no consensus within family circles whether the man was a victim of the JVP or of a state-sponsored death squad. The point, however, is that in their grief, it does not matter who abducted the man. According to Tilaka's mother, what matters is that "my daughter does not have a husband, and her little daughter does not have a father."

Like many others, along with paying regular visits to the police stations and military detachments and writing letters to various governmental and nongovernmental organizations, Tilaka also sought divine intervention. For almost everybody in similar circumstances, the combination of these activities became a routine. In these ventures Tilaka was guided by her mother as well as close kin and friends. In Tilaka's case, this was the first of two distinct phases of activity involving spirits and specific rituals of popular religion in which the primary objectives were to locate her husband, find out whether he was alive, and assure his safe return. Says Tilaka: "Everyone said that I should go to an *anjanam* specialist [a kind of spirit medium] to find out where my husband was. There is someone fifteen miles away who is very good. Everyone used to go to him before all these things started happening [i.e., the period of terror] whenever they lost something. Many people also come to him to ask about relatives who they have not heard from."

Anjanam experts are fairly common in many parts of Sri Lanka. They can be adult men and women or children who are deemed to have the power to ask favors from Anjanam Devi. The ritual involved here is a very simple one. For instance, when someone needs information on lost property or kin, he is supposed to ask for help from the medium, who in turn requests the intervention of Anjanam Devi, who appears to the medium in the flame of a clay lamp. Through the flame Anjanam Devi shows a number of images to the medium to indicate where the lost kin or property can be found. The medium is expected to interpret these images for the benefit of his clients. According to Tilaka her husband is still alive: "I was told that he was taken away by armed men, and that he is kept in a dark place surrounded by water. He is in pain, but he is still alive. This happened to him because of his karma. He [the spirit medium] told me that I should undertake bodhi pooja to bless my husband and ask the gods for his early return." Tilaka strongly believed that her husband was still alive, and she constantly told her child that her father had gone away but would return soon. While many of her neighbors and kin believed that her husband was in fact dead, they did not say so to her or to the child. The belief gave Tilaka some hope, which allowed her to continue with her other work. Interestingly, many kin of the disappeared that I have interviewed who have consulted spirit mediums say that they have been told that their loved ones are alive and that they are kept in "a dark place." Many say that the dark place is underground, in an island, or in a place surrounded by water. It is important to note that the spirit medium merely stated that according to Anjanam Devi's information, Tilaka's husband was still alive. He did not say that he would return. Instead, he simply advised her that she should undertake meritorious activities in order to assure his safety and his quick return home. He specifically mentioned bodhi pooja as the kind of meritorious activity that she should perform, but did not undertake to perform this ritual himself. In similar situations, however, many spirit mediums and other experts in spirit religion have not only suggested that the disappeared persons are alive but that they would return soon. They also undertake particular rituals in order to bless the disappeared and assure their safe return home. In some places this has become what one can only describe as a minor cottage industry, where victims of terror are bound to a cycle of grief, despair, hope, expectations of divine intervention, and ultimately financial ruin as well.

Following the advice from the spirit medium Tilaka consulted her village monk, and he undertook to conduct the bodhi pooja ceremonies in his temple, under his supervision. Bodhi pooja is a relatively new kind of Buddhist ritual which managed to capture the public interest in the mid-1970s. In its early days it was almost exclusively conducted by a young and charismatic monk called Panadure Ariyadhamma. According to Obeyesekere and Gombrich, the ceremony was a revitalized form of an older version of Buddha pooja (offerings to the Buddha) in which offerings such as lamps, flowers, incense, and so forth are made to the images of the twenty-eight Buddhas (twenty-seven former ones and Gotama, the last Buddha) accompanied by the recitation of a few Pali stanzas. The ritual also revives the custom of honoring the *bo* tree (*bodhi*) under which the Buddha is believed to have achieved his enlightenment (Gombrich and Obeyesekere 1988: 384). It was this latter element which gave the ritual the label of bodhi pooja. Though Ariyadhamma's bodhi poojas were not mandated to be held near a bo tree, today the ritual is always held near a tree which is the main object of worship. Another significant innovation in the popularization of bodhi pooja was the use of Sinhala in some of the verses, as opposed to Pali, which was the conventional language of Buddhist liturgy. This innovation probably made a significant contribution to the popularization and expansion of bodhi pooja. In its expansion, however, significant changes have occurred in its form and in what it means to participants (Gombrich and Obeyesekere 1988: 384).

It is in this transformed form that the ritual is significant insofar as the present discussion is concerned. Bodhi poojas are increasingly being held to achieve worldly ends, which was not the original intention of the ritual. As Gombrich and Obeyesekere observe, "If *bodhi puja* has been taken up by Sinhala Buddhists as a nation to serve their common purposes, it is . . . being still more commonly used specifically by individuals to serve their private worldly ends" (Gombrich and Obeyesekere 1988: 391). You no longer need a monk to perform or lead the bodhi pooja as in the days of Ariyadhamma. In addition to monks, priests of the spirit religion perform it for their clients now. Moreover, any individual can also perform it himself or herself by following widely available printed instructions. It is in the context of this general background that Tilaka's ritual activities have to be understood.

During the first month in which the bodhi pooja undertaken by Tilaka was performed (between late September and late October 1989), it was conducted by the village monk with the participation of her kin and friends. The rituals were conducted three times a week for about four weeks. Afterwards her kin suggested that they could do it themselves, and they could do it for longer periods at a time without the monk. Soon, however, the thrice-a-week rituals were conducted once a week. This was mainly due to financial considerations. After a period of six months, they were conducted on a monthly basis. In any case, Tilaka conducted bodhi pooja for the safe return of her husband for a total period of about one-and-a-half years. During this time she continued to visit the spirit medium, who suggested that the husband had been moved from one location to another, advised her to continue with the bodhi pooja, and so on. She also visited a close relative who composed for her a set of *seth kavi,* or auspicious verses, for her husband. Recitation of such verses on a regular basis is supposed to bring good luck for the person in whose name they have been composed.

After one-and-a-half years, Tilaka's hopes for her husband's safe return began to wane. Her kin and relatives advised her that she should make up her mind and concentrate on the future of their young daughter. At about the same time, the spirit medium told Tilaka that Anjanam Devi had shown him the body of her husband, and that he had died recently. He also suggested that she offer alms to the monks in the village temple and transfer the merit thus accrued to her dead husband. With the help of her kin and neighbors she offered alms to the monks. According to Sinhala Buddhist tradition, alms are given to monks seven days after the death, and later three months after the death; Tilaka followed this convention on the basis of the time of death calculated by the spirit medium. It was at this time that Tilaka entered a second distinct phase, wherein her primary interest was to bring misfortune upon the people who were responsible for her husband's abduction and murder. The problem was that Tilaka was unaware of the culprits, a dilemma faced by many kin of the disappeared. Only a very few can clearly identify those responsible for legal or ritual purposes. However, Tilaka requested an expert to compose a series of *was kavi,* which is the opposite of seth kavi, designed to bring misfortune to the person or persons

to whom the verses are directed. The verses were composed to seek
divine intervention in bringing harm upon anybody who was responsible.

She also visited a Suniyam shrine a number of times, where she asked
the *kapurala* (the shrine priest) to invoke the powers of Suniyam in order
to punish the culprits. Suniyam is specifically noted for his destructive
power. He is one god from whom one can request almost unrestricted
acts of revenge. For instance, consider the following segments of an
invocation to Suniyam by a kapurala on behalf of a woman whose husband had left her:

> O Siddha Suniyam, king of gods, victorious hero
> You who have the power of fiery destruction—
> Cast your divine eye upon the maker of this trouble.
> Gather your demon army. Raise your sword of Vadiga in judgement.
> Take hold of this evil husband. Seize him by the neck, squeeze the breath
>   from his body.
> Crush his wind pipe. Give him as a sacrifice to the
> Blood Demon—
> Smash his skull into pieces, no larger than grains of rice.
> Tear his body apart—
> O God! Infect him with diseases: smallpox, eczema, leprosy. Cause his skin
>   to itch—
> Make this woman's heart full of happiness by meeting out this punishment.
>   (Kapferer 1988: 31–32).

Tilaka, however, was not simply satisfied with invocations to Suniyam
at his shrines. She went a step further and began to light a small lamp
for Suniyam in her garden. According to popular belief, Suniyam would
specifically take care of those who regularly worshipped him. Moreover,
this allowed her to direct her invocations directly to the god herself
without an intermediate priest. It also saved money, since she did not
have to travel to distant shrines.

Tilaka lit the lamp and worshipped Suniyam every day, and seems to
have developed considerable faith in the god:

> I started lighting a lamp for god Suniyam, for our protection. If we had done
> this before my husband would have still been alive. But now that I light a
> lamp every day and have asked god Suniyam to punish those responsible for
> this crime, they will have to pay for this. There has to be some justice in this.
> I may get some compensation from the government. But that is not punishment. We cannot allow them to be free when they have killed my husband,
> and the father of my daughter. Only god Suniyam can do justice now.

After about two months of was kavi and invocations to Suniyam, Tilaka
was taken to the spirit medium by her mother, who was worried that
Tilaka was getting too obsessed with the idea of revenge: "Earlier the
only thing she thought about was the safe return of her husband. Now
the only thing she thinks about is revenge. That is not a very good thing.
She has to bring up her daughter in a normal house. She should not
grow up hearing her mother curse like that. I hoped that the spirit medium would say that god Suniyam had already punished those responsible." In fact, when the spirit medium was consulted, he told Tilaka
and her mother that he could see four bodies, which were unrecogniz-
able. He interpreted them as the bodies of the persons who abducted
and later killed Tilaka's husband. According to the medium, the god
Suniyam had punished them all. They had all met with terrible and
painful deaths. This last meeting with the spirit medium did have the
effect Tilaka's mother hoped it would. Tilaka's visits to Suniyam shrines
stopped, as did her rather loud recitations of was kavi and invocations
to Suniyam at home, but she continued to light the lamp regularly in
expectation of protection for herself and her daughter. Tilaka's last
words to me were, "Justice is something only the gods can deliver. The
government cannot do it. As you can see, the god Suniyam has punished
those responsible for my husband's death. He will continue to look after
my daughter and myself."

PROBLEMS OF ACCESS AND AVAILABILITY:
SECULAR SYSTEMS OF JUSTICE AND COPING
OR THE REVENGE OF DEITIES?

At the end of World War Two, George Orwell had the opportunity to
see some German prisoners of war responsible for mass human destruction in a prison camp. The appearance of many of them seemed rather
pathetic to Orwell, and he wrote later that revenge "is an act which you
want to commit when you are powerless and because you are powerless.
Somehow the punishment of these monsters ceases to seem attractive
when it becomes possible: indeed, once under lock and key they almost
cease to be monsters" (quoted in Time, 8 May 1995). Orwell's observations would make little sense to victims of terror in contemporary
societies of terror. Many torturers and murderers are not under lock and
key, and although the physical wave of violence may have ceased, the
ability to reinitiate processes of terror remains real. To most victims and

survivors, the perpetrators continue to be monsters that need to be locked up, exterminated, or brought to justice in some other way. As in the case of Sumanapala and his daughter, even in situations where people claim to have reconciled themselves to their fate and seem to be getting on with their lives, expectations of revenge and justice manifest themselves in other ways, such as in possessions and other supernatural experiences. Moreover, as Tilaka's case demonstrates, revenge and justice can become consuming obsessions until it is perceived that they have been delivered by divine intervention.

Thus it would be reasonable to argue that irrespective of the semblances of normalcy or claims to that effect by governments, expectations of justice and desire for revenge will continue to exist so long as memories of terror continue to exist. Given the reality of the dominant sociopolitical structures currently entrenched in postterror societies, however, including Sri Lanka, many survivors do not get an opportunity to realize their expectations of revenge or justice. Moreover, in situations such as these conceptual differences between revenge and justice tend to get blurred. In many cases, people tend to regard both concepts without differentiation.

Thus one of the fundamental features of postterror societies is the reality of having to live with torturers and murderers. Such a situation is particularly difficult for people who have directly experienced torture and terror. In such situations mental torment will surely continue. This is the reality captured in Ariel Dorfman's play *Death and the Maiden,* also known as the *Scars on the Moon* (1990). Dorfman's character Pauline is a victim of torture who recognizes her torturer and attempts to force him to confess. He refuses, and she is unable to prove her case legally even though her husband is head of a commission collecting testimony on such cases. Only the torturer and his victim are aware of the real nature of the past that bind them together. In Dorfman's play, even though the victim is able to confront her torturer and establish for a brief moment a relationship in which the torturer is at her mercy, he does not repent for his crimes (Dorfman 1991: 19, Perera 1995: 60–61).

The conclusion of the play is significant, precisely because it is ambiguous: two different endings are provided. In the first, unable to get a genuine confession, Pauline has to let Jorge, the torturer, go free, and later it is shown that Jorge, Pauline, and her husband, Gerardo, continue to coexist and move within the same social circles (Dorfman 1991: 5–20). In the second, she kills Jorge but the memory of her past continues to haunt her, as she keeps seeing visions of his image (Dorfman 1991:

19–20). Whatever the end of the play may actually be, the point it attempts to make is valid for all societies of terror: many people may be destined to live ambivalently with their tormentors for the rest of their lives. On the other hand, even if survivors manage to successfully seek justice or revenge, psychological torment will be part of their lives insofar as memories of torture and political murder continue to exist (Perera 1995: 60–61).

In most postterror societies the secular apparatus of the government claims to offer redress to the victims of violence. This normally amounts to legal mechanisms that fall far short of the victims' expectations of justice (Perera 1995: 47). The three commissions of inquiry the Sri Lankan government appointed after its electoral victory in September 1994 to investigate disappearances and political violence fall into this category of secular mechanisms of justice. If such mechanisms work, they can certainly help people cope with their experiences in some way. At the very least such commissions should be able to expose murderers and torturers in the manner the South African Truth and Reconciliation Commission expects to do, even though in most societies of terror the victims of violence and terror expect something far more than mere confessions from perpetrators of violence.

Even though a government can offer general amnesties, as many have, such amnesties will not cause the populace to be afflicted with collective amnesia. Thus despite the great hopes for justice many Sri Lankan victims of violence have placed on the recently appointed commissions of inquiry, the likelihood is that many of these people will be utterly disappointed in their quest for justice. The new government clearly has given too much hope to the victims of violence. Moreover, no government agency seems to have come to terms with the great psychological problems that a significant segment of the populace must be suffering from. There are no clinics established in the provinces to deal with such problems, nor is there a mental health program or policy to deal with this specific problem. Claims that "things have returned to normalcy" are perhaps the ultimate manifestation of this state-sponsored amnesia.

The emergence of ghost stories and experiences of spirit possession have to be placed in the context of a society where both the normal means of mourning and coping and the mechanisms of law and order have been radically subverted. Many people have lost faith in these mechanisms. In such a context, people have to devise mechanisms to cope with trauma and fulfill their own sense of guilt for surviving and their inability to do justice to those who perished. As in similar situations in Zimbabwe and Guatemala, victims of terror and torture in Sri Lanka have opted to find solace in accessible areas of the Sinhala popular religion. This includes people who sought help in the secular systems and were unable to have their expectations fulfilled, as well as people who seek solace in popular religion while attempting to utilize the secular systems as well.

Sri Lankans have shown a strong tendency to seek supernatural intervention in times of personal crisis, even under conditions not marked by sustained terror. In this regard Obeyesekere's study of sorcery practices as alternate means of channelling aggression in Sri Lanka provides some important insights. His study, undertaken in the early 1970s, clearly demonstrates that even under the best of circumstances people's perceptions of the law-and-order apparatus were quite negative. According to Obeyesekere's information collected from the sorcery shrines in Munneswaram, Kahapitiya, and Sinigama, 31 percent, 22 percent, and 33 percent respectively of the clients who visited the shrines had initiated some official action in an attempt to remedy the wrong they believed had been done to them (Obeyesekere 1993: 15).

Obeyesekere further notes that "practically everyone who expressed opinions on the subject spoke of the futility of reporting to the police. Respondents were unanimous in their view that police officers were corrupt and under the control of 'undesirables' and politicians" (Obeyesekere 1993: 15). However, 29 percent of the people in Obeyesekere's sample attempted at some point to seek police or other official intervention in their problems (Obeyesekere 1993: 16). As Obeyesekere has observed, such a pattern of behavior clearly indicates that we are dealing with individuals who seek rational solutions to their problems (Obeyesekere 1993: 16). I would further suggest that the tendency to find solace in popular religion under these kinds of circumstances is a practical extension of that rationality informed by the reality of the nonfunctional nature of the secular systems of justice.

Obeyesekere's description refers to relatively normal circumstances. Under conditions of terror, when the secular systems of justice and law completely collapsed, people's tendency to seek divine intervention through the recitation of was kavi and invocations to Suniyam is not only understandable but constitutes the only realistic option still open to them. Similarly, the ghost stories and experiences of possessions were clear manifestations of the complex frame of mind that has emerged in the postterror context.

In the postterror narratives of supernatural activity, the manner in which an individual's or a community's self has been constructed differs markedly from the construction of the self under "normal" circumstances involving the same individuals or collectives. It seems to me that the variations in the construction of the self between these two different states of consciousness reinforce my main argument thus far: these narratives and experiences are essentially mechanisms for remembering the past and coping with the experiences of terror as well as manifestations of the community's expectations of revenge and justice.

The difference in the construction of the self in normal and altered states of consciousness was most clearly marked as a variation between loss of hope versus hope, apparent manifestation of reconciliation versus strong expectation of justice and revenge, a sense of utter powerlessness versus strong sense of empowerment, and relative silence versus graphic expression. The case of Sumanapala and his daughter clearly exemplifies this duality in the construction of the self. In normal conversation they seem reconciled to their fate, but their expectation of justice and desire for revenge are graphically clear under possession. Ghost stories, on the other hand, are indicative of memories that cannot be erased, as well as expectations of justice irrespective of the public claims of normalcy and reconciliation to fate.

This duality was clearly a manifestation of the existential dilemmas faced by many victims of political violence and terror in southern Sri Lanka. Most of these survivors of terror were from economically and socially marginalized backgrounds, particularly from rural areas. It is no accident that a great majority of the narratives of supernatural activity and spirit possession which I have documented originated in the rural south. Under the best of circumstances, these people had relatively little access to real political or socioeconomic power, which was centered on the cities. Under possession and in ghost stories, people seemed to express what they desired but could not achieve in the secular world. This duality is also framed within the collective conscience informed by personal and communal emotions, as opposed to the reconstructed reality of normalcy imposed by the state. The state attempts to construct an alternate and preferable reality for the survivors of terror; and indeed, some survivors—at least in public—seem to accept these reconstructed realities of normalcy. But the experiences of spirit activity bring to the surface the actual reality of the survivors' experiences and expectations.

I would like to sketch out some of the basic strands in a situation documented by Kakar which is structurally somewhat similar and which

may shed some light on this issue. In a study of spirit possessions in
North India, a large number of malignant spirits possessing Hindu men
and women turned out to be Muslims (Kakar 1990: 136). In healing
rituals in which the spirits expressed themselves, their wishes turned out
to be wishes that would have horrified the conscious self of the average
Hindu (Kakar 1990: 136). As Kakar observes, all the negative fantasies
that a good Hindu could not imagine were able to come to the fore
when he was possessed by a Muslim spirit, because Muslim spirits were
"universally considered to be the strongest, vilest, the most malignant
and the most stubborn of the evil spirits." The Muslim, already demon-
ized in the popular consciousness, seemed to "symbolize the alien and
the demonic in the unconscious part of the Hindu mind" (Kakar 1990:
137).

The basic components of Kakar's argument can be utilized to explain
some aspects of the Sri Lankan situation. For instance, revenge is not
compatible with Buddhism, and most victims of the terror in the south
were Buddhists. While many people openly discussed their expectations
of justice, and to a lesser extent revenge, there were many others who
simply did not discuss any of these expectations. It was not merely a
result of problematic political circumstances but a problem of conscience. Revenge, as many victims of political violence themselves explained, was not good for the society. Many of those taking this position
referred to a famed Buddhist Jataka story whose main dictum is "hatred
begets more hatred."[9] But the possessions and ghost stories gave them
an opportunity to express their hatred as well as their expectations of
justice and revenge and the preservation of their memories in a socially
and ritually accepted fashion—particularly in a context where all of
these issues were discouraged by the secular systems of law.

The project initiated by this chapter, it might be argued, attempts to
romanticize the role of popular religions as a mechanism of coping in
the context of postterror societies; it discourages a Western type of psychiatric treatment to victims of terror and torture. Indeed, there are
many reasons not to romanticize popular religions: for instance, there
is already some evidence emerging from Sri Lanka indicating that some
spirit mediums and sorcerers are making use of the situation to generate
business for themselves at the emotional expense of victims of torture
and terror. Nevertheless, in many situations of terror as in Sri Lanka,
popular religions are sufficiently flexible and accessible to be practically
utilized in dealing with some of the problems of postterror societies.

This is not an argument for local methods of healing in preference to Western psychoanalytic models.

As I have already noted, the postterror Sri Lankan state has not implemented a clear mental health program specifically to deal with survivors of terror. The state has not even acknowledged that there is a potentially serious mental health problem facing a significant segment of the population. Even in the case of members of the military and the police, who in many instances have exhibited symptoms that may be indicative of post-traumatic stress disorder, there are no counselling or treatment programs. Moreover, Sri Lanka has only a handful of qualified psychiatrists and psychologists to deal with the problem at hand. Even they have not considered it necessary to work with sociologists and anthropologists as well as others familiar with Sri Lanka's political violence to devise realistic strategies of intervention or treatment.

In the context of such a reality one has to seriously consider the viability of formal methods of coping or intervention prescribed by mainstream psychiatry. Therefore I would suggest that local methods of healing and coping have to be situated in a context where formal, secular, and mainstream methods pose a serious problem in terms of availability and accessibility. On the other hand, healing of postterror trauma is primarily a social process, not merely an exercise in formal psychotherapy. Formal psychotherapy clearly has to play a part in the overall process of healing, but it is not the process itself. As psychologists investigating the case of the "Women of Calama" in Chile had observed, in some instances some form of collective treatment can be devised (Timmerman 1987: 29). However, even without such formal interventions, social healing of some nature usually takes place at the level of the community, where the community has a stake in making such a process work.

On the other hand, there are serious problems in medicalizing trauma and transforming victims into patients. According to Kleinman and Desjarlais, "The person who undergoes torture first becomes a victim—a quintessential image of innocence and passivity who cannot represent him or herself—and then becomes a patient with post-traumatic stress syndrome" (Kleinman and Desjarlais 1996). As they further point out, even to receive certain basic public assistance "it may be necessary to undergo a transformation from one who has lived through the greatly heterogeneous experience of political terror to stereotyped victim, to standardized sufferer of a textbook sickness" (Kleinman and Desjarlais

1996). In their view, given the "political and economic import of such transformations, the violated themselves may want, and may even seek out, the moral as well as the financial consequences of being ill" (Kleinman and Desjarlais 1996).

However, in the Sri Lankan situation, there are no moral or financial benefits to being afflicted with a textbook illness such as post-traumatic stress disorder. Perception of mental illness has negative cultural value in Sinhala consciousness. Such a situation will automatically label a person as *pissu,* or simply mad. There are no variations in the popular Sinhala categorization of mental illness. Once a person is perceived as pissu his or her social position tends to be devalued, irrespective of the manner in which that person came to be in such a state of mental illness. Under such circumstances there is great reluctance to visit mental health professionals even when it is deemed necessary and they are available. Local methods of intervention and coping associated with popular religion, on the other hand, have no negative cultural perceptions. At this point I would like to refer to the observations of Johnson, Feldman, Lubin, and Southwick in a recent paper (1995). They argue that ritual and ceremony can be effectively used in a therapeutic sense in the treatment of PTSD. Such ceremonies and rituals must be specifically constructed by mental health professionals to address specific issues of PTSD, and formally conducted in specially designed facilities (Johnson, Feldman, Lubin, and Southwick 1995: 286–96). However, such an approach can only work in a situation where the mental health infrastructure is extensive and well established and where trained professionals are widely available.

The situation in Sri Lanka is quite the opposite. In such situations, I would suggest that selected rituals and other aspects of religion which already exist in the cultural repertoire of the society can be used for therapeutic purposes, both by themselves and in association with processes of formal psychotherapy when available. Thus while formal methods of coping and healing have to be made more acceptable and accessible, available local methods need to be formally recognized and encouraged in situations where such methods are likely to help. Ideally, such a position should also be part of the state mental health policy.

In summary then, I would locate these particular ghost stories, experiences of spirit possession, invocations to gods, and other methods of popular religious coping as interventions in a single functional category. When confidence in secular systems of coping, healing, justice, and compensation are unavailable or have failed, it should not be surprising that people resort to traditional and more accessible mechanisms.

Though at a fundamental level ghost stories, spirit possession, and other aspects of popular religion mentioned above are traditional constructs, in terms of structure, symbolic inferences, and the context in which they are located, these particular narratives and experiences are clearly a postterror phenomenon molded by the experiences of terror. As such, they serve a number of purposes. Reports of supernatural activity generally arise from places where violent actions are known to have taken place. In the long run these narratives and experiences are mechanisms by which a community remembers the people it has lost, a mechanism that helps place in perspective the community's collective losses and memories of the violent past. Such memories are also constructed as expressions of the guilt of the living over the dead, a desire for justice and revenge, and the need to alleviate the otherworldly suffering of those who died unnatural deaths. The ghost stories in particular are indicative of a replication of the terrifying existential predicaments of the community's immediate past in its own collective conscience of the present.

Thus in the final analysis, taken collectively as narratives of supernatural activity, the ghost stories, the experiences with spirit possession, and the utilization of traditional methods of coping and intervention are clearly an integral part of the community's own healing process. Such traditional methods of coping and compensation may be their only hope in a society where the secular legal system is unlikely to deliver the justice it is supposed to, where the state has failed to protect its citizens, and where the normal methods of mourning have been subverted. As far as many survivors are concerned, all that is left is the revenge of yakku and the justice of the deities.

NOTES

The first version of this paper was presented at a seminar on Sri Lankan Society and Polity at the South Asia Studies Centre, University of Rajasthan, Jaipur, India, in November 1994, and a much extended version was presented at the Centre for Asia Studies in Amsterdam in June 1995. In October 1995, another expanded version, incorporating new field material from Sri Lanka, was presented at a conference on social suffering organized by the Social Science Research Council at the University of Cape Town, South Africa. Comments made at each of these conferences have helped me immensely in formulating this final version. I would particularly like to thank Arthur Kleinman, Veena Das, and Pamela Reynolds for their comments and literature provided.

1. The background to this paper is the political violence that occurred in southern Sri Lanka between 1988 and 1991. However, political violence in Sri Lanka was not merely restricted to its Sinhala-dominated southern areas. In the Tamil-dominated northern and eastern provinces, institutionalized political violence initiated by the state and Tamil guerrilla groups has been a dominant feature of the political landscape since early 1980s. The violence in the south cannot be considered as completely autonomous from the violence in the northeast. For instance, many military and police personnel who were responsible for the violence in the northeast were also responsible for the violence in the south. Similarly, many mechanisms of torture and violence which initially emerged in the northeast were later replicated in the south. However, to make this analysis more manageable, I will not refer to the violence in the northeast in this paper. That, I believe should constitute a separate project. On the other hand, whenever I refer to "postterror Sri Lanka" in this analysis, I specifically refer to the south. For the people in the northeast, terror continues to be a part of their daily reality.

2. *Yakku* and *yakshayo* are the plurals of *yaka* and *yakshaya*. In much of the contemporary anthropological literature on Sri Lankan religion and ritual, the word and concept of *yakku* has been translated into English as "demons" due to the influence of colonial and missionary perceptions on contemporary anthropology. However, in this discussion I will refer to these spirit forms in the original Sinhala as *yakku*.

3. "Duro" is a local trade name.

4. For a useful and informative discussion on this subject, see David Scott (1994).

5. Sumanapala is not his real name.

6. The new Peoples' Alliance government has decided to compensate all violent deaths that took place during the terror on the following basis: compensation will be paid to the kin of any person who is confirmed killed or who has disappeared and is believed to have been killed. To receive compensation for the latter category a police report must be submitted. If a Buddhist or Christian priest or the member of Parliament for an area states that a disappeared person is dead, the police are asked to provide a report. All deaths and disappearances between July 1989 and September 1991 will be covered under this program. Compensation for a married person who is believed to be dead will be Rs. 50,000 (approximately US$750) while for a single person it would be Rs. 25,000 (US$375). For every child killed a sum of Rs. 15,000 (US$230) will be paid (*Irida Lankadipa,* 21 November 1994).

7. Interviews with JVP activists in the 1971 insurrection have shown that many of them were detained by security forces because envious neighbors had sent anonymous letters to the police and military claiming that they were either sympathizers or activists. In many cases the reason for envy was their relative prosperity and access to a university education, as well as personal vendettas.

8. Tilaka is not her real name.

9. Jataka stories are fables detailing the exemplary lives of the Buddha before he achieved Buddhahood. In the Sinhala Buddhist tradition there are 550 of these stories.

REFERENCES CITED

Boddy, Janice. 1989. *Wombs and Alien Spirits: Women, Men and the Zar Cult of Northern Sudan.* Madison: University of Wisconsin Press.

Bourdillon, M. C. F. 1987. "Guns and Rain: Taking Structural Analysis Too Far." In *Africa* 57, no. 2: 263–79.

Brown, Cynthia, ed. 1985. *With Friends Like These: The Americas Watch Report on Human Rights and U.S. Policy in Latin America.* New York: Pantheon Books.

Bruner, Edward M. 1986. "Ethnography as Narrative." In *The Anthropology of Experience,* ed. Victor W. Turner and E. M. Bruner. Urbana: University of Illinois Press.

Das, Veena. 1990a. "Introduction: Communities, Riots, Survivors—The South Asian Experience." In *Mirrors of Violence: Communities, Riots and Survivors in South Asia,* ed. Veena Das, 1–36. Delhi: Oxford University Press.

———. 1990b. "Our Work to Cry, Your Work to Listen." In *Mirrors of Violence: Communities, Riots and Survivors in South Asia,* ed. Veena Das, 345–94. Delhi: Oxford University Press.

Davis, Shelton H. 1983. "State Violence and Agrarian Crisis in Guatemala: The Roots of the Indian Peasant Rebellion." In *Trouble in Our Backyard,* ed. M. Diskin. New York: Pantheon Books.

Dorfman, Ariel. 1983. *Widows.* New York: Pantheon Books.

———. 1991. "Death and the Maiden." *Index on Censorship* 20, no. 6: 5–20.

Gombrich, Richard, and Gananath Obeyesekere. 1988. *Buddhism Transformed: Religious Change in Sri Lanka.* Princeton: Princeton University Press.

Irida Lankadipa. 1 November 1992, 8 November 1992, 15 November 1992. Colombo: Wijeya Publications Ltd.

Johnson, David Read, Susan C. Feldman, Hadar Lubin, and Steven M. Southwick. 1995. "The Therapeutic Use of Ritual and Ceremony in the Treatment of Post-Traumatic Stress Disorder." *Journal of Traumatic Studies* 8, no. 2.

Kakar, Sudhir. 1990. "Some Unconscious Aspects of Ethnic Violence in India." In *Mirrors of Violence: Communities, Riots and Survivors in South Asia,* ed. Veena Das, 135–46. Delhi: Oxford University Press.

Kapferer, Bruce. 1988. *Legends of People, Myths of States.* Washington: Smithsonian Institution Press.

Kleinman, Arthur, and Robert Desjarlais. 1996. "Violence, Culture and the Politics of Trauma." In Kleinman, *Writing at the Margin: Discourse between Anthropology and Medicine.* Berkeley: University of California Press.

Kriege, Norma. 1988. "The Zimbabwean War of Liberation: Struggles within the Struggle." *Journal of South African Studies* 14, no. 2: 304–22.

Lan, David. 1985. *Guns and Rain: Guerrillas and Spirit Mediums in Zimbabwe.* Berkeley: University of California Press.

Last, Murray. 1999. "Violence in Northern Nigeria and the Process of Post-war Reconciliation." In *Violence and Subjectivity,* ed. Veena Das, Arthur Kleinman, Mamphela Ramphele, and Pamela Reynolds, 315–33. Berkeley: University of California Press.

Marcus, Paul, and Alan Rosenberg. 1995. "The Value of Religion in Sustaining the Self in Extreme Situations." *Psychoanalytic Review* 82, no. 1: 81–105.

Obeyesekere, Gananath. 1984. *The Cult of the Goddess Pattini.* Chicago: University of Chicago Press.

———. 1993. *Sorcery, Premeditated Murder, and the Canalization of Aggression in Sri Lanka.* Colombo: Studies in Society and Culture.

Obeyesekere, Ranjini, trans. 1991. *Jewels of the Doctrine: Stories of the Saddharma Ratnavaliya,* by Dharmasena Thera. Albany: State University of New York Press.

Perera, Sasanka. 1995. *Living with Torturers and Other Essays of Intervention: Sri Lankan Society, Culture and Politics in Perspective.* Colombo: International Centre for Ethnic Studies.

Ranger, Terrence. 1985. *Peasant Consciousness and Guerrilla War in Zimbabwe: A Comparative Study.* Harare: Zimbabwe Publishing House.

Reynolds, Pamela. 1990. "Children of Tribulation: The Need to Heal and the Means to Heal War Trauma." *Africa* 60, no. 1: 1–38.

Scott, David. 1994. *Formations of Ritual: Colonial and Anthropological Discourses on the Sinhala Yaktovil.* Minneapolis: University of Minnesota Press.

Suarez-Orozco, Marcello M. 1990. "Speaking of the Unspeakable: Towards a Psychological Understanding of Responses to Terror." *Ethos* 18, no. 3: 353–83.

Taussig, Michael. 1987. *Shamanism, Colonialism, and the Wild Man: A Study in Terror and Healing.* Chicago: University of Chicago Press.

Timmerman, Jacobo. 1988. *Chile: Death in the South.* New York: Vintage Books.

Warren, Kay B. 1993. "Interpreting *La Violencia in* Guatemala: The Shapes of Mayan Silence and Resistance." In *The Violence Within: Cultural and Political Opposition in Divided Nations,* ed. Kay B. Warren. Boulder: Westview Press.

Boundaries, Names, Alterities

A Case Study of a "Communal Riot"
in Dharavi, Bombay

Deepak Mehta and Roma Chatterji

FRAMING THE EVENT

There has been considerable recent interest in representing and imagining collective violence in India, the organized or sporadic effort to
destroy other communities (Engineer 1995; Das 1990; Nandy et al.
1995; Varshney 1993; Kakar 1995; van de Veer 1984, 1996; the list is
not exhaustive). With few exceptions (Das 1990) this literature either
deals directly with Hindu-Muslim conflict or focuses on it as its main
referent under the rubric of communalism. Briefly, the study of communal conflict moves in one of two directions. First, the emphasis is on
historical causation (Freitag 1990; Rao 1994) and its link with structural
factors (Engineer 1995), such as unemployment, illiteracy, and poverty,
in precipitating violence. The attempt is to arrive at a general explanation of communalism. Second, when sectarian violence is placed within
local communities (Das 1990) we see its impact on the lives of survivors
as it shapes their experiences and constitutes them as victims. Scholars
are at pains to portray voices telling stories drawn from a storehouse of
individual and collective memory. Their concern is not with the procedures of what happened as much as in documenting how it happened.
In this way the dynamic of violence and its pervasive and persuasive
hold over those touched by it is charted. Such experiences emerge from
the narrative accounts of survivors (Kakar 1995; Das 1990), and
are in more elliptical ways seen in the reorganization of daily life.

Reorganization entails a relationship between the local and the national, one that is asymmetric and often contradictory.

Both the historians and phenomenologists of the riot assume that after violence has run its course individuals and communities will return to normal life. This is often interpreted as the sign of the resilience of traditional Indian community life (see Nandy et al. 1995). Das (1990), in a sensitive paper on the survivors of the Delhi riots that occurred after the assassination of Indira Gandhi in 1984, shows the pathos of this movement. The recovery of the everyday is coming to terms with the fragility of the "normal." Taken-for-granted notions regarding community solidarity become deeply problematic when it is one's neighbors who are the perpetrators of violence, as was the case in the slums about which Das writes. Her paper makes it clear that there is a gap between the end of the riots and the resumption of everyday life. Our paper is located precisely in this gap. In seeing how people ravaged by violence resume everyday life, we establish links between collective disorder and rehabilitation work. In the process we see how local communities are refashioned. What remains after the riot is not a coherent moral and local world but a multiplicity of fractured communities, each charting, through rehabilitation work, its strategies of survival and coexistence. As stated above, this view runs counter to that proposed by Nandy et al. (1995), who argue that local communities are well-bounded moral wholes corrupted from the outside, in this case nineteenth-century European ideas of state and nationalism. This corruption, they argue, is stoutly resisted by the vibrant everyday life of local communities.

The riot we study occurs in a shanty town called Dharavi in Bombay.[1] It begins a day after the demolition of the Babri Masjid (6 December 1992) in Ayodhya, a town in eastern Uttar Pradesh, some 2,500 kilometers northeast of Bombay. A voluminous literature documents what is called the Babri Masjid–Ram Janmabhoomi controversy. It details the origin of the conflict and shows how the landscape of Hindu-Muslim relations is vitally affected by the destruction of the mosque. Our paper examines how this event of national importance is experienced in a local setting. First, a few words on the controversy.

BABRI MASJID

Situated in the temple town of Ayodhya, the Babri Masjid was built in 1528 by Mir Baqi, a noble of the Mughal emperor Babur (1526–1530). Sectarian conflict over this mosque dates back to at least the eighteenth century (Van der Veer 1989) with reports of intermittent clashes between Hindus and Muslims. In Independent India the controversy is dated to 1949 (Rao 1994). The details of that troubled history are not part of this paper. Suffice it to say that since 1949 the Babri Masjid has been a site of national concern, with Hindus, Muslims, and the nation-state actively engaged in determining whether the mosque was built after razing a Hindu temple, purportedly the birthplace of the Hindu god Ram. In 1990 members of "ultra Hindu" organizations,[2] claiming that the *masjid* was built after desecrating an ancient Ram temple, succeeded in partially damaging it by performing what they called *karseva* (religious work as service). Two years later (6 December 1992) more than two hundred thousand *karsevaks* (religious workers) congregated at the Babri Masjid and demolished it. This congregation, the result of careful planning, came from every region of India. Mass mobilization was complemented by the orchestration of political passions (see Nandy et al. 1995: 192–97). Following the destruction, mobs of karsevaks in Ayodhya killed Muslim men and children, burned their homes, and damaged mosques (Nandy et al. 1995: 197). This destruction was patterned: the mobs knew which houses to burn, almost as if they had access to voters' lists; the local police force and the provincial armed constabulary actively aided the rioters; and in some cases Hindu neighbors identified Muslim houses. Less than twenty-four hours after the demolition, large parts of India experienced communal violence.

The destruction of the masjid is an event of national importance in two related ways. First, the controversy raises the past (as heritage, tradition, and history) so that it transcends local geographies, local problems, and local communities (van der Veer 1989). Since 1992, Ayodhya signals Hindu nationalism and locates Hindu identity in a public and political space. Following the destruction of the mosque, riots in the rest of India are thought to carry an image of this nationalism (Engineer 1995; van der Veer 1996). In this way, the national constitutes the local under its shadow.[3] Second, the writing of communal riots is predictive. Depending upon one's political persuasion this writing constitutes a grid of representation (see Engineer 1995, Van der Veer 1996, even Nandy et al. 1995) which allows the riot to surpass the exigencies of the local. Thus it becomes possible to show the mimetic violence occasioned by Ayodhya. The inscription of the riot and the construction of a past are unified in their conception of the local. Is the violence of 1992–93 in Dharavi, a notorious slum and a product of urban squalor, a repetition of the carnage in Ayodhya? Before we address this question we will

describe Dharavi and the nature of our fieldwork. It may, however, be
necessary at this stage to take a slight detour to describe briefly how the
riots were dealt with in the public domain. Although our paper locates
the processes of recovery and rehabilitation within the local community,
we are not suggesting that the public domain has no role to play in this
process.

There are at least two reports on the Bombay riots by two separate
Commissions of Inquiry that also document efforts at rehabilitation and
offer suggestions for the improvement of Bombay's administrative machinery (see Srikrishna 1998; Daud and Suresh 1993; Bharatiya Janawadi Agadhi 1993). Since the reports have been influential in crystalliz-
ing the discourse on the Bombay riots in the public culture, a brief
discussion of the scope of the inquiry and its relationship to the government is important.

The report of the Indian People's Human Rights Commission, which
was published in July 1993, was the product of a people's tribunal pre-
sided over by two retired judges of the Bombay High Court, Justice
Suresh and Justice Daud. The tribunal held hearings in most of the riot-
affected areas of Bombay and collected first-hand accounts from the
victims. Based on these accounts, the report was presented as a testimony
of the people of Bombay. Apart from the eyewitness accounts of the
victims, the report also recorded activities of the various citizens' groups
and rehabilitation committees which had been set up after the riots. The
report of the Indian People's Human Rights Commission was seen as
the right and the responsibility of the Indian citizen in creating avenues
of legitimate access to knowledge in the face of government censorship
on the event.

The state government of Maharashtra instituted its own Commission
of Inquiry soon after the riots in January 1993, headed by Justice Srikrishna, sitting judge of the Bombay High Court. The coalition government of the Shiv Sena and the Bharatiya Janata Party (BJP), commonly
perceived as Hindu nationalist parties, which succeeded the Congress (I)
Government in Maharashtra in March 1993, decided to extend the
scope of the investigation of the Commission to include the serial bomb
blast that occurred in the aftermath of the riot and was commonly perceived as the work of aggrieved Muslim gangs of the Bombay Mafia. In
January 1996, the Srikrishna Commission was disbanded on the ground
that it had taken too long to release its report, which would at this stage
only serve to "reopen old wounds" (see Srikrishna 1998: 3). The public
outcry against this decision prompted the BJP national government

to persuade its ally in Maharashtra (the Shiv Sena) to revive the Commission, which was duly reconstituted in May 1996. Its report was presented to the state Assembly in August 1998, but its findings were rejected by the Assembly because they implicated the Shiv Sena in the instigation and organization of riots. It was then privately published and circulated among the wider public. Paradoxically, the inclusion of evidence from the unofficial reports published shortly after the riots made the Commission's report suspect in the eyes of the government.

It is interesting to note that the intertextuality of these various documents not only helped to crystallize a particular discourse of the Bombay riots in the public domain but also participated in the metanarrative of the "communal riot" that was formed in the colonial period (see Pandey 1990). The policy of investigating riots as a problem in public order goes back to the colonial period—a discussion of the genealogical linkages of contemporary instances of collective violence to the colonial construction of the category of the communal riot is important, but unfortunately outside the scope of this paper. We return to the specificity of Dharavi.

DHARAVI

Named after the goddess Dhareshwari, Dharavi is situated in central Bombay. It formed part of one of the seven islands that constitute the present city. Commonly known as the largest slum in Asia, it is located on 432 acres of land and houses approximately six hundred thousand people. Two-thirds of its inhabitants work in the slum. Muslims constitute 40 percent of the population (Masselos 1995: 211). The population density for Dharavi is estimated at 187,500 people per square kilometer, while for the city as a whole the figure is 17,676 (Masselos 1995: 210). We were told that in 1992 Dharavi transacted business of more than ten million rupees daily. It falls in the industrial belt of Bombay and is a center of entrepreneurial activity, specifically the manufacture of garments, leather processing, waste disposal, pottery, suitcase manufacture, and iron-smithery. Due to the acute housing shortage in Bombay it is not unusual to find doctors, lawyers, clerks, and members of political parties living in the area.

On the map Dharavi consists of five administrative subdivisions: Social Nagar, Mukund Nagar, Central Area, South Area and South-West Area. Much of this land belongs to the Bombay Municipal Corporation (BMC) and the Maharashtra state government. For this reason, many dwellings in Dharavi are considered to be unauthorized structures from which its residents may be evicted without notice (Patel and D'Souza 1987). Until 1985 there were approximately three demolition operations a day carried out by the BMC in Dharavi. The slum has a mixed population, further reinforced by the fact that virtually every region in India is represented here.

Data for this paper was gathered while doing fieldwork in Dharavi in 1994 and 1995. Data is provided by informants who live in *chawl*s in four colonies of Dharavi: Mukund Nagar, Social Nagar, Central Area, and South Area. A chawl is a segment of a colony which comprises anything from 130 to 250 single rooms, often with one or two floors built on top; sometimes there are as many as three conjugal units in a single room. Mukund Nagar, for example, has twenty-two chawls. Each chawl has communal bath and defecation houses with eight defecation segments and two showers.[4] Of the thirty-eight areas ravaged by violence, we have information for sixteen. Informants' accounts are in the nature of first-hand testimony. In all the cases they saw the violence as it occurred around them. Five informants, by their account, participated in the violence, and all of them, save one, were directly engaged in relief and rehabilitation. The exception is a woman with three children.

As people narrate their experiences we see not what happened but rather how the imagination of violence and relief work comes to be sedimented in language.[5] In significant ways violence exacerbates the tensions inherent in everyday life, but in other equally important ways it departs from it. Relief work, undertaken to absorb the impact of violence, shows how everyday life is reformulated. The two most important aspects of this reformulation are the reorganization of space and the refashioning of territorial boundaries. Boundaries are established only after the violence of 1992–93 was able to divide the actors into two contending parties: Muslim and non-Muslim. Territories are demarcated through naming. Boundaries, so divided, have constitutive force for those living within areas that witnessed violence. To bear a name and belong to a territorial community are bound up with one another. In addressing violence in the same terms, relief work reinforces such boundaries.

In their separate but related ways, both violence and relief work establish their genealogies, hence it is an error to see the latter as a direct and unmediated response to violence. As far as the genealogy of violence is concerned, the narration of the riots forges a link with prior instances of collective violence. Attempts are made to invest this genealogy with a telos. Rehabilitation too operates in similar ways, arrogating an agency for itself. In this sense, both violence and relief work in Dharavi, as articulated in language, break from earlier ways of dividing and sharing space. We understand this break through the category of event. Before discussing how the event of 1992–93 carves out spaces in Dharavi, we will show how our ethnography made Dharavi available to us as a site of violence and rehabilitation.

NARRATIVES OF DHARAVI

To an outsider Dharavi appears to be strikingly homogeneous in its appearance. Its inhabitants occupy spaces that are not immediately visible. The paths of access within Dharavi fulfill multiple functions: they are simultaneously roadways, garbage dumps, routes carrying sewer water, and extensions of the private space of the household to the outside. From the inside, however, each area of Dharavi is marked by the lived experience of its inhabitants, rather than by spatial divisions available on a map. Each neighborhood is a welter of fluid, intersecting boundaries. Rather than catalogue such fluidity in its myriad details, we walked the invisible spaces of Dharavi to speak to informants within a setting that had experienced the violence of 1992–93.[6]

The narratives frame Dharavi in two distinct ways. While walking through neighborhoods the narrators describe the effects of violence on buildings, they show where people fought, killed, or sought refuge. What we, the fieldworkers, see is a bustle of activity, people engaged in daily chores, populated dwellings, shops selling their wares: everything points to the absence of violence. However, it is clear that our narrators see an ensemble of past events and future possibilities. As narrator the walker transforms each spatial configuration into something invisible to us. Certain areas—walls, for example—are associated with prohibitions; others testify to the absence of friends through migration. Their places are occupied by strangers. While walking through a Hindu-dominated chawl in Central Area, Asif Ali, a Muslim resident, has this to say:

> I was the only Muslim living among three to four hundred Hindu families. I lived without the least fear. In my neighborhood there were about thirty to forty Muslim families, all of whom ran away when the *danga* [disorderly violence] began. Their houses were wiped clean. They weren't burned, mind you. Everything was looted. Even their shithouse slippers were not spared. But the Hindus took good care of me. They bought me food and water

regularly. The other Muslims ran away with the clothes they were
wearing, nothing else.

DM: Who did the looting?

ASIF ALI: Our neighbors, the sisterfuckers, are Dalits.[7]

During his walk he pointed to houses that had been burned. "That is
Sharik's house. It was burned." He pointed to an alley composed of
single-story asbestos roofs, and then gestured to another: "Jalil and his
entire family became naked. They didn't even spare the hens. Must have
had a good meal that night [laughs]. The Muslims who came back did
so for one reason. They wanted to sell as quickly as possible and return
home. . . . They came back a year later. They went naked, they returned
naked." This act of walking and Asif Ali's conversation reflecting on it
attempt to understand the violence by trying to remember the destruction. In this way he makes violence emerge in speech by looking at
physical topography as its signifier. In so doing he constitutes for himself
a near and a far and a here and a there. Simultaneously, he introduces
an other (Dalits) in relation to an I (himself, Muslims). It is almost as if
walking is an act of remembrance being embodied in speech, but an act
also that establishes the boundary between Hindus and Muslims. A
sense of this boundary comes across in the following account as we
returned from where Asif Ali had taken us.

> During the danga, when I was walking home at about eleven at night, from
> this very alley I heard voices: "Catch him" [isko pakro]. I stopped and
> stood my ground. I thought my mind was playing tricks on me since I
> couldn't see faces. When I started to walk again I heard the voices saying
> the same thing. I stopped, waited quietly for a while and said: "If you have
> a face, you sisterfuckers, show it. I am ready." I heard them going away.
> You see, you have to treat them like dogs. [He spits on the ground.]

Such narration creates a discreteness: the narrator provides a reading of
particular spatial signifiers and simultaneously displaces them through
the uses made of them. The one feature common to the narratives is that
the speaker constitutes a *here* and a *there* and associates such spaces
with personal pronouns linked to an *us* and *them, we* and *they*. Thus
violence is spatial, but it occurs randomly and anonymously. Territories
are marked, but the distribution of this mark does not obey a pattern.

   The walking narratives are counterpoints to more conventional
modes of speaking the violence.[8] Conducted in an enclosed space among
a group of speakers, these narratives are punctuated by crosstalk and
interruption. In sitting narratives Dharavi (more specifically, the neigh-

borhood) is seen differently. Here the neighborhood is initially a facsimile of physical spaces of the city populated by anonymous subjects. Dharavi is presented to us in its wretchedness and poverty; the one function it fulfills in relation to the city is to accommodate waste. Once talk of violence begins, this image is replaced by other, more fertile ones. Each neighborhood produces its boundaries that separate it from others. Just as in the walking narratives, here violence is limited to neighborhoods or to parts of neighborhoods. Unlike in the walking narratives, however, violence can be easily located. In this sense boundaries are carved. In a conversation that occurred in a community hall among eleven people,[9] Mohammad said:

> The trouble started on the seventh morning [7 December 1992]. Some two to three hundred people had surrounded Mukund Nagar. They started burning. We decided it was better to die fighting than to become [sacrificial] goats. We organized ourselves to meet the threat. We put out the fire and made sure our women and children were safe.

RC: How did you put out the fire?

MOHAMMAD: See, it's like this. Some of our boys created a diversion by attacking from one side while the others put out the fire. If we put out one fire another would start, but we made sure that it did not spread beyond the border. This drain [*Joglekar nullah*] that runs around Mukund Nagar was called the India-Pakistan border.

FARHANA: We were playing Hindustan-Pakistan.

MOHAMMAD: Again you have started. Quiet, I told you. [He put his index finger to his lip.]

Farhana is the mentally disturbed daughter of Mohammad.

These boundaries are both functional and invested with the quality of proper nouns—they are iconic. Naming is an important device in these narratives. In the process of constituting the event of violence, naming expresses identity. By giving it a name, danga, violence is a pervasive presence, embedded in experience as an object and story with a predetermined telos. The name "Dharavi" itself becomes a marker. This is echoed in the account of a resident of another slum in Bombay (in Antop Hill, Wadala): "We fear Dharavi. We wouldn't like to settle there. They have cut links from their communities. They have migrated to Bombay on their own [as solitary individuals]. We [referring to his neighborhood] came here as a group and we have retained ties with our community back home." We find an indexical relationship between the

mode in which Dharavi presents itself to outsiders and the location of
the danga. The one is the causal condition of the other. Naipaul (1990:
235), for example, says, "Seen from here Dharavi looked artificial, unnecessary even in Bombay, allowed to exist because, as people said, it
was a vote-bank, a hate-bank, something to be drawn upon by many
people. All the conflicting currents of Bombay flowed there as well; all
the new particularities were heightened there." In contrast to the slum
in Wadala, Dharavi appears porous and is susceptible because it does
not form identifiably coherent communities. But like all indexical markers a similarity is found between the mark and the condition it signifies.
The mark is, of course, Dharavi, where new "particularities" are crystallized. It is almost as if old customs and ways of life no longer have
the power to shape identity. Now all that is left is violence, the marker
par excellence of collective identity: to be a Muslim is to be in a relationship of conflict with the Hindu.

Naming, furthermore, is one way of fixing memory. It operates not
just as a mnemonic but also initiates the narrativizing process. With the
act of naming the narratives provide a way of stitching together everyday
life, whose fabric has been torn by violence. The expression of violence
leads to an extraordinary hardening of the present. The narrator always
identifies himself or herself with names of others. Asif Ali's account exemplifies this. It is as if the narrators live in two times: the present moment of violence and the memory of a more sober life. The present,
apprehended through the objects on which violence leaves its mark, is
lost in the narratives whenever one establishes a genealogy of violence.
For this reason the narratives assume an engagement with the present,
but tenuously. They make present a violence that previously existed by
implication. To be sure, endemic violence in Dharavi is thought of as a
quality of everyday life; it forms the backdrop on which the specific
contours of this specific event are etched: a Hindu-Muslim riot.

EVENT

How, then, do we understand the violence of 1992–93 in Dharavi? In
obvious ways it is linked to the destruction of the Babri Masjid. This
link is both temporal and spatial. There is a remarkable continuity with
the riots in Ayodhya and the rest of India, just as there are well-defined
targets of attack: mosques and temples. Can we, however, say that the
violence of 6 December 1992 in Ayodhya was replicated a day later in
Dharavi? To see it in this way is to create an uninterrupted linear text

that is referential and fixed. The demolition of the mosque in Ayodhya is a national event. At stake are both the identity and future of Indian Muslims and the forging of a sacred Hindu geography. For this reason, the violence following the demolition is distributed over large parts of India. Read in this way, the national inscribes itself over local territories. From the point of view of the local we are unable to see how it incorporates the national. We argue that the local as much as the national has the capacity to reformulate identity. In our conversations naming plays a crucial role in this reformulation:

> MOHAMMAD: I have never supported Pakistan. It means nothing to me. My honor lies in India. My name is Mohammad Ansari. The Ansaris have always voted for Congress. Even before Partition the Ansaris never supported Jinnah. . . .
>
> MAMU (INTERRUPTING): What does he know? He was a young boy during Partition. . . .
>
> MOHAMMAD: Where were you during the danga [in 1992–93]?
>
> MAMU: I know that the [Babri] Masjid fell and I left for home. Nothing else. In 1947 there were only two people, Jinnah and As-Salaam Abdul Ghaffar Khan, not even Gandhi or Maulana Azad.[10] There were four brothers in our family. One was dark and blind in one eye. Three of us voted for the Congress because Ghaffar Khan of the red cap asked us to do so. The dark one voted for the Muslim League. We were all born in UP. How could we vote for anything other than India? The Shiv Sena may not want us here. But can they deny my corpse its plot of land? Can they bury me in Pakistan?[11]

The names in these conversations are not simple references to the past, nor do they coexist with the present. Mohammad's account is remarkable for its investment of hope and subsequent betrayal as much as it is nostalgic for a lost home. For him, the name of his community must be remembered so that he shall not himself be forgotten. His refusal to see the Partition in sectarian terms is tied up with the reiteration of his name. This name resonates in the account of his biography. He talks of his mysterious journey to Bombay and the changing of his name from Muhammad Masud to Ansari because it looked better on a visiting card: "Ansari Brass Works." Mamu disturbs this memory. His speech establishes a stable relation between the interlocutor (the "I," in this case Mamu) and history. His identification, drawn from an onomastic table, denies the possibility of localizing Muslim (at any rate, his) identity. In contrast, the danga, in both these accounts, is the uttering of an alterity—an absolute difference between 1947 and 1992–93. Here, both Mohammad and Mamu are located by uttering statements that are fundamentally other.

Rather than argue for a mimetic explanation of violence, we suggest that its occurrence in Dharavi is, from the point of view of narrators, explained both through local geography and social relations. For example, we find repeated references to particular spots functioning as the India-Pakistan border, particular neighborhoods being named as foreign and therefore enemy. Mohammad identifies a local drain in his area as the India-Pakistan border. Similarly, another narrator shows us a wall that divides a Muslim neighborhood from a Hindu one and calls this the Kashmir border.[12]

The event of the Babri mosque and the violence of Dharavi make the narratives of violence possible. This point cannot be overstated enough. The event gives the narratives a foundation. In this sense the event is constitutive. However, it is grasped primarily through the narrations. Thus the event has a double structure. First, the narratives describe the present moment of the event's actualization, a moment when violence inheres in a state of affairs, designated by saying "It happened" (aisa hua). The future and past are evaluated through this definitive production and from the point of view of those who embody it. In this sense the event is realized and accomplished. Equally, there is the future and past of the event considered in itself, sidestepping each present. Here the event creates its genealogy, a secret part continually added to its actualization. The narratives are perpetually haunted by two types of description: What happened? What is going to happen? Concerning what happened, the narratives mark out an object: violated bodies, destroyed houses, burned bakeries, etc. As regards what will happen, we find that a story or tale is constructed: the significance of sudden noises, gathering of crowds, voices signaling future conflicts. The event is both object and story, never an actuality. In this way a genealogy is fashioned.

Following from the above, the event has two temporal dimensions. First, it constitutes the present by enveloping it in a time internal to the act of description. In this sense the event exists in the act of speaking. This speech, in drawing the contours of violence, inscribes the present. This present evaluates the effect of violence on bodies, buildings, and neighborhoods and depends upon the matter that fills it. The present, then, measures out the temporal realization of the event: its incarnation and embodiment in a state of affairs. But this present oscillates with an infinitive that formally divides the past from the future. Here, the past and future elide the present and are unlimited: they can be filled in numerous ways.

For this reason, the event is emergent. It sticks out from the everyday as an alternate temporal configuration providing new strands by which the world is experienced. The narratives crystallize the event, imagine it as unique so that it becomes a frame within which the everyday, now estranged, can be viewed reflexively. In describing violence the narratives authorize the event as well as show how the latter intersects with the narratives on relief. Relief work, we will show later, acts as a bridge between the violence of 1992–93 and a reformulated everyday life that succeeds it. It reformulates everyday life through collective action, enabling a resumption of normality and the remoralizing of local communities. Through collective action these communities enter, in Kakar's (1995) words, "normal time," as opposed to "riot time." In our case, normal time is not sharply polarized from riot time. It involves a forgetting of the violence, so crucial for the everyday task of coexistence. To understand this phenomenon we first show how violence carves out specific chawls and then how relief work reformulates the spaces marked by violence.

BOUNDARIES AND NAMES

Violence carves out boundaries. In the narratives boundaries are designated by national and sectarian names.

FARIDABI: A group of forty to fifty women came to me and said they wanted to meet Kane, a Shiv Sainik, who was then a corporator [an elected member of the Bombay Municipal Corporation]. I said there was no use in meeting him since his role in the danga was well known. The women were adamant. So I went along at the head of this procession. Near Pakeezah Hotel a police jeep was going past. I stopped it and the women fell on the jeep. The policeman came out with his *danda* [wooden stick]. He asked me what I wanted. I said the conditions in our chawl were very bad. The men could not come out of their houses, we had nothing to eat, everybody was afraid. The officer told me not to worry, he would request the military to come. I told the women to return since the police had promised to send the military. On the rooftops of houses along the road men were laughing and whistling at us. While coming back, near Sumitra Hotel, the men broke on

us [*hum pe toot pare*]. The police saw this and fired their tear
gas. Women were running all over the place. I took the women
towards the Masjid road, but a Madrasi [a generic term for a
person from South India] told us that there was a large group of
boys waiting there. He said to run towards Bismillah chawl. I
asked him to show us the way. He took us down the road and
left. Near Bismillah chawl the crowd pounced on us and took
two women away. A Madrasi got them back. One of the women
is Rafique bhai's wife. She had her head and jaw opened. While
taking them away, the crowd was shouting, "See, we are snatch-
ing your Pakistan away."

The India-Pakistan border becomes substantial and corporeal. Since a
territory (the body of women) is marked as an arena of violence, a legitimate theater of practical action is delimited.

Sarvate,[13] a Dalit Maharashtran living in Central Area, has this to
say:

> In the danga this place was known as the Kashmir Hindu-
> stan-Pakistan border. We didn't start the riots. They [Mus-
> lims] began it by throwing stones and after that hand
> bombs. . . . They would make these bombs in boxes and
> throw them.

SARVATE'S SON: They were put in *pan parag* [betel nut] tins. In these tins
yellow phosphorous and gunpowder were added to broken
tube light glass. Once they had made them they would
throw the tin. We would catch the tins and throw them
back. [He demonstrates how it was done.]

RC: Weren't you afraid they would explode and hurt you?

SON: No, they only explode when they are forcefully hit against
the wall. You have to catch them like this. [He demonstrates
by showing how one would take a catch.]

SARVATE: My children play bat-ball. They know how to catch.

At the end of this conversation Sarvate accompanied us outside his house
and showed us from where the attackers had entered. He took us to a
dead end and, pointing to a wall about eight feet high, said that the
attackers had scaled the wall. In retaliation, with a few others he placed
live electric wires across two houses that stood on either side of the wall.
This was, presumably, the Hindustan-Pakistan border. Taking us to the
other side he pointed to a narrow path from which other attackers had
come to burn Muslim houses.

This boundary, it is evident, is fragmented, miniaturized, and has
multiple meanings and effects built into it. It is fragmented in at least

two ways: we do not find one physical barrier running through Dharavi. Depending upon the neighborhood this barrier is a drain, a wall, a road, or something more intangible called the "other side" (*us par*): spaces that are public. Second, once public space is referenced in this way it is excised of neutrality, but in such a way that the referentiality replacing such excision is infused with multiple meanings. The drain is a place where bodies are disposed; the wall allows one side to think of the other as anonymous and dangerous; and the road is the site for random attacks. The miniaturized character of the boundary is found in the account of virtually every informant: lived space shrinks to the house, too precariously. This, in part, explains why narratives of the event reflect on domestic space and recount what happened to one's family. Correspondingly, most accounts of the violence that occur in public space are characterized by anonymity or expressed in rumor. Finally, this boundary is polyvalent because the existence of multiple narratives gives it a function that is localized to the territory within which narratives circulate.

A second characteristic of this boundary is that it is designated by naming. Once areas are designated as the Hindustan-Pakistan border a range of practices is ordered within: the name, in this sense, limits. In this way a link is established between collective identity and a personal name. The idea is that the name, redolent of the personal uniqueness of the individual, is also a sociological construction of the namegiver. From the perspective of the namegiver it is almost as if the narrators have no choice other than realizing themselves in a name which is characteristic simultaneously of a nation and a community. From the point of view of the namegiver the name of each male person of the other community is designated by general terms: *landia log* or *katua,* terms denoting circumcision as a stigmatizing mark.[14] Here, religion, nationality and personal identity all intersect. Consider the following examples.

MOHAMMAD: It was during the time of the Bhiwandi riots[15] when they [police] made us naked, took us in their trucks, and shoved their *lathis* [thick wooden sticks attached with iron at one end] up our arse. That's how they identified us. Whoever they caught they would ask to strip. If they found the fellow was a katua they would give him the lathi. [Laughter.] Munnalal Bidiwalla [a Hindu] was caught this way. The police caught him and asked him to strip. He is a katua, just like me. In spite of his protests they gave it to him. When his *bhatija* [brother's son] intervened they asked him to strip too. He was also circumcised. Now he walks like a pregnant goat.

ALI: You see, roads were under constant threat. Groups of boys
         [*tapori chokras*][16] from outside would wait on them. If they
         found anyone they would strip him to discover his identity.
         We would spare all those who are katua. They [Hindus] call
         us katua, people who are not male. Some of ours were knifed;
         others, more fortunate, were made to stand in a sewer and
         shout "Jai Siya Ram" [a form of greeting used by Hindu na-
         tionalists]. If they didn't they were beaten. . . . When they
         came in to attack we could hear them shouting, "Where are
         the katua?" [*katua kahan hain*], "Catch the circumcised" [*lan-
         dia log ko pakro*], "See, there's another katua, cut it off"
         [*dekho wahan katua hai, kat do uski*].

The term *katua* is difficult to translate because it has a complex of meanings associated with it. As synecdoche it refers to Muslims in general,
but also to the cut penis. The latter signifies castration. The term is
stigmatizing: the Muslim is hunted because of the mark he carries on
him. "Katua" always refers to the other, the enemy. It designates a violation because it indicates an insurmountable alterity, forever sealing
the difference between Hindus and Muslims in territorial and religious
terms. Branding Muslims males as katua is not merely the operation of
an anonymous force with injunctive power. To call the danga communal
is to remove it from the domain of individual agency and give it the
quality of a force immanent with particular identities. Thus identity becomes communal and is susceptible to violence.

Once the boundary is marked there are various ways by which its
insides are constructed. Asif Ali,[17] who walked with us to a colony called
Bagicha, sees this as being composed of rubble and stone. While at Bagicha we met two textile entrepreneurs, Sharique and Rafique, who had
suffered heavy losses during the danga. Initially reticent to talk, Sharique, the elder of the two, invited us inside his workshop, a large room
half filled with bales of cotton cloth. While Sharique and Rafique talked
of the loss to their business, Asif Ali continued where he left off:

> When this burning started we found that a Muslim worker of mine was
> stranded in Kala Killa [the place where Asif Ali has his workshop]. I went
> to rescue him. In normal times it is less than fifteen minutes away. Kala
> Killa has three or four Muslim establishments, the rest are Dalits. When I
> reached him a big crowd had gathered. I got him back with me, but with
> this danga it took us about an hour or two to reach here. When I reached
> it everything was razed to the ground. In one hour. I could see across to
> the other side of the road. Not a single Muslim house remained. Everything
> was stone and brick. If only I had stayed this would not have happened.
> Both sides listen to me. I could have stood in the middle and stopped them.

In those days children would fly kites and play bat-ball on the grounds where houses stood. We used those places to shit. Everything has changed. Muslims staying in this area want to sell out.

Asif Ali's account privileges an ambiguity. It recounts inversions and displacements and turns the boundary into a crossing. The house can be destroyed and made into public space: it is a disobedience of the law of habitation; the passageway back home is an ensemble of violent encounters and anonymous threats. The danga radically alters the physical landscape, perhaps forever. This alteration he believes could have been prevented if he had been present during the moment of violence. He sees himself as occupying the precarious middle ground between Hindus and Muslims. One of his neighbors, Barkatulla, said that during the danga Sarvate had taunted Asif Ali with the words "*O Mullah yahan sandas nahin karne ka*" ("O Mullah don't you use this shithouse." *Mullah* is a derogatory term used by Hindus for a Muslim priest). This precariousness emerges when Asif Ali talks of the last election:

> During the last election the booth was captured for forty minutes. For forty minutes. This is Hindustan. What can I say. Whoever has power has money and law. Today it is their day, tomorrow will be ours. Nothing can be done now. There was no relief given. All the Muslim houses were burned. The only politician who was honest during the danga was Dutt,[18] and we see the consequences of that. Nobody gave us anything. The sisterfuckers left us on the streets. People ran away with the clothes they were wearing, without slippers. This is Hindustan.

Asif Ali refused to meet us again. After repeated attempts to talk to him we were told that he felt threatened. He never mentioned Sarvate's name, his neighbor who had taunted him and yet whose son he is forced to employ in his factory. It is as if the affirmation of one's name is placed against an absence—the inability to name one's enemy and one's identity as an Indian Muslim, the fact that one's citizenship is in question.

Asif Ali's cynicism is countered by the guarded optimism of Mahmud, another leather worker, but not as prosperous as Asif Ali. Mahmud,[19] living in Central Area, conceives of his chawl as a fortification. If for Asif Ali the danga destroys the meeting ground between Hindus and Muslims, Mahmud says:

> There is a crossing [he crosses his two index fingers] between Hindus and Muslims. Both have become suspicious of each other. On the outside everything is okay, but now there is no trust. On the sixth evening, I had gone to offer prayers. While praying, we heard a noise. The mosque was being stoned. The *maulvi* [priest]

here is an innocent man. He asked me to find out what the noise
was about. I looked out of the mosque gate and saw a group of
people approaching. They were shouting slogans. . . . On the sev-
enth morning, the danga broke out. People were waiting for milk.
That day there was stoning and fire. All these houses are made
of wood, you see. If one house catches fire the entire road is in
flames. It continued for the entire day. . . . But the danga lasted
only for a day. At night my daughter woke up screaming. I
thought the crowds had come. I found my sons awake. They had
taken *gaslit* [kerosene] from the house. They were going to join
a group to burn the other side. They have become sensible now,
but then they were young and angry. I ran after them. They didn't
know they were being watched by a big crowd on the other side.
I told my sons not to do this. With God's grace, they saw sense
and came back. After that the Hindus realized that the Muslims
of this area didn't want to make trouble. That night the Muslims
had climbed on to a temple here. They had begun to chip away
but no damage was done.

DM: What happened to the Hindus here?

MAHMUD: We also looted them. They looted and burned and we did the
same. If Muslims were in a minority they looted and if they were
in a minority we looted. Their shops were destroyed. But there
was no killing here. See, we are not going to accept it meekly. We
would also retaliate. They knew this . . . . There were fights in
other chawls. We could see stones and bottles being thrown.
Sometimes two stones would collide and fall over our houses, but
we didn't create trouble. This area was safe. They knew that these
leather workers are honest but they become violent and angry
when troubled. We enjoy respect here and we know how to give
respect. We take care of our neighbors. This is only necessary.
[Pointing to a young man sitting next to him:] He is my brother's
son, my real brother. He lives across the road. But I will seek my
neighbor's help first and later my brother's. Why? Because I have
to live with them. I see them every day.

If in Asif Ali's narration the mediating role (between Hindus and Muslims) is played by the narrator, in Mahmud's account the neighborhood
combines Hindus and Muslims. His narration shows how communication and separation are made possible. More than that, the neighborhood is an in-between space, but one not without its pitfalls:

People are nice, but from the outside. During marriages, they will send us
cards but they will never come personally to deliver them. Are we interested
in their cards or in them? We personally deliver our cards and always take
something for them but they don't. This happens once, twice, thrice. In the
fourth instance we start to behave like them. We also know how to preserve

our self-respect. This is why there is suspicion and fear. If they are tight, we also know to be tight. [He sits up straight.]

Perhaps Mahmud's narration moves towards a political freezing of his neighborhood, one that is protected and stable because of the inherent strength of its inhabitants, a fixing that is impervious to the depredations of the outside. This narration is an attempt to delimit the neighborhood from the violence of the outside, but in this attempt at delimitation he expresses the alterity hidden inside the limits. The Hindus in his neighborhood, contemptuously dismissed as Dalits and *jahils* (untutored), are to be reformed so that they maintain the peace. The house in this neighborhood is a sanctuary:

> It is not as if all Hindus are bad. There are good Hindus and bad Muslims. Some of the Marathis gave us shelter. Their women used to bring my woman news of the danga. They would tell her not to send her children to troubled areas. There was a Muslim from here who got caught. A Maharashtran family gave him shelter in their house. He would eat in the house and also shit in there. When the danga ended they sent him back. We also helped them. We would send them food and water when they needed it. For this reason there was no trouble here after the seventh. Their women and children would run through here. We gave their women shelter in our house and helped them get their breath back.

In this narration the adverbs here and there have the function of introducing an other in relation to this I. In so doing they show how territories are being both conjoined to and separated from each other under the frame of a sectarian identity.

VIOLATED HOUSES

What happens when the house is violated? For Dina[20] the destruction of her house is experienced as the legal system literally inscribing itself on her husband's back.

> On 24 January the police came in firing. Late in the night when we were asleep, the sounds of firing awoke us. The police were here. My husband was in his *lungi* and vest on this bed with our youngest child. The police came in and picked up my husband. They were picking up every male above the age of fifteen. When I asked why they were doing this they said my husband was involved in the danga. They said he had fought against the police. I told them that wasn't possible since he was sleeping on the bed with his child. I spoke in Marathi, but they warned, "*Ai randi, Marathi men nahin bolne ka*" [don't speak in Marathi, whore]. He was wearing a lungi and vest. When I said this one of the men pushed me and abused me

in the vilest language. They were drunk, all these men were drunk. . . .
Whichever house they found bolted from inside they would break down
and drag the men away. They were bundled into a van, taken to the other
side of the road, and beaten with rifle butts. My neighbor came back the
next day, his back was blue and swollen all over.

Perhaps more for Dina than for the others there is a daily reality of the
violence of 1992–93. This painful recognition is forced:

> I pleaded with them to let my husband go, but he was jailed. My daughter
> here is attached to her father since he feeds her at night. When he was
> arrested she stopped eating. She wanted to be with her father. They
> wouldn't let me visit him in jail. If I was carrying food for him they asked
> for five rupees to let the food pass. One day my daughter said she would
> eat only from her father's hand. I begged them with my daughter in my
> lap. I was allowed to meet him after I had given them money. The lawyers
> kept telling me that my husband would be released any time. I gave them
> two hundred rupees. I haven't seen them since. My husband was in jail for
> eleven days. He got out on bail. . . . He has been charged with half murder.
> The case is in the Bandra courts. Whenever my daughter sees a policeman
> she cannot talk. My son says that when he becomes big he wants to hit
> policemen. [Giggles.]

Faridabi[21] shows how the invasion of her house occurs together with
that of her body. In her account we find a progression of violence from
her body to commodities in her house. For her too, 24 January is a
marked date:

> There were two alarm clocks, one Ajanta and one foreign. On the twenty-
> fourth the police came to my house. . . . The "scene-shot"[22] was like this:
> when I opened the door they asked me to show them where the men were
> hidden. I told them there was no one in this house. They wouldn't listen.
> They took my two clocks and a Citizen wall clock. When I protested they
> rifle-butted me in the stomach. Ever since my stomach has become hard.
> [She catches RC's hand and runs it down her stomach.] One of them kicked
> the cupboard. Now it doesn't close. They found fifteen hundred rupees and
> took that. When I objected they fired three shots. The third shot passed
> between my knees, grazing them. Because of this my knees fill with gas and
> swell up. I have difficulty walking. . . . People say that I am a rich woman.
> They say that I am a *randi* [prostitute], that I employ women. But the men
> here are impotent. You go to this balcony and shout, "You sisterfuckers,
> is there any male among you?" Not a single man will come out. They were
> scared when the police came. Do you think, *birader* [brother], they were
> going to take part in any *danga*? When I resisted the police hit me with a
> lathi on my wrist. [RC's hand is made to run over her right wrist.] . . . The
> police came to know I was giving food to others. They came to my house
> again, but I didn't open the door. The next day when I asked for permission

to buy rations they abused me in Marathi.[23] I understand this language. In Marathi they said [she repeats in Marathi], "These women's men have swollen cocks. The only way is to cut them." In Marathi I said, "It seems to me that you are a Poona-Nashik fellow." They replied back, "Let's cut this old bitch's fat breasts." These sisterfuckers, don't mind birader, are only good for drinking *bhevada* [country liquor].

The conversation ended with RC examining her knees.

Faridabi's account, filled with hyperbole and drama, talks of a resistance to police repression. This resistance is marked on her body as much as it is invested in the things stolen from her house. Her body both mirrors the violation of her house and remembers, in a physical sense, the invasion. It is almost as if proper nouns are corporeal. For Dina, the destruction of her house is a continuous presence. This destruction is made possible because her husband's alleged involvement in the danga allows the outside to become a permanent feature of her house. While for Faridabi her body is memory, in Dina's narration the event has not crystallized enough for her to establish a separation from it. Common to both accounts is the forced opening of the house to the outside.

As we see it, then, this boundary is a graduated one. In its most general sense it divides India from Pakistan, but also Maharashtra from the rest of India, Dharavi from Bombay, and, within Dharavi, one colony from another. It also divides neighbors living in the same colony and finally the house from itself.

DISPLACEMENTS AND ALTERITIES

The narratives show that violence leads to a sense of displacement, thematized as loss, something that is fixed and final. Often, associated with such loss is a conception of the other as the prehistory of the danga. When identified with members of other communities the other is either dangerous or dehumanized, one who is not removed to a distance but is constantly lurking below the surface. Displacement means moving into a different neighborhood within Dharavi, but in a few cases leaving Bombay altogether. Migration, however, is not merely a matter of physical boundaries, it also delimits cultural fields (the familiar versus the strange) and in this way allows for conceptualizing the other. One way in which delimitation is effected is by assigning names to spaces brutally torn by violence. Here proper names (as in Asif Ali's narration) carve out pockets of hidden and familiar meanings. Since names map neighborhoods, they change areas into passages. Boundaries so identified

rework the spatial division of the neighborhood so that the latter is
polarized into a Hindu and Muslim section. We will use a few examples.

RAKESH, A HINDU FROM RAJASTHAN: There is no aftereffect of the danga,
save one. Now I would not like to
stay in this colony. I don't feel safe.
This is natural, isn't it? If as a minority you are staying in a majority-
dominated area then you would not
feel safe. It is the same for Hindus living in Muslim-dominated areas. They
don't feel safe. . . . It has come to my
ear that a lot of Hindus want to leave.
It is natural. One has this feeling of
security among one's own. My house
has been broken once. I would not
like to have it broken again. In this
place there are approximately 30 percent Hindu families. They all want to
leave.

In a later conversation Rakesh said he would leave if he got a good price
for his house, but then immediately admitted, "During the riots some
said I belonged to the Shiv Sena. I heard of this and came out to this
compound. I said, 'Can anyone say this to my face?' I have been here
from the beginning when Dharavi was marshy land that boats used to
ply. I will leave for a Hindu colony because I don't feel safe." He refuses
to be drawn out on what he thinks of Muslims, except to say that he
exchanges greetings and sweets with them on festive occasions. If Rakesh is hesitant in talking of his feelings towards those he wants to leave,
his friend Mohammad is more forthcoming:

Let me tell you the truth. The Maharashtrans don't want to kill us, they
just want us to leave Bombay. What is the phrase: *hamara Mumbai, svach
Mumbai, amchi Mumbai* [our Bombay, pure Bombay, my Bombay]. Look
at him. The sisterfucker wears a *dhoti* [loincloth] that goes into his arse,
he drinks bhevada and lies in the gutter all day. In the evening he gets up,
goes home, and smashes his wife. My friend [pointing to one of the
PROUD workers who lives in Dharavi and is participating in the conver-
sation] does this sometimes.

This reduction of the other to an object is linked to the effect of the
danga. "The main object was to deprive us of our land. But that did not
happen. Instead this danga has helped us in getting rid of our fear. During the danga I didn't sleep for more than two weeks. Now if it were to

happen again I wouldn't be afraid. Let the Maharashtrans come. This time we are ready." But the fear is palpable in other accounts.

AYESHA: The effect of the danga is seen in kids. They didn't go to school for two months. Many dropped out. Others changed houses and had to find their feet all over again. Now we have *madarsas* [seminaries] all over the place.

MOHAMMAD: Arabic teaching is essential.

AYESHA: I'm not talking of mullahs. Will they teach my children English and mathematics? It's not only children who are afraid, but all of us, in spite of what Mohammad bhai [brother] here says. Even now at night if we hear shutters banging I get scared. If I hear people running or screaming I think we are in another danga.

In Mukund Nagar, a Muslim majority area, the one person explicitly talking of displacement is a Hindu. Rakesh would rather leave a chawl he has stayed in for the last twenty years and live among comparative strangers. For Mohammad the effect of the danga is that it allows him to recognize the other, but only to the extent that this recognition is available through acts of violence. For Rakesh the other is always repressed, perhaps because of his proximity to those who are now alien.

For Mohammad and Faridabi rootedness involves continuous negotiations with the other. Faridabi says:

Only after the Hindu areas were burned did Kane call for a meeting. He didn't want to meet us when our houses were being burned. We went to the meeting—there were Mohammad bhai, Momin bhai, and me. On the other side of the Joglekar Nullah, about four to five hundred Shiv Sainiks had gathered. They were standing with one hand behind their backs gnashing their teeth. They all had weapons . . . Kane asked us to stop this burning. I said we would when they stopped. He said we didn't seem sincere. I said, look, Momin bhai is here. His son's corpse is in his house.[24] He hasn't had time to bury it. After that we shook hands.

This effort of creating communication between a here and a there fixes areas into two opposing camps. In contrast to Mukund Nagar, displacement is much more pronounced among the Muslims of Central Area. Sharique says that his main problems started after the danga. During the violence he had gone back to his village in Uttar Pradesh. After returning he found his workshop gutted. He was left with three workers, where previously he used to employ more than thirty.

Many of those who came back have sold out. Others are waiting for a good price. I also want to sell. But Muslims will not buy this property.

DM: Who has bought this land?

SHARIQUE: Hindus, Maharashtrans. They are service people,[25] they don't do
          this work. . . . Dharavi has a bad name. Others are convinced
          there will be more dangas. . . . My elder brother went back to
          the *mulk* [home town or village]. He doesn't want to return.
          Muslims want to move to their neighborhoods. If I get the op-
          portunity I will move to Chamra Bazaar [Muslim majority area
          in Dharavi].

For Idris of Central Area, to move is an imperative. She stays in a chawl
inhabited primarily by Hindus, one of whom is an office bearer of the
Shiv Sena. During the danga her neighbors categorically warned her that
they were unwilling to protect her. She was subject to their taunts. Furthermore, while she was moving (temporarily, during the danga) they
refused to keep her goods. She took refuge first in the house of Mahmud
and later in the masjid. Upon returning she found her house looted. Her
neighbors, whom she identifies as Hindu and Maharashtran, have with-
drawn social contact, and her daughters-in-law are subject to verbal
abuse. She says that as soon as she finds a house near Mahmud's she
will move. For her the spatial order of her neighborhood organizes a
series of prohibitions. Her son's children cannot play with Hindu children of the neighborhood, her household cannot reestablish contact
with contiguous households, and she is afraid to share the same public
space.

Much the same story emerges in Social Nagar. Dina says,

> So great was the terror [after the danga] that people just left, leaving their
> entire businesses. After that there was silence, like that of a graveyard. This
> area has been populated in this last year, but not by those who left, who
> were mainly from UP. Those who have come are from Bihar. The Hindus
> did not leave. There are four Hindu households here. One left during the
> danga, one well before that. The other two continue to live here. They
> were not troubled by the police. How did they know not to touch them?
> Is it written on everyone's forehead that you are Hindu and you Muslim?

While walking out of her house we were accompanied by a stranger,
who had been listening in on this conversation. He drew alongside us
and said, "Here there used to be a bakery. You see, it was burned to the
ground. That is where a man and a woman were shot by the police. The
daughter came running with blood all over her. But the police would
not let her take her parents to hospital. They were removed to the masjid." Here, the places where people lived before the danga testify to
diverse absences. What can be seen designates what is no longer there:

"There used to be a bakery," but it can no longer be seen. Walking indicates the identities of the invisible. This seems to be the definition of neighborhoods ravaged by violence: the past is not removed to a distance but becomes the other of what remains on the surface. This phantom enunciates through the act of walking.

MEMORY AND GENEALOGY

What remains after territories are carved out, houses violated, and people displaced? We must remember that the danga is constituted for us as an act of memory. In this memory, names function as traces of memory. Often they point to an absence—an active forgetting of past events for the sake of coexistence—and yet the name makes present. Through names violated areas are marked. One of our informants shows us new houses, once Muslim-owned. They had been burned and later rebuilt with relief money by the one responsible for their destruction. The houses were sold to Hindu Maharashtrans. This landscape is both present in memory and marks the future as the anticipation of an inevitable violence.

In these narratives naming creates identity. All efforts to locate narratives in the particularity of individual agency or everyday life fail. Mohammad's narrative highlights the danger of a sectarian identity, one that lurks under the surface of his discourse. It emerges in lapses and asides, in elaborate third-person generalizations, analogic statements, and excuses. Another speaker, Babat, says, "I want to shift not because I am Hindu in a Muslim majority area. They run businesses in their houses. The machines keep me awake at night. I can't tell this to my neighbors. I have lived here long and they respect me. I can't hurt by telling them the truth."

We hear censored speech: circumlocutions and slips, the shift from first person to third person, an inability to name perpetrators. More than that, the physical contact necessary to conversation is threatened. This fear is most marked in the walking stories. Public spaces, especially roads, make one visible to the other. The danger of being overheard, of having words misinterpreted and returning as accusations, all contribute to a sense of foreboding.

Care is taken to regulate access to these narratives. The audience controls the story, yet there is a desire to tell it, to name. Barkatulla, introduced to us by Sarvate and asked to bear witness to Sarvate's role as peacemaker, makes a surreptitious appointment with us. When we meet in his house the desire to name the perpetrators gives way to rhetorical questions: "Who looted and who suffered? Did we loot from our own homes? The sisterfuckers, now they ask us to give the names of those who looted us. As if they don't know. They loot us and then pretend a concern for justice. Give us the names? The police know, they were with them." When pressed, he referred to the looters as "Ghati," a derogatory name for Maharashtrans, never more specific. Barkatulla, at least, is able to voice that which Mohammad cannot or will not: fear among Muslims, selling houses, resettlement of neighborhoods. Mohammad distinguishes between a genuine and illusory fear, the latter generated by rumors during the danga: bells ringing, shouts announcing the attackers' arrival, constant vigil. Finally the distinction collapses. This is why those affected, both Hindus and Muslims, wish to sell their houses, even after they have been renovated. This is the effect of the danga. Not only does it generate its past, it also molds the future. The danga is not merely a memory but also an anticipation of a possible future. It is thus not only an alterity coexisting with everyday life, but an event that makes the latter in its image.

The inevitability of this violence is placed within a genealogy. It is measured against the Bhiwandi riot of 1984 and against internal troubles within Dharavi, such as those fomented by liquor barons, drug lords, and land-grabbers. It is also placed against the Bombay blasts of March 1993. Mohammad mentions that the danga ended with the blasts. Implicit in this genealogy is the theme of sectarian war. Thus beyond the particular experiences and actions of people living in Dharavi is the broad theme of Hindu-Muslim conflict. Within this frame the genealogical mode acquires cogency. This mode crystallizes, in the process, forces that are anonymous, arbitrary, and yet inevitable. For Masih, a Christian member of the Peoples' Responsible Organization for United Dharavi (PROUD), the police are unable to control the violence since "communal spirit" has entered into the hearts of people. Rakesh, however, recognizes that sectarian conflicts often conceal self-interest. He places such hostilities within a genealogy:

In Mukund Nagar there was one other danga between 1984 and 1992. There was a man called Musa who had a hotel in Khambadevi. Musa was a *goonda* [hooligan]. He did all sorts of illegal things—drugs and prostitutes. There was some problem between him and the people of Khambadevi. They asked the Shiv Sena for help. Musa got to know that the Shiv Sena was after him. He decided to turn the problem into a Hindu-Muslim issue. He burned one row of households in Mukund Nagar and claimed that the Shiv Sena had done it. The situation became so bad that the police were unable to control it. Some people from here [Mukund Nagar] started fighting with those of Khambadevi. The special police were called. They waited near the shithouse and whenever people came to shit they caught them. People started leaving. In 1984 also people started running away. They would come back during the day and run away at night. I know because I stayed here. My children were very small. This danga [1992] was not between Hindus and Muslims. It was started by people who stood to gain from fighting. They were all goondas. It was done by outsiders.

In Rakesh's account the extraordinary dimensions of the danga are reduced to a problem of law and order:

> You see, before the danga there were goondas here. They would brew illicit liquor, shout at night, rob people. Rebeiro came here—he was the head of some committee.[26] I and Mohammad met him and we told him of our problems. Rebeiro asked us to show him the houses of these goondas. How could we? Later, they would catch us. He said to walk by their houses and throw matchboxes before them. His man, following us, would note down the number of that house. I and Mohammad did this. In this way we got rid of the goondas.

Rakesh, however, is certain that if an opportunity arises for him to sell his house and settle in a Hindu majority area he will take it. He does not feel safe. His attempt to measure the danga as a law-and-order problem must be seen together with his statements which reduce the communal nature of the conflict. In a conversation with seven others, Rakesh mentions that all those who looted Muslim houses were not Hindus. "These people have no *dharma* [religion]. They do it on behalf of Hindus. They are goondas. But it is not as if Muslims don't have their goondas. Where do these *taporis* [iron rods] come from?" Rakesh implicitly recognizes that even criminals fall within a sectarian divide. More than that, he tries to order the danga by linking it to earlier occasions of the breakdown of law and order.

This genealogy, then, remains present in memory through fear and danger associated with certain spaces and names. It marks the future as the occurrence of similar events. Thus, the event creates its future. It also marks the present by creating a memory for its practitioners, those who are constituted by a faculty of forgetting as much as remembering. Those touched by violence must create another memory, one that is collective, a memory of words and names and no longer a memory of things, a memory of signs and no longer of effects. The next section shows how relief work aids in this.

RELIEF AND REHABILITATION

The first part of this chapter has described how local communities are reconstituted through the narratives of violence. Through naming and the construction of genealogies, these narratives order memories of violence. Names carve out boundaries and reterritorialize communities so that Dharavi is increasingly torn between polar collectives, whose mark of identity is their difference and opposition to each other. Genealogies, the construction of teleological models of history, grapple with the extraordinary nature of the event. The genealogical mode operates in reversible time, creating a past that recurs endlessly. The future, then, is a fearful anticipation of similar events. Thus, the danga is now articulated as a metanarrative, located in the conflict between opposing sectarian groups—Hindus versus Muslims. Behind the effort of coming to terms with the unexpected nature of the event, we find also an awareness of its arbitrariness and absurdity. Violence spreads terror because it strikes in unexpected places. It is anonymous and yet palpable, incarnated in bodies and social relationships.

These narratives are recounted to us two years after the event. The question, then, is: What is the relationship of this violent event to everyday life? The question is important in the context of the reality that the narratives emerge from, already different from the one they describe. The present reality is shaped for us through zones of silence, the censorship they impose on memory and therefore on recounting aspects of everyday life that emerge after the danga. Silences point to the breach the danga creates in the everyday. Some of it has perhaps been closed with the passage of time, but its impact and the nature of the healing process are not easy to assess. The narratives of rehabilitation work provide one way of understanding the healing process.

In seeing how rehabilitation work absorbs violence, we do not view the former as being causally related to violence. Rather, the narratives of rehabilitation and of violence run on parallel tracks. Activities that are thematized into one or other of the two types of narratives occur simultaneously in people's discourse. What the rehabilitation narratives do instead is to help frame differently the relationship between violence and the everyday. If communal violence shapes everyday life in Dharavi in one particular way (seen, for example, in the effect of certain noises signaling violence), then acts of relief also structure violence, shifting our focus to a different register, so that its anonymity gives way to a recognition of face-to-face relationships and the uniqueness of particular incidents in the danga.

In the previous section we have seen how the danga transforms a violence endemic to everyday life. Persons are robbed of agency, even as perpetrators of violent acts. The narratives describe all actions as reactions, as responses to anonymous forces. No one claims to initiate an act for which he or she is accountable. In this mode of articulation those acts of violence, formerly characterized as part of everyday criminality, are now transformed into communal violence. Thus Ayesha states that what starts as a quarrel between two communities (*quomi jhagra*) is prolonged because local enmities take on communal color. She speaks of the looting of shops along the ninety-foot road. Mobs enter shops to take out commodities. These are separated—some piled up to be burned and others appropriated. Idris mentions the packets of "fancy" biscuits and tins of clarified butter found in a Maharashtran Hindu household in her neighborhood. Thus, what appears to be mob frenzy is a mask for greed and envy set adrift from normal everyday restraints. Both Ayesha and Idris imply that these prosperous Muslim shop owners are the envy of many of their neighbors, who, with violence, satisfy their greed.

In contrast, acts of relief work restore agency and allow for expressing individual voices. The rehabilitation narratives reconstitute the complex subjectivity of actors as they move between different subject positions— those of victim and perpetrator in the event. Through these narratives we see the manner by which day-to-day relationships are negotiated in an altered everyday—altered, that is, by the effect of the danga. As we have just stated, the danga initiates a state of normlessness (*magarmach ki niti,* "the law of the crocodile"). Agency is attributed to the force of violence, not to its individual carriers, who are merely its tools. They cannot be accountable. Consequently, everyone takes on the role of victim in the post-danga everyday. This allows for the restoration of normality, since different groups of people can coexist. However, it also reinforces the climate of impunity created by the danga. Relief action reflects this divided character of people's subjectivity: the simultaneous restoration of agency to individuals and its negation, because its goal is to restore an equilibrium between Hindus and Muslims. While relief work aids in the process of restoring everyday life it also reinforces the representation of the danga as an extraordinary event.

What happens to everyday life in this culture of impunity? What is the nature of coexistence when one's neighbor is made alien by violence?

Can the relationship between people in their everyday lives be construed
to form a moral community? To these questions we now turn.

THE BRIDGE

Much of the writing on relief work following the violence of 1992–93
in Bombay emphasizes the remoralizing effect of relief on social life. The
local community is seen as an integral unit able to withstand the effect
of violence. The spirit of coexistence, necessary for everyday life, is assumed to be based on a tolerance of difference, of religion and caste,
and on local-level structures of integration (Nandy et al. 1995; Padgaonkar 1993). The community is defined vis-à-vis violence, characterized as external to it. Relief work pits itself against this externality and
sees its agenda as the restoration of the moral community. The city of
Bombay becomes this community and the restoration of normality is
viewed as a renewal. Bombay's cosmopolitan character is stressed, one
that fosters tolerance. Relief work becomes a bridge connecting formerly
segregated class groups and different sectarian communities. The danga
takes on the qualities, positive and negative, of the sacred.

If the impact of violence affects the city, initiating a previously invisible communal divide, it also brings together "the rich and the poor in
non-denominational togetherness" to fight it (Karkaria as cited in Padgaonkar 1993: 171–72). Thus, on the one hand urban anomie arises
from the mushrooming of slums as a result or rural-urban migration;
on the other, this leads to tolerance as migration breaks communal bar-
riers. The shanty towns of Bombay contain the seeds both of violence
embedded in structural conditions caused by overpopulation, scarcity,
and poverty, and of tolerance, reflecting Bombay's cosmopolitan and
mercantile spirit. The assumption is that a set of common interests and
values makes Bombay a coherent whole, transcending differences. Relief
work taps this value system, thereby acting as a bridge between different
sections of people, but also between violence and the return to normality.

While we agree that relief work, by allowing survivors to reengage
with the everyday world, plays a significant role in restoring normality,
our narratives show that its quality as a bridge makes it ambivalent.
After the danga everyday life becomes a precarious balancing act between a multiplicity of divergent forces. Pragmatic concerns of livelihood are juxtaposed with irrepressible memories of neighbors turned

enemies. Thus Asif Ali is forced to employ Sarvate's son in his workshop and maintain a relationship of amity even though Sarvate insulted him during the danga. He is rumored to have instigated the looters in his area and even now is able to censor Asif Ali's speech by the fact of being his neighbor. Because Asif Ali, one of the few Muslims in this area, remained behind during the danga, he is now perceived as dangerous by Hindu neighbors. "People hesitate before giving me credit. They do not refuse outright since I am well known. But they make excuses like, 'We don't have your material in stock.'"

The everyday life that relief work reconstitutes is different from that which existed before the danga. Memories of the danga have to be set aside but they persist under a surface normality and imperceptibly affect social life. Thus, Mahmud's account reflects the upbeat mood of the relief narratives, but also the anxiety they seek to suppress: "We live in peace as we did before. The danga was an aberration. I have no pleasure in living here . . . I have managed to improve this neighborhood over the past two years by talking to people, holding meetings. We all need peace, our livelihood depends on it. People know who I am here . . . I believe in peace, not the use of force." Yet his story illustrating his powers of diplomatic persuasion reflects a stance of distrust, if not fear, of the outside world:

	This happened a few months ago. . . . It was nighttime and these boys [he pats his son's knee] found a stranger roaming in our neighborhood. They thought he was a thief and thrashed him. They were at fault—they didn't ask him what he was doing here, but you must understand, to be walking around at night and in these times. . . .
MAHMUD'S SON, INTERRUPTING:	We asked him but he said it was none of our business.
MAHMUD:	Yes, that was his fault. He came back the next morning with the police, searching for my boys. This boy [gesturing to his son] was taken to the police station and given a beating. We were scared to leave him there at night. I couldn't get that man to withdraw his case against my son. He wanted revenge. It is human nature. I spoke to the person who was with him. I took him out

for tea and asked him, "Where do you
live?" "Chamra Bazaar," he replied. "You
are a Hindu living in a Mohammadan
area?" I said. "Did you see the danga two
years ago? Do you know what it is like for
us here? We are five or six Mohammadan
households. My boys feel like they are
among strangers. Their fault was that they
beat him up without finding out what he
wanted. But he was at fault, too. To come
to a strange neighborhood at night is to put
your life at risk." I persuaded the man to
withdraw the case. I took them back to my
workshop, got a doctor to bandage the
man's wounds. We are friends now. They
come to my workshop for shoes. My policy
is to draw good people towards me, whatever their group.

MAHMUD'S SON [LAUGHING]:   The police came here for free shoes even
during the danga when the workshop was
closed.

These vignettes show how everyday life was reformulated after the
danga. We have seen how the renaming of spaces creates boundaries.
One of the effects of the danga is that people migrate to sanctuary
spaces—where their religious communities have a larger presence. Social
identities are increasingly determined along denominational lines. Solidarity is no longer determined by the quality of face-to face relationships, or class and occupational similarity. Many narratives of relief
work strengthen these divisions. Neighborhoods are marked as recipients or nonrecipients of relief supplies. This division is often conflated
with a Hindu/Muslim one and, implicitly, a victim/perpetrator one.
However, given the ambivalence of relief work—as mediator between
the danga and the everyday—it also reflects the opposite. As we will see,
relief work narratives carry the imprint of neighborhood relations, relations that characterize the heterogeneity of everyday life. Such relations endure through the danga, revealing its other face. It is in the
nature of the bridge that traces of violence lie in uneasy juxtaposition
with aspects of everyday life.

BOUNDARIES AND NAMES

Rehabilitation narratives, like those of violence, re-create the topography of Dharavi. External space is renamed, identified through relief

operations. Naming functions as a trace; it gives body to relief activities. Relief emerges as a theme in the walking narratives. They mark spaces in a manner that is the contrary to the narratives of violence. Public spaces are not feared. They become places for the distribution of supplies. They are associated with a breakdown of different identities, as they were in the narratives of violence. However, in the violence narratives, breakdown is associated with the terror of the faceless mob, while here it is a participatory and occasionally celebratory displacement. Thus, women move out of their homes into spaces that acquire a public character—unfinished buildings that flank Social Nagar, or into the two large mosques located in Dharavi. Public squares, community buildings, churches, and schools become places where supplies are collected and then distributed. In this way, spaces are reordered, reclassified with the availability of supplies or the lack of them. Other spaces, such as the ninety-foot road, function as boundaries by marking neighborhoods on either side as recipients or nonrecipients of relief.

MOHAMMAD: A crowd of people had gathered to watch it. The police forced the procession onwards but the crowd unloaded some sacks. We protested but the police said they too had been affected. Then a man got out of a white car that had been following the procession and told the police that this was meant for Muslims. But we gave them some of it and distributed the rest ourselves.

Courtyards and roads operate as boundaries of exclusion. They enable a differentiation and reorganization of the collective. The narratives detail the manner in which supplies are checked, portioned out, and readied for distribution. They highlight a systematic and ordered relief work, almost as an antidote to the confusion and chaos of the danga. Order is equated with normality initiated by an organized agency—in this case PROUD. Masih, a member of PROUD, has this to say:

Ashok is a goonda from Jaideep Society, which is next to us. He tried to break through the queue that we had organized. He threatened us with a revolver and said that PROUD favors Muslims. But we convinced him of our intentions. We had made lists of needy people, we knew who had lost what and could show him our record. And that drunk Anil [another hooligan], we sent him away with hundred rupees in his pocket.

Here, the work of relief reinforces the divisions created by violence. Other tellings stress the opposite. In several stories domestic space becomes a shelter for people in more vulnerable positions. Ayesha and

Farida both speak of their homes as open to all those needing protection.
Vulnerability created by the threat of violence cuts across sectarian
boundaries. Unlike in the violence narratives we find no platitudes about
Hindu-Muslim amity. People are identified through names, not through
sectarian identity. Thus Ayesha says:

> Ratan's whole family, Jalal's mother, Arif, his wife's sister, they were all
> here. The men here, the women there. We partitioned the room. This went
> on for eight days: everyone cooked here. Anna, the Madrasi shopkeeper,
> would give us things on loan. He would say, "Take it now, I have no use
> for it. Give me the money later." I would take separate shopping lists for
> different families sheltering here and get the provisions.[27]

Relief work reaffirms neighborhood ties, reflecting structures of everyday coexistence. Earlier we suggested two foci that embody different
trajectories for relief and reinforce relationships. The public/private polarity—between, for example, roads and courtyards as a focus for relief
distribution and the interior of the home—is not merely a concrete spatial one. It also reflects an opposition in the organization of relief between the outside (concerned private citizens, NGOs both sectarian and
secular) and the neighborhood. Yet even though the former is important
in renegotiating Dharavi's relationship with the outside, the latter is emphasized. Even when speaking of relief supplies provided by outside
agencies the stress is on procedures over which they have control—distributing supplies and thus overcoming threats to disorder. Accounts
that replicate a sectarian divide do so for the initial phase of distribution.
The sectarian bias in relief is described as a misapprehension or rumor,
soon rectified by personal initiative. The shift from "they" to "I" and
"we" is restored. The "we" refers to the familiar collective of the neighborhood speaking from within Dharavi.

THE DISPLACED AND RETRIEVED SELF

The argument as it has developed emphasizes the contrast between two
types of narratives. Those of violence show how the danga displaces
self-identity by destroying the structures that affirm individual agency.
These narratives do not name persons responsible for acts of violence,
they describe effects. They transform all particularities into generalities,
as we see in the following framing utterance: "The Hindus rose up and
the masjid fell. Then the Muslims responded. They rose up against the
Hindus." Even when asked to name persons speakers become evasive.

"Everyone knows who they are," or "It's not my duty to name them, the police were there, it's their job to investigate such matters."

The relief narratives move back to particularity. A plethora of names are mentioned. Specific individuals are described as both looters and recipients of relief. Those relief distributors who kept resources for themselves are named.

NILUFAR: I know who did it, I saw them looting—Meena, Rajesh, Madhu, Joseph, Ganesh. Madan and Rajesh used to cut grass before. Now their wives wear new saris everyday. As the fires of the riot cool the loot emerges [*jitna thanda ho raha utna note ab nikal raha hai*]. They took relief also. Whoever has the power has the right. . . . I went to mosques all over Bombay asking for relief. All the *maulavis* [priests] were running away. Their women were sitting at home getting fat. I know them all—Zakir, Ahmed, Usmanullah, Nasim, Asit Ali, Banne, Apa Jaan. They all thought I had stuffed my house with milk powder the way they did. They said, "You are a social worker so you must have kept the relief for yourself." But I never took any. I was satisfied with *kanji* [a cooling drink made from carrots]. I did not need milk powder.

Nilufar does not fear to name. In direct contrast to the violence narratives, proper names proliferate. Agency is located in persons, not anonymous forces. She does not even balk at showing her son-in-law in an unsavory light. "I got five thousand rupees for my son-in-law because he was shot through the ankle. I did not let him go to work because of the *lafra* [fight]. So he went out. Stones were falling and doors were being broken, so he started to break a small temple, calling the Maharashtrans and Muslims to join him. The police fired on him. I had the case against him removed and got him relief. I did it for my daughter." Violent acts are described in carnivalesque imagery. Her son-in-law calls Muslim and Hindu passersby alike to help him in destroying the temple, without discriminating along sectarian lines. Similarly, there are stories of ration shops distributing stocks to all in the neighborhood. The carnivalesque tone is echoed by Mohammad when he talks of two thugs, Rizwan and Nawabuddin, who had looted a cigarette shop during the Bhiwandi riots of 1984. Mohammad laughed and said that he too was inadvertently implicated, since he had smoked a Panama cigarette offered to him without realizing it was looted wealth. In 1992–93 the two thugs forced open a ration shop to distribute supplies when no relief was available. Here, actions and their consequences are rejoined. The act is reidentified as social and recognizable within the moral community.

It is not as if there are no references to displaced agency or to a sectarian divide. However, these are framed as rumor and therefore to be discounted. A rumor is spread that relief is only for Muslims. A private truck carrying goods for distribution as relief to Mukund Nagar (a Muslim majority area) is stopped at the ninety-foot road by the police, who start distributing it along Kumbharwada (a Hindu majority area, from which many say the first attacks came). They are stopped by people accompanying the truck and told that the provisions are meant for Muslims. (We were told that the Jamaat-i-tablighi and privately formed Muslim bodies were active in organizing long-term relief and rehabilitation.) The conversation concerning the distribution of relief follows sectarian lines.

MOHAMMAD: Outsiders were sending in supplies. The trucks would come here, we would distribute them.

RAKESH: This relief was only for Muslims. It was not meant for Hindus.

AYESHA: That's not true. We made no distinction between Hindus and Muslims. Everybody got it.

RAKESH: The Hindus did not, I don't mean that I did not. My house had provisions.

Masih gave us another variant: "We used to check the relief trucks as they entered Dharavi. Once we were examining the contents of a relief truck sent by a big Muslim businessman and we caught a glimpse of some guns among the sacks that contained relief provisions. They hadn't realized that we would check the truck. They hustled us away and left." We met later but Masih refused to elaborate further, save to say that initially Muslims were being favored because there was an impression among social workers and activists that the Muslims were victims. This was soon corrected.

We met the director of the Reclamation Society, Kadri Madam. Their method was like this: they give food in emergencies, wheat, sugar, milk powder. We had problems amongst ourselves. Social workers should help everyone equally. The first time they came they had loaded everything on a truck. There were biscuits, milk powder, even boiled eggs. They gathered the Muslims and distributed it to them. But when the second truck came, escorted by the military, doubts arose in our minds. They had prepared themselves, they would not let us inspect the supplies. Our request was that we were all hungry, everyone should get relief. I went on behalf of PROUD. It is a famous name. I consulted Kadri Madam. She had come in the evening. She had sent four bags of supplies of four hundred kilograms.

But this was not enough. We measured it out in the community hall and distributed a little to everyone—sugar, eggs, bread. Kadri Madam must have sent it for everybody but her workers were giving the supplies only to Muslims. Kadri Madam took some entry [interview] from me. She asked, "Who started the lafra?" I said, "Both sides were present. The police had no control." Then she said directly, "You people provoked them." Her people consulted the Muslims. News would reach them every hour. Mohammad *chacha* [kin term for father's younger brother] used to speak to them on the phone. She said, "Why do you want relief?" I replied, "You are a social worker, you must give equally." Then we went to the ration shop and made a collection. The *chakki* [wheat-grinding shop] was closed, but we took from the owner and from people who had extra. We collected one quintal of wheat. We made *chappatis* [wheat bread] and a curry and distributed it. We also sent some of it to Ganesh Vidya Mandir in Dhorwada. The Hindus there had severe problems, their children had no food and milk.

What is the significance of labeling certain incidents as rumor? In the narratives of violence we find references to rumors that milk and bread are poisoned. These rumors function as reasons for burning Muslim bakeries. Rumors play a significant role in polarizing sectarian identities. They operate through obfuscation, since they cannot be traced to a source (see Das 1995). They also add to the uncertainty of everyday life and condition people's relations to their neighbors so that neighbors are seen through a religious identity.

In the narratives of relief work, rumors covertly reinforce the sectarian divide while denying it on the surface. There is, however, a more complex process at work. By labeling as rumor the allegation that only Muslims are the recipients of relief, one implicitly complies with the blurring of the victim/perpetrator distinction. People are caught in a double bind. To claim relief is a statement of one's innocence, but in this case it also becomes a sign of greed. We have already mentioned stories alluding to those who demand relief in bad faith: looters and those claiming amounts far exceeding what they lost. Relief here is construed as an unexpected fortune and is sometimes thought of in the idiom of the gift that establishes an asymmetrical relation between givers and receivers. Thus, several people hold that they did not ask for relief even though they suffered damage to their property.

The relief narratives thus show how self-identity is renewed through the reappropriation of agency, but also displaced. Rumors are an important trope by which this happens. More dramatically, displacement is demonstrated in the style in which the narratives are rendered. At first impression stories of relief work seem prosaic when contrasted with the impassioned tone of the violence narratives. We glimpse this in Masih's account: precise details of supplies and their quantities and qualities are enumerated in a style reminiscent of bureaucratic record keeping. Even the "discovery" of guns in the truck carrying relief supplies is not dramatized.

This is even more marked in Ayesha's account. When asked how many people she had seen die, she said:

> Four. Two were married and two were not. One had one child and the other two. She was supposed to get one *lakh* [Rs. 100,000] for her son. Then two lakhs were declared—thirty thousand in cash and seventy thousand in fixed deposit. As far as the Bihari boy was concerned I knew that his relatives would try to claim the money. I said, "Call his mother from Bihar and give her the money." This was done.

The matter-of-fact tone here contrasts starkly with Faridabi's melodrama, Asif Ali's bitterness, even Mohammad's passionate defense of Hindu-Muslim coexistence. The danga, an extraordinary event set in extraordinary time, must be portrayed dramatically, its mystery enhanced. Relief work narratives restore a sense of the everyday by trying to reduce the extraordinary dimensions of the violence. The prosaic, recordkeeping style of many of the narratives can be interpreted as part of the effort to return to normality. As we have shown, this return is not to the normality that characterized the pre-danga everyday. This altered everyday is marked by a new knowledge and a memory of loss, but also by a practical wisdom of negotiating this loss. It tells one that reparation cannot take the form of justice, that coexistence is possible only if the past is deliberately set aside.

Here, forgetting is an active and deliberate choice, reflected in the mocking tone that narrators use. The recuperation of individual agency, so evident in the narratives, is presented through mockery. Bettelheim (1980: 19–37), in his moving account of survival after incarceration in German concentration camps, speaks of laughter as a distancing device, masking the knowledge that one has to live with evil. Are the utterances of the "I" in our narratives a mocking of the self, an acknowledgment, perhaps, of the helplessness that the "I did" or "I said" tries to cover? Faridabi's mimetic account of the invasion of her home by the police exemplifies this. Interspersed with the details of the possessions that the police steal—the Citizen wall clock, and so forth—are passages of dialogue:

> They tried to force the door of the cupboard. The daughter of my co-wife
> pleaded with them. Blood had oozed into her mother's throat with cough-
> ing—she had TB. She said, "We only have money left for the doctor and
> medicine. You have taken everything else, let that be." [Faridabi's face
> takes on the exaggerated aspect of a Hindi film star on her death bed.]
> They didn't listen. They had already dented the almirah. I quickly opened
> it. They were drunk tight and I thought that they might destroy the other
> furniture if I argued with them.

By describing the objects she has lost, she also recounts the police's du-
plicity, highlighting their greed and cowardice. She thereby recovers her
sense of self, albeit diminished by the loss of property. These commodities are the repositories of her identity, not her relationship to her neighbors and husband. She has no children, only things. Her mocking tone
expresses her powerlessness at the police invasion. Whining and plead-
ing, she mimics a false supplication to the arbitrary power of the police.
Appropriately, she refers to each account of police action as a "shot,"
as in a film:

> The police would not let the women go down to fill water. Each one waited
> for the next to approach them. I went up to the SRP [State Reserve Police]
> with my blue water pot. The others were watching from the roof-tops,
> waiting to see what would happen. [Her face takes on a pitiful expression
> as she whines.] "We are poor people, *sahib* [master], there is not even a
> drop of water in the house." They let me fill one pot before pushing me
> away.

Faridabi's mockery implicates everyone—police and victims alike: "I
will drink your urine, brother, if any of those boys had the courage to
leave their home, let alone participate in the looting." The articulation
of the personal voice is a performative device distancing the self from
its past humiliation. Equally, the use of a mocking tone implies a recognition of complicity in the danga, even if this is through silence, an
acceptance of a new regime of censorship. By making use of mockery,
these narratives become critiques. Yet because they distance the selves
of the narrators (by being rendered in a nonserious mode) they also
function as protective devices. In the process, they collude with the regime of censorship that presents the danga as an agentless, anonymous
force.

THE GENEALOGY OF RELIEF WORK AND
REMORALIZING THE COMMUNITY

The narratives of relief work point to the failure of the moral community
in the attempt to achieve normality. Consensus or mutuality as a base

for social life gives way to a collaborative silencing of specific memories. Yet we glimpse face-to-face relationships based on previous associations, on some acknowledgment of the uniqueness of voice, of the specificity of an individual's suffering in spite of the disappointment with societal resources. Thus Ayesha's account links the extraordinary violence of the danga with known faces and groups of people who, even if they are characterized as criminals, are still part of her everyday life.

> On the second day of the danga in December I was walking past the Khamba Devi temple early in the morning when I saw this boy with stab wounds in his chest. I managed to drag him up to the ninety-foot road because I thought I could stop a car or a two-wheeler and take him to the hospital. No one stopped, not even police jeeps. It was Ashok Kale [a known hooligan with links to the underworld and the Shiv Sena] who stopped for me. He took us to the hospital. Actually, many of these boys have become like this because their mothers are not at home to check them. They go out to work and their boys mix with criminals.

Her account tacitly admits that coexistence is based on the recognition of differences. It assumes that different, and sometimes conflicting, moral values compose the identity of the other person. Similarly, Mahmud is able to contain the violence on the first day because he recognizes some of the people among the horde of attackers and is able to stop them. On this occasion he uses their common affiliation as PROUD members. Later, he is able to avert the danger from his household by drawing on his previous alliance with the police. "Some of my neighbors are Shiv Sainiks. But they are impotent because they know that my sons and I have a line to the police station. That runs through our shoes." (It was said that policemen on duty would come to his workshop, even during the violence, when all work was at a standstill, to try on shoes.) At another time he uses his connection with the mosque, as its treasurer, to keep the peace in his neighborhood and to prevent a group of Muslim boys from damaging a temple. He says that normalcy can only be restored through negotiation, by appealing to different identities in terms of what the situation demands.

An attempt is made to normalize the extraordinary event by linking it with everyday acts of violence and potentially violent situations and times. Barkatulla speaks of certain festival days, such as Shiv Jayanti, when the gathering of large crowds in front of temples may spark off violence. Ayesha mentions taporis from neighboring Mangwada who sit outside their defecation house and snatch valuables from passersby.

Here, the recognition of nearness and care for one's neighbor complements a knowledge, also based on familiarity, arising from a nearness of the other's weakness. Different moral values are allowed to coexist and to make up the identity of the other person. The potential for violence that they present is thought to be manageable because it is known. The fear generated by the danga is a fear of the unknown and the unrestrained. Therefore it must be set aside.

The violence narratives explicitly recognize that local forms of violence have no relation to the event. The relief work narratives present the danga in the frame of local and familiar violence, but only apparently. They do not judge or demand justice, thus indirectly confirming the extraordinary character of the danga. When these narratives name persons it is to concede that narrators share a diversity of experiences. The restoration of an altered everyday is not a return to a former innocence but a recognition that coexistence involves some element of usurpation of the other's space. Distrusting one's neighbor implicates oneself—one may appear to be a perpetrator of violence.

If everyday life is to be restored, it is necessary to maintain an equilibrium between sectarian collectives. This restoration has the unfortunate side effect of fostering a culture of impunity. This issue concerns our narrators, and it is to such accounts that we finally turn.

Masih, in creating a genealogy of relief work, substantiates a sense of an altered everyday. In his narrative an attempt is made to embed rehabilitation work after the danga in accounts of collective agitation against oppressive forces from the outside—the Bombay municipality and important commercial enterprises. The attempts of PROUD to forge a coherent community out of the disparate sections of Dharavi through "action programs" now become the context within which relief actions are understood. Masih's account creates a genealogy for relief work by linking it to past action programs.

> Don Bosco school sent us milk and also PROUD. The milk came in a truck, with a banner fixed on it. Then later, through CISRS [Christian Institute for the Study of Religion and Society], we conducted a survey and fixed a central area for distributing money based on the percentage of loss. The CISRS relief fund had given us fifty thousand rupees to distribute. But PROUD has problems of its own. Prabhu [a PROUD community organizer] had a beard. It was unclear whether he looked Hindu or Muslim. I phoned him to tell him not to come here, but he didn't listen to me. The film *Bombay* shows the reality of the situation—whose fight it was and who got the blame. Small people were provoked to violence. Every

individual has some communal spirit and this was deliberately inflamed
by political leaders. I have heard that builders had a hand in it as well.
There have been proposals for redevelopment in the past. The Kerkar Committee came from Delhi. They sat in a five-star hotel and made a scheme.
They proposed that 80 percent of Dharavi's population should be removed.
We protested and had the scheme removed. Then the Rajiv Gandhi slum
redevelopment scheme sanctioned 37 crore [one crore equals ten million
rupees] for Dharavi. But there are problems. Land is scarce and the public
plentiful. There are problems about proof of identity. Many people have
not bothered about getting proof made. They are uneducated, they go out
to work in the morning, come back at night to sleep. They don't have the
time to get ration cards made [which would provide documentary proof
that they are legitimate residents of Dharavi].

There was a tar factory that used to crush rocks to make macadam.
The people who lived here were affected by it. Their health suffered. Many
people got TB. Bits of stone would settle on children's food. We organized
a medical camp. The doctors from Sion hospital checked the people and
we made a record of all TB cases. Our action achieved success in 1983.
We took a procession to the head office in Worli. It was made of marble
stone. We went up in a big lift but they barred our entry. This tar factory
was part of the Shah company. They make roads in Iran and Arab countries. We decided to try again but this time we made a plan. We put chick
peas and betel leaf in our pockets. We chewed them on our way up in the
lifts and spat them out when we reached the office. They called the police
and said that a danga had broken out. But we had gained entry to the office
and we found out that the Shah company had leased the land in Dharavi.
The lease had run out but they had managed to extend it by bribing municipal officials. We organized action and demonstrated three times. They
pretended they had not been sanctioned alternative land to move out of
Dharavi. We found out they were lying and forced them out.

PROUD's long-term goal is one of forging links of solidarity within
Dharavi by turning common problems into social causes. The following
is a description of tactics used to implement their collective action programs: "Procedural applications are first made to the authorities concerned for obtaining amenities. If the government official fails to act,
problems are presented in a manner that startles or embarrasses him
into conceding their demands. The people/agencies ignoring their demands are called 'the enemy' and the collective battles won are depicted
as 'victories'" (Patel and D'Souza 1987: 20). PROUD's success in
achieving its goal is based on its ability to periodically organize public
rituals that generate solidarity through collective effervescence.

PROUD's task today is to address communal violence and strengthen
community solidarity—cutting across territorial and religious divisions.
However, whether communalism can be cast as the enemy and collec-

tively challenged is a question that cannot be easily answered. So also the allegation made by Raju Moite: "PROUD favors Muslims." Even though this claim can be dismissed when coming from a known hooligan, there are others like Sarvate who voice the same sentiment, though in a more moderate tone. PROUD's internal organization has suffered considerably because of the Hindu-Muslim polarization after the danga. Several of its Hindu members are known to have participated in the danga, and yet they participated in previous actions of protest in alliance with non-Hindus.

One such person is Sarvate, a major player in the agitation against the Shah company and in the antidemolition agitations in the 1980s. Barkatulla is bitter about Sarvate's role in creating fear by driving out his Muslim neighbors and looting their houses. However, Barkatulla agrees to mediate and establish a peace committee with Sarvate.

> Jharia ["fat man"; in this case, Sarvate] helped create the tension. He would make up stories of armed gangs coming from Chamra Bazaar. How could they come here when he had strung up live wires on all the boundary walls? He caught two *chokras* [boys] and brought them to me saying, "Look Seth, they have come to loot us." I recognized them; they had come to find out whether their relatives were safe. Then he changed his story: "I saved them from being beaten up." Jharia helped foster the fear and then he used to come to my house for settlement meetings.

Sarvate had earlier introduced us to Barkatulla, wanting him to bear testimony to his role in the peace process:

SARVATE: Barkatulla Seth, tell these people, did even one Muslim die in our neighborhood? And who organized the settlement committee?

BARKATULLA: It's true no one died, but there was arson and looting.

SARVATE: But no deaths, and who helped restore peace and get the Muslims back? It was I.

Only after we met Barkatulla in his house did he answer Sarvate's rhetorical question: "Yes, Muslims did come back, but most left within six months of returning, selling their houses that had been rebuilt after the danga. They are scared. Why should we be looked at with suspicion by Maharashtrans when it is we who have suffered and not them?"

These questions remain unanswered. Sarvate has made a public confession and been officially pardoned for his role in the violence. PROUD needs him to maintain its heterogeneous image in the difficult task ahead. Yet even now Sarvate's role in the danga, whether he robbed and stabbed people, is unclear. Masih speaks only in general terms: "Some of these local politicians [party bosses] foster communalism by forming gangs for them. This is not the way in which PROUD works. PROUD's method is socialism and equality." But do these values have enough vitality to rebuild a moral community? Kakar (1995) says that the claim to the possession of a future makes belonging to a community attractive—a future seen as shared cultural myths and archetypes. The appeal of a community identity based on religion may lie in the idea of a shared primordiality, a shared destiny. Secular symbols embodying values of socialism and equality do not have the same charismatic force, especially when personal identity is besieged. Contrarily, a shared perception of a future punctuated by a series of violent events may draw otherwise diverse sections together, forcing them to redefine their identities. Here, unifying cultural symbols could become the basis of organizing social life.

Together with a common set of symbols and the perception of a shared future, there is also a sense of the other who, by functioning as a scapegoat, defines commonality within the community. He is the ghati, the drunkard and cowardly Shiv Sainik, the jahil. Conversely, he is the mullah, the katua. The emotional charge of these stereotypical images highlights an insecurity after the danga. It is here that the efforts of Mohammad and Masih to embed relief programs in PROUD's past attempts to create community solidarity must be framed. Kakar (1995: 21–22), quoting Durkheim, would say a collective needs a sense of continuity with its past to maintain its identity. Otherwise, its memories have no relevance for its present. This is the reason for presenting the relief narratives in a genealogical mode, an attempt to tap sources that once were able to generate a more inclusive self-identity.

NOTES

We are grateful to the people in Dharavi who shared their experiences so generously with us, and to the members of PROUD who have been working in Dharavi. We thank all members who participated in the workshop on community coping in Cape Town in 1995—especially Arthur Kleinman, Veena Das, and Pamela Reynolds for their extensive comments. The names of informants have been changed.

1. The city of Bombay has been recently renamed Mumbai. However, we have chosen to retain the older name, as it remains the common name for the city in everyday contexts.

2. Such members belonged to the Rashtriya Swayamsevak Sangh (RSS), the Vishwa Hindu Parishad, the Bajrang Dal, the Akhil Bhartiya Vidyarthi Parishad and their parliamentary party, the Bhartiya Janata Party (BJP). There is no agreed-upon term to describe these Hindus. They are termed militant, fascist, and communalist. Our usage is borrowed from Nandy et al. (1995).

3. An example of this is found in the slogans raised during the destruction of the mosque, quoted in Nandy et al. (1995: 195):

Jai Shri Ram, say Jai Shri Ram
Jinnah say Jai Shri Ram
Gandhi say Jai Shri Ram
Mullah say Jai Shri Ram

Jinnah was the founder of Pakistan; *Mullah* is a derogatory term used by Hindus for a Muslim priest. "Jai Shri Ram" is a greeting often used by Hindu nationalists. Jinnah, Gandhi, and Mullah are not local names, just as Ram cannot be localized (see Ramachandra Gandhi 1992).

4. In 1981, one such house served approximately twenty people, excluding children. In 1995, one house served about one hundred and twenty people, excluding children.

5. In discussing violence in Northern Ireland, Feldman (1991: 14) argues that the event of violence is that which can be narrated. Such narration is characterized both by a "semantic excess" and an instrumental imagination of violence as it is inscribed on various material artifacts. This paper follows Feldman's line of argument but also suggests that the event of violence makes possible its narration. Following Deleuze (1990) we argue that the event pre-inheres in the narration.

6. These narrations are fragmented: we do not find a linear sequence of ideas or episodes, or indeed a complete story with coherent and complete themes. But insofar as they dwell on violence, it is evident that violence functions in such a way as to arrogate to itself both a distributive power and performative force, whether this be the power to refashion the nation, effect displacement, or reterritorialize areas that are thought to be depopulated. A further characteristic of such narration is the inscription of violence on the body. This narration, then, operates on multiple registers. If, in one case, violence appears to be nomadic, occurring randomly and with great variation and intensity across different neighborhoods, in another it is seen as the conscious plotting of the police to systematically terrorize specific segments of a population within a neighborhood.

7. The term *Dalit* is the most commonly accepted term for the former "untouchables," especially in Maharashtra. In the accounts of the Muslim survivors of the riots, the term took on derogatory connotations.

8. Implicit in this schematic classification is that narration is an art of saying (de Certeau 1984: 79). Rather than indicating, such narration exercises itself by employing various styles of saying.

9. This conversation occurred in a community hall among a group of people. A total of eleven people participated in the conversation, six of whom were

residents of Dharavi. Besides the two fieldworkers, there were three community organizers from an NGO known as People's Responsible Organization for United Dharavi (popularly known by its acronym, PROUD). The composition of the group was fluid, with people walking in and out. There were several Hindus present.

10. The political figures mentioned here were important actors in the nationalist movement as well as the movement for Pakistan. Mamu is referring to the divison in families in terms of those who supported Jinnah and the demand for a separate Muslim state, and those who supported Abdul Ghaffar Kahan, also known as Frontier Gandhi, who was a supporter of the Gandhian idea of a single independent state for all religions.

11. The theme of the Partition of India occurs repeatedly in these narratives. Here it gives Mamu's story a mythic quality. Jinnah, the architect of Pakistan, and Mamu's dark, one-eyed brother coalesce to become the embodiment of otherness—an otherness that has to be expelled for Mamu to integrate his identity as both Muslim and Indian.

12. The Kashmir border again refers to the Partition and the continuing conflict between India and Pakistan over Kashmir. It is interesting that it is not the event at Ayodhya that is seen to be replicated in the riots in Dharavi but the event of Partition. A similar dispacement occurs in the Srikrishna Commission Report, in which a seamless continuity between the Partition and the riots is assumed.

13. We almost forced Sarvate to talk to us. On two prior occasions we had made appointments, but for one reason or another he was unable or unwilling to meet us. On this occasion we barged into his house while he was sleeping. Sarvate's participation in the violence is controversial. Our Muslim informants were firm in their belief that he had actively colluded with, if not organized, crowds of Hindu attackers. Sarvate is a powerful man in his neighborhood. He and his family own extensive land in Dharavi. It is rumored that in 1992 his sons were arrested for rioting.

14. Goffman (1979) argues that the name is a peg to hang an identity on. He shows how the name, together with physical handicaps, character defects, and phylogenetic handicaps of race, religion, and nationality, is open to stigmatization. See also Bering (1992).

15. Bhiwandi is a textile center neighboring Bombay. Early in 1984 it witnessed extensive warfare between Hindus and Muslims, part of which seeped into Bombay and Dharavi.

16. *Tapori* refers to thin iron rods that groups of young men carry as weapons. This is a favorite weapon of intimidation in Dharavi.

17. This was the only occasion when we could talk to Asif Ali, for subsequently he refused to meet us. One of the PROUD workers, who had introduced us to Asif Ali, said that the latter had been threatened by "Jharia" ("fat man"—referring to Sarvate). This worker had himself been receiving anonymous telephone calls threatening him. He believed that a coworker had, perhaps unwittingly, provided his telephone number to the "wrong people." An atmosphere of fear and suspicion persists.

18. Sunil Dutt, a popular film actor and subsequently a member of Parliament from Bombay, was one of the few visible politicians who surveyed the violence-ravaged areas during December 1992 and January 1993. His statements were construed as being sympathetic to Muslims, perhaps because he had married a famous Muslim film actress, Nargis. Their son, Sunjay Dutt, also a film star, was in 1994 charged under the Terrorist and Disruptionist Activities Act (TADA) for possession of unlicensed weapons. TADA allows for people so charged to be taken into police custody without the provision of bail and habeas corpus. Asif Ali's statement refers to the travails of the Dutt family.

19. We talked to Mahmud on the first floor of his house. This conversation was conducted between six people: Mahmud, his son, his brother's son, a leather worker, and the two fieldworkers.

20. Dina met us in her house. She was with her three young children, two girls and one boy. Dina says she is from Madras and her husband, absent during this conversation, from Uttar Pradesh. She is fluent in Hindustani. Her speech reflects Urdu training.

21. The conversation with Faridabi occurred on the first floor of her house. Besides the two fieldworkers, there were six others present: four members of PROUD, Faridabi, and a middle-aged lady from the same chawl. Faridabi's house is very well maintained, and she seems to be richer than most others we met in Dharavi.

22. The use of filmic imagery in her narrative is particularly marked.

23. Marathi becomes the language of the aggressor in the narratives of the Muslim women of Dharavi. These women are characterized as "outsiders" by the aggressors and therefore not Marathi speakers. This is in spite of the fact that they are fluent in Marathi and use it for many routine purposes.

24. Momin's son was killed in police firing. Apparently he was standing outside his house when this happened. For three days the corpse remained in the house, and it was only after the intercession of a policeman that a proper burial could be given. Despite repeated requests, Momin refused to meet us. After the danga he became an active member of the Jamaat-i-tablighi, an Islamic organization that some say is fundamentalist.

25. "Service" denotes work in an office, as distinct from unskilled and skilled manual work here.

26. Rebeiro was, until his retirement, one of the most famous police officers of the Indian police. In the media he was known for his honesty as much as for adopting a hard line against "terrorists" and common criminals.

27. The precise detailing of names in Ayesha's narrative is significant. It draws attention to the fact that both Hindu and Muslim families are drawn together by their common plight.

REFERENCES CITED

Bering, Dietz. 1992. *The Stigma of Names*. Trans. N. Plaice. Cambridge, England: Polity Press.

Bettleheim, Bruno. 1980. *Surviving and Other Essays.* New York: Vintage Books.

Bharatiya Janawadi Agadhi. 1993. *The Bombay Which the Fascists Could Not Burn!* Bombay: M. D. More.

Das, Veena. 1990. "Our Work to Cry, Your Work to Listen." In *Mirrors of Violence: Communities, Riots and Survivors in South Asia,* ed. Veena Das, 345–94. Delhi: Oxford University Press.

——. 1995a. *Critical Events: An Anthropological Perspective on Contemporary India.* Delhi: Oxford University Press.

——. 1995b. "Rumor as Performative: A Contribution to the Theory of Perlocutionary Speech." S.K. Bose Memorial Lecture, St. Stephans College, Delhi.

Daud, S., and H. Suresh. 1993. *The People's Verdict: An Inquiry into December 1992 and January 1993 Riots in Bombay by the Indian People's Human Rights Tribunal.* Bombay: Indian People's Human Rights Commission.

de Certeau, Michel. 1984. *The Practice of Everyday Life.* Trans. S. Rendall. Berkeley: University of California Press.

Deleuze, Gilles. 1990. *The Logic of Sense.* Trans. M. Lester. New York: Columbia University Press.

Engineer, Asghar Ali. 1995. *Lifting the Veil: Communal Violence and Communal Harmony in Contemporary India.* Hyderabad: Sangam.

Feldman, Alan. 1991. *Formations of Violence: The Narratives of the Body and Political Terror in Northern Ireland.* Chicago: University of Chicago Press.

Freitag, Sandria. 1990. *Collective Action and Community: Public Arenas and the Emergence of Communalism in North India.* Delhi: Oxford University Press.

Gandhi, Ramachandra. 1992. *Sita's Kitchen: A Testimony of Faith and Inquiry.* Delhi: Penguin Books.

Goffman, Erving. 1979. *Stigma: Notes on the Management of Spoiled Identity.* Englewood Cliffs, N.J.: Prentice Hall.

Kakar, Sudhir. 1995. *The Colours of Violence.* Delhi: Viking.

Masselos, Jim. 1995. "Postmodern Bombay: Fractured Discourses." In *Postmodern Cities and Spaces,* eds. Sophie Watson and Katherine Gibson, 199–215. Cambridge, Mass.: Blackwell.

Naipaul, V. S. 1990. *India: A Million Mutinies Now.* London: Minerva.

Nandy, Ashis, Shikha Trivedy, Shail Mayaram, and A.Yagnik. 1995. *Creating a Nationality: The Ramjanmabhumi and Fear of the Self.* Delhi: Oxford University Press.

Padgaonkar, Dileep, ed. 1993. *When Bombay Burned.* Delhi: UBS Publishers' Distributors.

Pandey, Gyanendra. 1990. "The Colonial Construction of Communalism: British Writing on Banaras in the Nineteenth Century." In *Mirrors of Violence: Communities, Riots and Survivors in South Asia,* ed. Veena Das, 94–134. Delhi: Oxford University Press.

Patel, Hutokhshi, and Nafisa Goga D'Souza. 1987. *A Review of "Proud": A People's Organisation in Dharavi.* Delhi: Indian Society for Promoting Christian Knowledge.

Rao, Nandini. 1994. "Interpreting Silences: Symbol and History in the Case of Ram Janmabhoomi/Babri Masjid." In *Social Construction of the Past: Representation as Power,* ed. George C. Bond and Angela Gilliam. London: Routledge.

Srikrishna, B. N. 1998. *Report of the Srikrishna Commission Appointed for Inquiry into the Riots at Mumbai During December 1992 and January 1993.* Bombay: Privately Published by Concerned Citizens.

Van der Veer, Peter. 1984. *Gods on Earth: The Management of Religious Experience and Identity in a North Indian Pilgrimage Centre.* Delhi: Oxford University Press.

———. 1996. *Religious Nationalism: Hindus and Muslims in India.* Delhi: Oxford University Press.

Varshney, Ashutosh. 1993. "Contested Meanings: India's National Identity, Hindu Nationalism and the Politics of Anxiety." *Daedalus* 3: 227–61.

Speech and Silence

Women's Testimony in the First Five
Weeks of Public Hearings of the South
African Truth and Reconciliation
Commission

Fiona C. Ross

Describing the faculties with which one may mourn a lost lover, Jeanette Winterson (1993: 135) speaks of hearing thus:

> Hearing and the Ear:
> The auricle is the expanded portion which projects from the side of the head. It is composed of fibro-elastic cartilage covered with skin and fine hairs. It is deeply grooved and ridged. The prominent outer ridge is known as the helix. The lobule is the soft, pliable part at the outer extremity.
> Sound travels at about 335 metres per second.

The starkness of Winterson's description of the physical characteristics of the ear, a description that is followed by a deeply personal account of loss and grieving, is an appropriate beginning for a paper that describes stories of loss told to the Truth and Reconciliation Commission.[1] The description of the physical ear acts as a counterpoise to my argument on the difficulties involved in listening and attending to stories of pain and loss.

AMBITS OF THE ACT

The Truth and Reconciliation Commission was established under the Promotion of National Unity and Reconciliation Act, Number 34 of 1995, and its amendments (hereinafter referred to as the "Act"). Its aims, set out in the preamble to the Act, were extensive:

To provide for the investigation and establishment of as complete a picture as possible of the nature, causes and extent of gross violations of human rights committed during the period from 1 March 1960 to the cut-off date contemplated in the Constitution, within or outside the Republic, emanating from the conflicts of the past, and the fate or whereabouts of the victims of such violations; the granting of amnesty to persons who make full disclosure of all the relevant facts relating to acts associated with a political objective committed in the course of the conflicts of the past during the said period; affording victims an opportunity to relate the violations they suffered; the taking of measures aimed at the granting of reparation to, and the rehabilitation and restoration of the human and civil dignity of, victims of violations of human rights; reporting to the Nation about such violations and victims; the making of recommendations aimed at the prevention of the commission of gross violations of human rights; and for the said purposes to provide for the establishment of a Truth and Reconciliation Commission, a Committee of Human Rights Violations, a Committee on Amnesty and a Committee on Reparation and Rehabilitation; and to confer certain powers on, assign certain functions to and impose certain duties upon that Commission and those Committees; and to provide for matters connected therewith. (The Act, 2.)

The Commission drew on the experiences of similar bodies set up to record painful periods in other countries' recent pasts (Hayner 1996 identifies nineteen such bodies to date). South Africa's Commission was unusual in that it linked witnessing, amnesty, and reparation together into a single institution. It was also unusual in that it was set in place by a democratically elected Parliament, did not grant automatic or blanket amnesty to perpetrators, and held public hearings. It was the product of negotiations between major political parties during the process of forming the Interim Constitution that enabled the first democratic elections to be held in South Africa in 1994. The postamble of the Interim Constitution states that "amnesty shall be granted in respect of acts, omissions and offenses associated with political objectives committed in the course of the conflicts of the past" (the Act, 2).

The Truth and Reconciliation Commission represents an intention to forge a common memory predicated on making public particular kinds of knowledge. Memory and knowledge are imbricated. In part this springs from the definition of violation devised in the Act:

(a) the killing, abduction, torture or severe ill-treatment of any person; or (b) any attempt, conspiracy, incitement, instigation, command or procurement to commit an act referred to in paragraph (a), which emanated from conflicts of the past and which was committed during the period 1st March 1960 to the cut-off date [a date that was changed from December 1993 to May 1994] within or outside the Republic, and the commission of which was advised, planned, directed, commanded or ordered by any person acting with a political motive. (The Act, chapter 1(1)(ix).)

Victims are defined by the Act as "Persons who, individually or together with one of more persons, suffered harm in the form of physical or mental injury, emotional suffering, pecuniary loss or a substantial impairment of human rights . . ." (the Act, chapter 1(1)(xix)). Subsequent paragraphs of the Act indicate that victims are also those who suffered "as a result of such person intervening to assist persons contemplated in paragraph (a) who were in distress or to prevent victimisation of such persons," and "such relatives or dependents of victims as may be prescribed" (ibid.).

The definitions of violation set out in the Act are largely to do with what can be done to the body—it can be abducted, tortured, killed, "disappeared." In the Commission's hearings the main focus was on bodies and on the visible embodiment of suffering.[2] In other words, the Commission tended to seek for experiences that were both literally and visibly embodied. As I show, this has important implications for the ways in which women's testimonies can be heard.

The Commission was empowered to investigate violations committed by the state in its pursuit of apartheid policies.[3] The Commission was also required to investigate human rights violations committed by the liberation movements, one of which, the African National Congress (ANC), had already held two Commissions of Enquiry into violations in its training camps outside South Africa (Motsuenyane 1993; Skweyiya 1992).

The Commission, consisting of seventeen commissioners and divided into three committees (a Human Rights Violations Committee, an Amnesty Committee, and a Committee on Reparations and Rehabilitation), was constituted in December 1995. Through its work, particularly its public hearings,[4] it provided an opportunity for new kinds of witnessing: witnessing that was metaphorically envisaged as national catharsis, cleansing, or exorcism.[5] The possibilities of new forms of seeing and acknowledging past violence in South Africa raise questions to do with effective witnessing, a process rendered more complex by the retrospective nature of testimony on offer.

The Human Rights Violations Committee invited people to make written and oral statements before it. Approximately ten percent of these were heard in public hearings held throughout the country. Selected episodes or portions of public testimony were screened on television and broadcast on radio. The Commission created the opportunity to observe and witness a public event of recall: a doubling of witness. The difficulties arising from such a project are the subject matter of the remainder of the paper, in which I explore testimonies made by women before the Commission. I examine on whose behalf women speak, what they say, and how it is said. Implicit in such a project is a question about the nature and contexts of telling and hearing. What does it mean to be asked to speak or to listen, and to do so in a place that has only recently and very tentatively become amenable to such public affirmations of knowledge? In a South Africa where, before, during, and perhaps even after apartheid, danger resided in too public a confession of certain kinds of knowing, how do women express their experience? And with what understandings are we to listen? How can their experiences, both of apartheid and of the Truth and Reconciliation Commission, be represented?

The stories that women told to the Commission during the first five weeks of its hearings differ from one another in many respects. In one important way, however, there is a similarity between their testimonies, and that is that for the most part women told stories about the human rights violations experienced by others. It seems to me that in their testimonies about others women described their own experiences of the pernicious effects of apartheid on domestic life, families, intergenerational relations, and gender roles. Taken as a whole, their testimonies illustrated the gaps in women's public speech: absences and silences that, for the most part, had to do with representation of their own physical experiences of violation.

WHOSE VOICES?

During the first five weeks of public hearings, held in East London, Cape Town, Johannesburg, Durban, and Kimberley, 204 people testified about 160 cases of human rights violation. Most of those testifying were women (58 percent). Only 13 percent of cases reported were directly concerned with violations perpetrated against women. In other words, for the most part, both men and women appearing before the Commission did so in order to report violations against men. Table 1 categorizes testimonies by gender. Table 2 disaggregates testimonies to show relationships.

TABLE 1

TESTIMONIES BY GENDER, AS PERCENTAGE OF
TOTAL TESTIMONIES

	Testimonies by women about	Testimonies by men about
Women	10	2
Men	46	35
Men and women	3	3
Total	59	40

NOTE: Figures have been rounded and therefore do not add up to 100 percent.

TABLE 2

PEOPLE TESTIFIED ABOUT, AS PERCENTAGE OF
TOTAL TESTIMONIES

	Women speak about	Men speak about	Total
Themselves	4	20	24
Their mothers	0.5	0.5	1
Their fathers	1	3	4
Their sisters	1.5	0	1.5
Their brothers	8	4	12
Their spouses	11	0	11
Their sons	25	3.5	28.5
Their daughters	1.5	1	2.5
Other women	2.5	1	3.5
Other men	1	4	5
Unrelated women and men	3	3	6
Total	59	40	99

NOTE: Figures have been rounded and therefore do not add up to 100 percent.

Approximately 28 percent of testimonies heard by the Commission
in this period concerned sons. Men's testimonies about their own experiences of violation comprised 20 percent, while women's testimonies
about their experiences made up less than 5 percent. Women testified
primarily about violations committed against their sons, husbands, and
brothers, while men described their own experiences of abuse. Men also
spoke about their comrades and friends (4 percent of cases), their brothers (4 percent), their sons (3.5 percent), and their fathers (3 percent).
Men testified for five women (comprising 2.5 percent of the cases heard
by the Commission) during the period about which I write. These were
a mother, two daughters, and two female friends. Women's testimonies
about women included accounts of violations against a mother, three

daughters, five comrades or friends, and three sisters. This figure makes up 6 percent of the total testimonies heard by the Commission during the period I analyze here.

Women gave scant account of their own brutal treatment. Their silence should not be taken to suggest that women were not physically abused. A submission, "Gender and the Truth and Reconciliation Commission," made to the Commission by Beth Goldblatt and Shiela Meintjies (1996) documents the violence, both direct and indirect, that women suffered under apartheid. The authors state that between 1960 and 1990, physical abuse of women in detention increased. They suggest that it is not easy for women to speak of such violations: there are strong cultural and social reasons that women do not (and are not allowed to) tell of their experience (see Reynolds 1995b). After the first five weeks of hearings, commissioners expressed their concern that women did not present their experiences of pain.[6] Nevertheless, rape, beatings, and torture were both implied and stated in testimonies. One young person testified that because girls could not run as fast as boys, when the police shot tear gas and rubber bullets at protesting students, it was the girls who were worst affected. Another person testifying pointed to the scars on her body from birdshot and hinted at rape by the police. Yet another told of genital torture. One young woman told of how, after her beating in detention, she had been taken to the district surgeon. She explained to the panel of commissioners before whom she was testifying, "I smelled of blood. There was clotted blood everywhere. [Yet] the doctor said that nothing was wrong" (Mamagotle Mohale, Gauteng hearings, 30 April 1996). The Commission and the media called women "secondary witnesses" because they testified mainly about the experiences of men. Underlying the stories that women told to the Commission, however, are stories of their own experiences that resonate with metaphors of political consciousness.

In the following discussion it is important to keep in mind the diversity of stories. I begin with the story told on 25 April 1996 by Nyameka Goniwe in the ornate buildings of East London's City Hall, site of the Commission's first public hearings. Nyameka Goniwe has told the story of the death of her husband, Matthew Goniwe, many times before to inquests and commissions of inquiry. Her testimony to the Truth and Reconciliation Commission was clear and direct. Events were given in sequence and were chronologically ordered. The focus of attention was on Matthew. The story as I tell it is distilled from her words to the Commission that day.[7]

She began her testimony at 9:30 A.M., in a hall full of people silent in expectation. She sat on a podium with the widows of three other activists who had been killed with her husband, facing the semicircle of commissioners. National flags flew from the corners of the stage behind the commissioners, and a large banner bearing the words "Truth and Reconciliation Commission: Healing Our Past. First Hearing, East London, 15–18th April 1996" lined the wall at the back of the stage. A lighted altar candle burned at the edge of the stage, flanked by tassled maroon velvet curtains and potted palm trees. Nyameka Goniwe read her statement in English, commencing, "To talk of Matthew Goniwe and my life is a daunting task. I'll try to bring together the events that led to his death." She then told one of the most well-known stories of activism in South Africa. Matthew Goniwe was a teacher and an anti-apartheid activist. Frequent arrests and imprisonment, the first of which occurred in 1975, marked his marriage to Nyameka. Arrested under the Suppression of Communism Act, he spent fifteen months as a prisoner awaiting trial before being sentenced to four years' imprisonment, a sentence he served in Umtata. Nyameka Goniwe had meanwhile enrolled at the University of Fort Hare, which meant living some one hundred kilometers from her eight-month-old baby, whom she left with Matthew's mother in Cradock.

In 1982, shortly after his release from prison the preceding year, Matthew was transferred by the Department of Education and Training to the small town of Graaff-Reinet. The following year he was moved to Cradock, where he became deputy-principal of the high school and one of the founders of the Cradock Residents Association and of CRADOYA, the local youth organization. Both organizations were affiliated with the newly launched United Democratic Front (UDF) in 1983.[8]

In December 1993, Matthew was transferred back to Graaff-Reinet. Seeing it as an attempt to curtail his political activity, he refused to go. The community and youth of Cradock supported him in his decision. The Department of Education and Training suspended him from his position. Youths boycotted school, demanding his reinstatement. In March 1984, he was detained under section 28 of the Internal Security Act and spent six months in detention.

The situation in Cradock deteriorated, as protests against state action increased and the state responded with ever harsher repression. Matthew was released from prison. He immediately returned to his political work, creating street committees and rallying youth leadership. He was elected as regional rural organizer for the UDF. On 27 May 1985, the South

African Defence Force sealed off the township. Helicopters dropped pamphlets denouncing Goniwe. Police searched the houses of known activists. The Security Branch, the feared branch of the South African Police tasked with internal security matters, closely monitored Matthew's movements. The surveillance affected not only Matthew but also his family. Nyameka Goniwe described that period thus: "The whole family bore the wrath of the security police which took the form of harassment, early morning house raids, constant surveillance, death threats, phone bugging, short term detentions for questioning, mysterious phone calls, tampering with cars. . . ." The last time his wife saw him was when he left home with Fort Calata, Sparrow Mkhonto, and Sicelo Mhawuli to attend a UDF meeting. When he did not return that night, Nyameka Goniwe said, she knew that something had happened. The next day she telephoned around, seeking information, then traveled the route he usually drove home to look for him. She alerted the press. The community began boycotts of shops and schools. The next day, 29 June, Sparrow and Sicelo's bodies were found. Those of Matthew and Fort were found five days later.

Nyameka Goniwe presented the Commission with her analysis of the likelihood of police involvement in the deaths.

> We have stated why we believe that Matthew had to die. We think that it was because he was seen as a person who was responsible for the collapse of the community council's discipline in Lingalihle. We also think that he was held responsible for disrupting the schools by instigating the students to engage in school boycotts and for the resignation of all school communities in Cradock. He was also accused of mobilising the people of Cradock and the neighbouring towns under the banner of the then banned ANC. They hated him for raising the level of political awareness of people in the rural areas. He was seen as a communist, a terrorist and therefore a dangerous man, who was a threat to the state.

Nyameka Goniwe told the Commission of the harassment suffered by the family as a result of his activism, and of how the message that his body had been found had been left by the police with a child. She described the first inquest into his death as a "circus," and told the commissioners that although the second inquest found the state security forces to have been responsible for Matthew's death, the official verdict was that no one could be named as culpable. When asked by a commissioner whom she thought had killed her husband and his comrades, she said, "We have a picture of what happened, although we can't prove it to the courts," and went on to describe the similarities between the deaths of the "Cradock Four" and the "PEBCO Three."[9] She displayed a deep knowledge of the connections between the South African Defence Force, the police, the Security Branch, the State Security Council, and death squads.[10] Her presentation was clear and implicated the state in sustained and sanctioned violence and horror.

The statement that Nyameka Goniwe presented to the Commission focused on Matthew and the family's attempts to locate his killers. Other than a brief comment on the harassment of the family, she did not address the question of her own experiences or those of her family until expressly asked to do so.

Her story was not the only one to be presented in a clear chronology. Elizabeth Floyd, Ria Solagee, and Maggie Friedman, among others, testified in similar fashion. Elizabeth Floyd spoke in Johannesburg (2 May 1996) of the death in detention of Neil Aggett—unionist, medical doctor, and conscientious objector—who was found hanging in his cell on 5 February 1982. She described his activities as a unionist, commenting on the dangers that he faced and adding, "We were well aware of what we were up against." She said that after Aggett's death, "The question really for everyone was, was he killed in interrogation and hung up or did he in fact take his own life?" She added that even if Aggett had killed himself, the state was still responsible for having pushed him to the point where suicide seemed to be his only option. She described the effects of his death on the activist community inside South Africa: "With his death our worst fears about detention were confirmed. He was the first white to die in detention. For the black people involved, this was very significant; he had not held back in the struggle and had paid the price. . . . When I was released from detention, our community was shattered. Neil's death was a watershed, as was David Webster's death."[11]

Floyd told the Commission about the effects of torture practices commonly used against detainees. These included sleep deprivation, solitary confinement, and electric shocks. She described the inquest into Aggett's death, its finding that he had committed suicide and that "legally, no-one was to blame." She described a chronology of violence that included changes in torture practices over the thirty-four years that the Commission investigated. She made a clear and precise connection between Aggett's death and the systems that underpinned apartheid, and linked the violent treatment of detainees to practices of inflicting pain used elsewhere in the world. She added that the security services still harbored those accused of abuses of human rights.

"A civil war was fought over people's personal lives," Floyd commented, and made it clear that the reason that she chose to testify to the Commission was in order to inform those people "who did not know or did not want to know." She added, "I think it's critical that people do know—and not just about the events of 1981 or 1982." Like Nyameka Goniwe, Elizabeth Floyd presented her understanding of the chronology of state attempts to halt activism, indicating, through her familiarity with state processes, a kind of political literacy.

Her testimony differed from many of the others heard by the Commission, as we shall see, in that she did not identify herself as a victim but as someone imparting expert knowledge. Her credibility as a witness was predicated on her knowledge and the way she was able to present it to the Commission.

The kinds of testimony I have described above offered a coherent chronology of good and bad and were presented in accord with a detailed understanding of state structures and personal awareness of the processes of violence. The information given was stark, presented linearly, and with emotion carefully held in check. The attention of the audience was easily focused on the stories of Matthew Goniwe and Neil Aggett, rather than on Nyameka Goniwe and Elizabeth Floyd. Testimony of this kind located the speaker as someone who "knows" and who has valuable information to impart. The women spoke from two positions of authority in this context—as what Mamphela Ramphele (1996) has called the "political widows" of activists and as women familiar with the state's bureaucratic processes. Their testimonies do not directly impute victimhood to self.

HEROES AS MODELS:
TIME AND THE DOMESTIC

The stories I now present followed different sets of narrative conventions. These testimonies were explicitly located within idioms of the domestic sphere. The accounts reflected the tropes found in oral tradition, locating individuality in a social and cultural context in ways that resonated with many of the people in the audience. The women who testified in this way seemed to testify to layers of experience entwined in wide sets of social relations. Hidden in such discourses of domesticity, I suggest, are powerful forms of knowledge and agency that need to be carefully recognized and sensitively heard.

Three stories by Nonceba Zokwe, Sylvia Dlomo-Jele, and Eunice Miya described the deaths of their sons. Their accounts offer themes that were reflected in other women's testimonies, using narrative forms that embedded experience firmly in a domestic world marked by daily struggle.

On 17 April 1996, shortly after Nyameka Goniwe had described Matthew Goniwe's death, Nonceba Zokwe testified about the death of her son Sithembile. She introduced herself to the Commission by her clan name: "a daughter from the Nogaka Family at Inymakwe." She told the commissioners how she had met the man who was to become her husband, describing him as "a propagandist of human rights." At this point her story took on the lyric repetition which was to characterize it throughout the telling. "I went to work and I met the activist Sipha-balala Zokwe. I met him there during the difficult times of struggle and oppression, when the government was removing people from place to place."

The couple had four children—Thobela, Sibongile, Sithembile, and Sibusiso. Mrs. Zokwe gave an account of two of her children's political activities. Thobela had gone into exile to join the ANC. There he used the pseudonyms Tony and Trinity. He had escaped the illegal crossbor-der raid made by the South African Defence Force on Maseru, Lesotho, in 1982, and had gone into exile first in Zimbabwe and then in Australia. He returned to South Africa after the 1994 elections. Another son, Sith-embile, had died. It was his story that Mrs. Zokwe had come to tell before the Commission.

As a schoolchild, Sithembile had become involved in the struggle against the apartheid regime, and after writing his school-leaving ex-aminations he had gone to join the liberation forces in Botswana. He returned briefly to South Africa to tell his mother that he had joined "the struggle" and then he left again for Lesotho, Angola, and East Germany. The family received scant news of him. Mrs. Zokwe was told he had disappeared and later she learned from human rights lawyers that he had been arrested in Bophutatswana.[12] She was told he was being held in a prison in Soweto, and that there he addressed the prison guards as "oppressors," demanding that he be charged or released. Mrs. Zokwe told the Commission that her son would recount his family's history of political activism to the prison guards and taunt them with his desire to destroy apartheid.

Mrs. Zokwe sought her son. She wrote to the Commissioner of Police and was told that Sithembile had been sent back to Transkei (the "independent state" in which his mother resided) to serve a prison sentence.

In 1988 he was released and returned to his mother's home at Butterworth in the Transkei. There he worked "at the cellars, carrying beer up and down, in and out." She added, "He was in and out of jail also, accused of being a communist born of a communist mother." Mrs. Zokwe told the Commission about three attempts on her son's life by the police. She had a premonition of his death before one of the attempts: "I had a premonition. . . . I dreamed that this child of mine was looking into death's eyes, and I think this was the second premonition on a Tuesday because I dreamed the same dream again."

She described Sithembile's involvement in politics to the commissioners: "Then this youth would sit without doing anything. He did not want to do anything but the struggle."

In June 1988, he was killed at home. "On that day I was [returning] from the wholesalers," said Mrs. Zokwe. "I met him on his way to town with my grandchildren on his shoulders. . . . He saw me and hugged me." Sithembile told his mother to accept what would happen to him and warned her that the police would kill him. She told him to go home and wait for her. She went to Chicken Licken (a fast-food outlet), where she was stopped and told that her son and his friend had been arrested. Stopping at a salon, she was told the story again, in more detail.

When she returned home she saw a policeman silhouetted against the house, and was greeted by "the leader of the Apartheid regime, a policeman, the head of the Security Branch, who said, 'Here's that communist mother.'" She was angry and challenged him, saying, "On these premises I am the government!" and, when he threatened to kill her, she replied, "The only pain I know is the pain of giving birth." She attempted to attack him and was restrained by neighbors. She tried to leap over the wall surrounding her property to reach her son, lying near the police van in the street, and then she described to the Commission the moment of his death: "A few minutes later I heard the sound of a revolver. I knew I had to close my son's eyes, but I could not." Amid threats from the police, the van reversed into the yard, breaking the gate and wall and destroying the flowers.

Her testimony did not explain how she verified that her son was dead and his body in the morgue. Instead, she continued her testimony with the search for her son. She spoke of visiting the police station and hospital and a relative, a policeman, who promised to try to find out what had happened.

She did not talk of the ironies of asking her kinsman to assist her when he was employed as a policeman by the same government that her son—and she—worked against. She concentrated instead on how she traced her child's whereabouts, learning of his death. She told the commissioners that when she returned home without having found him she saw signs of struggle everywhere. She listed them carefully: they included a burned passage, bullet holes in walls, wardrobes and suitcases scattered on the floor, a patch of blood between the wardrobe and the bed, a jacket still hanging in the burned cupboard, and torn curtains. Her other children were crying.

Then her testimony moved to the identification of her son in the mortuary: "He was on a stretcher, smiling in death. He would tell us to be strong. . . . He was dead but smiling. . . . I was proud because I knew why my child had died." Later she described the return of the policeman who had promised to find out about her child. He had not performed the appropriate rituals after the death of her son, and so came to the house but would not enter. He bore news that the policemen who had killed her child had been imprisoned but had escaped from prison. She greeted him and told him that her son had been buried and that he should "wash his hands."[13]

Mrs. Zokwe's story is about her own experiences in relation to her child's death. In her story she describes herself as protector of the child, as boss in her home, as mother. Later, when asked about her strength, she replied:

> It depends on your upbringing. . . . My home was a traditional home. . . . Nobody was regarded as a stranger in this house. . . . We had the examples of heroes as models. They gave strength. I saw they could survive and therefore said I could survive, too. I know my struggle. I am proud of womanhood. It is womanhood which brought me this strength . . . You have to decide for yourself who you are and what you'd like to be tomorrow.

Her testimony was elliptical, using repetition and pause, gesture and silence. Mrs. Zokwe saw her strength as being based on traditional values, and her narration gave form to these ideas. The largely black audience responded audibly to her narrative. Nods and repetition of well-known names punctuated her testimony.

Other women used metaphor differently. Eunice Thembiso Miya, testifying in Cape Town, used the domestic world and chronological time as hangers on which to place her experience of the death of her twenty-three-year-old son in what has became known as the case of the "Gugulethu Seven." Jabulani was shot by security forces on 3 March 1986.

Approximately three hundred young people were officially acknowledged to have been killed by security forces between 1984 and 1986 in the "Unrest."[14] Jabulani was one of them.

Mrs. Miya described to the Commission how she learned of the death of her son:

> On the 3rd of March 1986 I was working in offices in town. I left the house at half past four in the morning as usual, to be at work at six o'clock. Just before I left, my son [who lived in a room in the back yard] knocked on the door. I opened it—it was about quarter past four or twenty past—and he came and got bread and cold water and asked for two Rand. I said that I only had five Rand and would be short if I gave it to him. But I gave it to him because I wanted him to work. He said he wanted to accompany me to the station. I said "This is the first time!" but he insisted.
>
> He left to go to his bedroom and I closed and bolted the door. The garage is next to the house and he came through the garage and insisted on accompanying me. I was suspicious and I said "Turn back," but he accompanied me to NY59 [a nearby block]. I told him to turn back. That was the last time I saw him. I went to work on the quarter-to-five train.

Her story is precisely located and framed: at a given time in the morning of a specific day, as she was preparing to go to work. The events she described are placed squarely within the domestic domain that then introduces her position within the economy, as she prepares for a double shift in her work as a cleaning woman, and her encouragement of her son's job search. The story is framed in space: the scene moves from the kitchen, now locked and bolted and secured from the dangers outside, to the garage, and outside into the street; from the relative security of domesticity into the unknown of the world at large. The testimony about her son's death was not simply the recall of an event but of the conditions of life that characterized and shaped it.

The beginning of the day was marked in her mind because her son's behavior was unusual. Her description of the day as out of the ordinary indicates a retrospective prescience of violent change. It points also to the ebb and flow of violence: Mrs. Miya did not expect the intrusion of violence and death into her home, notwithstanding the contexts of violence and repression that marked both that time (mid-1980s) and the place (a black township).

Her son's insistence that he accompany her transformed it from an ordinary day into one marked out of the ordinary. The way in which the story is specifically located in daily experience is sustained in the next part of her testimony where she hears of the violence in Gugulethu that day.

As usual, she went to clean offices and then went to work in a private
home:

> I worked as usual, but at about half-past ten my boss, Mrs. . . . , came to me
> and said, "Eunice." I said, "Madam." She said, "I heard on the news there
> are Russians[15] in Gugulethu who were killed. Is your son in politics?" "No,"
> and I continued working.
>
> At about two o'clock I went home. On the way I did the shopping, and
> caught the five o'clock train. [I got home] and put on the TV for the news.
> My daughter put it on. [Pause while she weeps.] When the music started for
> the news, then I was told that seven children were killed by Russian guer-
> rillas.[16] One was shown on TV with a gun on his chest and I saw it was my
> son. My daughter said, "It's him!" I said, "No. I saw him this morning and
> he was dressed warmly." I prayed that the news would rewind.

Again, her testimony is situated in her daily experiences: at work, responding to the "Madam," shopping, then the return home, watching
the news, and recalling what her child had worn that day.

Many women testifying to the Commission placed their accounts
within the domestic. Perhaps domesticity is used to mark a world that
is relatively ordered and predictable, in which kinship relations have a
degree of coherence, and time, too, flows predictably—"as usual." Yet
many of the women spoke explicitly about the loss of loved ones as
changing their expectations of time, and of aging. Sylvia Dlomo-Jele,
for example, said that the death of her son Sicelo had altered her future,
and that his activism had affected her life. She explained,

> The harassment and pain [we experienced] did not start when my child died.
> It started in 1985 when he began to be harassed by police as a student activist.
> He was harassed at school; the police and Defence Force went to the school
> and the headmaster would hide him with other children. . . . The house was
> petrol-bombed. I suffered a lot and my mother nearly died. . . . The police
> used to come in and out of my house and told me to tell my son not to be
> political.

In response to their warnings she said that she did not know what they
were talking about, and that she knew nothing about politics. She passed
on their warnings to her son, but he would not desist from his activities.
Instead, concerned about the continuing police harassment of his family,
he stopped sleeping at home, and her expectations of family life—that
children should sleep under the same roofs as their parents—were disrupted. She described her last moments with Sicelo in her testimony:

On the Wednesday before his death he came to me and said, "Mother, Father, I've come to sleep at home." I was relieved because he had been sleeping with other people or outside. He looked tired and had a headache. I used to give him my nerve tablets. A child, he knew what he was fighting. He told us to be strong if he died: "Pick up my spear and continue my struggle," he said.

I told him to sleep at home. He refused, saying that it would not be nice for his parents to see the police killing him. He left. He did not like to be followed, but I did so. I think he slept in the passage [the strip of ground separating houses].

On Saturday he phoned his aunt and told her to cook for him. He did not return on Saturday to fetch his food. We were worried, but prayed. On Sunday, while still preparing new food for him, at about ten o'clock, the phone rang. It was Sicelo who asked if I was okay, then kept quiet. I thought he did not have money for the phone. That was the last time I spoke to him. The next day the police arrived with his pocketbook. I said, "Have you killed my son?" and he [the policeman] denied it.

The failure of her son to collect his meal was an indication that something was amiss, a further breach in a social order already shaped by the apartheid regime's intrusion. After identifying Sicelo's body, Mrs. Dlomo-Jele commented, "the pain did not end there." The police at the police station accused her of having a "big mouth" yet of being unable to control her own child. When her other son grew angry at their taunts he was detained. Later, at the funeral, police threw tear gas and her niece almost suffocated as a result. Family members were harassed even after Sicelo's death. His killers were not found.[17]

Mrs. Dlomo-Jele's health suffered as a result of Sicelo's activism and death.[18] She spoke of the change in the shape of her future, saying that Sicelo had been a good student who would have found work and supported her. Her husband's mental health was unstable and he had not worked for three years. Her own state of health prohibited her from regular work, and her expectations of support from Sicelo had been dashed. Her future was no longer predictable, and the way she had envisaged time, prompted by cultural expectations that emphasize the obligations of children to parents, could not be fulfilled.

At the funeral, Mrs. Dlomo-Jele said, she was unable to mourn her child as her own (personal communication, November 1995). He had become a child of the community, a symbol of resistance. The outpouring of public grieving that accompanied his funeral was such that she felt unable fully to admit the loss of her son. His death and burial became a public opportunity to make political statements that were otherwise impossible. The children in the community had given her their lunch moneys on that day in commemoration of Sicelo's death. She explained that they did so because they recognized that her child would not be able to fulfill his obligations to her. Collectively, they took symbolic responsibility for a short period.

THE LAYERING OF EXPERIENCE

Four themes drawn from the testimonies of Nyameka Goniwe, Elizabeth Floyd, Nonceba Zokwe, Eunice Miya, and Sylvia Dlomo-Jele resonate with testimonies of most of the women who spoke before the Commission. These have to do with the location of self in stories; with experiences of family life; with expectations of time; and with silence and secrecy. Each is implied in the other.

THE LOCATION OF SELF

Hidden in the stories of loss of men that women told are stories about themselves, in which they are both narrators—facing the commissioners and audience—and performers. Most testimony began with an event that located the speaker firmly as a witness in space and time. Sometimes the commissioners sought this information, but even when they did not, women prefaced their stories by placing themselves firmly in the plot. Yet we are required to pay careful attention to locate precisely how women place themselves. For example, when speaking to the Commission about Neil Aggett, Elizabeth Floyd did not state that she had been a political activist. Her political consciousness and its price were implicit in the way she framed her statements, prefacing them with comments such as, "When *I* was released from detention" and "*We* knew what we were up against." Other women position themselves differently. For example, Nonceba Zokwe's political consciousness was evident in her statements about her son, whom the police sought for being "a communist born of a communist mother." Sylvia Mabija described the death of her brother Phakamile in 1977 while in detention to the Commission at a hearing held in Kimberley on 10 July 1996. She said, "On the 7th of June, the police came. *We* were all in the dining room.[19] They came with Phaki who was haggard. . . ." Sylvia Molekeli, also testifying in Kimberley, began her statement with a specific temporal framing: "It was the 16th of June, 1993, in the morning, between nine and ten.[20] *We* were toyi-toyiing, just a small group of people" (10 June 1996), while

Mabu Mokhuwane, who testified about the death of her grandson, Christopher, said: "When Christopher died, *I* was with my younger daughter. *I* was very ill" (10 June 1996). Busiswe Kewana's testimony about the death of her mother, Nombulelo Delato, opened with a comment on the separation of families: "While *I* was in Grahamstown [at school], I received a telegram from my grandmother to say my mother had died [in Colesburg]. She was burned"[21] (Cape Town hearings, 24 April 1996).

Notwithstanding the differences in the ways that women positioned themselves, the testimonies that they made to the Commission implicated themselves almost immediately. These are not only stories about the loss of loved ones but women's stories of loss. And, as I have commented, many women testified about their losses using metaphors drawn from their domestic roles. These roles in turn are imbricated in the social, political, and economic realities of South Africa, past and present. I do not wish to imply that women are confined to domestic roles. I wish rather to draw attention to the ways in which women used domesticity to map the interpolations of violence in their lives.

FAMILY

The domestic metaphor encompassed family life. Stories told using domestic tropes are not concerned only with an event but with the contexts of daily life, in which women are the linchpins as they seek to make and maintain homes, to work and raise children. Women's testimonies, largely about the loss of men, explicitly and implicitly marked male absences. Women testified about the death and disappearance of men, yet they were silent on the subject of men as actors in their domestic worlds.[22] Indeed, it is partly this silence that draws attention to the contingencies of family life in South Africa (see Reynolds 1995a): the absence of men from family life.

Women described the disruption of family life at many levels by the state and the political activities of loved ones. They also spoke of the ways that families were separated. Mrs. Gwedla (see below) was brought from her rural home to Cape Town by her son. Mrs. Kewana was attending school far from her mother's home when she received the news of the latter's death. Nyameka Goniwe had to leave her son with his paternal grandmother whilst she continued her studies.

Women's testimonies tell of their attempts to maintain families, both by providing economic resources and by trying to protect family

members from the incursions of the state. Frequently their responses to
state incursions into the domestic were violent. Mrs. Zokwe shouted
that on her property she was boss, even as a policeman aimed a gun at
her and tried to arrest her son. Mrs. Adonis told the Commission that
she hit a policeman on the head with a chair when he came to arrest her
son.

Women described the distances that they traveled in order to find or
obtain news of missing kin. They sought lost ones in police stations and
mortuaries, in hospitals and prisons. Mrs. Godolozi described sneaking
past policemen guarding a court in order to find her husband, who had
been detained. Women traveled to nearby towns and across borders to
Lesotho, Botswana, Zambia, Angola, and Tanzania. The search as motif
is diffuse, spanning huge geographical spaces and immense periods of
time. Women told the commissioners of their desire that the searching
be ended appropriately: with the discovery of a body, correct burials
and funerary rites, appropriate reparations, and sometimes retributive
justice.

Sometimes women were not successful in maintaining families. Maria
Mthembu spoke of how her brother was killed "by accident" by police
seeking for her (Gauteng, 29 April 1996). The death of one child in lieu
of another points to the ways in which the body was not necessarily a
signifier of individuality to the state. Maria Mthembu's story points also
to the vulnerability of boundaries: self and other were interchangeable
in terms of state action. The violation of bodily boundaries is reflected
in the violation of domestic spaces: Mrs. Zokwe's catalogue of destruction in the house was repeated by other women, who asked for compensation for goods destroyed in searches.

Women's testimonies point to the contingencies of home and of
domesticity. Locked doors could not protect families from either random or directed violence; individual activism brought harassment and
death to kinsfolk. The emphasis on domestic context in women's stories
highlights the failures of home to protect and contain, and points to
state intrusion at many levels. The specificity with which women detailed
their domestic worlds and time points to the depths of state irruption in
them.

There are two further themes drawn from what women say about
families that I shall explore briefly. They have to do with expectations
of time and continuity as these relate to family life, and with silence and
secrecy. Both themes emerge from the words of domesticity that women
used to describe their experiences.

TIME AND CONTINUITY

Earlier, I described Sylvia Dlomo-Jele's expectations of a time when her child would provide for her, and how these expectations were changed by her son's death. Her expectations are reflected in the story that Mrs. Gwedla told to the Commission in Cape Town, on 24 April 1996. She said that her son, Zongesile, had brought her from her rural home and had built a shack for her in Crossroads. Three weeks after she arrived in the city, police shot and severely injured Zongesile during the *witdoek* violence.[23] With her son seated beside her, she told the Commission that their roles are now reversed; instead of being cared for in her old age by her son, she looks after him. Her husband abandoned them. She said that he left "because he could not stay with an abnormal son." She told the Commission that she was afraid to sleep at night because her son roams the streets (Cape Town, 24 April 1996). Other women repeated elements of her story, describing the expectations they had held of their (male) children. Frequently prefaced "He was a good boy," or "He was good in school, and would have supported me," or in Mrs. de Bruin's words, "My son was like a daughter to me" (Worcester, 25 June 1996), the women's requests of the Commission were oblique and frequently limited. Yet implicit in their testimonies and requests were commentaries about the ideal shape of social relationships, the role of the family, the kinds of support that should be available to the aged. Sindiswa Mkhonto, speaking of the death of her husband, Sparrow, at the hands of the Security Forces, said, "Because I have no husband, my child has no father. . . . Today I don't have a husband and my son has no father. The family is lost" (East London, 16 April 1996). Her lament points to the construction of family and its location in time; the death of a father in this case irrevocably changes the family and its relationships through time.

SILENCE AND SECRECY

Women spoke of secrecy, of the multiple levels at which activism and violence created silences within family life. Some women claimed not to know that children, husbands, kinsfolk were politically involved. Women such as Sylvia Dlomo-Jele used claims of ignorance to resist police demands for information about kinsmen. Nquabakazi Godolozi said that she and her husband used passwords to gain access to their own home. Secrecy shaped conversation, too; information about activism was hidden from parents and children, sometimes even from spouses. Silence and secrecy played themselves out in gender struggles, and in conflict over roles. "We are not allowed to ask our husbands about politics in my culture," said Feziwa Mfeti (East London, 16 April 1996); a wry comment greeted with nods and laughter from the audience, and later confirmed by Govan Mbeki, who addressed the Commission. A stalwart of the struggle against apartheid, Mbeki told the Commission of the difficulties that family life had generated in the early days of the struggle. "After work we went into the township to educate. The police were looking for meetings. So when you left you did not tell your wife where you were going, and when you returned, at twelve or one in the morning, they were asleep and your food was on the stove. . . . Women created problems for the [liberation] movement because they wanted to know" (Cape Town, 28 April 1996). Women's stories told before the Commission detailed the complexities of managing daily life in the apartheid state. Women spoke of the absences of men, the diffusion of family over large geographies, the silences that political activism wrought, and the effects of these silences on the ways that political consciousness could be shaped and expressed. It is perhaps in these kinds of stories, rather than those which speak more directly to the embodied experience of violation, that the depths of apartheid are revealed. Hidden within women's words are narratives of the destruction of kinship, the alteration of time's expected flow, the power of economies in shaping experience, the intrusion of the state. Their stories bear testimony to attempts to create and maintain families against the odds.

In their testimonies about others, women tell of their own experiences. Through the stories that they told before the Commission, women described layers of experience and, through their oration, invited audiences to participate with them in their performances of memory and meaning. The narrative forms that women used speak to different levels of experience and meaning in the world. The stories some women told drew on forms that have deep cultural resonance, even as the contexts in which the forms were narrated were new. Harold Scheub (1975) suggests that, like culture, genres of oration shift and flow. He also suggests that successful performance of oral narrative is dependent on audience imagination (Zenani and Scheub 1992). Thus women who use such narrative forms were telling their own stories, but in doing so were also telling the stories of those who listened. The question is, how it is that we who listen—whether in the audiences of the public hearings, or to the televisions and radios—are to witness the stories that women tell.

Joyce Carol Oates once argued that language is "all we have to pit against the death and silence." Quoting her, David Morris (1996: 31) points out that she does not, however, guarantee "that the opposite of silence is truth." In a Commission whose aim is to elicit spoken and written commentary on human rights violations of the apartheid era, the relationships between words, silences, and meaning become especially pertinent. I wish to suggest that what is taken for silence in women's speech is itself meaningful, a language. We need to take note of what it is that women say and also to recognize what they keep silent. I suggest not that we excise and excavate words in order to reveal women's experiences but that we reformulate a context, in which the silences give meaning.

We need sensitive ways to map the reverberations of violence and horror outwards from the individual to kin and friends and communities. The physical experience of pain is but a part of a far wider awfulness against which people pitted their strengths. Veena Das, quoting Wittgenstein, asks whether it is not possible to experience another's pain in one's own body (1996: 69–71). She comments that this question begins to provide a philosophical grammar for the exploration and experience of pain; pain becomes amenable to expression and sharing, rather than being that point which demarcates the self most distinctly from the world, as Elaine Scarry (1985) and Lawrence Langer (1991) would have it. Pain is not confined to the individual body in this formulation but is shared and possibly transformed by the relationships between people.

I suggest that by focusing too closely on bodily experience, we narrow our gaze and close our ears, disallowing the veracities of experience of which women speak. By saying that the body is truth, we ignore their experiences and their words. A focus solely on the body and its violation fixes an experience of violence in time, in an event, and draws attention away from ways of understanding that experience as a process that endures through time.

The testimonies presented by women before the Commission point to different ways of telling their experiences. How do we listen? Das and Kleinman suggest that witnessing should be through tear-blurred eyes (this volume). We need to develop ways to attend to such effects as the dissolution of the everyday and the taken-for-granted nature of time and relationships that underlie the testimonies of many women.

The ways that women describe their experiences is important for the ways we hear. Part of what women described before the South African Truth and Reconciliation Commission was the disruption of the communal, the social and cultural expectations of time and place. They told of the ways that apartheid shaped their daily contexts and those of their families and of their attempts to oppose it, to maintain families in the face of great odds. I argue that these aspects of experience need to be witnessed, and that, at the same time, witnessing needs to take into account that which is left unsaid in testimonies.

Witnessing is neither simple nor automatic. Das argues that failure to recognize an affirmation of pain ("I am in pain") is to perpetuate and participate in violence, and that this failure is not a failure of intellect but of spirit (1996: 88). Maya Todeschini (this volume) shows the ease with which hibakusha women's experiences of the atom bombs dropped on Hiroshima and Nagasaki are delegitimized in official scripts of women's social roles. She shows that women have used a diversity of mechanisms, including support groups, prose, and protest, to make their experiences of violence known. She shows how easily experience is subsumed in stereotypic representations of gender and suffering. Das has commented, in relation to the violence of the Partition of India and Pakistan, that for women it was "part of their obligation as women to bring to the collective consciousness the grievous wrongs that had been done to them" (1994: 363). Yet, she suggests, some horror is not and cannot be articulated. Silence marks particular kinds of knowing, and that silence is gendered. In other words, silence too is a legitimate discourse on pain—if it is acknowledged. The recognition of pain may be heavily reliant on acknowledgment of the meaning of silence, and of the validity of silence as a means of communicating particular kinds of experience.

Das's writing differs from that of Langer, who also writes of the inexpressibility of some experiences of horror and pain (1996; 1995; 1991). Das is insistent that the silence of Indian women about the violations they experienced during Partition is an act of conscious agency. Langer argues that massive violences, as in Holocaust experience, are not knowable in common language and that time is fractured in such a way as to make experience unrepresentable. Showing how some women create silence of their experiences of violation, Das points to new constructions of agency. In her formulation, agency does not lie in linguistic competency but in the refusal to give experience words, in the ability to do something with the experience (i.e., to hold it inside, silent). As she comments elsewhere, "In reading history we must learn how to read silences, for the victim rarely gets an opportunity to record his or her point of view" (1987: 13).

Kirsten Hastrup has suggested that the anthropological exercise is characterized by "the imaginative ability to see strange people as fellow sufferers" (1993: 736). The study of suffering, Hastrup argues, is essential. In this chapter I have explored some of the problems of hearing to which testimonies of pain and suffering give rise. Interrogating the "silence" and "absence" of women's stories of their own experience in testimonies made before the Truth and Reconciliation Commission illustrates that different ways of telling require that the attention be differently focused. Some women represent their experiences in narrative forms which appear on the surface to mark silence. Their telling of experience is couched in metaphor and implied in the narrative structure of stories and their performances. The resolution of this apparent contradiction is only partial: women's "silence" can be recognized as language, and we need carefully to probe the cadences of silences, the gaps between fragile words, in order to hear what it is that women say.

Words can be weapons; giving voice to the voiceless, the specific aim of the Commission, assumes—perhaps patronizingly—that the world is knowable only through words and that to have no voice is to be languageless, unable to communicate. "An ear for this, an ear for that. Who to believe? . . . The struggle for truth continues ever afterwards. Because afterwards is where we live. . . . Afterwards is where stories begin" (Nicol 1992: 1).

NOTES

Thanks to Pamela Reynolds for her encouragement, advice, and readings of this manuscript. My thanks too to Stuart Douglas, Patti Henderson, Linda Waldman, Sally Frankental, Rob Turrell, Richard Wilson, and Susan Levine, all of whom gave valuable comments, criticism, and support. They, of course, bear no responsibility for either my errors or my interpretations.

1. This chapter reflects on the public hearings held between April and May 1996, before the Human Rights Violations Committee of the Truth and Reconciliation Commission. I have updated sections of the paper in endnotes using data collected from research conducted throughout 1996 and 1997 in the Western and Northern Cape Provinces of South Africa. For the most part, the trends I describe in the paper were sustained throughout the period of public hearings (i.e., April 1996 to December 1997). At the time of publication of the volume of which this chapter is a part, the Commission has already made its Final Report (5 vol., 1998). However, the amnesty process of the Commission is not yet complete, and public hearings into amnesty applications have continued and are expected to be completed in mid-2000.

2. Notwithstanding the inclusion of the phrases "pecuniary loss" and "substantial impairment of human rights," public hearings of the Human Rights

Violations Committee tended to focus on physical suffering and on mental and
emotional suffering. The draft recommendations regarding Reparation and Rehabilitation Policy submitted by the Truth and Reconciliation Commission to
the government (see Reparation and Rehabilitation Committee, TRC, 1997)
made few recommendations regarding pecuniary loss and impaired human
rights that fall outside of the definitions of "gross" human rights laid out in
chapter 1(1)(xix)(a) of the Act, as described above.

The Commission later described its work as having been concerned with the
violation of rights to bodily integrity (Report, 1998 Volume One: 64).

3. At the height of repression in 1985–86, ten thousand children were detained under the Emergency Regulations promulgated in that period, and under
Security Legislation that had provided increasing powers for the state since
1960. Fourteen hundred black people were killed at the hands of security forces
(International Defence Aid Fund 1991: 69) in 1985–86. The period under review
by the Commission (1960–1994) saw also enforced racial classification and seg-
regation; mandatory military conscription for young white men; unacknowledged "destabilization" by the state against neighboring states; and assassina-
tions of political activists. Legislation, States of Emergency, and draconian
Emergency Regulations eventually provided for detention without trial for up
to 180 days. Torture and harassment were frequent (see Chabani Manganyi and
du Toit 1990; Foster, Davies, and Sandler 1987). Banned political organizations
established offices outside South Africa and conducted a covert war against the
apartheid state. Inside South Africa, campaigns to render the country ungovern-
able were implemented in the mid-1980s by those opposing apartheid. The intention was to force the National Party–led government of the day to abandon
its apartheid policies and implement reforms that would include universal suf-
frage.

4. The Commission's main public focus shifted from hearings of the Human
Rights Violations Committee to hearings held by the Amnesty Committee in
mid-1997. The initial focus of the Human Rights Violations hearings was a
deliberate attempt by the Commission to "restore human and civil dignity" to
victims by allowing them a public forum in which to testify without distraction.
It may also have been an attempt to divert attention from the unpopular task
of the Amnesty Committee.

5. Does this form of witnessing presage a "new" society where the gaze is
equated to knowledge? Describing the violence that erupted in Delhi in 1984
after the murder of Indira Gandhi, Srinivasan says that "the very act of witnessing . . . was a function of the breakdown of structure which permitted a
certain kind of gaze to be directed at that which would normally have remained
hidden from view" (1994: 318).

6. The concern was manifested in other ways. For example, the form
used by the Commission to record statements of human rights violations was
refined throughout the two-year process of public hearings. By April 1997, it
had been modified to include a cautionary note to women applicants: "IMPOR-
TANT: Some women testify about violations of human rights that happened to
family members or friends, but they have also suffered abuses. Don't forget to

tell us what happened to you yourself if you were the victim of a gross human rights abuse" (Statement Concerning Gross Violations of Human Rights, Version 5, 1997: 3).

In addition, special Women's Hearings were held in Cape Town (8 August 1996), Durban (24 October 1996), Johannesburg (29 July 1997), to highlight women's experiences as political activists, agents and victims. The Cape Town hearing on 8 August 1996 was held to celebrate National Women's Day on 9 August. The day—a national holiday—is a commemoration of women's protests against the pass law system, which enforced residential separation on the basis of race and determined employment opportunities. Women's antipass protests culminated on 9 August 1956, when twenty thousand women marched to one of the seats of Parliament, the Union Buildings in Pretoria, to protest against pass laws. The Commission's Women's Hearing in Cape Town was held "to celebrate, honour and pay tribute to women," and to debunk the "myth that women played a secondary role" in the struggle, according to one of the Commissioners, Glenda Wildschutt. Ironically, the year of the women's pass protests, 1956, falls outside of the Commission's mandate period, and abuses suffered by women during and as a consequence of the march did not directly inform the Commission's findings and report.

Testifiers at the Cape Town Women's Hearings recounted the violations committed against nine people, six of them women. Agnes Gounden told the Commission about the death of her sister, Avril de Bruyn, who had been returning from work when she killed in crossfire between the police and protesters. Selina Williams described the death of her sister, Coline, a member of Umkhonto weSizwe (Spear of the Nation—the ANC's armed wing, commonly known as MK) who was killed in a grenade explosion. Coline was killed alongside Robert Waterwitch, whose uncle, Basil Snayer, described the event to the Commission. Monica Daniels described her injuries incurred as a result of a police attack; Sarah Martin testified on behalf of the de Bruin family, whose son, David was killed by police. Hilda Levy spoke about the death of her son, Ricardo. He had been watching protesters and was caught in the police crossfire. Sarah August told the panel about her daughter Sarah van Wyk, who had also been caught and killed in crossfire. Shirley Gunn, an MK member, was one of few women activists to testify about her experiences. She described the wrongful arrest of herself and her baby son, and told the Commission about the torture she had endured. Zubeida Jaffer, a journalist, told the Commission that she had become an ANC member and a trade union organizer after her first detention and torture.

7. There are eleven official languages in South Africa. Testimony to the Commission is made in the witness's language of choice and is translated simultaneously into English, Afrikaans, and the other major language spoken in the area. My writings are drawn from the English translations where these were necessary. A great deal of idiom is lost in the simultaneous translation, but my analysis relies on the plot of the story as witnesses tell it rather than directly on people's words. Quotation marks indicate verbatim recordings from the English translation.

8. The UDF was an umbrella organization whose membership consisted of approximately five hundred organizations. It was banned by the apartheid state in 1988 and formally disbanded in 1991.

9. Sipho Hashe, Champion Galela, and Qaqawuli Godolozi, who came to be known as the "PEBCO Three" after their disappearance in May 1985, were political activists in the Eastern Cape. They were arrested and imprisoned and were never seen again. In 1994, their deaths were linked to "hit-squad" operatives based at the police farm, Vlakplaas. Applications brought before the Amnesty Committee of the Commission in November 1997 by members of the Security Branch and Vlakplaas operatives revealed that the three men had been tortured and killed in May 1985. Their bodies were set alight and their remains thrown into the Fish River.

10. Death squads (or hit-squads) were said to be organized groups of assassins that worked for the state security forces. Many members of the apartheid government continue to deny the existence of such squads (Submission to the Truth and Reconciliation Commission by the National Party, 21 August 1996), notwithstanding convictions in the criminal courts of two leaders of the police unit C-10 based at Vlakplaas, and the testimonies made both in court and before the Commission of witnesses involved in operations at Vlakplaas and in "covert operations" (see Pauw 1997).

11. Floyd did not describe her detention and made no further reference to it, a point to which I return later in this chapter.

David Webster, a social anthropologist, worked at the University of the Witwatersrand. He was assassinated in 1989. His companion, Maggie Friedman, testified to the Commission on 3 May 1996 in Johannesburg. She accused the state and the legal system of covering up his death. Ferdi Barnard, a member of the apartheid state's covert organization, the CCB, later admitted to a journalist that he had killed Webster (*Mail and Guardian*, 21–27 November 1997, 23–24; Pauw 1997). At the time of writing, Barnard is facing criminal charges for Webster's death.

12. Bophutatswana was one of four "Independent States" (ethnic homelands) created as part of the apartheid plan for Separate Development.

13. A reference to burial rituals. Death is considered polluting, and those who have attended funerals wash their hands outside the house of the deceased before crossing the threshold for the culmination of the burial service. See Hunter 1979.

14. The decade of the 1980s was marked by an increase in state violence and an "ungovernability" campaign in townships. Severe legislation was set in place by the state, ostensibly to control the violence. There is, however, increasing evidence that the state itself was responsible for fomenting some of the violence (Goldstone Commission of Enquiry 1993).

15. A slang term used to describe members of the armed wings of liberation movements.

16. This appears to be a mistranslation. The police stated that the dead youths were "Russian terrorists."

17. During a public hearing into violations committed by the Mandela Football Club, a lead article in the *Mail and Guardian* (21–27 November 1997)

stated that new evidence would emerge that would link Winnie Mandela-Madikizela (Nelson Mandela's ex-wife) to Sicelo Dlomo's death. On 31 January 1999, the *Sunday Times* newspaper ran a short front-page article that claimed that four men had applied for amnesty for killing Sicelo Dlomo. They were members of MK. They claimed that Sicelo was killed because he was suspected of being a police informer. At the time of writing, the amnesty applications have not yet been heard in public. Sicelo Dlomo is not reported as a victim of gross violations of human rights in the Commission's 1998 report.

18. On 13 March 1999, Mrs. Dlomo-Jele died. I was notified of her death by an e-mail sent by the Centre for the Study of Violence and Reconciliation in Johannesburg, with which she had worked in establishing the Khulumani Support Group, a support and lobby group for survivors of violence. The message explained, "Her son, Sicelo Dlomo, lost his life on the path to freedom in South Africa. Sylvia not only completed his journey while carrying the heavy burden of his death, but took many with her. Ironically, in the end, it was the stress of his death and the partial truths about him being killed by his fellow comrades that was too much for her. In this regard she symbolises the plight of so many in South Africa who have only been left with half-truths about the past. Her death reminds us that it is people like Sylvia who ultimately paid the price for the democracy we now enjoy. . . ."

19. All emphases in this paragraph are mine.

20. The temporal framing is specific in this instance: June 16 was known as "Soweto Day" and commemorated the student uprisings in Soweto in 1976. It is now celebrated as Youth Day.

21. Sometimes people suspected by members of their communities of having been police informers were set alight and burned to death. The method of burning was to fill a tire with paraffin or gasoline and put it around the victim's neck before setting it alight. This method was known as "necklacing."

22. My thanks to Linda Waldman for pointing out the absence of representation of men in women's testimonies.

23. The witdoeke (Afrikaans; literally, "white headcloths") were so named because of the white fabric they wore as identification. In the 1980s in the Cape there were ongoing conflicts between witdoeke and surrounding squatter camps aligned to progressive political organizations such as youth, women's, and civic organizations and unions aligned to the UDF. See Cole 1987.

REFERENCES CITED

Chabani Manganyi, N., and Andre du Toit, eds. 1990. *Political Violence and the Struggle in South Africa*. Halfway House: Southern Book Publishers.

Cole, Josette. 1987. *Crossroads: The Politics of Reform and Repression, 1976–1986*. Johannesburg: Ravan Press.

Das, Veena. 1987. "The Anthropology of Violence and the Speech of Victims." *Anthropology Today* 3, no. 4: 11–13.

———. 1990. "Our Work to Cry, Your Work to Listen." In *Mirrors of Violence: Communities, Riots and Survivors in South Asia*, ed. Veena Das, 345–94. Delhi: Oxford University Press.

————. 1996. "Language and Body: Transactions in the Construction of Pain."
    Daedalus 125, no. 1: 67–92.
————. 1997. "The Act of Witnessing and the Healing of Culture." In *Social
    Suffering,* ed. Arthur Kleinman, Veena Das, and Margaret Lock. Berkeley:
    University of California Press.
Detainees' Parents Support Committee. n.d. *A Woman's Place Is in the Struggle
    Not behind Bars.* Johannesburg: Detainees' Parents Support Committee.
Foster, Don, Dennis Davies, and D. Sandler. 1987. *Detention and Torture in
    South Africa: Psychological, Legal and Historical Studies.* Cape Town: Da-
    vid Philip.
Goldblatt, Beth, and Shiela Meintjies. 1996. *Gender and the Truth and Rec-
    onciliation Commission: A Submission to the Truth and Reconciliation
    Commission.* Johannesburg: Department of Political Studies and Gender
    Project, Applied Legal Studies, University of the Witwatersrand.
Goldstone Commission of Enquiry. 1993. *Goldstone Commission of Enquiry
    into Public Violence and Intimidation: Role of the South African Defence
    Force.* Pretoria: Goldstone Commission of Enquiry.
Hastrup, Kirsten. 1993. "Hunger and the Hardness of Facts." *Man* 28: 727–
    39.
————. 1995. *A Passage to Anthropology.* London: Routledge.
Hayner, Priscilla. 1996. "Commissioning the Truth: Further Research Ques-
    tions." *Third World Quarterly* 17, no. 1: 19–29.
Hunter, Monica. 1979. *Reaction to Conquest: Effects of Contact with Euro-
    peans on the Pondo of South Africa* (abridged paperback edition). Cape
    Town: David Philip.
International Defence Aid Fund. 1991. *Apartheid: The Facts.* London: IDAF.
Langer, Lawrence. 1991. *Holocaust Testimonies: The Ruins of Memory.* New
    Haven, Conn.: Yale University Press.
————. 1995. *Admitting the Holocaust: Collected Essays.* Oxford: Oxford Uni-
    versity Press.
————. 1996. "The Alarmed Vision: Social Suffering and Holocaust Atrocity."
    Daedalus 125, no. 1: 47–67.
Morris, David. 1996. "About Suffering: Voice, Genre and Moral Community."
    Daedalus 125, no. 1: 25–46.
Motsuenyane Commission Report. 1993. *Reports of the Commission of En-
    quiry into Certain Allegations of Cruelty and Human Rights Abuses Against
    ANC Prisoners and Detainees by ANC Members.* Report made to the African
    National Congress. Johannesburg.
Nicol, Mike. 1992. *In This Day and Age.* New York: Alfred A. Knopf.
Pauw, Jacques. 1997. *Into the Heart of Darkness: Interviews with Apartheid's
    Assassins.* Johannesburg: Jonathan Ball Publishers.
Promotion of National Unity and Reconciliation Act Number 34 of 1995. Gov-
    ernment Gazette No. 16579. 1995. Cape Town: Government Publishers.
Ramphele, Mamphela. 1996. "Political Widowhood in South Africa: The Em-
    bodiment of Ambiguity." *Daedalus* 125, no. 1: 99–118.
Reparation and Rehabilitation Committee, South African Truth and Reconcil-
    iation Commission. 1997. *Proposed Policy for Urgent Interim Relief and*

Final Reparation. Published on Truth and Reconciliation Commission website: http://www.truth.org.za/reports/index.html. April.

Reynolds, Pamela. 1995a. *The Ground of All Making: State Violence, the Family and Political Activists*. Pretoria: Human Sciences Research Council.

————. 1995b. "'Not Known Because Not Looked For': Ethnographers Listening to the Young in Southern Africa." *Ethnos* 60, no. 3–4: 193–221.

Scarry, Elaine. 1985. *The Body in Pain: The Making and Unmaking of the World*. New York: Oxford University Press.

Scheub, Harold. 1975. *The Xhosa Intsomi*. Oxford: Clarendon Press.

Skweyiya, T. L. 1992. *Report of the Commission of Enquiry into the Complaints by Former African National Congress Prisoners and Detainees*. Johannesburg: African National Congress.

South African Truth and Reconciliation Commission. 1998. *Report of the South African Truth and Reconciliation Commission*. Cape Town: Juta.

Srinivasan, A. 1995. "The Survivor in the Study of Violence." In *Mirrors of Violence: Communities, Riots and Survivors in South Asia*, ed. Veena Das. Delhi: Oxford University Press.

Winterson, Jeanette. 1993. *Written on the Body*. Toronto: Vintage.

Zenani, Nongenile Masithathu, and Harold Scheub. 1992. *The World and the Word: Tales and Observations from the Xhosa Oral Tradition*. Madison: University of Wisconsin Press.

Contributors

Naomi Adelson, Associate Professor, Department of Anthropology, York University

Roma Chatterji, Lecturer in the Department of Sociology, University of Delhi

Komatra Chuengsatiansup, Head of the Health Socio-Cultural Policy Unit in the Bureau of Health Policy and Planning, Ministry of Public Health, Thailand

Veena Das, Krieger-Eisenhower Professor of Anthropology, Johns Hopkins University

Arthur Kleinman, Professor in the Departments of Anthropology and Social Medicine, Harvard University

Margaret Lock, Professor in the Department of Social Studies of Medicine, McGill University

Deepak Mehta, Lecturer in the Department of Sociology, University of Delhi

Sasanka Perera, Senior Lecturer and Anthropologist in the Department of Sociology, University of Colombo

Mamphela Ramphele, Managing Director of the World Bank and former Vice Chancellor, University of Cape Town

Pamela Reynolds, Professor in the Department of Anthropology, University of Cape Town

Fiona C. Ross, Lecturer in the Department of Social Anthropology, University of Cape Town

Maya Todeschini, Research Associate, Center for Japanese Studies, Ecole des Hautes Etudes en Sciences Sociales

Index

aboriginal, 76

aboriginality: as construction, 93, 95–97; definition of, 80; as political tool, 80–81, 95; in social response to suffering, 80–81; reimagining, 76. *See also* Indigenous peoples

Adelson, Naomi, 10, 20, 76–101

aestheticization, 7

African National Congress (ANC), 252, 275n6

agency, 20, 216; collective violence as robbing, 229, 234–35; and domesticity, narratives of, 259; marginalization and loss of, 52; relief work as restoring, 229, 235–36, 237–39; as resistance, 20–21; silence as, 272. *See also* identity; subjectivity; voice

agentive moments, 6, 63

Aggett, Neil, death of in detention, 258, 259, 266

agriculture, 65, 66

Akin Rabibhadana, 39

Akom Chanangkura, 57

alcohol consumption, 87, 93

altered states of consciousness: and construction of self, 158, 193; narratives of, *see* supernatural activity, narratives of

alternate public spheres, 3, 8–10, 19, 25, 27n2; definition of, 63; hibakusha women and, 104, 105, 132–46; Kui and, 9–10, 51, 68; lack of, 19; life cycle and access to, 133, 147; marginality and, 32, 63–64, 68; networking and, 67; officially sanctioned

narratives prompted by, 51–52; politics of exclusion combatted by, 68; as prerequisite for social movements, 63

ambivalence: and relief work, 18–19, 230–32, 233, 234, 241; victim/perpetrator distinction and, 17, 18, 19, 24, 162–63

amnesty, 191, 251, 274n5

ANC (African National Congress), 252, 275n6

Anders, Günther, 130

Anek Laothamatias, 58

anthropology: alternate public spheres created through, 63; involvement vs. detachment and, 64; methodology of, 26–27; objectivity and, 64; repressive structural order legitimated through, 64; and suffering, study of, 273

apartheid, 1; commission investigating abuses of, *see* Truth and Reconciliation Commission; policies of, 252, 255, 256, 263, 274n3, 276nn8–12, 14; recovery from, community responses in, 13–14

architecture, 49–50, 51

atom bomb: delayed effects of radiation, 102, 107–8, 113, 117–20, 150n1; and memory of humankind, 11. *See also* hibakusha *entries*

Atomic Bomb Casualty Commission (ABCC), 117–20

"atomic maidens," 151nn6–7. *See also* hibakusha women; "Hiroshima Maidens"

self *(continued)*
    158, 193. *See also* identity; subjectiv-
    ity; voice
sentimentality, 25, 26
Seremetakis, Nadia, 9, 32, 67
*Shamanism, Colonialism, and the Wild
    Man* (Taussig), 164–65
Shils, Edward, 47
Shiv Sena, 204, 205, 222
Siam. *See* Thailand
silence: and apartheid, 269–70; collective
    violence and, 225–26, 239; of hibaku-
    sha women, 133; language of,
    women's testimony as, 253, 269–73;
    listening and, 159–60, 270–73; relief
    work and, 239–40; and return to every-
    day, 228; in terror, reasons for, 159–
    60; and traditional narratives, 163
Sinhala people: language of, 157, 158,
    198n2; mental-illness stigma among,
    196; religion of, Buddhism, 168–69,
    170, 175–77, 180–81, 186, 194,
    199n9; religion of, popular, 158, 168–
    69, 173–74, 175–77, 183–89, 192;
    and terror, *see* Sri Lanka, terror in;
    supernatural activity, narratives of
Snayer, Basil, 275n6
social empowerment, 79
social movements: alternate public
    spheres and, 63; local movements net-
    working to, 62, 64; in Thailand, 34,
    60–61. *See also* civil society
social organization, vertical vs. horizon-
    tal, 59–60. *See also* class
social suffering, 2, 3, 27, 32, 76–78; an-
    thropological practice and, 31, 64; au-
    tonomy as necessary in solutions to,
    76, 78; healing of, *see* healing; inter-
    subjectivity of, 34–35; as local expres-
    sion, 20; marginality, *see* marginality;
    medicalization of, *see* medicalization;
    recognition of, as healing mechanism,
    19; social response to, 79–81
Social Suffering (Das, Kleinman, Ram-
    phele, and Reynolds), 2, 18
Solomos, John, 32
South Africa: apartheid, *see* apartheid;
    and context, loss of, 17; family life of,
    267; languages of, 275n7; police in-
    formers, community and, 276–
    77nn17, 21; Truth and Reconciliation
    Commission of, *see* Truth and Recon-
    ciliation Commission
Southwick, Steven M., 196
Soyinka, Wole, 22–23
Spencer, Jonathan, 28n12
spirit mediums, 161, 178, 183, 184–89
spirit possession. *See* possession

spirit religions. *See* popular religion
spirituality: Japanese women's movement
    and, 138; Native, shift to, 79, 88,
    97n3, 99n16; of Whapmagoostui
    Cree, 88, 91–92, 94, 97n3, 99nn16,
    19. *See also* religion
Spivak, G. C., 69n1
Srikrishna Commission, on Dharavi ri-
    ots, 16, 204–5
Sri Lanka, terror in *(beeshanaya)*, 4, 157–
    58, 178–79, 198n1; and bodies, lack
    of, 166–68, 183, 184–89; compensa-
    tion and assistance by government,
    167, 179–80, 195–96, 198n6; inter-
    personal relationships and, 159, 181–
    82, 190–91, 198n7; memory and,
    158, 190, 191; psychological treat-
    ment of, 191, 194–96; silence and,
    159–60, 163; supernatural narratives
    in response to, *see* supernatural activ-
    ity, narratives of; surrealism of, 165–
    66; as temporal marker, 159
Starr, Paul, 67
state, 33–34, 48; agencies of, 18; civil
    society and, 34, 57–62, 70n13; he-
    gemony of, 41, 57; medico-judicial
    category and, 123; myths of, 52; and
    natural resources, control of, 61; pub-
    lic sphere conflated with, 53–54; reifi-
    cation of, 52, 62. *See also* nationalism;
    nation-state; officially sanctioned nar-
    ratives
stereotypes: hibakusha women and, 11–
    12, 109, 122, 124–31, 147; of Kui,
    marginalization and, 35, 49, 54; rele-
    vance of, 5. *See also* otherness
stigma, 109
storytellers, 11, 103, 104, 140–43,
    150n3
Suarez-Orozco, Marcello M., 162
subaltern counterpublics. *See* alternate
    public spheres
subject, 6
subjectivity, 2, 6, 103; agentive moments
    and, 6, 63; complicity with violence
    and, 16–17; formation of, 5–7; inter-
    subjectivity and, 34, 35, 67, 68; reha-
    bilitation narratives and, 229; voice
    and, 20–22. *See also* agency; identity;
    voice
suffering, 2, 7, 11, 25, 31, 32, 35, 104,
    122, 272–73
supernatural activity, narratives of, 158,
    197; context of, 158–60, 166–68; as
    coping mechanism, 15, 158, 170, 177–
    78, 180–82, 183, 193, 194–97; ghost
    stories, 158, 168–75, 193; justice and
    revenge and, 160, 174–75, 190, 191–

voice *(continued)*
22, 239; as distancing device, 239;
genre and, 5, 25; hibakusha women
finding, 133–36; mockery and, 238–
39; polis as requiring, 4; recontextual-
ization of narratives and, 6; relief
work and, 239; retrieval of, 20; words
and, 4. *See also* agency; identity; subjectivity
voices, 14, 27n3, 34, 168, 212

war, 1, 11, 12, 24, 28n12; spirit mediums and healers and, 161. *See also*
terror
Warren, Kay B., 159, 163
Weber, Max, 47
Webster, Daniel, 258, 276n11
well-being, reimagination of, 10
Whapmagoostui Cree, 97n4; elders of,
88, 90, 91–92, 97n3, 99n18; Gatherings of, 88–97, 99nn15–19; identity
of, 6, 7, 8, 89–97; language of, 87,
98nn10, 13; livelihoods of, 86, 98n9;
municipality of, 85–87, 98nn8, 12;
reinvention and reclaiming of culture,
10, 79, 88, 91–92, 94, 97n3, 99nn16,
19; resistance to hydroelectric project,
82, 83–84, 88, 89, 90; social suffering
of, 87; spirituality and, 88, 91–92, 94,
97n3, 99nn16, 19; transnational Indigenous culture and, 79, 93
Widows, The (Dorfman), 166
Winterson, Jeanette, 250
witnessing, 13, 20, 24, 252–53, 272,
274nn4–5
Wittengenstein, Ludwig, 3, 7, 271
women: abuses of, apartheid and, 255,
274–75n6; alternate public spheres
and, 32; and atomic bombing, *see* hibakusha women; bodies of, *see*

women's bodies; marriage and status
of, 110; and motherhood, *see* motherhood; narratives of, *see* women's narratives *and* women's testimony; as the
other, 106, 136. *See also* gender
women's bodies: as particularly vulnerable, 105–6, 115, 145; as polluted, 107–
8; social contradictions played out on,
147; as territory, 214
women's narratives: body in, 105; of hibakusha, 132, 134–36, 139–40; maternal authority in, 134–36; suffering
of others as central to, 132, 253–55,
259, 274n6. *See also* women's testimony
women's testimony (South Africa): co-
herent-chronology type, 256–59; do-
mestic-focus type, 259–66, 267–69,
271–72; as focused on suffering of
others, 253–55, 259, 274n6; and self,
location of, 266–67; silence as language in, 253, 269–73; time and continuity and, 264, 265–66, 269, 271–
72; Women's Hearings, 275n6. *See
also* Truth and Reconciliation Commission
Women Tell of Hiroshima, 134

Yagnik, A., 202, 245nn2–3
Yamaoka Michiko, 104; on bodies, 137;
as "Hiroshima Maiden," 109; illness
as war, 105; injuries and illness of,
109; as *kataribe* (oral storyteller), 141–
43; livelihood of, 111
Yamashita Group, 103–4, 133, 135
youth: atomic bombing of Japan and,
106–7, 108; marginalization of, 32

Zar cult, 176
Zimbabwe, 161–62

Text: 10/13 Sabon
Display: Sabon
Composition: Binghamton Valley Composition
Printing and binding: Maple-Vail